Value Shift

Value Shift

*Why Companies Must Merge
Social and Financial Imperatives
to Achieve Superior Performance*

Lynn Sharp Paine

McGraw-Hill
New York   Chicago   San Francisco
Lisbon   London   Madrid   Mexico City   Milan
New Delhi   San Juan   Seoul   Singapore
Sydney   Toronto

The **McGraw·Hill** Companies

1 2 3 4 5 6 7 8 9 0 AGM/AGM 0 9 8 7 6 5 4 3 2

ISBN 0-07-138239-9

 This book is printed on recycled, acid-free paper containing a minimum of 50% recycled de-inked fiber.

In memory of
Geneva Welch Browning (1904–1978)
and
Robert Perry Teater (1898–1991)

Contents

Preface

This book is about changing notions of corporate performance—what it is and how to achieve it. Although addressed principally to those who want to build high-performing companies—managers, executives, directors, entrepreneurs—its message has relevance for a much wider audience. Given the extensive role played by companies in the world today, corporate performance is something that concerns virtually everyone. And that fact, more than anything else, is driving the developments discussed in the pages that follow.

If readers take only one idea from this book, I hope it will be an understanding of what I believe to be an emerging new standard of corporate performance—one that encompasses both moral and financial dimensions. We are, I believe, in the midst of a fundamental value shift that is altering how companies are thought of and how they are expected to behave. The deep sense of betrayal provoked by the past year's revelations of misdeeds at Enron, Arthur Andersen, Worldcom, and many other U.S. companies is just one of the most recent and most visible indicators of this shift.

This book has grown out of my research, teaching, and consulting over the past 20 years. It is a description, an interpretation, an argument, and a guide to practice all rolled into one. It unfolds pretty much in that order. The first part describes what I term the "turn to values." By this, I mean the growing emphasis on values, culture, ethics, stakeholders, citizenship, and so on that has emerged in many companies around the world during the past several decades. In this part, we will see what executives say about these topics and why they are embracing initiatives to promote them. The second part offers an interpretation of this phenomenon—how it is best characterized, what is motivating it, and why it is significant. Here I argue that the turn to values reflects an evolution in what has sometimes been called the "personality" of a corporation—the attributes that define its essential character. The third part then spells out the implications of this evolution for management practice. The final three chapters explore the implications for decision making, organizational design, and corporate leadership.

Chapters 4 and 5 present the intellectual underpinnings of the book's central argument, while Chapter 6 addresses the objections and counter-arguments. These chapters place the contemporary corporation in histori-cal context and show that companies today are being measured against a performance standard that is qualitatively different from past standards. Unlike traditional measures that have been purely financial in nature, the new yardstick is more complex. In order to excel under this new standard, companies must not only turn in superior financial results, they must also demonstrate moral intelligence in their dealings with their employees, cus-tomers, and other constituencies. Although this may sound like a modest requirement, I argue that it has profound implications for how companies are managed and led.

The book traces the emergence of the new standard to the corpora-tion's expanding presence and growing stature in the wake of the great movements of the past century, and particularly of recent decades. Liberali-zation, privatization, globalization, advances in knowledge and technology—all these have simultaneously heightened the corporation's importance and given rise to new expectations for its performance. Once thought of as little more than a convenient device for pooling capital, the corporation has come to be viewed as itself an actor on the social stage.

Today's leading companies are expected not only to create wealth and produce superior goods and services but also to conduct themselves as "moral actors"—as responsible agents that carry out their business within a moral framework. As such, they are expected to adhere to basic ethical principles, exercise moral judgment in carrying out their affairs, accept responsibility for their deeds and misdeeds, be responsive to the needs and interests of others, and manage their own values and commitments. Contrary to theorists who for centuries have declared the corporation to be an entirely amoral creature and thus incapable of such behavior, society today has endowed the corporation with a moral personality.

Evidence of this development is all around us. Corporate reputation studies, best-company rankings, employee commitment surveys, polls of cit-izens worldwide, expanding investor concerns, the daily news—all these indicate that employees, customers, citizens, and even some investors are using both ethical and economic criteria to evaluate the companies they deal with. Even if it is profitable to conceal product risks, misreport earnings, evade the law, or rely on suppliers who use forced labor, these practices are increasingly viewed as unacceptable and unworthy of a leading corporation. Even more striking is the growing body of evidence pointing to the positive benefits of an ethical orientation—benefits that flow not only from better risk management but also from improved organizational functioning, increased market attractiveness, and better relations with the public and public officials at large.

To build companies that can deliver sustained performance under this new standard, managers will need to go well beyond the ethics programs, values initiatives, and stakeholder activities that have become *de rigueur* add-ons in recent years. They will need instead to build new organizational capabilities and embrace new ways of thinking and managing. As I argue in the chapters that follow, the superior performers of the future will be those that can satisfy both the social and financial expectations of their constituencies.

Writing this book has presented a number of challenges. One of the most vexing has been the problem of language. Part of this problem is captured in an experience I had almost 10 years ago when I was invited to present a seminar for key executives from a leading financial services company. Although the group wanted to hear about my research, I was told they would prefer that I not use the word "ethics" in my presentation because it made people feel "uncomfortable."

Such a request might seem bizarre, but from the vantage point of traditional corporate theory, it is quite normal. If you have been acculturated to think of the corporation as an amoral entity to be run as if it were an efficient machine, then it can be awkward and difficult to begin thinking about questions of values in the context of your professional role. It's really not so different from asking doctors who have been taught to think only about patient needs to begin thinking about health-care finance.

Recognizing the "discomfort" problem but also believing that a new era in thinking about corporate management is upon us, I have freely used terms such as "ethics," "values," and "morality." As a purely practical matter, I am not sure how I could avoid using such words, given my subject matter. Still, I have tried to be reader friendly, and I hope that readers who feel challenged by this language can brace themselves for a brief journey that may at times take them outside their comfort zone.

Another aspect of the language problem has to do with the generality of many words in this domain. Language is laden with philosophy, and the words we use in everyday discourse have widely varying meanings depending on the context in which they are spoken. The word "social," for example, has many different uses and connotations—some appealing and some not so appealing. It can often substitute for "societal," "civic," "moral," "ethical," "sociable," "shared," "communal," "deriving from society," "owed to society," and so on. Thus, the phrase "corporate social responsibility" can be used as an expansive category encompassing the many types of corporate responsibility that derive from societal arrangements—financial, legal, civic, functional, environmental. In some circles, however, "social responsibility" has come to be understood as a narrower category and made to contrast with financial, legal, moral, civic, or environmental responsibility.

After trying to construct a precise and consistent lexicon of terms to use in writing this book, I found that the price of precision was excessive awkwardness in expression, so I abandoned the effort. I also found it difficult to maintain the boundaries I had tried to set up in this artificial language system—which perhaps says something about the fluid nature of reality. In the end, I opted for ordinary language with all its inherent ambiguity. However, I have usually chosen to use the term "social responsibility" as an all-purpose category for nonfinancial responsibilities. If I were a language czar, I would favor the more expansive usage that treats financial responsibility as a subcategory of social responsibility. This usage would more accurately reflect the grounds of corporate financial responsibility, but it would not reflect what I take to be mainstream contemporary usage.

Developing a comprehensive picture of the corporation's role and how it is changing around the world also proved challenging. Libraries contain studies of large corporations, multinational corporations, privatized corporations, commercialized corporations (formerly nonprofits), corporations in this or that industry, and so on. However, aggregate data on corporations in general is in short supply. The picture I sketch in Chapter 4 is thus highly impressionistic and far from complete, but I believe that the essential features are correctly drawn. The increasing reliance on for-profit companies to carry out the work of society—in contrast to government, nonprofit, and noncorporate organizations—is a clear trend in a significant number of regions.

Finally, my own limitations have made it inevitable that this work will contain errors. In attempting to address an issue that cuts across many domains of knowledge, I have necessarily had to go beyond the bounds of my formal academic training and experience. And in my efforts to sketch the big picture, I have undoubtedly overlooked important details and gotten some things wrong. But here again, I believe the overall argument to be sound in its essentials.

Readers looking for answers to substantive moral questions facing today's companies will not find very many in this book. While there are some ethical basics—as found in the emerging set of "generally accepted ethical principles" for business—many of the moral questions confronting companies are complicated. Just as developing a traditional corporate strategy or a business plan requires careful consideration of particular facts and circumstances, finding workable answers to many moral questions requires research, analysis, and creative thinking. For the most part, however, companies have not thought it important to apply themselves to such questions. This book will explain why they must now endeavor to do so and how they can begin going about it.

To the extent that the book succeeds in making sense of the complex and changing corporate world, it is largely because so many have contributed to the ideas presented here. Over the years, I have benefited from opportunities to work with executives and managers from many companies and many parts of the world on issues discussed in the text. Teaching in the MBA and executive education programs at the Harvard Business School for the past 12 years has given me a unique laboratory for testing and exploring these ideas. I am particularly indebted to the executives who have allowed me into their companies as a researcher and case writer. Whether studying their successes or their mistakes, I have been impressed by their willingness to share their experiences and humbled by the awesome responsibilities they bear.

The school's Division of Research provided funding not only for the book itself but also for the many case studies and preliminary papers on which it is based. Without the school's financial support and its unique research environment, this book could not have been written. Dean Kim Clark provided me with the gift of time to launch this project. In allowing me to step down from my duties as head of the General Management unit, he opened up the space I needed at a crucial time in the creative process. Much of the writing was carried out during my tenure as a Novartis Fellow from 1999 through 2001. The school's Henry B. Arthur Fund for business ethics has also provided funding for my work.

Among the many colleagues who have contributed to the ideas presented here, I am especially indebted to the more than 30 who have been part of the teaching group for Leadership, Values, and Decision Making, a required module for MBA students that I have taught for the past 12 years. Perhaps my greatest debt, however, is owed to Joe Badaracco and Tom Piper, the two colleagues with whom I have worked most closely on issues of leadership, values, and corporate responsibility. Joe's writing on individual decision making and Tom's ideas about ethics and financial performance have had an enormous impact on my thinking, as will be apparent to anyone who knows their work. In this book, I have drawn liberally on some of Tom's insights—particularly his use of Venn diagrams as an explanatory tool—though I hasten to add that the ideas presented here do not necessarily reflect his views.

My debt to the late R. M. Hare will be apparent to anyone familiar with his work on moral thought. As a graduate student at Oxford University many years ago, I benefited as much from Dick's insistence on clear thinking as from his tutorials on moral reasoning. If I have managed to make the argument here clear and understandable, it is largely because of Dick's influence. He thought that business, among all the professions, presented the most challenging moral questions, and he was a firm believer in the power of reason to illuminate the way toward answers in this domain as in others.

To the extent that this work reflects distinctively Asian ideas and concerns, it is the direct result of interests sparked when I spent a year in Asia as a Luce Scholar during graduate school. That year, I discovered the rich traditions of Chinese thought from which I draw at several points in my argument. For that extraordinary experience, I will be forever indebted to the Henry Luce Foundation and especially to Hank Luce, the Luce family, and the many friends and colleagues affiliated with the foundation's activities.

I am particularly grateful to other friends and colleagues who have taken time to read and comment on parts of this manuscript as well as on earlier papers, presentations, and case studies that have fed into it. In addition to Joe Badaracco and Tom Piper, I also wish to thank Connie Bagley, R. Bhaskar, Sissela Bok, Laura Nash, Joshua Margolis, Hank Reiling, Kathy Spear, Guhan Subramanian, Sandra Sucher, Richard Tedlow, Dennis Thompson, Ken Winston, Per Molander, Marian Radetzki, and Claes Lundblad. I have also benefited from discussing the ideas presented here with members of the school's Ethics, Law, and Leadership group. In addition to the members already mentioned, Rohit Deshpandé, Ashish Nanda, Mike Wheeler, and Mihir Desai have enriched my thinking on many of the central topics addressed in the text.

Many others have gone out of their way to help track down important sources and points of information. In particular, I would like to mention Chris Coulter, Marc Drizin, Nien-hê Hsieh, Bill Laufer, Carolyn Mathiasen, Bill Megginson, Trex Proffitt, Mike Sharp, and Heidi Welsh. The Caux Round Table has generously allowed me to include in the appendix an assessment tool I developed based on the Round Table's 1994 Principles for Business. The nine principles of the Global Compact announced by the United Nations Secretary-General at the World Economic Forum in 1999 are reproduced in the appendix with U.N. permission.

Invaluable help has been provided by Kim Bettcher, my research associate, who has worked tirelessly in challenging the ideas presented, filling in data gaps, tracking down facts, and wrestling inconsistencies to the ground. Jeff Cronin and Erika McCaffrey, analysts with the Harvard Business School research services group, have also provided essential research support at various points along the way. And Trudi Bostian, my administrative assistant, has not only assisted with research, citation checking, and manuscript preparation but also kept everything else running smoothly while the book has been in progress.

Thanks also to my agents Rob McQuilkin and Ike Williams, and to my editor Mary Glenn at McGraw-Hill.

Finally, I would like to acknowledge those who have assisted me with the case studies on which parts of the book are based. These include colleagues Karen Hopper Wruck, Michael Watkins, Prompilai Khunaphante, Louis B. Barnes, and Eiji Mizutani as well as former doctoral students and now colleagues Mihnea Moldoveanu, Michael Santoro, Li Jin, Sarah Mavrinac, and Bronwyn Halliday. Carin-Isabel Knoop and Ann Leamon, both accomplished case writers with the Harvard Business School Division of Research, have helped with various projects, as have many outstanding research associates who have worked with me on the case studies that inform the book: Michele Lutz, Harold Hogan, Suma Raju, Robert Crawford, Jennifer Gui, David Kiron, Howard Reitz, Charles Nichols, III, Jane Palley Katz, Sarah Gant, Lexanne Abbott, Albert Choy, Chris Paige, and Andrea Strimling.

I am deeply grateful to all these people and to my family. On the home front, my husband Tom has served as a sounding board, consulting wordsmith, graphic arts adviser, and indefatigable optimist whose relentless encouragement has been essential to my seeing the project through. My children's contributions—Sumner's critical reading of the manuscript, Mallory's expert tech support, and Lydia's buoyant spirit—have also been invaluable. An author could not wish for a more supportive family.

I conclude this project all too aware that it raises many more questions than it answers. But I look forward to exploring these new questions and hope others will join me in doing so. The quest grows ever more urgent. As this book goes to press, companies worldwide are facing an unprecedented level of scrutiny, and many, including some mentioned here that have heightened their emphasis on values in recent years, have been charged with serious misconduct. These developments, I believe, only reinforce the book's central thesis and indicate, as I suggest in the final three chapters, that most companies will need to do much more to achieve the higher standard expected of them today.

1

The Turn to Values

Business has changed dramatically in the past few decades. Advances in technology, increasing globalization, heightened competition, shifting demographics—these have all been documented and written about extensively. Far less notice has been given to another, more subtle, change—one that is just as remarkable as these more visible developments. What I have in mind is the attention being paid to values in many companies today.

When I began doing research and teaching about business ethics in the early 1980s, skepticism about this subject was pervasive. Many people, in business and in academia, saw it as either trivial or altogether irrelevant. Some saw it as a joke. A few were even hostile. The whole enterprise, said critics, was misguided and based on a naïve view of the business world. Indeed, many had learned in their college economics courses that the market is amoral.

Back then, accepted wisdom held that "business ethics" was a contradiction in terms. People joked that an MBA course on this topic would be the shortest course in the curriculum. At that time, bookstores offered up volumes with titles like *The Complete Book of Wall Street Ethics* consisting entirely of blank pages. The most generous view was that business ethics had something to do with corporate philanthropy, a topic that might interest executives *after* their companies became financially successful. But even then, it was only a frill—an indulgence for the wealthy or eccentric.

Today, attitudes are different. Though far from universally embraced—witness the scandals of 2001 and 2002—ethics is increasingly viewed as an important corporate concern. What is our purpose? What do we believe in? What principles should guide our behavior? What do we owe one another and the people we deal with—our employees, our customers, our investors, our communities? Such classic questions of ethics are being taken seriously

1

in many companies around the world, and not just by older executives in large, established firms. Managers of recently privatized firms in transitional economies, and even some far-sighted high-technology entrepreneurs, are also asking these questions.

Ethics, or what has sometimes been called "moral science," has been defined in many ways—"the science of values," "the study of norms," "the science of right conduct," "the science of obligation," "the general inquiry into what is good." In all these guises, the subject matter of ethics has made its way onto management's agenda. In fact, a succession of definitions have come to the forefront as a narrow focus on norms of right and wrong has evolved into a much broader interest in organizational values and culture. Increasingly, we hear that values, far from being irrelevant, are a critical success factor in today's business world.[1]

The growing interest in values has manifested itself in a variety of ways. In recent years, many managers have launched ethics programs, values initiatives, and cultural change programs in their companies. Some have created corporate ethics offices or board-level ethics committees. Some have set up special task forces to address issues such as conflicts of interest, corruption, or electronic data privacy. Others have introduced educational programs to heighten ethical awareness and help employees integrate ethical considerations into their decision processes. Many have devoted time to defining or revising their company's business principles, corporate values, or codes of conduct. Still others have carried out systematic surveys to profile their company's values and chart their evolution over time.

A survey of U.S. employees conducted in late 1999 and early 2000 found that ethics guidelines and training were widespread. About 79 percent of the respondents said their company had a set of written ethics guidelines, and 55 percent said their company offered some type of ethics training, up from 33 percent in 1994. Among those employed by organizations with more than 500 members, the proportion was 68 percent.[2]

Another study—this one of 124 companies in 22 countries—found that corporate boards were becoming more active in setting their companies' ethical standards. More than three-quarters (78 percent) were involved in 1999, compared to 41 percent in 1991 and 21 percent in 1987. Yet another study found that more than 80 percent of the *Forbes* 500 companies that had adopted values statements, codes of conduct, or corporate credos had created or revised these documents in the 1990s.[3]

During this period, membership in the Ethics Officer Association, the professional organization of corporate ethics officers, grew dramatically. At the beginning of 2002, this group had 780 members, up from 12 at its founding 10 years earlier. In 2002, the association's roster included ethics officers from more than half the *Fortune* 100.[4]

More companies have also undertaken efforts to strengthen their reputations or become more responsive to the needs and interests of their various constituencies. The list of initiatives seems endless. Among the most prominent have been initiatives on diversity, quality, customer service, health and safety, the environment, legal compliance, professionalism, corporate culture, stakeholder engagement, reputation management, corporate identity, cross-cultural management, work-family balance, sexual harassment, privacy, spirituality, corporate citizenship, cause-related marketing, supplier conduct, community involvement, and human rights. A few companies have even begun to track and report publicly on their performance in some of these areas. For a sampling of these initiatives, see Figure 1-1.

CORPORATE INITIATIVES — A SAMPLER

COMPREHENSIVE (APPLYING TO ALL ACTIVITIES AND FUNCTIONS)

Internally oriented:
- ethics programs
- compliance programs
- mission and values initiatives
- business principles initiatives
- business practices initiatives
- culture-building initiatives
- cross-cultural management programs
- crisis prevention and readiness

Externally oriented:
- reputation management programs
- corporate identity initiatives
- corporate brand-building initiatives
- stakeholder engagement activities
- societal alignment initiatives
- nonfinancial-performance reporting initiatives

FOCUSED (APPLYING TO PARTICULAR ISSUES OR CONSTITUENCIES)

Employee oriented:
- diversity initiatives
- sexual harassment programs
- employee health and safety initiatives
- work-family initiatives
- workplace environment initiatives

Customer oriented:
- product and service quality initiatives
- customer service initiatives
- product safety initiatives
- cause-related marketing

Supplier oriented:
- supplier conduct initiatives

Investor oriented:
- corporate governance initiatives

Community oriented:
- environmental initiatives
- corporate citizenship initiatives
- community involvement initiatives
- strategic philanthropy

Issue oriented:
- electronic privacy
- human rights initiatives
- anticorruption programs
- biotechnology issues

FIGURE 1-1 VALUES IN TRANSITION

To aid in these efforts, many companies have turned to consultants and advisors, whose numbers have increased accordingly. A few years ago, *Business Week* reported that ethics consulting had become a billion-dollar business. Though perhaps somewhat exaggerated, the estimate covered only a few segments of the industry, mainly misconduct prevention and investigation, and did not include corporate culture and values consulting or consulting focused in areas such as diversity, the environment, or reputation management. Nor did it include the public relations and crisis management consultants who are increasingly called on to help companies handle values-revealing crises and controversies such as product recalls, scandals, labor disputes, and environmental disasters. Thirty or 40 years ago, such consultants were a rare breed, and many of these consulting areas did not exist at all. Today, dozens of firms—perhaps hundreds, if we count law firms and the numerous consultants specializing in specific issue areas—offer companies expertise in handling these matters. Guidance from nonprofits is also widely available.[5]

What's Going On?

A thoughtful observer might well ask "What's going on?" Why the upsurge of interest in ethics and values? Why have companies become more attentive to their stakeholders and more concerned about the norms that guide their own behavior? In the course of my teaching, research, and consulting over the past two decades, I have interacted with executives and managers from many parts of the world. In discussing these questions with them, I have learned that their motivating concerns are varied:

- An Argentine executive sees ethics as integral to transforming his company into a "world-class organization."
- A group of Thai executives want to protect their company's reputation for integrity and social responsibility from erosion in the face of intensified competition.
- A U.S. executive believes that high ethical standards are correlated with better financial performance.
- An Indian software company executive sees his company's ethical stance as important for building customer trust and also for attracting and retaining the best employees and software professionals.
- A Chinese executive believes that establishing the right value system and serving society are key components in building a global brand.
- The executives of a U.S. company see their efforts as essential to building a decentralized organization and entrepreneurial culture around the world.

- Two Nigerian entrepreneurs want their company to become a "role model" for Nigerian society.
- A Swiss executive believes the market will increasingly demand "social compatibility."
- An Italian executive wants to make sure his company stays clear of the scandals that have embroiled others.
- A U.S. executive believes that a focus on ethics and values is necessary to allow his company to decentralize responsibility while pursuing aggressive financial goals.
- A U.S. executive answers succinctly and pragmatically, "*60 Minutes.*"

These responses suggest that the turn to values is not a simple phenomenon. Individual executives have their own particular reasons for tackling this difficult and sprawling subject. Even within a single company, the reasons often differ and tend to change over time. A company may launch an ethics initiative in the aftermath of a scandal for purposes of damage control or as part of a legal settlement. Later on, when the initiative is no longer necessary for these reasons, a new rationale may emerge.

This was the pattern at defense contractor Martin Marietta (now Lockheed Martin), which in the mid-1980s became one of the first U.S. companies to establish what would later come to be called an "ethics program." At the time, the entire defense industry was facing harsh criticism for practices collectively referred to as "fraud, waste, and abuse," and Congress was considering new legislation to curb these excesses. The immediate catalyst for Martin Marietta's program, however, was the threat of being barred from government contracting because of improper billing practices in one of its subsidiaries.

According to Tom Young, the company president in 1992, the ethics program began as damage control. "When we went into this program," he explained, "we didn't anticipate the changes it would bring about. . . . Back then, people would have said, 'Do you really need an ethics program to be ethical?' Ethics was something personal, and you either had it or you didn't. Now that's all changed. People recognize the value." By 1992, the ethics effort was no longer legally required, but the program was continued nonetheless. However, by then it had ceased to be a damage control measure and was justified in terms of its business benefits: problem avoidance, cost containment, improved constituency relationships, enhanced work life, and increased competitiveness.[6]

A similar evolution in thinking is reported by Chumpol NaLamlieng, CEO of Thailand's Siam Cement Group. Although Siam Cement's emphasis on ethics originated in a business philosophy rather than as a program of damage control, Chumpol recalls the feeling he had as an MBA student—

that "ethics was something to avoid lawsuits and trouble with the public, not something you considered a way of business and self-conduct." Today, he says, "We understand corporate culture and environment and see that good ethics leads to a better company."[7]

Siam Cement, one of the first Thai companies to publish a code of conduct, put its core values into writing in 1987 so they "would be more than just words in the air," as one executive explains. In 1994, shortly after the company was named Asia's "most ethical" in a survey conducted by *Asian Business* magazine, Chumpol called for a thorough review of the published code. The newly-appointed CEO wanted to make sure that the document remained an accurate statement of the company's philosophy and also to better understand whether the espoused values were a help or hindrance in the more competitive environment of the 1990s. In 1995, the company reissued the code in a more elaborate form but with its core principles intact. The review had revealed that while adhering to the code did in some cases put the company at a competitive disadvantage, it was on balance a plus. For example, it helped attract strong partners and employees and also positioned the company, whose largest shareholder was the Thai monarchy's investment arm, as a leader in the country.

A very different evolution in thinking is reported by Azim Premji, chairman of Wipro Ltd., one of India's leading exporters of software services and, at the height of the software boom in 2000, the country's largest company in terms of market capitalization. Wipro's reputation for high ethical standards reflects a legacy that began with Premji's father, M.H. Hasham Premji, who founded the company in 1945 to make vegetable oil. The elder Premji's value system was based on little more than personal conviction—his sense of the right way to do things. Certainly it did not come from a careful calculation of business costs and benefits. In fact, his son noted, "It made no commercial sense at the time."[8]

When his father died in 1966, Azim Premji left Stanford University where he was an undergraduate to assume responsibility for the then-family-owned enterprise. As he sought to expand into new lines of business, Premji found himself repeatedly having to explain why the company was so insistent on honesty when it was patently contrary to financial interest. Over time, however, he began to realize that the core values emphasized by his father actually made for good business policy. They imposed a useful discipline on the company's activities while also helping it attract quality employees, minimize transaction costs, and build a good reputation in the marketplace. In 1998, as part of an effort to position Wipro as a leading supplier of software services to global corporations, the company undertook an intensive self-examination and market research exercise. The result was a reaffirmation and rearticulation of the core values and an effort to link them more closely with the company's identity in the marketplace.

Managers' reasons for turning to values often reflect their company's stage of development. Executives of large, well-established companies typically talk about *protecting* their company's reputation or its brand, whereas entrepreneurs are understandably more likely to talk about *building* a reputation or *establishing* a brand. For skeptics who wonder whether a struggling start-up can afford to worry about values, Scott Cook, the founder of software maker Intuit, has a compelling answer. In his view, seeding a company's culture with the right values is "the most powerful thing you can do." "Ultimately," says Cook, "[the culture] will become more important to the success or failure of your company than you are. The culture you establish will guide and teach all your people in all their decisions."[9]

In addition to company size and developmental stage, societal factors have also played a role in some managers' turn to values. For example, executives in the United States are more likely than those who operate principally in emerging markets to cite reasons related to the law or the media. This is not surprising, considering the strength of these two institutions in American society and their relative weakness in many emerging-markets countries. Since many ethical standards are upheld and reinforced through the legal system, the linkage between ethics and law is a natural one for U.S. executives. In other cases, executives offer reasons that mirror high-profile issues facing their industries or countries at a given time—issues such as labor shortages, demographic change, corruption, environmental problems, and unemployment. Antonio Mosquera, for example, launched a values initiative at Merck Sharp & Dohme Argentina as part of a general improvement program he set in motion after being named managing director in 1995. Mosquera emphasized, however, that promoting corporate ethics was a particular priority for him because corruption was a significant issue in the broader society.[10]

Despite the many ways executives explain their interest in values, we can see in their comments several recurring themes. Seen broadly, their rationales tend to cluster into four main areas:

- Reasons relating to *risk management*
- Reasons relating to *organizational functioning*
- Reasons relating to *market positioning*
- Reasons relating to *civic positioning*

A fifth theme, somewhat less salient but nevertheless quite important for reasons we will come back to later, has to do with the idea simply of "a better way." For some, the rationale lies not in some further benefit or consequence they are seeking to bring about but rather in the inherent worth of the behavior they are trying to encourage. In other words, the value of the behavior resides principally in the behavior itself. For these executives, it is just *better*—full stop—for companies to be honest, trustworthy, innovative, fair, responsible, or good citizens. No further explanation is necessary any more than further explanation is required to justify the pursuit of self-interest or why more money is better than less.

A few examples of companies that have turned their attention to values in recent decades will show how these themes have emerged. Notice that each company has emphasized a somewhat different set of values.

Risk Management

Some managers have turned to values as a way to manage, and, ideally, eliminate certain risks, particularly those associated with misconduct but also those associated with carelessness, neglect, and insensitivity. By focusing on the values that guide people's behavior, they hope to minimize the incidence of malfeasance and its damaging consequences.

In some cases, managers are concerned about *individual* misconduct—misdeeds against the company by employees acting in their personal capacity. Petty larceny, embezzlement, and diversion of business opportunities that properly belong to the company are serious problems for managers in many parts of the world. In the United States, for instance, individual misconduct is said to cost companies some 6 percent of their revenues annually. Between 1997 and 2000, U.S. retailers saw their losses from employee theft jump by 34 percent to an estimated $12.8 billion. And this does not include costs that are more difficult to quantify, such as lowered morale among conscientious employees.[11]

However, most managers who have turned to values as part of their risk management strategy are most concerned about the risks associated with *corporate* misconduct—misdeeds committed by those acting in the company's name or on its behalf. In recent years, these risks have escalated to the point that even seemingly minor misdoings can spawn problems of crisis proportions, particularly if they become known to the public. As most recently illustrated by the experiences of Enron, Arthur Andersen, Tyco, and others, a company caught in misconduct can quickly find its reputation in tatters and its core relationships shattered. It can also find itself saddled with millions of dollars in fines, litigation expenses, and legal fees. This is especially true in the United States, where companies may be subject to large punitive damage awards and where failure to guard against misconduct can mean increased fines and penalties. Perhaps managers' greatest concern, however, is what will happen if misconduct undermines the public's trust in the company or its products and drives customers to other suppliers.[12]

Misconduct threatens not only the corporation, but also individual executives, board members, and corporate officers who can find themselves on the firing line. Even those who are not personally involved can suffer reputational, legal, and financial damage from their mere proximity to malfeasance.

Such concerns underlie the heightened emphasis on values in many companies, particularly those that have experienced firsthand the repercussions of misconduct. A dramatic case in point is Salomon Brothers, the former Wall Street trading and investment firm. Salomon no longer exists as an independent company; it was acquired in 1997 by Travelers Group, which then merged with Citicorp the following year. In 1991, however, Salomon was a leading Wall Street firm and the most active among 39 "primary dealers" involved in the U.S. Treasury's weekly securities auctions. The firm, with earnings of about $300 million for the previous year, was in the midst of a five-year effort to improve its management processes when misconduct on its government trading desk triggered a corporate crisis.[13]

Impatient with the Treasury's rules limiting the size of bids and awards to any single firm in a given auction, several trading desk officials took the liberty of submitting false bids in the names of Salomon customers. Not once, but on several occasions beginning sometime in the second half of 1990, traders borrowed the names of well-known firms including London-based S.G. Warburg and Mercury Asset Management. These fraudulent bids, entered without customers' knowledge or consent, enabled Salomon to circumvent the Treasury's limits and in some cases gain control of securities beyond the prescribed maximum.

When Salomon's senior executives learned in April of 1991 about one such bid, they convened and debated an appropriate response. In the end, though, they did nothing to correct the situation or inform auction officials. Nor did they discipline the employees involved until the possibility of an investigation led them to disclose the matter publicly several months later. In August 1991, Salomon issued a press release announcing the discovery of trading-desk "irregularities" and other "rule violations." Then, five days later, the firm issued a second release, which revealed that top executives had known about at least one of the unauthorized bids for nearly four months prior to the disclosure.

These announcements sent shockwaves through the world financial community. Salomon was on the front page of virtually every major newspaper in the world. In London, financiers were stunned to learn that traders had submitted an unauthorized bid in the name of Warburg, one of the city's most respected institutions. In Japan, where Salomon's debt was widely held and traded over the counter, creditors were astounded. In New York, meanwhile, Salomon was bombarded with calls from clients, creditors, employees, shareholders, insurers, regulators, the media, and various government officials seeking an explanation. The Federal Reserve Bank notified Salomon that its primary dealer status was in jeopardy, and threatened to bar the firm from bidding in Treasury auctions.

What would later be called the "billion-dollar error of judgment" set off a chain reaction among the firm's core constituencies. Their confidence shaken, many felt they could no longer do business with Salomon. Creditors balked at holding the firm's unsecured debt, and banks threatened to cut its credit lines. Suddenly and unexpectedly, the highly leveraged firm was faced with a major funding crisis. At the same time, Salomon's share price plunged from $36 a few days before the first press release to $22 a week later.

Within days of the first disclosures, Salomon lost a number of important clients, including CalPERS, then the world's largest private pension fund, and the World Bank. Some clients, particularly in the United States and United Kingdom and to a lesser extent elsewhere in Europe, felt it necessary to penalize what they saw as a breach of trust and a serious threat to the financial system by withdrawing their business from Salomon. Others moved to protect their own assets and reputations. Many government and quasi-government clients severed their relationship because of legal requirements that forbade them to do business with any firm charged with wrongdoing. Salomon was dropped or its investment banking role reduced in a number of transactions, including a planned $8.5 billion public offering of British Telecommunications. Its moral authority diminished by the misdeeds, Salomon was in no position to enforce its contractual rights in these deals. As a Salomon official noted, "In this situation, you simply have to go along [with the customers' wishes]."

Employees, too, were shaken. "Basically, our lives fell apart," recalled one manager. As events unfolded, supervisors spent much of their time reassuring nervous subordinates or trying to talk them out of leaving. One executive joked that in London, headhunters had two stacks of resumes, one for Salomon employees and one for everyone else. Employees also had to cope with the stress and uncertainty of having to deal with skeptical clients and other outsiders—experiences described variously by Salomon personnel as "embarrassing," "demoralizing," "torture," and "insulting to your professional pride."

As Salomon's core business relationships unraveled, the firm faced a barrage of investigations. Employees spent much of their time responding to the deluge of requests for information from myriad authorities including the Securities and Exchange Commission (SEC), the U.S. Treasury Department, the Justice Department, the Federal Reserve Board, the FBI, the Manhattan District Attorney's office, and the New York Stock Exchange (NYSE). Congress geared up for hearings and new legislation. Meanwhile, customers, shareholders, and other parties filed lawsuits charging the firm with various offenses and seeking compensation.

Following the second press release, it was clear to everyone that Salomon's top executives had lost their ability to lead. Under pressure from senior managers and government officials, CEO John Gutfreund and the firm's president both resigned. Gutfreund later commented that he knew his days were numbered when he opened his front door, picked up his copy of the *New York Times*, and saw his photo on the front page.

Salomon board member and well-known investor Warren Buffett took over as interim chairman with the immediate task of designating a new executive team. Appointed by the board in an emergency meeting, the team faced a crisis of major proportions. "Nothing could go 'on hold,'" said Deryck Maughan, who was named chief operating officer and later became CEO. "With one engine on fire, we had to keep in forward motion to avoid going down."

Not surprisingly, this series of events turned management's attention to questions of ethics. Within a few days of taking office, Buffett sent the firm's senior managers a letter advising that, with the exception of minor infractions such as parking tickets, they were "expected to report, instantaneously and directly to me, any legal violation or moral failure on behalf of any employee of Salomon." For Maughan, what happened on the trading desk signaled a need to "reassert the traditional values of the firm." "In some way, in some fashion, we had lost our way," he said. For Robert Denham, appointed CEO of Salomon's parent company after the scandal broke, the brush with disaster served to underscore the CEO's role as standards bearer. In Denham's view, establishing and maintaining the firm's ethical standards was as much a CEO's core function as was assisting the board, allocating resources, and managing key personnel.[14]

In the wake of the crisis, Salomon took a number of steps to tighten standards and strengthen self-discipline. These included a thorough overhaul of the firm's compliance and control systems, the creation of a board-level compliance committee, and the designation of a firm-level business practices committee to advise on ethical issues connected with Salomon's various businesses. The executive team breathed a collective sigh of relief in May 1992 when the U.S. government's case against Salomon was settled for

$290 million in fines and damages. The settlement meant that criminal charges, which might well have been the firm's undoing, would not be brought.

Thanks in large measure to the rescue program carried out by the Buffett-Maughan-Denham team, Salomon weathered the crisis. But the effects of the scandal lingered. Two years after the crisis, the company had still not fully recovered its lost underwriting business. When the merger with Travelers Group was announced in 1997, several observers linked the favorable terms extended to Travelers to the scandal. Maughan seemed to confirm their analysis. "We had to spend two years fixing [the firm] before we could start driving forward," he said. "The opportunity cost was very substantial."[15]

Organizational Functioning

For some managers, the turn to values is less about preventing missteps and more about organization building. It is not so much a defensive measure as a positive effort to build a well-functioning company. These managers talk about values as essential for encouraging cooperation, inspiring commitment, nurturing creativity and innovation, and energizing the organization's members around a positive self-image. They see ideals like respect, honesty, and fair dealing as the building blocks of a high-performance culture.

Such themes are much in evidence at Sealed Air Corp., a U.S.-based specialty packaging company whose products are sold throughout the world. The company is perhaps best known to consumers for Bubble Wrap®, the sheets of see-through plastic bubbles used as a protective packaging, but it makes a wide range of products including padded mailers, protective food packaging, and molded plastic packaging systems used by computer makers. The company's sales in 2001 were $3.1 billion.[16]

At Sealed Air, the focus on values cannot be traced to a particular triggering event or crisis. Rather it has grown naturally from an evolving awareness among the company's successive leaders. Many of the values emphasized today are a legacy of the company's founders who, in the late 1960s, implanted them unselfconsciously through their example and sheer force of personality. It was Sealed Air's second CEO, T. J. Dermot Dunphy, who first articulated a set of guiding principles and made them a deliberate focus of management attention. Dunphy, who served as CEO from 1971 until early 2000, felt instinctively that values and attitudes could profoundly influence an organization. He acknowledged that values were difficult to articulate and perhaps impossible to quantify, but nonetheless he believed them to be an important management concern.

Dunphy and his colleagues, including Bill Hickey who became CEO in 2000, also believed that "virtue was a competitive advantage"—to use

Dunphy's words. They felt that by nurturing a positive set of values, they could build a dynamic, self-governing organization made up of people willing to contribute their best ideas and efforts. The key to their vision, however, was trust. As one executive explained, they reasoned that trust depended on behavior and behavior depended on values. That is, a high level of trust and mutual regard could only arise if people took responsibility for their actions, dealt fairly with one another, and treated one another with respect. Thus, to build and maintain the organization they envisioned, values would have to be addressed on an ongoing basis.

Guided by this line of thinking, Sealed Air's leaders have sought to instill a strong commitment to the values they identified as crucial—personal accountability, respect for the individual, truth, and fair dealing. Hickey and others refer to these ideas collectively as Sealed Air's "bedrock values." Surrounding this bedrock are supporting values that express the company's stance on such matters as hierarchy and bureaucracy (to be minimized), open communication (to be practiced and encouraged), and work life ("work hard and play hard," but save time for family.) Sealed Air's value system also emphasizes resourcefulness, known as "doing more with less," as well as innovation, customer focus, and world-class manufacturing quality. Although employees are encouraged to participate in community activities—for example, a primary-school "buddy" project in Connecticut, a cancer-patient assistance program in Holland, and a monastery rebuilding effort in France—the company plays down such civic involvement. "We don't run it up the flagpole," explained on executive, "otherwise people will do it just for the recognition."

Longtime employees across the organization credit this value system with driving creativity and helping Sealed Air maintain a healthy balance between two ideals often thought to be incompatible—a deep belief in the individual and a strong emphasis on teamwork and cooperation. In interviews conducted at five locations in 1997, seasoned employees across the organization described an extraordinary degree of freedom, openness, trust, and regard for the individual. Production employees, sales reps, managers, and staff professionals alike spoke about the recognition and rewards given for individual contributions, solicited and unsolicited. But they also cited uncommon levels of cooperation and communication as seen, for example, in the extensive use of cross-functional teams, consensus decision making, mutual assistance among colleagues, and open lines of communication extending right to the CEO's office.

Sealed Air's values were intended not just to regulate internal relations among employees but also to carry through to relations with customers, suppliers, competitors, and others. Trust and fair dealing, for instance, have been central to Sealed Air's approach to the customer, and the company's sales force regards itself as a group of genuine "professionals," with both the knowledge level and ethical standards implied by that term. They practice a brand of selling known in-house as "consultative selling" whose aim is not just to sell packaging products but to provide "packaging solutions" that solve customers' problems in a way that creates real value for the customer. This approach is based on the theory that sustainable success depends on mutual gains—for the customer as well as Sealed Air and its employees.

The company reinforces this professional identity in its training programs and business practices. Sales reps learn, for example, to diagnose customers' problems and recommend objective, appropriate solutions—even if this sometimes means losing the sale. New-employee training covers a wide range of skills—everything from setting up appointments and asking for orders, to presenting health, safety, and environmental issues. In a similar spirit, Sealed Air employees are taught to take the high road in their approach to competition. Competing on the merits is expected, and slamming the competition is frowned on. Corrupt payments to win a customer, even in regions where this is common practice, are forbidden, as is poaching competitors' employees in order to acquire proprietary information.

Sealed Air's bedrock values have been elaborated and documented in a code of conduct. Hickey characterizes the code's provisions as the basic terms of membership in the organization—its "nonnegotiable, inviolate principles." The code calls on everyone not only to comply with the law but also to apply standards of "basic morality" and "common decency" in all their dealings. As one employee noted, the code of conduct is viewed not just as "law" but as "how we are expected to treat one another."

Beyond the specifics of the code, however, the company's values have been reflected in a wide range of attitudes and practices. Extensive employee stock ownership, for instance, reflects and reinforces both individual accountability and cooperative effort. So do the company's reward programs such as the "Keys to Success" and "Winning Performers" awards that recognize individual as well as team contributions. Hiring and firing practices are another example. Apart from employees who join Sealed Air as part of an acquisition, new people are brought on board only after an intensive interview process. "This is the Mayo clinic of interviewing," quipped one manager referring to the traditional seven-person consensus required to hire someone new. Another employee, only recently hired, described five rounds of interviews with 17 people before he received an offer.

Given the careful attention paid to hiring, firing for cause is relatively rare, but it does happen from time to time. One way to "end the relationship," as one employee put it, is by breaching the code. Other grounds for dismissal, said another, include "talking down to employees, being disrespectful to people who work here, putting form over function, or posturing without knowing the story." One hourly employee commented, "To get fired, you really have to be a dunce, on drugs, or disrespectful of people." Even so, the firing process contains checks and balances to guarantee fairness and respect for the individual involved. And despite the broad authority delegated to employees, even corporate officers are required to consult the CEO before firing anyone who has been with the company for more than five years.

Sealed Air's top executives have held themselves to the same standards of accountability that they expect of others. Believing in the salutary effects of exposure to the market, they have foresworn "poison pills" and other takeover deterrents and have not sought golden parachutes or protective contracts for themselves. In fact, the company has generally avoided formal employment contracts of any type.

Both Dunphy and Hickey attribute much of Sealed Air's past growth and profitability to the company's value system. What is the connection? They cite the company's ability to function with fewer layers of management, larger spans of control, and lower overhead compared to other companies of comparable size. These benefits, they believe, are a direct result of adhering to values that respect and cultivate people's capacities for self-direction and self-coordination. The company's loose structure and its reliance on self-management, moreover, have made for a high degree of organizational flexibility.

Sealed Air's distinctive mix of freedom and responsibility also seems to nurture a high level of initiative and creativity. As one long-time U.S. sales rep put it, working at the company is "as close as you can get to having your own business without actually doing it." An hourly worker echoed the sentiment: "Here, people have more pride in what they do. . . . They contribute and do a decent job. Other places I've been, people try to do as little work as possible. It's a game to see whether you can put something over on the company." Many employees spoke about Sealed Air as a place that encouraged experimentation and learned from mistakes. In fact, said one, "Around here you get almost as much credit for trying something and having the courage to shut it down as you do for a commercial success."

Certainly, though, Sealed Air has had plenty of commercial success. It has grown smartly over recent decades, both through the development of new products and through more than 50 acquisitions and at least a half-dozen significant deals aimed at extending its technological and geographical reach. Sealed Air's revenues increased from $7.6 million in 1971 to

$2.8 billion in 1999, having tripled in 1998 with the acquisition of Cryovac, a division of W. R. Grace. In the 1990s, prior to the Cryovac acquisition, annual returns on the company's common stock averaged some 39 percent, an amount substantially in excess of the S&P 500. Since 1999, the pattern has been more volatile due to the general economic slowdown as well as investor skittishness over unresolved legal issues related to the Cryovac acquisition agreement. But these difficulties have not so far diminished the company's emphasis on values.

To the contrary, Hickey sees a "seamless corporate culture" based on the company's stated values as the key to successful globalization. Such a culture, he believes, is necessary to foster effective working relationships across the company's various divisions and with its many customers around the world. Moreover, it is in his view crucial to growing the company without becoming a highly centralized, bureaucratic organization. Still, from Hickey's perspective, Sealed Air's values are more than just financial tools; they represent a very "human" approach to people both inside and outside the company. They not only contribute to good financial results, but they also, in his judgment, make Sealed Air an enjoyable place to work.

Market Positioning

A third cluster of themes fueling the turn to values is market oriented. For some managers, positioning their company vis-à-vis markets and industry rivals is paramount. These managers focus on the importance of values for shaping their company's identity and reputation, building its brands, or earning the trust of customers, suppliers, or other business partners. One important concern for many of these managers is what customers and other market-actors expect of the products and services they buy and the companies with which they deal.

At the Haier Group, one of China's leading household electronics and appliance makers, a focus on values has been an important aspect of the group's drive to become one of China's first global brands. In the early 1990s, this goal was little more than a gleam in the eye of CEO Zhang Ruimin. But even then, he felt the company would need a strong corporate culture to achieve a worldwide reputation for excellence. And this culture would have to be based on individual responsibility, uncompromising quality, meticulous attention to customer preferences, and continuous innovation.[17]

Zhang had come to focus on these values through a combination of personal experience, observation, and study. An ardent reader of management literature, he devoured the books that began pouring into China in the early 1980s after Deng Xiaoping's economic reforms opened the country's doors to outside influences. When Zhang, then a vice-general manager of the municipal government's household appliances division in the northern port city of Qingdao, read about the management methods of leading Japanese and American firms, he realized that many of them melded easily with the wisdom of such traditional Chinese thinkers as Confucius, Laozi, and Sun Tzu. Zhang was particularly impressed with the level of initiative and self-monitoring displayed by employees of General Electric: "By leading themselves, funneling their energies in the company, they were realizing their identities. I wanted to do the same in my company."

Putting these values into practice, however, was something else again. Personal responsibility, quality, and customer service were concepts that had no place in the thinking of China's managers and workers prior to the reforms initiated under Deng's leadership. In China's centrally planned economy, the manager's role was simply to fulfill production quotas handed down by government authorities, not to satisfy the needs of customers and end users or to experiment with improvements and new ways of doing things. Personal responsibility and initiative, far from being encouraged, were positively frowned upon. Instead everything was done, or supposed to be done, according to plan, with a focus on quantity, not quality.

Equally alien was the concept of rewards for individuals' contributions. Chinese workers were accustomed to a strongly egalitarian distribution of wages and lifetime employment, regardless of effort or contribution. Under the prevailing communist ideology, it would have been unfair to reward people any other way. Moreover, most employees took the existence and survival of their enterprise as a given, not as something to which they had to contribute every day. The concept of the customer in a Western sense was unknown, and consumers had few if any alternatives to the shoddy products churned out somewhat unreliably by designated local producers.

The net result of this system was pervasive passivity and mediocrity. Employees commonly spent the better part of their workday drinking tea and reading newspapers. Rather than seeking advancement by contributing to the enterprise, many spent their time cultivating political connections with higher-ups in the hope of winning future favors. Managers awarded contracts to friends and connections more to lubricate personal relations than to meet the needs of the enterprise. Financial accounts and production records were often a mess and seldom bore any relation to reality. Inventory was frequently lost or unaccounted for, receivables often went uncollected, and responsibilities were so vague that no one could be held accountable.

Zhang Ruimin experienced such attitudes firsthand as head of the Qingdao General Refrigerator Factory, the predecessor to what would later become the Haier Group. In 1984, impressed that long lines of customers were suddenly waiting to buy the factory's refrigerators despite their shoddy quality, Zhang convinced his colleagues in the municipal government to name him factory chief. This was not difficult, because the factory was burdened with debt and had been losing money steadily. Yet Zhang saw an opportunity in the rising consumer demand generated by China's reforms. While other local producers adapted to the new environment by selling their inferior and virtually identical products at lower and lower prices, Zhang thought that competing on price alone was a losing strategy. Instead, he planned to take an alternate route—to differentiate the company by building a reputation for quality and reliability. Zhang persuaded a government colleague, Ms. Yang Mianmian, to join him in the new venture, and with government backing they set about transforming the moribund factory.

Their first step, acquiring modern refrigerator technology from the German white-goods maker Liebherr-Hausgeräte, was easy compared to the task of changing the values and attitudes of managers and workers. "Workers were not used to thinking about how to do a good job or take personal responsibility and initiative," Zhang recalled. "Their refrigerators came off the assembly line in terrible shape, and they had no idea what good service was." Zhang, whose aim at the time was to become China's number-one producer of refrigerators, knew that he could succeed only by changing the prevailing value system and establishing new standards of conduct. One day, to make a statement about the importance of quality— a point he had found difficult to communicate—he gave his workers a graphic demonstration. He pulled 76 flawed refrigerators out of inventory and ordered employees to smash them with sledgehammers. "That got their attention," Zhang recalled. "They finally understood I wasn't going to sell just anything, like my competitors would. It had to be the best."

By 1991, Haier had become China's number-one refrigerator maker. With his earlier goal achieved, Zhang now determined to expand into other markets and to transform Haier into a brand name known around the world. With government support and encouragement, the company embarked on an energetic program of acquisitions in China and partnerships with international companies. Between 1991 and 1998, Haier assumed control of some 18 Chinese enterprises, many of them in worse shape than the refrigerator factory that had launched his career.

Recognizing the importance of transforming the cultures of these enterprises, Zhang sought to codify and devise methods for institutionalizing the values he had come to regard as essential to Haier's success: personal accountability, hard work, innovation, outstanding quality, reliability, and extraordinary attention to the customer. Among other things, Haier would offer customers after-sales service on their purchases, something unheard of in China. Suppliers, moreover, would be selected on the basis of competitive bidding. Individual employees would be held accountable for their own work, and advancement would depend on skills and performance. According to Yang Mianmian, the goal was to motivate employees to work to the best of their potential.

At the same time, Haier would seek to establish itself as a technological leader and a good corporate citizen. One project would be a line of environmentally friendly products, including a CFC-free, low-energy-consumption "green refrigerator." The company sought and attained international certifications for reliability and quality, and it sponsored such activities in the community as a children's opera troupe and a popular science magazine for young people. Zhang knew that greater openness and financial transparency would eventually be required, too, especially if Haier, which was structured as a collective enterprise, sought to raise capital outside China.

To move the organization in the desired direction, Zhang established a "culture center" intended to educate employees about Haier's values and rules of conduct. This group engaged employees in small-group discussions and promoted the new standards through the employee newsletter, video materials, bulletin board displays, and other communications channels. With each new acquisition, Zhang and his management team sought to instill Haier's values both through personal example and through the management systems and work processes they put in place. Clear objectives, backed by rewards for success and penalties for failure, were introduced as a matter of course. In several cases, managers even fined themselves for their subordinates' poor-quality work.

Although many Chinese employees have welcomed the value system introduced by Haier, it has not gone unchallenged. According to Zhang, "the biggest problem is getting people to recognize the goals" of the culture. At one acquired enterprise, formerly state-owned, a group of employees went on strike to protest Haier's demanding practices and performance-oriented values. It didn't help that Haier was cleaning up the kickback system that had kept the sales force happy under previous management—while creating a huge backlog of uncollected accounts. Employees also chafed at such Haier practices as requiring poor performers to stand on a designated spot on the factory floor and explain their failings to assembled colleagues—a practice reminiscent of China's now-reviled Cultural Revolution. The triggering event for the work stoppage, however, was the introduction of employment contracts to replace the previous system of lifetime employment.

Despite such experiences, Haier has been working to forge a set of values worthy of a global market leader. How far it has come is difficult to say without more information. However, by the end of 2001, Haier's products were being sold in more than 160 countries, including the United States, where the company was said to have 25 percent to 30 percent of the small-refrigerator market. In 1998, Haier made the *Financial Times* list of the Asia-Pacific's most respected companies—the first mainland Chinese company to break into the Asian top 10. And in early 2002, an online Chinese poll voted it China's most-respected company.

Haier's expansion and rapid growth have received generous support from China's government and banks, and access to technology has, of course, been crucial. But Zhang Ruimin and Yang Mianmian also point to Haier's distinctive value system as playing a key role in its success to date.[18]

Civic Positioning

A fourth set of themes behind the turn to values has to do with corporate citizenship or civic positioning. For many managers, the principal issue is their company's standing and reputation in the community, not just in the marketplace. Some seek to establish their company as a progressive force for social betterment. Others want to build good relationships with non-market or "civic" constituencies such as governments, nongovernmental organizations (NGOs), and local communities. Still others wish to establish their company simply as a solid citizen that obeys the law, pays its taxes, and respects society's basic ethical standards.

Citizenship themes have played a prominent role in recent discussions of values at Royal Dutch/Shell, for instance. In 1996, the Anglo-Dutch oil giant undertook a major review of its values and business principles. Motivated in part by reputational concerns, the review was triggered by a series of critiques that had been leveled against the company.[19]

One critique was financial. Lagging behind its competitors in terms of the oil industry's key financial metric—return on average capital employed—Shell had in 1994 set in motion a top-to-bottom review of the organization. The result was a far-reaching multi-year transformation plan. In 1995, the Shell Group put in place a new organizational structure, abandoning its nearly 50-year-old matrix organization, and re-engineered many of its management processes. These changes were intended to encourage innovation and make better use of the organization's vast human potential. But as the new processes were being implemented and before Shell embarked on the final values and behaviors phase of the plan, the company was hit with another critique. This time it was about the environment.

In June 1995, Shell became the target of an international controversy over its plan to dispose of the Brent Spar, a North Sea oil storage buoy. On

the advice of independent scientists who had studied the options intensively, Shell had decided that the safest and environmentally best alternative was to tow the Brent Spar to the deep Atlantic and sink it in 6000 feet
of water. The company met no objections from the relevant ministers of the
various European governments it had consulted, and the British government gave its permission for the plan.

Shortly after the plan was announced, however, the international environmental advocacy group Greenpeace boarded the Brent Spar in a dramatic and beautifully staged protest of Shell's plan. Greenpeace's footage of the
event was broadcast on television news throughout Europe. The gasoline-
buying public, especially in northern Europe, reacted strongly. In Germany,
angry automobile owners boycotted Shell stations and sales volumes at
some stations dropped by up to 50 percent during the media coverage.
More worrying for the people at Shell, however, were the bombing and
shooting in some German locales.

The intensity of the public reaction stunned Shell's executives. Phil
Watts, the Shell Group's regional coordinator for Europe at the time and
group chairman since 2002, called it "a life-changing experience in business
terms." "You can't imagine the tensions inside," he recalled. "It was not just
a question of a CEO in Germany losing market share. Staff members were
deeply affected. Their kids at home were asking, 'What on earth is your
company doing?'" He added that his own "awareness level on the broader,
softer issues went up by a factor of 10 to 100."

Although Greenpeace later acknowledged that its statements about the
toxicity of the Brent Spar's contents had been mistaken, the experience
made an indelible impression on many people at Shell. "You don't really
know what it's like unless you experience it in the first person," said Watts.
"[It's] like being in a plane crash." The experience was all the more unset-
tling because, unlike the Salomon traders who knew they were violating the
Treasury auction rules, Shell officials had thought they were doing their
professional and technical best when they decided to sink the Brent Spar.
Faced with so much opposition, Shell abandoned its disposal plan and
instead, with the permission of the Norwegian government, had the spar
towed to shelter in a Norwegian fjord.

Soon after the Brent Spar outcry, Shell again found itself a target of
international criticism. In late 1995, environmentalists and human rights
advocates joined forces and took Shell to task for its activities in Nigeria,
where it operated an oil production joint venture whose members were the
Nigerian government and the European oil companies Elf and Agip as well
as Shell itself. One challenge centered on the extent to which Shell had

contributed to Nigeria's environmental problems, particularly in the Niger Delta region, where the venture's operations were concentrated. The critics also questioned whether Shell had contributed enough to the region's communities, considering the benefits that Shell had reaped from its oil production activities there.

Most important, however, the critics charged Shell with failing to intervene in the Nigerian government's 1995 trial and execution of Ken Saro-Wiwa, an outspoken environmentalist and leader of an indigenous people's group known as MOSOP (Movement for the Survival of the Ogoni People). Saro-Wiwa himself had been a vocal critic of both Shell and the Nigerian government, and MOSOP, from the early 1990s, had been demanding rights and reparations from both. From Shell alone, MOSOP had asked for a payment of $10 billion, $6 billion in compensation for damage to Ogoniland and $4 billion in lost revenues from the sale of oil abroad. Saro-Wiwa and 13 other Ogoni activists had been brought before a special military tribunal on what were widely believed to be trumped-up charges of inciting the murder of four Ogoni chiefs. After a trial that many, including an eminent human rights lawyer who observed the proceedings, found to be deeply flawed, Saro-Wiwa and eight of his codefendants were executed.[20]

This series of events had a palpable impact inside Shell. Coming on the heels of the Brent Spar incident, the problems in Nigeria were all the more troubling. After all, Shell had long been considered one of the world's best-managed companies. Being the target of such strident criticisms was inconsistent with the image Shell personnel had of themselves and the company for which they worked.

The situations, moreover, were genuinely difficult. "Brent Spar was a big wake-up call," commented Watts, but "Nigeria keeps us awake all the time." The Nigeria controversy had thrown into question Shell's stance on human rights and sustainable development, issues on which the group had taken no official position. It had also put to the test Shell's position on political involvement, a topic addressed by the group's official business principles. Formally articulated in 1976, the principles stated explicitly that Shell companies were to endeavor to avoid involvement in politics. However, Mark Moody-Stuart, group chairman from 1998 through 2001, acknowledged that in a country like Nigeria, "it's just not true you don't get involved in politics."

In the wake of the Brent Spar and Nigeria controversies, Shell's executive group decided it was time to go back to basics by expanding the previously planned values and behaviors phase of the transformation process to include a thorough review of the group's standards and business principles. Commented Moody-Stuart, "We thought we had well-established and well-implanted principles, but the outside world questioned whether our principles were appropriate and whether we followed them." The review process would include extensive consultations with managers and employees all across the group as well as with external stakeholders, opinion leaders, and other companies.

Aimed at better understanding the world's expectations for a company like Shell, these discussions encompassed a wide range of issues including human rights, corruption, the environment, and political and community involvement. A major focus was implementation—what the company could actually do in any of these areas. "We spent the most time on human rights," recalled Moody-Stuart, "testing what we wanted to say to see if we could live with it."

These discussions led eventually to a revised set of business principles; new policies on health, safety, and environmental standards; and new accountability mechanisms related to both. The upshot, however, was a corporate commitment to the concept of sustainable development, along with the creation of a five-year roadmap for making it an integral part of the business. It had become clear to Shell's leaders that the company needed to begin thinking more broadly about its activities. The concept of sustainable development, which integrated social and environmental factors with economic concerns, offered an appealing anchor for their efforts.

Working out what this meant in practice would take time and would not be easy, but Shell's leaders saw no other option. "Many companies don't want to go this route," said one member of the team who worked on the roadmap. "But we saw it as facing up to reality. These expectations are out there, and, if you fall short, you can lose your license to operate. You also fall short of your own values."

A Better Way

For some managers, the turn to values needs no corporate justification. For this group, the very idea of values evokes something worthwhile in and of itself. These managers talk little about risk management, organizational functioning, or corporate reputation. Their language is one of responsibility, humanity, and citizenship. For them, values are fundamental principles whose rationale lies not in their commercial advantages but in their life-affirming nature. Even if adhering to these principles turns out to be commercially advantageous, their justification has much broader and deeper roots.

The late H. T. Parekh was one such manager. When he first envisioned the housing finance company he would establish in Bombay (now "Mumbai") in 1977, he most certainly thought of its values in this way. Having spent much of his life studying the problems of economic development, Parekh wanted to do something about India's vast need for housing by making it possible for middle- and lower-middle-class Indians to achieve their dream of home ownership without spending their entire lives accumulating the necessary funds. After retiring as chairman of one of India's leading industrial lending institutions, Parekh put into motion an idea he had originally conceived in the 1930s while a student at the London School of Economics. At age 69, he became an entrepreneur, mobilizing funding and other resources to launch India's first housing finance company. In October 1977, Housing Development Finance Corporation Limited (HDFC) offered its shares for the first time on the Bombay Stock Exchange.[21]

From the beginning, Parekh envisioned a company that would be guided by the principles of professional integrity, customer service, and civic responsibility. At the same time, he imagined a company that would be highly efficient and effective—it had to be or it would not survive. Parekh was a strong proponent of openness, and he also wanted customers to feel they could trust the new company. In turn, he took the view— incomprehensible to others in the lending business—that most borrowers wanted to be honest, too. For dealing with delinquent borrowers, he had in mind a "follow-up" function that would help them meet their obligations rather than a "recoveries" function that would scare them into doing so.

Parekh also believed in teamwork and employee involvement, practices alien to the time. Employees, he felt, should know what was going on with the business, regardless of their level in the organization. They should also feel free to raise questions and make suggestions. In turn, the organization should offer training and development to encourage the potential in every individual. From the start, HDFC practiced a high degree of transparency in its operations as well as its financial reporting. Parekh's standing advice to HDFC employees was to make decisions they could stand by forever and to do nothing they would find embarrassing if it became public.

In the late 1970s, Parekh's plan seemed wildly idealistic. At the time, Indian business was rife with inefficiency and corruption. The construction industry, with which HDFC would have to work, was notorious in this respect. Most business was transacted behind closed doors, and the reins of power were closely guarded. Customer service was virtually unheard of, especially in the financial-services sector. The country's banks operated as if they were doing customers a favor by serving them, and it was normal practice for customers to offer "speed money" to move their transactions along. Most Indians, moreover, were wary of borrowing money and suspicious of those who wished to lend it. Parekh's contemporaries gave his plan little chance of success. Deepak Parekh, HDFC's chairman since 1993 and nephew of H. T. Parekh, recalled the skeptics' prognosis: "People will borrow, and they will not pay you back, the legal system is weak, and you won't be able to collect your payments," they warned.

The skeptics were wrong. Developing HDFC's business was not easy, of course. And support from international financial institutions, including a $250 million loan from the World Bank, was crucial to the company's growth. But the approach Parekh brought to the business made a strong impression on employees, customers, and the community alike. One regional manager who joined the company as a management trainee in 1984 recalled his reaction to meeting Parekh for the first time. Parekh, then over 70, entreated the newly-minted college graduates to be patient and to give him a chance. "All of us nearly fell off our chairs," recounted the manager. "Here was a man we had only read about in textbooks and newspapers, a figure to be reckoned with in India's financial world, and he was asking *us* to give *him* a chance."

Another long-term employee commented that although customer service in the early days left something to be desired, it was a "customer's delight" by the standards of the time. Instead of waiting 6 to 12 *months* for loan approvals, as was typical for public-sector banks, HDFC customers waited only six *weeks*. Customers were also impressed by HDFC's efforts to protect their confidentiality. Recognizing the social stigma attached to borrowing money, HDFC set up private areas protected with sound-absorbent partitions to ease customer concerns. On bribery, however, the company took a hard line. Employees were instructed to terminate discussions with any customer who offered a bribe. "It was harsh," recalled Deepak Satwalekar, HDFC's managing director from 1993 until late 2000, "but we wanted the message to get out loud and clear that this was not an institution that you offered bribes to."

By the mid-1980s, HDFC was growing rapidly and gaining recognition for its practices. Being the only game in town had helped, but HDFC made a point of not exploiting its monopoly status. Instead, it constantly pushed to keep its costs low and its loans affordable. As the company's success began to attract the attention of potential rivals in the late 1980s, HDFC's response was to encourage rather than quash the competition. In an effort to promote a healthy industry and discourage reckless lending, HDFC decided to work with three public-sector banks interested in creating housing-finance subsidiaries. HDFC took an equity stake of not more than 20 percent in each, and provided start-up management as well as employee training.

The credibility amassed during its early years enabled HDFC to weather the life-threatening crisis it faced in 1991, when India's international credit rating was downgraded due to the country's economic disarray. At the same time, as part of India's economic liberalization, domestic interest rates were unleashed and rose several percentage points within a matter of months. In this environment, HDFC faced the dual challenge of attracting wholesale money to fund its operations while also lending at rates people could afford. The company had two options: shut its doors or seek new sources of funding. It chose the latter and turned to retail deposit-taking in the hope that Indian consumers would trust HDFC with their money. The venture succeeded. By 1996, HDFC had become India's largest deposit-taking institution outside the banking sector.

Like many companies facing the new competition spawned by liberalization, HDFC has in recent years spent time reviewing its core values. In 1995, after a period of internal brainstorming and consultation with external experts, HDFC's managers rejected the idea of developing a formal code of ethics—not because ethics was considered unimportant, but because of the potentially deadening effect of codification. According to Satwalekar, the management group felt that norms were best transmitted by example and that codes were often ignored in practice. "We would rather live it," he said, "and that is what our founding chairman, H. T. Parekh, did."

HDFC's low employee turnover and long employee tenure testify to the appeal of the company's founding values. In 2000, the average tenure was 8 to 10 years and the turnover rate was about 2.5 percent. Explained one long-time employee, commenting on employee loyalty, "Most of the people here don't work only for a salary. We work here because it is such a unique work atmosphere. . . . At the end of the day, we experience a high. We have helped another human being achieve one of his biggest aims in life—buying a house."

Today HDFC is widely regarded as one of India's best-managed companies, with a long list of awards to its credit. Virtually every aspect of its operations has earned recognition—its governance systems, accounting practices, customer service, and civic activities, particularly its contributions to housing development for the poorest sector of Indian society. Parekh's seemingly naïve trust in borrowers has been translated into a sophisticated system for dealing with delinquencies. The result has been an unmatched level of nonperforming assets—just 0.9 percent in 2000. The company's unlikely marriage of humanity with efficiency, enabled by technology, has helped it maintain a cost-to-income ratio that analysts say is one of the lowest among Asian financial institutions.

All this has made HDFC a favorite of foreign institutional investors, who in the late 1990s gobbled up its shares to the maximum extent allowed under Indian law. Despite the emergence of numerous competitors in the decade following India's liberalization, as of 2001 HDFC was still the country's premier housing finance institution, with about 50 percent of the housing loan market. As the company has embraced new technologies, faced intensified competition, and moved into new lines of business, it has sought to remain true to its guiding principles—integrity, transparency, sharing, customer service, civic responsibility, and genuineness of purpose. Says Chairman Deepak Parekh, "These values are not only good in themselves; they make sound business sense."[22]

Beyond Value-Free Management

As these profiles show, the paths to values are many and varied. Some companies arrive by way of a crisis or a scandal. Others come by way of an executive's personal conviction or a process of logical reasoning and reflection. Some are problem-driven. Others are opportunity-driven. Most arrive through a mix of both positive and negative factors.

Whatever the path, though, more and more companies are rejecting traditional ideas of management as a "value-free" science and business as an "ethics-free zone." Executives are coming to see attention to values not as a frill or an indulgence but as an integral part of effective management, touching all aspects of a company's operations. Many now believe that adhering to the core principles found in virtually all the world's ethical traditions is neither naïve nor a sign of weakness, but rather smart and a source of organizational strength. And some are coming to view moral judgment as a help rather than a hindrance in doing business.

What accounts for this shift in attitudes? Is it a passing fad or a symptom of fundamental change? Are the driving forces financial, or are other factors at work? To answer these questions, we must look more deeply at the themes introduced in this chapter and place the turn to values in a larger context.

2

Does Ethics Pay?

When AES Corporation went public in 1991, its prospectus described the company's commitment to four values—integrity, fairness, fun, and social responsibility. This list, although in some ways unremarkable, was at the time unusual for an independent power producer like AES, and it apparently set off alarm bells at the SEC, which insisted that the company mention its values in the section of the prospectus dealing with "risk factors."

Perhaps the SEC was taken aback not so much by the values themselves as by what the prospectus said about them: "[T]he company seeks to adhere to these values not as a means to achieve economic success, but because adherence is a worthwhile goal in and of itself." Should a conflict between these values and profits arise, the prospectus stated, the company would try to adhere to its values, even if doing so might result in "diminished profits and foregone opportunities."[1]

The stance taken in the AES prospectus is unusual. Rarely do executives state publicly and without qualification that their company's values have intrinsic worth. Rarer still are statements that such commitments may be allowed to override profits. Instead, in recent years, as values have come to the forefront, executives have tended to emphasize their financial benefits while downplaying the potential for conflict between ethical and economic considerations. As we saw in Chapter 1, many companies have turned to values as a way to create "value," through improved risk management, better internal functioning, enhanced market positioning, and improved standing in the community.

The shift in rhetoric over the past few decades has been striking. Not so long ago, concerns such as safety, quality, diversity, and environmental responsibility were deemed unaffordable luxuries. In 1971, Lee Iacocca, then president of Ford Motor Company, reacted defiantly when the subject of auto safety came up in a meeting with President Richard Nixon. "Hold it . . ." said Iacocca. "What do you mean they want safety? . . . We cannot carry the load of inflation in wages *and* safety in a four-year period without breaking our back." Today, the safety of products and people is frequently said to be a source of competitive advantage.[2]

As the ultimate financial benefits of addressing safety, quality, environmental, and other social interests have become more widely appreciated, concerns about potential conflicts between shareholders and other stakeholders also seem to have diminished. In its 1997 report on corporate governance, the Business Roundtable stated that it did not view shareholder and stakeholder interests as being in conflict. An advisory group to the Organisation for Economic Co-operation and Development (OECD) project on corporate governance took a similar view in a 1998 report: "Attending to legitimate social concerns should, in the long run, benefit all parties, including investors." And the majority of CFOs polled by *CFO* magazine in 1995 agreed with the Harnischfeger Industries executive who said, "I just don't think being responsible to stakeholders is in conflict with shareholder value."[3]

These statements, if taken at face value, suggest that many executives are coming to believe that an ethical stance pays off—and not merely in the metaphorical sense of being beneficial. These executives seem to think that adhering to a set of values and respecting the interests of others actually cash out in terms of real dollars and cents. Their view is similar to that of James Burke, the former CEO of Johnson & Johnson who steered the U.S.-based health products company through the legendary Tylenol crisis of 1982.

The story is well known. When Burke and other key managers found themselves unable to account for seven mysterious deaths linked with the company's popular Tylenol capsules, they took the dramatic and unprecedented step of pulling 31 million bottles of the pain reliever from store shelves and kitchen cabinets across the United States. The decision came after intensive debate and discussion during which the executives concluded that a nationwide recall was the course of action most consistent with the company's responsibilities. At the time, Tylenol was Johnson & Johnson's most important brand name and the market leader in the pain reliever category. The drug accounted for something like 8 percent of annual sales and 16 to 18 percent of net profit.[4]

Following the recall, which cost the company more than $100 million, Johnson & Johnson immediately mobilized the industry to work with regulators in formulating new product packaging requirements. Just six weeks later, Tylenol capsules, in new tamper-resistant packaging, were back in the marketplace. Not only did Johnson & Johnson recover the market share lost from what was later determined to have been product tampering, but the Tylenol brand surged ahead even further. Asked to explain his company's handling of the crisis and the remarkable recovery that followed, Burke answered simply, "I think the answer comes down to the value system. . . . What's right works. It really does. The cynics will tell you it doesn't, but they're wrong."[5]

What should we make of this new attitude? Does ethical commitment enhance shareholder value, or was the SEC right to regard AES's values as a risk factor for investors? Put more simply, does ethics pay? Answering this question requires a closer look at the arguments on both sides. As the analysis will show, the financial case for values has much to recommend it, but in the end "ethics pays" is a poor guide for companies aspiring to positions of leadership in today's world. To achieve truly superior performance, managers will need to think rather differently about the role of values. But this is getting ahead of the story. Before we look at what's wrong with "ethics pays," let's look more carefully at what's right about it. A later chapter will discuss the experience of AES.[6]

The New Math

The profiles sketched in Chapter 1 suggest that the financial case for values is quite robust. There we saw various ways in which economic advantage may accrue to companies that embrace even a modest set of ethical commitments. Compare two hypothetical companies. One practices the strict form of moral neutrality or indifference associated with value-free management. Let's call this company Indico (for "Indifferent Company"). The other has adopted a modest set of ethical commitments—to principles of honesty, reliability, fairness, consideration for others, and respect for law—to govern its activities. The members and agents of this company try to adhere to these principles in their dealings with one another and with the world at large. Let's call this company Comco (for "Committed Company").

Notice that Comco's people are not pure altruists, in the classic sense of that term. They are not interested in sacrificing themselves for the good of others, but they do believe in reciprocity and doing their fair share. They try to be honest and fair in their dealings, and conscientious in carrying out their responsibilities. They honor their agreements and promises even in circumstances when breaking them would appear advantageous, and they avoid free riding on the efforts of others. They also respect the law and try to follow it, and if they believe the law is wrong or unwise, they use lawful channels for seeking to change it. They are what we might call "mutualists" for their belief in fairness and reciprocity.

The people of Indico, on the other hand, are neither malevolent nor deliberately out to harm anyone. They simply see business as an "ethics-free" zone, where considerations of truth and falsity, fairness and unfairness, benefit and harm have no relevance. Concerned only to maximize their own financial gain, Indico personnel are indifferent to the rights, interests, and concerns of others. From the standpoint of Indico's people, the law is a list of prices for certain specified behaviors rather than a set of normative standards to govern their conduct. Like the "rational man" of neoclassical economic thought, they obey the law only if the risk of penalties makes it financially prudent to do so. Otherwise they ignore it. Indico's people are quite happy to free ride on the efforts of others, and they consider themselves clever when they manage to shift the costs of Indico's activities to other parties while capturing the benefits for their company.

Which company is best positioned for financial success? And should we consider Indico "focused" (which is good) or "myopic" (which is dangerous)? A deeper look reveals that Indico's single-minded approach has some severe limitations and that Comco's commitments have some significant benefits. Rather than being handicapped by its values as is frequently assumed, Comco actually enjoys a number of economic advantages relative to Indico.

Perhaps the most commonly cited advantage is a lower cost of complaints. Because Comco adheres to basic standards of law and ethics, it is likely to face fewer complaints about its behavior. This means less time and money spent in dealing with charges brought by those who feel they have been wronged or injured by its activities, and less time and money spent dealing with law enforcement officials, lawyers, and the whole apparatus of the legal system. Comco is also less vulnerable to the kind of misconduct-triggered crises that have crippled many companies and nearly destroyed others over the past few decades. As numerous examples show, the financial costs associated with these high-profile scandals can be enormous.

The Salomon case described in Chapter 1 is a good example of how a "small" deception, compounded by management inaction, mushroomed into a crisis from which the company never fully recovered. Although we do not have a precise breakdown of the costs associated with that "billion-dollar error in judgment," a tally of possible out-of-pocket and opportunity costs would certainly include:

- revenue losses due to customer defections and lost sales
- revenue losses due to a two-month suspension from trading with the Federal Reserve Bank of New York
- higher operating costs due to diminished productivity
- higher funding costs imposed by lenders and investors
- higher turnover costs due to employee defections
- higher recruiting costs stemming from damage to the firm's reputation
- increased marketing and public relations expenses needed to overcome reputational damage and restore public confidence
- additional consulting fees connected with investigating the allegations and implementing management and operational changes to correct past errors and prevent future malfeasance
- additional legal expenses associated with investigating, defending, and settling charges brought by the U.S. government, Salomon investors, and other private parties claiming to have been injured by the firm's actions
- fines, penalties, damages, and settlement costs resulting from legal proceedings, including $290 million paid to settle charges brought by the U.S. Department of Justice
- the discount secured by Travelers Group when it acquired Salomon in 1997

We should not forget that Salomon was lucky. Unlike E. F. Hutton, Drexel Burnham Lambert, and Kidder Peabody—three other Wall Street firms brought down by misconduct—Salomon survived its crisis. The recovery was due in large measure to Salomon board member Warren Buffett's stepping in as interim chairman after the crisis broke. "No Warren, no firm," was then-COO Maughan's succinct assessment six months after Salomon's trading "irregularities" hit the front page.[7]

Buffett brought a reputation for unquestionable integrity and uncommon financial acumen to a dire situation. Recognizing that Salomon had to "earn back its integrity," he adopted a posture of candor and cooperation, and vowed that he would follow the facts wherever they led and get them out. Buffett even promised to waive the attorney-client privilege and turn over all reports and notes prepared by the firm's lawyers in investigating the trading desk transgressions.[8]

This unprecedented degree of openness proved helpful in persuading clients that Salomon could recover. As one investment banker noted, "We had a very bad hand. But Buffett gave us a card." Buffett, Maughan, and Denham set about systematically rebuilding Salomon's relationships with its key stakeholders by communicating intensively with employees every day and going on the road to speak with customers, creditors, investors, and governments around the world. Even so, as noted earlier, it was a good two years before Salomon was able to put the crisis behind and begin driving forward again.

Although the Salomon case was dramatic, the pattern it revealed is not unique. When misconduct, or even the suspicion of misconduct, is made public, the financial effect is never positive, and researchers studying U.S. companies have found that firms convicted of wrongdoing often experience lower returns in succeeding years. As the Salomon case illustrates, the financial situation can sometimes deteriorate very quickly. The downward spiral often begins with public allegations that set off a chain reaction starting with the stakeholder group most immediately affected.[9]

Customer-related allegations, for instance, often trigger customer defections. These, in turn, have a depressing effect on revenues. When revenues shrink, employees begin to have doubts about the company's future and their own prospects. Meanwhile, injured parties begin their quest for recompense, filing lawsuits and broadcasting their complaints far and wide over traditional media as well as E-mail and the Internet. Before long, investigations are set in motion as managers, lawyers, and regulators try to sort out what went wrong, who is accountable, and what is to be done.

These investigations complicate the lives of employees and managers who must respond to repeated requests for information while at the same time operating the business and reassuring colleagues and customers. Uncertainty grows with the gradual emergence of the underlying facts— and the inevitable rumors about who knew what when. Investors, sensing increased risk, begin demanding higher returns, and rating agencies may downgrade the company's credit ratings. Funding costs rise, as do the financial pressures felt throughout the organization. Politicians and lawmakers may enter the fray with calls for public hearings and more investigations that exacerbate the deterioration.

In this vicious downward spiral, each constituency's loss of confidence reinforces everyone else's. One after the other, key relationships unwind as the fragile bonds of trust give way to distrust and doubt. In serious cases, the loss of confidence may extend all the way to the company's top managers, undermining the basis of their authority and their ability to lead. As in the Salomon case, key executives may be fired or forced to resign. For professional service firms and others whose wealth resides principally in people and liquid assets, the unraveling may be impossible to halt.

The ultimate result may even be bankruptcy, as Enron's meltdown in December 2001 vividly demonstrated. To be sure, the bankruptcy of this once-renowned energy trading giant cannot be attributed solely to the ethical breaches revealed to the public in the late fall of 2001. Investors had begun to grow wary of Enron's economic prospects many months before they learned about the company's misleading accounting practices and its executives' flagrant self-dealing. Between January and September 2001, Enron's share price fell from $80 to $30 as a growing number of investments failed to pay off and changing market conditions weakened the company's earnings picture.

The revelations of ethical breakdowns, however, proved the *coup de grâce*. As evidence of improper accounting, questionable financial engineering, and executive conflicts of interest came to light, criticism of the company's dealings took on a new tone. Enron's CFO, it turned out, had not only managed certain off-balance-sheet partnerships that did hundreds of millions in business with Enron but had also personally benefited from the arrangement in amounts said to exceed $45 million. The highly intricate and too-clever-by-half partnerships had allowed Enron to inflate profits while at the same time concealing debt that would have hampered its ability to raise the funds needed for its ambitious growth plans. Enron's board of directors had approved the partnerships and even voted to relax the company's rules against conflicts of interest to allow the CFO to serve as their general manager. What's more, as the company's increasing difficulties became obvious to its highly paid executives, they had sold off their own Enron shares while continuing to tout them to employees and others as sound investments. During one period, as the stock price was tumbling, employees were even prevented from selling Enron shares held in their retirement accounts because of a "lock-down" or freeze on the assets to allow the company to change retirement fund administrators.[10]

Following the pattern outlined earlier, these disclosures set in motion a series of reactions among the company's constituencies and various watchdog groups. Regulators geared up for investigations, while shareholders, creditors, employees, and other injured parties began lining up to press legal claims. Rating agencies downgraded the company's credit. Meanwhile, customers and investors fled in droves. Federal prosecutors turned their attention to possible criminal probes, and Congress prepared for public hearings. After the failure of a last-ditch effort to line up an acquirer for the ailing company, a further credit downgrade triggered repayment obligations that Enron could not meet. The company, which at its peak boasted a market capitalization of $70 billion and ranked seventh among the *Fortune* 500, filed for protection from its creditors. By January 2002, when the New York Stock Exchange suspended trading in Enron shares, they were valued at

$.60. Copies of the Enron code of ethics, some advertised jokingly as "never been read," were trading on eBay for as much as $10 to $20 each.

Although the full costs of Enron's collapse will not be known for a long time to come, the amounts look to be staggering. Even without considering the collateral damage inflicted on innocent parties around the globe, it is already clear that investors, employees, and creditors have lost tens of billions of dollars in what at the time was the largest bankruptcy in U.S. history. Given its magnitude, the Enron debacle has done more than perhaps any previous corporate scandal to underscore the linkage between values and corporate financial performance.

Invisible Savings

No company wants to be an Enron or a Salomon Brothers. But if the economic case for values depended only on avoiding such high-profile scandals, it would not be that compelling. True, the costs of these episodes can be substantial. On the other hand, from a purely financial point of view, the risk might be worth the gamble since even in our information age, most misconduct does not become front-page news. Sometimes it goes on for years without attracting public notice or even the attention of senior management.

But the economic case for values does not rest solely on the avoidance of high-visibility scandals. An even more compelling line of reasoning concerns unexposed wrongs and low-grade misdoings that are typically hidden from public view—what one manager characterized as "behavior that people today just shouldn't have to put up with." This category includes workplace irritants and demoralizers such as belittling comments, betrayals of confidence, neglected promises, self-serving half-truths, behind-the-scenes manipulation, misappropriation of credit, half-hearted effort, unwarranted favoritism, angry outbursts, *ad hominem* attacks, careless execution, evasions of responsibility, refusals to admit mistakes, and various other forms of inconsiderate behavior.

To the extent that its principles rule out such conduct, Comco can anticipate cost advantages along a number of dimensions. Monitoring costs—the costs of supervising and overseeing the work of others—are just one example. Even the modest ethical commitments adopted by Comco would appear to yield substantial benefits in the form of lower monitoring costs, for if people are truthful, reliable, and conscientious in doing their work, the need for expensive oversight and surveillance is lessened.

Moreover, if people can be counted on to act responsibly—exercising their best judgment on the company's behalf and putting the company's interests ahead of personal concerns—they can be entrusted to make important decisions. Authority can thus be decentralized and dispersed across the organization, and people's knowledge and energies better utilized. As suggested by the Sealed Air profile, companies in which such values are deeply embedded can function with larger spans of control, fewer layers of supervisory management, and less time devoted to overseeing the work of others—all of which add up to ongoing and cumulative cost savings.

Or consider coordination costs—the costs of assuring that the parts of the organization work together smoothly and effectively as a whole. In this area, too, gains in efficiency result when people are truthful, reliable, considerate, and fair. To put it another way, the costs of coordinating the work performed by different organizational units, be they individuals, teams, departments, or divisions, are likely to increase as the level of adherence to these values declines. Consider what happens when people transmit false information or shade the truth; when they fail to meet their commitments on time; when some try to do less than their fair share of the work or capture more than their fair share of the rewards; or when they are so focused on their own narrow interests that they ignore the needs of others with whom they must interact. The results in such cases are apt to be slower cycle times, misspent energy, and poor execution—all of which undermine the organization's ability to serve its customers.

A similar logic applies to contracting costs. When the parties to a transaction perceive each other as honest, reliable, fair, and considerate, they are apt to trust one another more. When the level of trust is high, the costs of contracting are likely to drop because there is less urgency to negotiate the resolution of remote contingencies in advance. Also, the process of reaching agreement is likely to proceed more smoothly and with less need for external verification. Moreover, the resulting formal contracts can be briefer and less rigid, giving both parties greater flexibility to adapt to changing circumstances over time without the expense and inconvenience of renegotiating prior agreements. These benefits apply to internal agreements among employees as well as to dealings with external parties such as prospective customers or suppliers.

Of course, the parties must still define their goals and specify their basic rights and responsibilities. In this sense, trust is not a substitute for contracts, as is sometimes claimed. However, greater mutual trust does reduce the time, effort, and emotional wear and tear involved in devising detailed agreements that try to protect both parties against the opportunism of the other. This is likely to be a losing proposition in any event for genuine opportunists care little for the agreements they make and readily find ways around obligations that become inconvenient.

Political and regulatory cost advantages are another little-noticed benefit. Companies that are seen to be trustworthy and civic-minded frequently have an easier time dealing with regulators and other public officials. Assuming that the process is not corrupt (an important caveat to be discussed in more detail later), such companies are more apt to be heard sympathetically and more apt to be believed when presenting an argument or applying for a license or product approval, for instance. Strong credibility can sometimes give companies greater voice in regulatory and policy matters that affect their business. HDFC, for example, has long been considered a trustworthy spokesperson for India's housing finance sector, and the Indian government has often adopted its policy recommendations—for example, to extend tax benefits to borrowers for home financing.

Furthermore, when things do go wrong, as they inevitably will from time to time despite everyone's best efforts, a company's track record of honesty, reliability, and good citizenship can well prove to be its strongest defense against the punitive tendencies of politicians, law enforcement officials, and juries. In this regard, it is interesting to compare Salomon's $290 million settlement with the $650 million in penalties levied against Drexel Burnham Lambert. When asked about this difference, SEC Chairman Richard Breeden pointed not only to differences in the underlying offenses but also to Salomon's open and cooperative response to resolving the matter once it was disclosed. In fact, a U.S. attorney for the southern district of New York called Salomon's cooperation "virtually unprecedented." So even when it comes to legal fines and penalties, ethical commitment can translate into a cost advantage.[11]

Comco's self-imposed commitments may also reduce its compliance costs. Here again Salomon is a case in point. After the Treasury auction crisis, the firm implemented a new compliance system requiring extensive documentation of bids, orders, and confirmations, as well as compliance department approvals of many transactions and even of correspondence with officials at the Treasury and Federal Reserve. Compliance officers were moved out of their offices and onto the trading floor, and some were stationed near the trading desk to monitor compliance during Treasury auctions. In a firm that achieves self-discipline through adherence to values, the compliance function can be far less extensive and far less intrusive than this.

In addition, such self-discipline also helps curb compliance costs by reducing the need for restrictive laws and regulations. Corporate overreaching, malfeasance, and questionable business practices have been decisive factors in mobilizing public support for many of the U.S. business laws and regulations now on the books: antitrust, food and drug safety, truth in advertising, securities regulation, employment discrimination, workplace safety, consumer safety, anticorruption, environmental protection, and so on. As of spring 2002, the U.S. Congress and various government agencies were considering an array of new regulations to contain the abuses revealed by Enron's collapse and the previous year's accounting failures at numerous companies. Had these companies held themselves to Comco's standards, new laws and regulations might well have been thought unnecessary.[12]

Underlying all these specific instances of cost advantage, however, is a more general point: the linkage between basic values and efficiency. The case studies cited so far demonstrate how commitments to truth, reliability, fairness, and respect can enhance management and group efficiency. Conversely, virtually any management activity becomes more difficult and more time-consuming—and thus more costly—in their absence. Even such routine tasks as evaluating a proposal, resolving a dispute, or mobilizing a team to address an important issue become far more difficult in environments plagued with the gamesmanship, self-promotion, and information spinning characteristic of moral indifference.

One pervasive problem in such environments is that nothing can be taken at face value. Managers must devote time to verifying information and correcting it for bias and exaggeration. Communication is more difficult. People stop saying what they mean and meaning what they say. As explicit messages lose their credibility, managers must find other ways to signal what they "really" mean. Truth-tellers tend to self-censor for fear of stepping on powerful toes. Because promises cannot be relied on, more time and effort must go into anticipating and preparing for contingencies as well as in checking up, overseeing, and otherwise making sure that what has been promised is in fact delivered. People become obsessed with "getting it in writing" and keeping "CYA memos" to protect themselves in the likely event of future mishaps and disputes.

By contrast, managers in companies that practice high standards of honesty, reliability, and fairness can spend far less time on such redundancies. Instead, they can focus on more productive activities such as supporting their people, serving customers, or developing new business. When people really care about what is true, more than about jockeying for position, they can see the world more objectively and evaluate things more dispassionately. Thus, we would expect a high regard for truth and honesty to contribute to better planning, better decision making, and more efficient problem solving. Why? Because the underlying information is more apt to be accurate, the analysis more objective, and the decision makers freer to acknowledge problems and risks. We would also expect to see fewer resources wasted on unrealistic projects undertaken for reasons of ego gratification or political accommodation.

No company openly espouses anything other than truth and honesty. However, what these values are thought to require and the extent to which they are actually practiced vary widely. Not long ago, I was on a plane when the man sitting next to me struck up a conversation. He was on his way home to Europe from a business trip abroad. Soon he began talking about his work, and eventually I asked about his job. At that point we had not talked about my line of work at all, so he was unaware that I might take a professional interest in what he was about to say.

With the look of someone expecting a reaction, he responded by telling me that he was a "liar." Every month, as regional manager for a particular division of this rather sizeable company, he fabricated reports to send to headquarters. He explained that his company had been bought a few years earlier by a large global concern. The new management's response to his first truthful report was so hostile that he never again dared to tell the truth. But, he went on, he would have to lie for only a few more years because he would soon be eligible for retirement.

As I listened to this man, who appeared increasingly troubled as he talked about his predicament, I thought about his company's planning process and the decisions that its senior managers were probably taking on the basis of his fabricated reports. Even if he was the only person in the company submitting false information—not very likely, based on what he had told me—the scenario did not seem promising. Quite apart from the risk of potential liabilities related to financial misreporting, the company was undermining its own ability to make realistic plans and projections. How could management do a decent job of allocating resources or formulating strategy without accurate information? And how many employees had, like this man, become so demoralized and cynical that they were simply marking time until retirement or the next takeover?

Without knowing more, it is impossible to say whether responsibility for this situation lay principally with the man I met or with the company's management. Surely, he was in the wrong for submitting false information, but his managers were also at fault for creating an environment so hostile to the truth. Their reactions to his first and only truthful report and their satisfaction with his subsequent false reports conveyed a clear message that truth was expendable.

This example offers a glimpse of the damaging but often invisible costs of chronic, low-grade misconduct. We have no evidence that this company was engaged in outright deceit, and the likelihood of legal challenge appears quite remote. Nonetheless, the low regard for truth and honesty evidenced in management's behavior was taking a subtle toll on the company's financial performance through its effect on planning, decision making, and the morale of employees like the troubled, disillusioned man sitting next to me on the plane that day.

A Positive Angle

So far, this chapter has focused on the negative case for values—the ways in which they help contain costs. A more positive side of the argument has to do with revenue and productivity gains. Some of these positive advantages flow from the heightened engagement and creativity associated with a commitment to values such as honesty, fairness, and respect for the individual.

As we've already noted, when adherence to these values is high, employees and managers can devote their energies to their work instead of worrying about protecting themselves and saving their ideas from being poached by others. They're also likely to have a more favorable attitude toward contributing. After all, who among us will voluntarily exert our best efforts or share our best ideas unless we feel confident of being treated fairly in return? Moreover, companies with fair and open hiring processes stand to benefit by attracting and retaining the best talent.

Employee empowerment plays a crucial role here. For many people, respect and recognition are sources of positive energy. When people are trusted and treated equitably, they are inspired both to do more and to do a better job. When their contributions are acknowledged, they take more pride in their work and are more interested in how it relates to the work of others and the good of the whole. Many people—assuming they have or can acquire the skills and knowledge necessary to do their jobs—are energized by opportunities to display their capabilities. Such employees actually contribute more when given discretion and responsibility than when they are carefully monitored, or tightly constrained by narrow job descriptions. When centralized companies decentralize decision making and expand employee discretion, they not only speed up decisions and eliminate costly layers of management but also tap into reservoirs of human energy.

By this reasoning, the ethical commitments of the hypothetical Comco should contribute to greater employee engagement and creativity. Comco calls on everyone to assume an attitude of responsibility and to practice honesty, fairness, and consideration for others. In contrast to Indico, which is indifferent to people's moral needs and capabilities, we might also expect the people of Comco to show greater initiative in identifying opportunities and solving problems outside the defined domain of their specific jobs. Because Comco's employees have a higher level of concern for and trust in one another, they are also more likely to share information and knowledge among themselves. In principle, then, we would expect Comco to have an edge along a whole series of dimensions important for sustained profitability in today's environment—creativity, problem-solving, opportunity-identification, and knowledge-sharing.[13]

This scenario may sound overly idealistic, but a number of studies have found links between values and such benefits. Researchers have found, for instance, that:

- Trust, helpfulness, and fairness in rewarding creative work are associated with higher levels of work-group creativity. Less creative work groups are more likely to have experienced dishonest communications, destructive competition, and political problems.[14]
- Employees are more likely to support management decisions that have been reached through a fair process. By the same token, employees are more likely to subvert decisions that benefit particular groups at the expense of the organization as a whole.[15]
- Employees are more likely to engage in discretionary behavior (that is, beyond the defined requirements of the job) to benefit the organization if they trust their supervisors to treat them fairly and perceive that the organization operates fairly.[16]
- Employees look for integrity, competence, and leadership in their bosses. They judge the trustworthiness of their supervisors by behavior that demonstrates honesty, reliability, forthrightness, principled conviction, and a willingness to trust others.[17]
- Employees are more likely to take pride and feel ownership in their organization when they perceive top management to have high credibility and a coherent set of values.[18]
- Employees are more likely to share knowledge and learn from one another in an environment of mutual trust and respect.[19] Conversely, low trust impedes the flow of knowledge.[20]
- Members of an organization are more likely to share sensitive information when they have trust and confidence in one another.[21]

- Partnerships between manufacturers and retailers are more profitable when they are based on high levels of mutual trust. High-trust partnerships emerge when the parties are honest, dependable, and mutually attentive to one another's welfare.[22]

These findings have their roots in the positive attitudes typically engendered by honesty, fairness, and consideration. Such attitudes are much in evidence at a company like Sealed Air, which, as noted earlier, has tried to base its development on these values. Asked to compare Sealed Air's culture with that of other companies they knew, many longtime employees offered comments similar in spirit to those of the hourly employee quoted in Chapter 1 who described his colleagues as taking pride and interest in their work:

- "Here there's lots of freedom to do good things and be noticed for it. . . . No one in the middle grabs the glory. People are recognized for their contribution. That's where the creativity comes from."
- "There's more accessibility, more freedom in speaking up, raising problems, working in cross-functional teams."
- "You can walk into an office and talk to anyone here to get something done."
- "They listen to you here. You may not get what you want, but they're listening. . . . You feel that Sealed Air cares for you."
- "People trust that if things don't work out, Sealed Air will do the right thing. Their severance will be fair."
- "Here, people are very honest and direct. You can communicate easily without thinking five sentences in advance and wondering, 'Is it okay?'"
- "If the emperor has no clothes, someone around here is going to tell him."
- "People pitch in wherever and whenever necessary. People wear lots of hats. We try to keep the company as flexible and nimble as possible to take advantage of opportunities as they arise."
- "It's a company on the move . . . . Here you continue growing, improving . . ."
- "You're treated like an adult here . . ."[23]

In general, the linkage between values and employee engagement would lead us also to expect tie-ins between values and employee loyalty.

Loyalty, in turn, translates into lower turnover and recruiting costs, as well as better knowledge retention because of greater employee continuity. People who are engaged in their jobs and feel they are being fairly rewarded are less likely to be seeking other opportunities. And even if opportunities come along, such employees are less likely to want to leave. Sealed Air is again a case in point: Its traditionally low turnover rate is unsurprising in view of employees' attitudes toward their jobs and the company. One employee who turned down an offer for higher pay at a different company put it quite directly: "I'm not a person who has trouble with change. I like change and do well with it. . . . It was the way I felt . . . . Sealed Air was giving back more than just money. Here I would be able to develop."

We saw similar attitudes at HDFC. As noted in Chapter 1, the company's employee turnover rate hovers around 2.5 percent, compared to 20 percent at other financial institutions. When asked why they stayed, employees talked about the company's openness, opportunities for high levels of responsibility, participatory decision making, and the nature of the business itself. As important as what people said was how they said it—with enthusiasm and obvious pride.

Several recent studies bear out a connection between values and employee loyalty. A 1999 study of U.S. employees found a higher percentage of "truly loyals"—those who voluntarily went the extra mile at work and intended to stay with their companies despite having other options—among people who regarded their companies as highly ethical. Some 55 percent of this group were found to be truly loyal, compared to 24 percent of those who saw their companies as ethically neutral and 9 percent of those who felt their companies were not ethical. A 32-country study of employee commitment conducted by the same organizations in 2000 found that employees worldwide cited fairness at work (including fair pay), care and concern for employees, and trust in employees as the top factors influencing their commitment to their organizations. The study also found that employees regarded these same areas as those in most need of attention from employers.[24]

Managers have frequently told me that their ethics efforts have aided their quality initiatives. If the line of reasoning presented here is correct, such effects are only logical. To the extent that quality of output, whether of goods or services, is a consequence of employee focus, energy, and conscientious effort, we would expect a positive relationship between company values and quality. This relationship is further reinforced by the linkages noted earlier between values and coordination. As quality experts have long pointed out, high-quality output requires a high level of cooperation among people, teams, departments, and divisions. Optimal cooperation, in turn, requires high levels of trust. And trust, as we have seen repeatedly, is itself the result of adhering to basic values such as honesty, reliability, and consideration for others. It is through such behaviors that people demonstrate their own trustworthiness and thus in turn activate others' willingness to trust them.[25]

Evidence for links between values and quality can also be found in recent research on the characteristics of outstanding service companies. A key determinant of service quality, it turns out, is how companies treat their employees. The research indicates that employees show more concern for their customers when their bosses and employers show more concern for them. This concern for customers translates into greater success in meeting customers' needs, which leads in turn to a more loyal clientele. And a more loyal clientele contributes to greater profitability. Similarly, other researchers have found that adhering to humanistic values can contribute to higher levels of loyalty among customers, employees, and investors.[26]

These findings appear to reflect a series of underlying principles of human interaction. Most people are not indifferent to how they are treated, and many practice a kind of interactive moral accounting based on a principle of mutuality. So, for example, employees who feel they are being misled or taken advantage of often feel little compunction about doing the same to others. As one employee who was caught in a dubious sales scheme put it, "An unhappy [employee] who figures he's been shafted is going to shaft someone else." Sometimes the "someone else" is actually the "shafter," as in the case of former Enron employees who, after the company's collapse, took to selling sensitive corporate information online. The "someone else" may also be a third party such as a customer, end user, or family member who bears the brunt of an employee's frustration.[27]

In another variation of this pattern, an employee responsible for competitor intelligence gathering felt justified in funneling his company's confidential information to a rival firm because of his own managers' cavalier corporate espionage activities. As this employee saw it, management deserved to get the same treatment it was giving to others. The same underlying dynamic applies to customer and other relationships as well. Consider the Salomon clients who, according to an executive of the firm, took advantage of the Treasury auction crisis to get even for past slights, such as "the time a trader slammed the phone down in my ear."[28]

By the same token, decency often begets decency. As already noted, employees are more likely to engage in voluntary behavior that benefits their organization when they feel that the organization has treated them fairly. Similarly, as also noted just above, employees who feel they are well treated are more apt to treat customers well. Another example is HDFC's successful recoveries function, mentioned in Chapter 1, whose design reflects the principle of reciprocal decency. Instead of automatically browbeating delinquent borrowers, the approach was to learn the reasons for delinquencies and then to work with borrowers to solve problems that stood in the way of fulfilling their obligations. On occasion, this approach has led HDFC to take some unusual steps to support its borrowers. In one case, an HDFC employee who learned of an upcoming strike at a factory showed up at the gates at 1.30 A.M. to reassure HDFC borrowers who had been caught in the ensuing management lockout. "The first thing they wanted to do [when they got back to work] was pay us back," recalled the head of recoveries.

Such positive behaviors, like their negative counterparts, seem to be guided by an underlying principle of general as well as specific mutuality. That is, many people tend not only to engage in payback and reciprocal assistance but also to carry forward moral credits and debits to their interactions with other third parties.

Recent research on human emotions is beginning to show that merely witnessing good deeds can enhance people's motivation to do such deeds themselves. Moreover, the observer need not be the beneficiary for the response to be triggered. This is not merely an instance of mimicry, though the power of example, both positive and negative, is quite important. Rather, the effect has both a psychological and physiological base, according to experts. This research may help explain the persistence of traditions emphasizing virtue as an aspect of leadership, as well as the power of exemplary behavior to command respect since both may have roots in human biology.[29]

A line of research in the field of game theory lends further support to the notion that decency begets decency and reinforces what moral philosophers have long taught—that mutuality is superior to selfishness as a guide to conduct. This research, which focuses on a highly stylized puzzle called the "prisoners' dilemma," involves two parties who stand to gain from cooperating with one another. However, a problem arises because one party can gain even more by not cooperating, called "defecting" in the jargon of the game, so long as the other party is trying to cooperate. There's a catch, though. If both parties pursue this self-centered course of action, both end up worse off than they would have had they both cooperated. That is, if both play a game of winner-take-all, the result is lose-lose.

Given the puzzle's structure, it might seem as if the ultimate "winner" in a series of prisoners' dilemmas would be the party who can most often get away with not cooperating while the other party tries to cooperate.

However, the research suggests that those who persistently pursue the self-ish option are apt to do less well for themselves than those who are more willing to cooperate. For one thing, those harmed by selfish defections tend to retaliate, thus negating the earlier gains of the self-interested actor. It turns out that the most advantageous strategy from a purely self-interested point of view is what the researchers dubbed "tit-for-tat."[30]

"Tit-for-tat" is a strategy of positive reciprocity that begins with a will-ingness to cooperate but thereafter simply mimics the behavior of the other party by repaying defection with defection and cooperation with coopera-tion. Two parties committed to this strategy can cooperate indefinitely—at least, this has been the result when computers have played this game tour-nament fashion. Life is considerably more complicated than a computer game, to be sure, but this research gives us additional reasons for thinking that Comco might benefit from the values it has adopted.

The prisoners' dilemma research points to another important principle of human interaction: Like the players in researchers' games, most people in real life prefer to deal with "cooperators"—people and companies they can trust. To put it another way, how many of us voluntarily do business with companies that we believe to be dishonest, unfair, unreliable, or unre-sponsive? Given a choice, most of us shun such companies. Whether we're making a purchase, choosing an employer, making an investment, or select-ing a business partner, we look for evidence of trustworthiness and respon-siveness. Sometimes we have direct evidence based on our own experience. Often, however, we must rely on indirect evidence through word of mouth or reputation.

The Reputation Connection

Reputational benefits are yet another linkage between values and the top line. As we saw in Chapter 1, reputational considerations have played a cen-tral role in many companies' turn to values. Shell, for instance, initially framed its Brent Spar and Nigeria-inspired reforms as reputation manage-ment efforts. When Warren Buffett took over as interim chairman of Salomon after the Treasury auction crisis, his first concern was the firm's reputation. Besides instructing senior managers to report "instantaneously and directly" any legal violations or moral failures by Salomon employees, he told the firm's assembled personnel: "Lose money for the firm, I will be very under-standing; lose a shred of reputation for the firm, I will be ruthless."[31]

Executives like Buffett and Shell's top management understand instinc-tively what researchers have begun to document—that a commitment to values like honesty, fairness, and responsibility is crucial for building a good reputation. Companies that display these qualities are not just meeting their immediate constituencies' needs for truthful information, fair treatment, or on-time delivery; they are also sending out messages about their attractiveness as business partners. These messages, which are then perceived, interpreted, and passed along by the parties involved or by third-party observers, play a key role in shaping how a company is regarded and thus in the overall impression of its attractiveness held by potential employees, customers, investors, and other audiences. It is through this process that companies build a reputation and amass the goodwill that is sometimes called reputational capital.[32]

Given this dynamic, we would expect a close correlation between a company's level of ethical competency and its reputation. Although research on this linkage is lacking, corporate reputation experts advise that a good reputation depends on management practices that prevent reputation-destroying misconduct, foster quality and customer service, respect the natural environment, and demonstrate corporate citizenship.[33] And what are these if not specific examples of responsibility, fairness, and consideration toward a company's constituencies? Furthermore, *Fortune* magazine, which periodically ranks America's companies, reports that the most admired companies tend to be "good guys." Conversely, as shown by the cases examined earlier, involvement in wrongdoing or failure to deal responsibly with crises or technical mishaps, can shatter a company's reputation almost overnight.[34]

A good reputation may be desirable, but does it have economic value? Here again, research is beginning to document what the profiles in Chapter 1 suggest—that a good reputation pays off in myriad ways. Most obviously, it helps to attract business, in the form of prospective customers, employees, and investors. Given how hard it is for us to obtain direct information before making decisions about where to shop, work, and invest, we have little choice but to rely on reputation, or at least to take it into account. Corporate decision makers face a similar problem, and they, too, frequently rely on reputation to simplify the selection process. It is safer and easier to award an important contract to a well-respected company than to one of unknown or dubious repute.[35]

Companies with good reputations also make for attractive business partners, especially for firms interested in burnishing their own image or keeping a good reputation intact. According to a recent study, a positive reputation can actually contribute to the success of corporate alliances.[36]

In financial terms, then, a well-regarded company can benefit from increased potential revenues and market share, greater access to talent and ideas, and, in some cases, lower recruiting, marketing, and funding costs. A good reputation can also translate into premium prices for a company's goods and services—or for the company itself—or into a larger or more selective set of opportunities. For instance, Siam Cement, long held in high regard in Thailand, was much in demand among overseas companies entering Thailand in search of a strategic partner in the early 1990s. As one analyst observed, "Almost any company that comes to Thailand will probably want Siam Cement as a partner. So Siam Cement is getting proposals almost daily, and they get to pick the cream of the crop."[37]

Conversely, as we saw in the Salomon case, reputational damage can mean lost opportunities, higher costs, and diminished market value for the company. After the Treasury auction scandal, some Salomon clients pulled away to protect their own reputations, while others were wary of further dealings with the company. Salomon's rank and market share in terms of underwriting proceeds fell sharply in the period following the crisis. Or, as we saw in the Shell profile, sales at some German Shell stations plummeted after the Brent Spar controversy erupted.

Research suggests that investors as well as customers and business partners appreciate the importance of reputation. According to one study, most of the decline in stock price following an announcement of corporate illegality, either alleged or proven, reflects reputational damage. The prospect of legal penalties such as fines and civil damages accounted for only a little more than 6 percent of the drop.[38]

Other payoffs from a good reputation are more diffuse and thus less easily identified. Reputations tend to feed on themselves, and well-respected companies are often in the spotlight as recipients of awards, subjects of media commentary, and grantees of scarce opportunities. Such validation only reinforces their standing and reduces their need for spending on marketing, recruiting, and public relations. Moreover, companies that have built up a stock of reputational capital may enjoy an extra measure of goodwill in times of difficulty or crisis. This goodwill can cash out in varied and sometimes surprising ways—as other parties refrain from using their superior bargaining power, remain willing to forego costly and time-consuming formalities, or tolerate mistakes they would otherwise challenge.

The HDFC case profiled in Chapter 1 again provides a nice example. HDFC began building a positive reputation from day one by shunning the corrupt practices pervasive in other parts of India's financial-services industry and seeking to behave in ways that were honest, fair, and considerate toward its constituencies. Civic responsibility was not an add-on, but a core element of its value system. Thus, from the beginning, HDFC differentiated itself as a professionally run and customer-oriented financial services organization. Furthermore, even though it had a virtual monopoly on the housing loan business for nearly 12 years, HDFC declined to take advantage of its monopolist position. Instead of charging monopolistic rates, it maintained thin profit margins and concentrated on keeping costs low to make its loans affordable for more consumers. And when competition did come along, HDFC took the role of promoter, believing that a healthy industry was in the country's best interests.

By the time the nationwide economic crisis hit in 1991, HDFC had amassed a considerable store of credibility among Indian consumers. Without that goodwill, it is doubtful that the deposit-taking business would have succeeded. Having established itself as a trustworthy institution, though, HDFC was able to attract enough customers willing to entrust it with their savings. The new business took off, and by 1996, as mentioned earlier, HDFC had become India's largest deposit-taking institution outside the banking industry. HDFC continues to benefit financially from its reputation. In 2001, its marketing expenses were among the lowest in its industry due in part to its strong reputation. Moreover, management attributed more than 55 percent of the company's business to word-of-mouth referrals.

A similar reputational dynamic helped Johnson & Johnson during the Tylenol episode. There, too, the company was able to draw on a huge store of institutional trust built up over the years. Even before the cause of the Tylenol-related deaths was identified, many consumers were willing to give Johnson & Johnson the benefit of the doubt. Talk-show host Phil Donahue invited CEO Burke to use his show as a "48-minute commercial," explaining that he regarded Johnson & Johnson as itself a victim in the tragedy.

In Burke's view, the widespread predisposition to view Johnson & Johnson favorably was a reflection of the high level of public trust in the corporation—a trust that was in turn a legacy of previous managers and all those who, through their individual actions, had contributed to this accumulated confidence. Said Burke, "All of the previous managements who built this corporation handed us, on a silver platter, the most powerful tool you could possibly have." That tool was institutional trust—elusive to define and hard to quantify but nonetheless, in Burke's words, "real, palpable, and bankable."[39]

Such high-visibility instances of exemplary conduct paying off have added momentum to the "ethics pays" movement. So has the increasing attention being paid to brand equity. Today, managers everywhere recognize the economic significance of a strong brand. Because the value of a brand, much like a reputation, derives from the favorable judgments of others, it is not surprising that executives and brand experts alike are coming to appreciate the role of ethics in brand building. It is hard to imagine how a company could build a positive brand identity without adhering at least to the basic values adopted by our hypothetical Comco, especially in dealings with the customer. And experts also say that civic values such as environmentalism, fair employment, and community involvement are increasingly required as well.[40]

As we saw in Chapter 1, the goal of building China's first global brand was the driving rationale behind Zhang Ruimin's effort to reshape the Haier Group's value system. Unlike some executives who think of brand building as only a matter of marketing or public communications, Zhang recognized that attaining his goal would require a companywide effort to instill a set of values that governed all activities, from sourcing and production to personnel and compensation. He knew that Haier would have to produce high-quality products that exceeded customer expectations and that the Haier brand would have to be associated with quality, reliability, accountability, and good citizenship. Only by infusing these values throughtout the organization could he position the company for leadership and economic success.[41]

From Values to Value

The "ethics pays" argument derives its credibility from the linkages explored in this chapter. Based on the evidence reviewed here, the economic benefits of a set of Comco-like commitments are numerous. The path from values to value is not easy to track, however, because some of these linkages are indirect, remote in time, and mixed with offsetting costs. For instance, the economic value generated by keeping an inconvenient promise to a customer may take time to be realized, either through future interactions with the customer or through reputational effects that are diffuse and dispersed throughout the customer base. In the meantime, the act of fulfilling the promise may itself generate an immediate cost.

The "ethics pays" argument depends on taking the broader view and looking to longer-term effects. If we appreciate that values represent certain patterns of thinking, behaving, and interacting with others over a period of time, then we can begin to see the logic of the argument. For example, Comco's commitments link to a long list of effects that can lead directly or indirectly to financial gain—through better cost control and risk management; through enhanced employee creativity and contribution; through strengthened reputation among key constituencies; and through expanded access to resources and opportunities, to name only broad categories. Within each of these, we have seen explicit ways in which economic gains are generated or preserved—through lower complaint costs, lower monitoring costs, lower compliance costs, greater trust, more knowledge sharing, improved product or service quality, strengthened brand equity, increased access to talent, and so on.

Given this extensive list of positive financial effects, might we therefore expect companies with higher levels of ethical competency to enjoy superior overall profitability? Intuitively, this would seem unlikely, considering that many factors affect a company's ultimate financial performance. Just as an overly optimistic stock market can make bad companies look good, an unexpected currency devaluation can instantaneously turn a good company's profits into losses. A wrong bet on technology, a forecast gone awry, the collapse of a major customer, a change in government policy, a fad, a flood, a terrorist attack—any one of these events can throw a monkey wrench into simple equations of values and profitability. Definitional and measurement difficulties are also a problem for both sides of such equations.

Nonetheless, a number of researchers have come up with suggestive findings. For instance, one study that compared higher- and lower-yielding U.S. companies in 10 industries over the period from 1977 to 1988 found a striking difference between the two groups. The more financially successful companies valued leadership, fairness, and the interests of their constituencies more highly than did the lower-yielding firms. Companies that were internally focused or that valued only one constituency over others—whether the most highly valued group was employees, customers, or shareholders—performed less well.[42]

Similar findings emerged from a widely reviewed 1985 study of 81 high-growth, mid-size U.S. companies. Here again, researchers found that leading companies had certain distinctive features. Most had articulated a guiding set of principles defining how value would be created for customers, the rights and responsibilities of employees, and what the organization stood for. The authors found that executives of these companies were motivated not only to make money but also to make a difference, and that profit was generally viewed as a by-product of doing other things well. This is not to say these executives were unconcerned about financial performance; they had rigorous systems to monitor financial performance, operations, and competitive position. But they also worked consistently to instill a strong sense of mission and shared values in their organizations.[43]

Yet another study of U.S. companies—this one covering 18 pairs of companies all founded before 1950—concluded that an enduring value system was a key driver of superior long-term financial performance. Notably, however, the study's authors concluded that the content of the values mattered less than their authenticity. In other words, according to these researchers, genuine belief in the values was more important than what the values actually were, although a compelling sense of purpose beyond making money was a shared feature of the leading companies' value systems.[44]

These three studies started with superior financial performance and then worked backward to try to identify its antecedents. Others have looked explicitly at some measure of ethical commitment and tried to determine its financial consequences. For instance, a recent study of the 500 largest U.S. companies appearing on the *Business Week* 1000 list found that those with a defined commitment to ethical principles outperformed their peers. This study used a composite measure of financial performance for 1997 and the previous two years and determined commitment to ethics by reviewing statements in the companies' annual reports. But statements in an annual report are scarcely a convincing measure of corporate ethical competency, and a three-year window on financial performance is too narrow to be of much significance, especially considering that the reported results are undoubtedly due in large measure to actions taken earlier in time.[45]

Perhaps the best perspective on the ethics–economic performance issue comes from a recent review of some 95 academic studies of the relationship between corporate financial and social performance. The studies, of mainly U.S. companies, used some 70 diverse measures of financial performance and examined 11 domains of social performance including human resource practices, environmental performance, product safety, and community investment. Eighty of the 95 studies sought to determine whether "ethics pays"—whether better social performance was a predictor of better financial performance. Nineteen considered the reverse—whether stronger financial performance could predict higher social performance. (Several of the studies examined the relationship in both directions.)

Although there is much to question about these studies, it is worth noting that only 4 of the 95 studies found a negative relationship between social and financial performance. Fifty-five studies found a positive correlation between better financial performance and better social performance. Twenty-two found no relationship between the two; and 18 found a mixed relationship.[46]

Although no study has convincingly measured corporate ethical competency and shown its positive relation to financial performance, one thing is quite clear. Ethics and financial self-interest are no longer the implacable enemies they have sometimes been thought to be. In this respect the growing acceptance of "ethics pays" is a remarkable shift from the "ethics costs" stance of only a few decades back. Today, thanks to a growing body of academic research and corporate experimentation, we have a better understanding of the linkages between companies' values and their financial performance.

We now understand that ethics and economic advantage often do go hand in hand. As research is beginning to document, companies that bring ethical discipline to bear on their activities and tap into the moral capabilities of their people stand to reap a variety of economic benefits from doing so. Many of these benefits follow from the very simple fact, noted earlier, that, given a choice, most people prefer to work and do business with companies that are honest, reliable, fair, and considerate. The cases and research cited so far show that respect for these values is essential to mobilizing people's energies, building trust, and maintaining constituency confidence. These effects, in turn, generate a variety of payoffs—inside the organization, in the marketplace, and in dealings with governments and the broader society.

3

Time for a Reality Check

Based on the argument so far, "ethics pays" might seem to be a plausible position. It's certainly an attractive one. But this conclusion comes too quickly. Although the financial case for values is quite powerful, it is not entirely satisfactory. For one thing, it does not tell us *why* the economics of ethics has changed in recent decades. What has precipitated the shift in attitudes from "ethics costs" to "ethics pays"? We have considered the reasons given by executives for their turn to values, but we have not looked behind those reasons to consider the larger forces at work.

In addition, there is a fundamental problem with the harmonious portrayal of values and financial self-interest presented in the last chapter. The difficulty is not so much that the argument is wrong. There's no question that the economic benefits we've discussed are "real, palpable, and bankable," to recall the words of Johnson & Johnson's Jim Burke. It's that the picture is incomplete. Lacking any trace of the tensions that sometimes arise between profit and other values, the discussion so far can only seem a bit surreal. Unless the financial case for values comes to terms with the possibility of this conflict, it is unlikely to prove convincing in the end. Moreover, even though ethical commitment has its financial rewards, moral indifference can frequently be quite profitable, too.

Most readers will know this from history as well as their own experience. Anyone who has even a passing acquaintance with history can think immediately of vast fortunes made on the backs of fraud and injustice. Think of the slave traders and plantation owners of America's antebellum South, or the wealth amassed by the early nineteenth-century New England merchants who traded opium in China. One trader writing to his wife in 1839 valued the opium business at nearly $15 million (in 1839 dollars). He readily conceded that this lucrative trade, though engaged in by many "respectable" people, was morally odious—"contrary to Law . . . demoralizing [to people's] minds, destroying [their] bodies, & draining the country of money."[1]

Then again, it is hard to imagine atrocities worse than those committed by European and American merchants seeking ivory and rubber in the African Congo at the turn of the last century. Using mayhem and other barbaric methods to coerce conscripted workers, they extracted vast wealth for themselves and their sponsors. Trivial by comparison, though hardly exemplary, were the competitive tactics used by National Cash Register in the United States around the same period. These included sabotaging rivals' products so they would malfunction, placing spies in rival companies, and intimidating the competition's prospective customers. Clearly, the full country by country, industry by industry story of the debts wealth has incurred to justice over the course of history would fill many volumes.[2]

But, readers may protest, all that is past. Today, things are different. There's more transparency, more freedom, more democracy, more law—and all these favor the convergence of ethical commitment and economic self-interest. Although this is true and in fact anticipates the discussion later in this chapter, the convergence is far from perfect. A few examples will show how and why the correspondence between profits and values frequently breaks down. These examples will also help explain why the financial case for values has grown stronger in recent decades, and why the case for values cannot rest entirely on a financial rationale. As we will see, the extent to which ethical behavior is economically advantageous depends on societal expectations and the design of society's institutions.[3]

Another Side of the Story

One afternoon a few years ago, I was working quietly in my office when a former student, "Eric," knocked at my door. Clearly distressed, he apologized for not having set up an appointment in advance and explained that he had just flown back from the country where he and his wife had been living and working for several years. His agitation increased as he began to tell me what had precipitated their hasty departure. It had all revolved around a question of values—more precisely, a question of what to tell lenders about the financial condition of the company where he worked.

Until this issue arose, Eric had been working quite intensively on a turnaround plan for the company. His team had been making good progress toward lining up resources to fund a new strategic initiative—or so he thought until one day a top executive pulled him aside. In the course of discussing an unrelated project, the executive asked Eric if he'd like to see the company's "real" financial records—the confidential ones. Until that moment, Eric had assumed that the accounts he had been working with *were* the real ones. In fact, he and his team had relied on them as the basis of all their projections and negotiations with prospective lenders.

When confronted with the discrepant sets of books, Eric's thoughts turned immediately to what he'd told prospective lenders about the company's finances. It was important, he suggested to the executive, to give the lenders the updated financial information as soon as possible. The executive, clearly startled, stated that such clarification was not necessary and abruptly dismissed Eric.

It wasn't long before Eric felt a chill in the air at work. He was no longer invited to important meetings or even consulted on day-to-day issues. Coworkers who had previously sought him out seemed to ignore him. Even more troubling were the strange incidents—mysterious callers, threatening messages—that began to happen at home. Eric and his wife began to fear that their lives might be in danger. Eventually, they decided they had no choice but to flee the country.

To anyone who's been through an experience like Eric's, "ethics pays" comes across as hopelessly naïve. His company was to all outward appearances a profitable and reputable concern. In fact, however, it was deeply involved in a systematic and ongoing fraud. What's more, the firm was apparently succeeding not only with the fraud but also with intimidating anyone who threatened to undermine it. Taking into account the potential hidden costs and risks of the scheme, its financial benefits might not have been all they appeared, but to those involved, the financial risks no doubt seemed worthwhile, especially compared to the risks of reporting the company's finances accurately. Accurate reporting would certainly have increased the cost of borrowing, might have made it impossible to secure funds for the planned expansion, and might even have imperiled the company's existence.

Those who argue for values on financial grounds often fail, it seems, to take such quandaries into account. Yet questionable if not blatantly wrongful or injurious behavior often results in financial gain. My research has brought me into contact with cases that span the entire ethical spectrum: garden-variety deceptions and betrayals, falsified books and records, defective and even dangerous products shipped out to unsuspecting customers, abusive behavior and hazardous conditions in the workplace, unwarranted favoritism and discrimination, bribery and extortion, unfair and predatory competition, misappropriation of information, and environmental degradation, to name just a few.

The prevalence of misconduct today is hard to gauge. Survey findings vary considerably. One U.S. survey conducted in late 1999 and early 2000 found that about one in three employees (31 percent) said they had witnessed misconduct either often or occasionally in the previous year.[4] Another U.S. survey conducted at roughly the same time found that three out of four employees (76 percent) said they had observed violations of law or company standards during the previous 12 months.[5] Respondents deemed many of the offenses serious. Of those in the second survey who had observed violations, about half (49 percent) said that if what they had seen were to become publicly known, the organization could "significantly lose public trust." Yet another study found that many executives were willing to violate financial reporting standards to maintain the appearance of stronger profitability. Depending on the issues presented, the percentage willing to misreport some aspect of their company's finances ranged from 14 percent to 47 percent.[6] Imprecise though these studies are, they strongly suggest that serious misconduct can and does occur rather frequently at all levels and across all corporate functions.

In more cases than we might care to acknowledge, the driving factor is the prospect of financial gain. While the gains are not always realized, or may be wiped out by later exposure or penalties, they materialize often enough to make their pursuit worthwhile. Consider the global cartel accused of price-fixing in the vitamin business over the past decade. The elaborate schemes created to govern the cartel as well as to conceal its existence suggest that the companies involved knew that their activities were wrong and indeed unlawful. Nonetheless, the profits were great enough that the firms ran the risk of detection and prosecution. In fact, one company continued to fix prices in its vitamin business at the same time that it was being investigated for price-fixing in another business.[7]

Clearly, ignoring or evading laws and regulations can be profitable. In some situations, it can be profitable to ignore even the most basic of human rights. Why else do some employers exploit child workers, deny employees their legal rights, or subject them to hazardous working conditions? In a recent documentary on child labor, a South Asian factory owner explained quite candidly his reasons for using child workers in his carpet factory—and for chaining them to the looms where they worked from morning until night. He said that children, besides costing less and doing twice as much work, were more obedient than adults. "The adults often take a break and go to the toilet," he explained, adding, "I chain them [the children] up so they don't steal or take drugs."[8]

Price-fixing and child labor are both illegal, but other examples illustrate the financial rewards of moral indifference in the context of activities generally regarded as entirely legitimate.

As one example, consider the "point-and-shoot" video games that represent some 5 percent of the $5 to $6 billion video game industry.[9] These games, which are played by millions of teenagers and adults around the world, were developed from technologies used by the U.S. military to break down new recruits' natural resistance to killing. The games became front-page news in 1999 after two teenagers in Littleton, Colorado, shot and killed 13 of their classmates at Columbine High School. The killers, it turned out, had honed their weapons deployment and marksmanship skills through countless hours playing a particularly popular point-and-shoot game, the object of which is to kill everything in sight using the chosen lethal weapon. Two years earlier, another avid player of point-and-shoot games shot and killed three students and wounded five others at his Kentucky high school.[10]

According to one expert in this field, these games do precisely what the makers of their military prototypes intended—they erode resistance to killing.[11] In the process, they also increase players' comfort with lethal weapons, desensitize them to the weapons' deadly effects, and develop their marksmanship skills. Indeed, a police officer commenting on the Kentucky killing deemed it a stunning display of marksmanship for a 14-year-old teenager who, apart from video game simulations, had had no previous practice with handguns.

For a neophyte soldier heading into deadly combat, these games perform an important and legitimate function. But for youngsters heading off to high school or junior high school, the assessment is surely rather different. If this expert is only partially correct, the widespread and indiscriminate use of point-and-shoot games should be a matter of serious moral concern. Restraint in the use of force against the innocent—particularly deadly force—is a fundamental tenet of civilized society, and activities that undermine this restraint should be undertaken with caution. Even if these games had never been associated with any school killings, however, their widespread use would still be troubling. Whatever entertainment value they might provide appears to be more than offset by the risks of dulling their young players' moral sensibilities and desensitizing them to the power of lethal weapons. At a minimum, moderation should be advised.

Told that "ethics pays," the makers of these point-and-shoot games would surely burst into laughter. As one journalist put it, "digital blood and guts mean serious money."[12] Precise figures are not readily available, but this segment of the game market is without doubt highly lucrative. Moreover, commentators have pointed out, the lure of these games is the "thrill of the kill"—the very feature that makes them morally problematic.

This insight has not been lost on game makers who seem only too eager to promote an antisocial "bad boy" image. "Get in touch with your gun-toting, cold-blooded murdering side," says one ad.[13] The president of one leading producer trumpets, "A few years from now, we're going to be able to do things that are really reprehensible."[14] Says another game maker, "[P]repare for the most intense mutant-laden, blood spattered action ever. You don't just play [the game]—you live it."[15]

A More Complicated Relationship

Moral indifference clearly has its financial attractions. Although these examples do not prove that ethical commitment and economic success are incompatible, they do remind us that the ethics–economics relationship has many variations. In some circumstances, attention to ethics can be essential for economic success. In others, like the ones just described, ignoring ethics can be quite profitable. Certainly, ethical scruples can sometimes be an economic handicap.

Corrupt officals present a classic dilemma. Most companies have encountered corporate purchasing agents who expect cash, motorcycles, or holiday trips in exchange for placing an order, or even high-level government officials who demand cash payments or other remuneration for awarding a major contract. One executive at a medical supplies company told of receiving a call from the government minister in charge of a major tender who made his demands perfectly clear: "It will cost you 10 percent to get this contract."[16]

A similar dilemma arises when rival companies compete by offering personal inducements to purchasing agents and officials. In such situations, a company that declines to offer expensive gifts, provide lavish entertainment, or render other special favors runs the risk of being excluded from consideration altogether. This is the familiar "pay to play" phenomenon. When corruption is involved, a company that seeks the higher moral ground will often be at a disadvantage unless it has market or other power to use as leverage.

Such examples undermine the neat convergence of ethics and economic advantage implied by the discussion in Chapter 2. The argument there enumerated an extensive array of financial benefits associated with ethical commitment. Depicted as a Venn diagram, Chapter 2 might be summed up by the perfectly congruent circles on the right side of Figure 3-1.[17] But just as Chapter 2 challenged the view that "ethics costs," the examples in this chapter have challenged the view that "ethics pays." In the final analysis, both strains of conventional wisdom sketched in Figure 3-1 are inadequate.

Neither the unalloyed antagonism of "ethics costs" nor the perfect congruence of "ethics pays" reflects the more complex reality that most

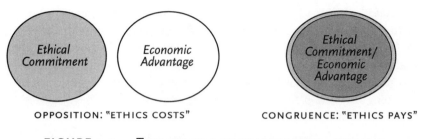

OPPOSITION: "ETHICS COSTS"   CONGRUENCE: "ETHICS PAYS"

FIGURE 3-1 Two strains of conventional wisdom

companies face. A more realistic depiction is captured by the diagram in Figure 3-2.

Figure 3-2 is a graphic acknowledgment that ethical commitment and economic self-interest are compatible in some situations but conflicting in others. Put another way, if we compare the class of ethically desirable actions with the class of financially beneficial actions, we will find that some actions belong to both categories. These fall within the area of overlap at the center of the diagram. Outside this zone of overlap, however, lie two other areas. One represents actions that are ethically problematic but financially attractive, such as the examples discussed earlier: misleading prospective lenders about company finances, exploiting child workers, or marketing video games that undermine the social fabric. The other area represents actions that are ethically attractive but financially problematic, such as resisting the illicit demands of corrupt purchasing officials, among many other possible examples.

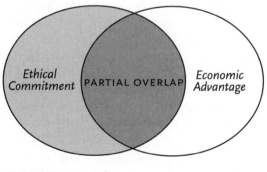

FIGURE 3-2 A more realistic picture

Consider a situation faced by AES, the independent power producer mentioned in Chapter 2 whose values set off alarm bells at the SEC. In 1994, an AES team that was designing a new plant in India faced a troubling conflict between the company's ethical commitments and its economic circumstances. In keeping with AES's environmental values, the team proposed equipping the new plant with circulating fluidized bed (CFB) boilers like those used at several of the company's recent projects in the U.S.[18]

Because CFB boilers were superior to standard pulverized coal (PC) boilers from an environmental point of view, they were a particular point of pride for AES, which at the time had more CFBs than any other company in the world. The team was eager to set a positive example by building a CFB plant in India, even though standard PC boilers would have met all local and World Bank environmental standards. Recognizing that CFBs would likely be harder to finance and would require many more government approvals, the team nonetheless decided to solicit bids for CFB technology after a preliminary investigation suggested that it might actually be feasible. As a backup, the team also asked for bids using standard boilers.

Unfortunately, the CFB bid was significantly higher than the PC bid because the contractor charged a higher risk premium for using an advanced technology in a developing country. The AES team knew that Indian officials would be unwilling to approve the higher capital cost required to achieve the higher environmental standard, given the society's pressing need to keep electricity prices down. In this situation, the ethically preferable course of action was not financially feasible. The AES team worked on an alternative plan that, although not their preferred option, would have met all required environmental standards. For other reasons, however, the project did not go forward and was eventually cancelled.

When confronted with such counterexamples, "ethics pays" proponents frequently invoke a longer-term perspective. And the time span involved can certainly make a crucial difference in assessing the financial benefits of any ethical stance, as it does in financial accounting more generally. Obviously, the most profitable company, as measured over a one-year period, may not necessarily be the most profitable as measured over a five-year period. Similarly, the financial effects of holding to ethical commitments—be these truth-telling, promise-keeping, legal compliance, or environmental responsibility—can be negative in the short term but nevertheless positive over a longer period.

As noted in Chapter 2, this is partly the effect of taking into account not only an action's immediate consequences, but also consequences that are more remote in time. Just as the benefits of holding to an ethical commitment may take some time to be realized, so too the costs of ethical shortcuts may become evident only over time—and, in some cases, long after their benefits have been forgotten. A falsehood that secures an advantage today may bar a company from a larger benefit that will become available a year from today. A bribe that wins a government contract this quarter may become a matter for prosecution when the political climate changes or the next administration takes office.

The importance of the chosen time frame is illustrated in the experience of a nationally established building contractor that was besieged in August 2001 by home buyers complaining about deceptive marketing and shoddy construction practices. Until the complaints surfaced, this builder had received plaudits from Wall Street for its rapid growth and high profit margins. But, almost overnight, the very practices that had earlier resulted in financial benefits became financial liabilities.[19]

A longer-term perspective strengthens the "ethics pays" argument in another way—by directing attention beyond single actions to the whole series of actions implied by committing to a set of values. A commitment is by definition not a one-time event but a pledge of continuing allegiance to a way of behaving and interacting with others that involves an entire "package" of attitudes, emotions, and beliefs. Honesty, for example, implies far more than infrequent lying. An honest person is someone who cares about truth, who strives to be truthful, who is troubled by dissembling, and who feels guilty and uncomfortable being involved in deceit or misrepresentation.

Taking into account the effects of the whole package over time can dramatically affect the financial calculus. This is, in part, due to the simple arithmetic of adding up the costs and benefits of many actions over some reasonably long period of time. But the expanded time horizon also brings into view certain benefits that, because they do not accrue case-by-case in an additive fashion, are often overlooked when analysis focuses only on short-term effects.

The financial benefits of honesty are an example, for they can be earned only through behavior that is consistently conscientious over time. A single instance of truthfulness means little, particularly if it would be financially advantageous in any case. Indeed, as we will discuss later, being truthful precisely when it is not to one's own advantage may be the best way to earn a reputation for honesty. The important point here, however, is that it takes time to establish such a reputation and to realize the benefits of the behavior that underlies it. Divergences between ethics and financial self-interest that appear acute in the short term can narrow or disappear if a longer-term perspective is taken.

Presented with this appeal to the long term, however, a realist like Eric might retort by quoting economist John Maynard Keynes's famous observation that "in the long run, we are all dead."[20] Just how long is the long term? And what is to be done in the meantime? Certainly, a longer-term perspective strengthens the argument for congruence between ethics and financial self-interest. In practice, however, managers may not find it easy or even possible to take the longer-term perspective. As the AES team learned in India, the present cost of preventing future harm may exceed the company's ability to pay, if it wishes to remain a competitive and fundable concern.

The speed of change and the short accounting periods customarily used in business today often exacerbate these conflicts. In a fast-paced environment marked by rapid technological change, companies must be careful about incurring present costs in anticipation of remote future benefits lest that envisioned future never materialize. Although we might wish it to be otherwise, our ethical ideals do not always square easily with our economic circumstances given the time frame within which we must function.

Unscrupulous rivals can also undercut a conscientious company's efforts to compete on an aboveboard basis. Suppose one company pays its full share of duties on imported supplies while its rivals escape those taxes by paying off customs officials. The conscientious company, with its higher cost structure, may be unable to match its rivals' lower prices and suffer shrinking sales and market share as a result.

This is what happened to Russia's Cherkizovsky Group in late 1997. Widely regarded as one of the best-managed companies in Russia's post-Soviet food-processing industry, the company faced a perplexing situation at that time. Suddenly, sales of its low-end hot dogs and sausages plunged to nearly half their normal volume as rivals' cheaper products flooded the market. About the same time, allegations appeared in the media charging that Cherkizovsky and certain other food processors were selling hot dogs made from tainted meat. A Cherkizovsky executive took it upon himself to ferret out the origins of the low-priced goods and the mysterious rumors.[21]

After some determined sleuthing, he discovered that a group of Russian meat importers had teamed up with Russian customs officials and European meat brokers to dump excess supplies of low-end, low-priced hot dogs from the United States on the Russian market. The hot dogs entered the country under a little-used tariff category and thus escaped the higher duties imposed on correctly declared, properly classified goods. Thanks to the elaborate fraud, participants in the scheme were able to underprice their goods and dramatically increase their profit margins.

The damage to Cherkizovsky, whose CEO had made a point of insisting that the company operate lawfully and pay its taxes—an unusual stance among Russian companies, by the way—was not trivial. The scheme took a substantial bite out of the company's share of the Moscow market, slowed its fundraising campaign, and necessitated even more costly efforts to build the fledgling brand. The source of the rumors was never identified.

Even when ethics does pay, it doesn't always pay enough. Consider a case from South Africa. Between 1996 and 1998, two of the country's leading banks followed quite different strategies. One bank, as part of a plan to reduce costs and increase efficiencies, *closed* 800,000 accounts held by low-income South Africans. Instead of servicing these "low-value" accounts, the bank decided to focus its energies on the higher-margin accounts opened by middle- and upper-income South Africans. During this same period, the second bank *opened* some 2.5 million low-value accounts. The financial results at the end of 1998 would have disappointed "ethics pays" proponents. The bank that had closed the low-value accounts reported a 23 percent return on equity, while the bank that opened them reported a return of only 18 percent. Though the difference in financial performance reflected a variety of factors, the higher proportion of low-value accounts held by the second bank did not help.[22]

This situation arises in many industries that provide essential services required by rich and poor alike. Banking is only one example; health care is another. Unless they can find ways to make up the difference, companies that serve their share of poorer customers are likely to have difficulty matching the returns of rivals that serve only the wealthy. The problem is not necessarily that serving poorer customers doesn't pay but rather that serving the wealthy is frequently easier and pays more. One Wall Street official made the point succinctly in this E-mail to his company's brokers not long ago: "If we're going to be financial consultants to wealthy and successful individuals and businesses, then we don't have time to provide personal services to the poor."[23]

As we've discussed, corporate citizenship of the type practiced by the second South African bank is not without economic benefits. Good citizenship can enhance a company's reputation in the marketplace, strengthen employee morale, and generate goodwill among civic constituencies and public officials. However, we do not know whether or how often the economic gains generated by these factors will be sufficient to offset the opportunity and other costs incurred. Moreover, as we've noted, such reputational benefits necessarily lag behind the behavior that generates them. Thus, the

payback for this type of citizenship may come too late. Indeed, in 1999, the
South African bank with the 23 percent return, citing opportunities for cost
savings and the potential to create a bank that could compete in an international arena, began trying to take over its rival.[24] After nearly a year of
wrangling, however, the country's finance minister blocked the takeover bid
to preserve competition in the banking sector.[25]

Today, companies all over the world are under pressure to deliver not
simply a return, but an outstanding return. Meeting the expectations of
investors who freely roam the globe in search of the highest possible earnings can put severe strain on a company's local citizenship commitments.
So can changing market conditions. Even companies with impeccable cre-
dentials as corporate citizens can face situations in which their only economically feasible choice is to cut back on these commitments if they wish
to remain competitive.

Consider U.S. apparel maker Levi Strauss, a company with a long-
standing reputation for high ethical standards in dealing with its employees
and local communities. Traditionally a progressive force in the communities
where it has operated, Levi Strauss managed to keep its employees on the
payroll in the aftermath of the 1906 San Francisco fire and earthquake, and
again during the Great Depression in the 1930s. At a time when racial segregation was the norm in the U.S. South, Levi Strauss took steps to integrate
its factories in that region. In the 1990s, it was one of the first global companies to begin looking into the welfare of workers in its supply chain,
many of whom were toiling in appalling and unhealthy conditions. The
company put in place a set of supplier standards and determined to do
business only in countries that recognized basic human rights.[26]

Even a century-old reputation for good citizenship, however, could not
protect Levi Strauss from financial difficulties in the late 1990s. Despite
soaring profits in the early 1990s, by the second half of the decade changing tastes had begun cutting into the company's share of the casual apparel
market. Younger customers were forsaking the Levi's® jeans favored by
their parents and turning to other brands. Faced with shrinking sales and
rising costs, the company in 1997 announced plans to close 11 of its 32
U.S. plants and lay off nearly a third of its U.S. workforce. Two years later,
it shut down 11 more U.S. plants and laid off an additional 6000 employees. By 2000, Levi Strauss had closed 30 of its 51 plants worldwide and dismissed 15,000 people, 40 percent of its global workforce. Notably, the
company offered departing employees generous notice and severance
packages, including as much as $6000 for education, job training, and mov-

ing expenses, as well as health insurance for as long as 18 months. It also offered $8 million in grants to affected communities.[27]

Here again, we see that ethics may pay, but not enough to eliminate the tough choices imposed by changing market conditions. Nor is good citizenship a substitute for market responsiveness. Though Levi Strauss's many civic contributions over the years have undoubtedly yielded financial benefits in terms of sales, employee pride and loyalty, and so on, it is hard to say whether the benefits have exceeded the costs involved. Obviously, however, the benefits were inadequate to shield the company from a very pronounced recent shift in consumer tastes. The Levi Strauss case foreshadows an important conclusion that lies ahead—namely, that a leading company's enterprise model must be both ethically and financially sound, for no company can sustain a civic stance unless it is integrated with a viable economic model.

A Closer Look

As these and earlier examples demonstrate, the relationship between ethics and economic advantage is neither simple nor fixed. A closer analysis suggests that several factors play a role in determining the extent to which ethical commitment is financially beneficial. In addition to the chosen time frame and desired economic return, factors discussed in the previous section, the presumed ethical standard is also crucial. Depending on what this standard requires, the financial case for values is more or less robust. Put differently, the strength and significance of the links between ethics and economic advantage depend in part on the specific values in question.

As a general rule, for example, the financial case for values like fairness and honesty is more robust than the case for altruism or charity. Recall that much of the argument in Chapter 2 appealed to payoffs from honesty, fairness, and reliability. The financial case for shunning wrong and respecting basic rights is often thought to be even more robust—or at least more visible—than the case for fairness and honesty, given that many forms of wrongdoing are officially condemned and punishable by law. The fourfold matrix shown in Figure 3-3 provides a useful framework for looking more systematically at the ethics/economics relationship in different ethical domains.

This matrix is based on two distinctions found in many traditions of ethical thought. The first, shown on the horizontal axis, is between two groups of values, those associated with justice and those associated with humanity. Justice, in this schema, has to do with what is truthful, right, and fair. These are values that appeal to our sense of probity and rectitude

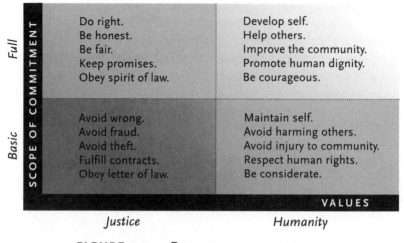

FIGURE 3-3   DOMAINS OF COMMITMENT

and rest on our need for moral order and self-discipline. The humanistic values, by comparison, spring from our impulse toward growth and self-extension. This cluster has to do with human flourishing, care and concern for one another, community betterment, and the like.

This distinction between justice and humanity, or something very like it, has played a prominent role in the ethical traditions of both East and West. It is somewhat akin to the contrast marked in Chinese thought by the Confucian concepts of *li* and *ren*. *Li*, often translated as "rightness" or "propriety," has to do with civility and conformity to standards of correct behavior.[28] *Ren,* usually translated as "humanity" or "benevolence," is concerned with human well-being and fellow-feeling.[29]

Similarly, Western ethics has sought to differentiate between "virtues of conscientiousness" such as honesty and trustworthiness and "virtues of compassion" such as generosity and charity.[30] This contrast mirrors a distinction between law and equity that has run throughout the Western legal tradition. A related comparison is found in contemporary research on moral psychology. Some researchers in this field have posited a difference between individuals who think about moral questions in terms of justice and right, and those who think in terms of care and concern for others.[31]

The second distinction, shown on the vertical axis, has to do with the scope of commitment. The matrix depicts two extremes of what is actually a continuum. Basic commitment involves adherence to only the minimum standards associated with these values, whereas full commitment implies dedication to a more extensive and more demanding set of precepts. This distinction, also recognized across many ethical traditions, marks the difference between elementary requirements presumed to be within the capacity of any mentally competent human being and a more advanced set of requirements that calls for higher-order capabilities or greater expenditures of resources and effort.

Applied to the realm of justice, the difference between basic and full commitment is captured in these contrasting pairs:

- avoiding wrong versus doing right
- fulfilling contracts versus keeping promises
- avoiding theft versus being fair
- avoiding fraud versus being honest
- obeying the letter of the law versus obeying the spirit of the law

Applied to the domain of humanity, the difference is reflected in such contrasts as:

- maintaining oneself versus developing oneself
- not harming others versus actively helping them
- respecting human rights versus promoting human dignity
- avoiding damage to the community versus contributing to community improvement
- being considerate versus being courageous

Notice that many of the basic standards take the form of negative injunctions, whereas the more advanced precepts are expressed in affirmative, open-ended language. These differences are reflected in our expectations of one another and in our practices of praising and blaming. Although we expect *everyone* to meet the minimum standard and feel entitled to criticize those who fall short, we often expect those with greater wealth, power, or capability to go beyond the minimum. Also, we are generally slow to blame people for falling short of these more demanding standards, but we do bestow praise and recognition on those who succeed.

Many executives speak about "ethics" and "values" with little awareness of the immense territory covered by these terms. Even the basic distinctions shown in this matrix seem alien to many. I recall one manager at Salomon Brothers, who, expressing puzzlement about the former CEO's failure to do anything about the trading-desk misconduct, made a comment that struck me at first as self-contradictory if not incomprehensible. "You know," he remarked, "John could be brutal to people, but he was very sensitive to ethical issues."[32] As our conversation continued, however, I realized that this individual's notion of ethics was confined entirely to the lower-left quadrant.

The matrix in Figure 3-3 provides a framework for understanding how the links between ethics and financial self-interest vary in different domains. We can also see more clearly why the financial case for values might be thought strongest for commitments in the lower-left quadrant. As noted earlier, many of the world's legal systems impose penalties for violating standards in this domain. Whether or not these precepts are backed by law, however, they define a fairly specific set of duties whose breach can result in formal and informal sanctions.

Few people voluntarily consent to being deceived, stolen from, or otherwise deprived of their contractual and legal rights, and if they are, they will likely take their business elsewhere. They may well do more, by demanding compensation, reporting the offense to authorities, seeking legal redress, contacting the press, posting a complaint on the Internet, or organizing a boycott, to name just a few responses. If none of these avenues is available, some victims, such as wronged employees, may respond by psychological withdrawal of effort and commitment. In short, someone who has been wronged, as opposed to slighted or treated poorly, is more apt to seek recourse against the offender, typically has more channels for doing so, and is more likely to receive a sympathetic hearing from third parties. This can be very costly for the offender, as we have seen.

In the lower-right and upper-left quadrants, the financial case becomes more complex and more subtle. In both quadrants, the financial argument depends as much on the rewards that can come from adhering to these norms as on the penalties triggered by their breach, though legal penalties play a less important role in both these domains. Recall that the higher-order precepts of justice go beyond the requirements of law or contract, so legal recourse by definition is not available for breaches in this quadrant. Similarly, activities that offend basic standards of humanity by harming innocent people or damaging the community may or may not be legally actionable. Market retaliation is less likely to occur as well, especially if the offenses involve injuries that are diffuse or subtle, as in the case of the point-and-shoot games discussed earlier.

On the other hand, adhering to the precepts in these domains often elicits positive reactions from those affected. As we saw in Chapter 2, many people respond positively to being respected, treated fairly, and dealt with honestly. These behaviors contribute to the formation of loyalty, trust, respect, and goodwill, which in turn yield economic rewards such as enhanced effort, creativity, repeat business, reputational gains, efficiency, flexibility, and others already discussed. And although today's laws may not require compliance with the norms in these quadrants, the law is not static, nor are legal rules as clear as they are often believed to be. So there's an economic case for adhering to the precepts in these domains, if only as a precaution against future legal risks. For all these reasons, and contrary to first appearances, the economic case in these quadrants is at least as strong as, if not stronger than, the case for the lower-left quadrant.

It's in the upper-right quadrant that the financial case appears most tenuous. The higher-order imperatives in this domain challenge us to improve ourselves, help others, and contribute to our communities. These are what moral theorists have traditionally called "imperfect duties," to mark their open-ended and nonspecific nature. In contrast to the "perfect duties" associated with elementary justice (lower-left quadrant), imperatives such as "help others" and "better society" do not create specific obligations to particular individuals. As a consequence, their neglect gives no one in particular a right to complain or seek redress.

By the same token, the benefits created by their observance are often diffuse and may go unrecognized or undervalued by the recipients. Because the beneficiaries may be unknown, or at least not individually identifiable, the benefactor's largesse cannot be directly reciprocated. For conduct to have economic traction, it must ultimately affect market or workplace behavior by, for example, enhancing organizational effort, stimulating a favorable response in the marketplace, or earning regulatory advantages. Otherwise, no matter how exemplary the conduct, it cannot have a discernible effect on the actor's financial well-being. Given the nature of the precepts in the upper-right quadrant, the connection between good deeds and financial gain can only be a loose one at best.

Imperfect duties are also open-ended in the sense that there's no natural or obvious limit to their fulfillment. When people talk about care and assistance for the needy, the standard seems to be "the more, the better." However, for someone running a business, unlimited generosity is a recipe for bankruptcy. This, no doubt, is why some economists balk at talk of corporate ethics. In the lexicon of economics, ethics is often equated with altruism, understood as selflessness. The very thought conjures up images of Mother Teresa giving away corporate assets.

It is unfortunate but true that rendering assistance to people who are genuinely powerless, or even forbearance from harming them, seldom yields much of an economic payoff for the benefactor. Don't misunderstand. There are many reasons to assist the poor and the powerless, but the prospect of riches is not one of them. To the extent that economic benefits do accrue to companies that engage in the generalized good deeds envisioned in the upper-right quadrant, they accrue due to enhanced employee commitment or to reputational gains in the eyes of third parties such as customers, regulators, policy makers, and the like.

As we have seen in Chapter 2, such economic benefits often do result. To add yet another example to those already mentioned, consider Timberland, a U.S. boot and apparel company that has based its strategy on a culture of service that encompasses active engagement with the community as well as customer service of the more usual sort. Among other things, the company sponsors a generous employee volunteer program and annual company-wide community-service days. According to Timberland's management, this strategy has paid off handsomely in terms of recruitment, motivation, and teamwork. Since 1998, the first year of *Fortune*'s "best companies to work for" rankings, Timberland has been a regular on the annual list.[33]

However, as the examples of Levi Strauss and the South African banks illustrate, the economic case for commitments in the upper-right quadrant can be fleeting, given their vulnerability to rising financial expectations and changing market conditions. Whether and to what extent a company garners economic rewards for conduct in this quadrant depends heavily on the broader social and institutional context in which it is operating.

This analysis of the matrix suggests a "ladder of commitment" consisting of three levels, each more comprehensive and more demanding than the previous one:

- The first involves adherence to a minimum set of standards having to do with basic justice. Because legal norms are so central here, we might associate this level with an ethic of compliance or mutual forbearance.
- The second level involves a more far-reaching commitment that encompasses not only basic justice but also basic humanity and higher-order precepts of justice. Companies at this level practice what we might call an ethic of consideration or positive mutuality. This is the realm of mutual-gains thinking and cooperative endeavor.
- The third level includes the two lower levels and in addition calls for a contribution beyond what strict mutuality might require. Companies that contribute to community problems they did not create or that take the lead in defining better practices would belong here. This is the level of active leadership and self-improvement, or what we might call an ethic of contribution.

At each level, the logic of the economic argument differs. At level one, the economic case is heavily cost and risk driven. At level two, it is based on a combination of penalties and rewards, as well as risk management. At level three, it is driven mainly by rewards. At all three levels, however, whether the economic costs and benefits actually materialize—and how significant they are—depends entirely on the responses of other parties.

The Importance of Context

The social and institutional context is perhaps the most important factor shaping the relationship between ethics and economic advantage. Much of the discussion so far has tacitly assumed a context characterized by economic and political freedom, free-flowing information, an educated populace, and a functioning legal system. When these conditions are lacking, or when power disparities become too great, the economic case for values weakens dramatically in all four quadrants of the matrix. In the absence of these conditions, even fraud and other forms of blatant injustice can be quite profitable. This is not to say that ethical norms cannot take hold under such conditions, but rather that, if they do, it will be for reasons other than financial self-interest. Moreover, the motivations for adherence will need to be quite strong to overcome the attractions of financial gain.

The role of these contextual factors is implicit in many of the examples considered earlier in this chapter. However, their importance comes into sharper focus if we consider a case study I have sometimes used to illustrate the linkage between ethics and financial performance. The actual case— let's call it the "tainted inventory" case—occurred in the United States. However, interesting conclusions emerge if we imagine it taking place in a different context that lacks crucial features identified above.[34]

The case concerns a marketing decision that arose in the early 1980s when executives of a U.S. baby food company learned that their principal vendor had been supplying bogus ingredients. At the time, the company was wholly owned by a major European multinational. One vendor, instead of shipping apple juice concentrate as specified in the supply contract, had been delivering apple-flavored sugar water. This concentrate had made its way into a wide variety of the company's products, including its critical lead-in item—apple juice for babies marketed and labeled as "100 percent pure" and "all natural." When the deception was discovered, the company had 700,000 cases of finished apple juice product in inventory. The question was what to do about it.

Rather than incur the costs of destroying the inventory, the executive team decided to push it through the pipeline. According to the company's internal documents, the decision was made to minimize the potential economic loss conservatively estimated at $3.5 million—the amount it would have cost to destroy the unused inventory—and to "minimize any damage to the company's reputation." At the time, the company was struggling to achieve profitability after several bad years, and destroying the inventory would have eliminated even the meager profit of some $600,000 projected for that year. Executives worked with the company's lawyers to sell off the adulterated juice to an unsuspecting public while holding FDA regulators at bay. The company was largely successful in this effort, and, by the year's end, executives felt they had salvaged a potentially explosive situation.[35]

This sigh of relief, however, proved premature. Six months later, a company employee wrote a letter to the U.S. Food and Drug Administration. Under the name "Johnny Appleseed," the employee detailed the entire operation, down to employees' glee over federal inspectors' failure to see the deception going on under their very noses. FDA officials promptly launched an investigation that generated enough evidence to turn the case over to the U.S. Justice Department for possible criminal prosecution. The Justice Department decided to pursue criminal charges against not only the company but also against two of its top executives. Meanwhile, the investigation had triggered a series of civil suits, including a class-action suit by a group of supermarket retailers that distributed the company's products.

In the end, the company pled guilty to federal counts of fraud and misbranding and settled the civil suits by making substantial payments to the plaintiffs. One of the two executives went to jail. The other, the CEO, pled guilty to several misdemeanor counts, paid a fine, and received five years' probation. The case received prominent coverage in newspapers across the United States and was featured as a cover story for the *New York Times* Sunday magazine. The publicity took a significant toll on the company's sales and market share. Despite efforts to revive the brand with a new trust-oriented marketing campaign, the company was unable to shake off the stigma of misconduct. Six years after the event, an unrelated purchaser bought the company at a steep discount attributed by observers to the reputational damage caused by the adulteration incident. The new management also tried to restore the company's reputation, but had only limited success.

All told, the company's strategy of deception backfired badly. Out-of-pocket costs alone were estimated at $25 million, far exceeding the predicted cost of destroying the adulterated inventory. Considering the damage to the company's brand and the impact on its market value, this case is a strong testament to the financial wisdom of strict adherence to basic norms of honesty.

However, imagine this case taking place in a very different context. Consider a hypothetical society in which whistleblowing is culturally forbidden, employment mobility is severely limited, and no rules or regulations govern food purity or commercial advertising. Suppose in addition that the society's legal system is ineffective because it is inefficient, or underfunded, or corrupt, or all of these. Imagine further a controlled press that is forbidden to publish negative or embarrassing news, and assume that the public lacks access to reliable information about goods and services offered for sale. Finally, imagine that the juice producer has a monopoly or near-monopoly over the juice market.

In this hypothetical context, the economic consequences of continuing to ship the tainted inventory would have been radically different. In the first place, no employee would have blown the whistle because such actions are culturally forbidden and would only get the whistleblower in trouble. In the absence of an effective regulatory or legal system, the parties injured by the company's deception would have had no obvious means of recourse. Nor, because information is tightly controlled, would the general public have been alerted. In any event, in the absence of competition from alternative suppliers, consumers would have been unable to show their disapproval by taking their business elsewhere.

In short, rather than costing the company $25 to $75 million, the decision to ship the juice would very likely have cost nothing—and it would certainly have saved the company enormous trouble. However, the ethical quality of the decision would have been no different. Marketing an impure product as a pure one would be just as deceptive in this hypothetical context as it was in the actual one.

In this respect, the decision to ship the questionable product breaches a basic norm recognized across many different ethical systems.[36] Scholars tell us that deceit has been consistently rejected by very diverse traditions—Buddhist, Confucian, Islamic, Hindu, and Judeo-Christian—and forbidden by virtually all legal systems.[37] Injunctions against deception can be found in works as different as the ancient Egyptian *Book of the Dead* and *The Metaphysic of Morals* by the eighteenth-century German philosopher Immanuel Kant.[38] Moreover, marketing an impure product as a pure one violates many contemporary codes of business ethics.[39]

As this example illustrates, the relationship between ethics and economic advantage cannot be understood in isolation from the context in which a company is operating. This example also suggests that the financial case for values is likely to be most robust when the following conditions obtain:

- when information is free-flowing
- when authority is decentralized and widely dispersed in the society
- when members of the society have economic freedom and actual choice in terms of employment, investment, and consumption
- when members of the society are educated and well informed on matters relating to these choices
- when members of the society expect companies to operate from an ethical framework, and
- when the society has an effective legal or regulatory system to enforce basic ethical norms.

A Dynamic Relationship

Taken as a statement of fact, "ethics pays" is at best a crude generalization whose truth varies from time to time and from place to place depending on prevailing attitudes and institutions. The extent to which it is true at any given point reflects in large measure the extent to which society's institutions are arranged and operated in ways that support it. Unless we know something about the social and institutional context in which a company is operating, we cannot possibly say whether adherence to even basic norms of justice is likely to be economically advantageous. Although there is undoubtedly some degree of natural overlap between ethics and economic advantage, given the principles of reciprocity discussed earlier, this overlap can be more or less strong and more or less extensive. Moreover, it can be undercut if the principles of reciprocity are blocked or denied effect.

Many of the examples discussed in this chapter involved just such blockages. In one set of cases, the parties that suffered injury lacked the ability to retaliate. Recall the lenders who were being defrauded by Eric's company, the child workers who were chained to their looms, or the food-processing company that was unfairly disadvantaged by its tax-evading rivals. All were powerless to take action for want of information or clout in the marketplace. In the absence of legal, political, educational, or other mechanisms that would have allowed the victims to redress these power and information disparities, the perpetrators were able to profit from their wrongs.

In other cases we considered, the positive relationship between ethics and economic advantage failed because companies' good deeds were inadequately rewarded. The beneficiaries of those acts may not have known they were benefiting or lacked the means to show their appreciation in market and monetary terms. For example, because the beneficiaries of AES's proposed environmental precautions are not yet born, they can scarcely reward the company for its contributions to their well-being. And, as I have noted, the economic rewards of serving the poor are often dwarfed by the rewards of serving the better-off for the obvious reason that the poor have less ability to pay. To make serious money serving the poor generally requires a large market and extra effort.

As both sets of cases illustrate, tensions between what's right and what's profitable are exacerbated as information, knowledge, and power are more unevenly distributed across a population. When injurious conduct is not penalized and beneficial conduct is not rewarded, the paths of virtue and profitability inevitably diverge.

This analysis helps explain why "ethics pays" is better received in some contexts than in others. Executives who try to promulgate this philosophy in free-wheeling markets that lack law, transparency, and democratic institutions are often seen as irritatingly self-righteous or incredibly naïve. Neither these executives—many of whom take for granted media scrutiny, litigation, punitive damages, consumerism, and competitive markets—nor their skeptical audiences seem to appreciate the contextual conditions that are necessary to make the financial argument for ethics plausible. Of course, both sides are right. It *is* naïve to think that ethics pays anytime and anyplace. However, it is also naïve to assume that values and profitability can never be pursued in combination.

The best that we can probably expect, however, is a partial and somewhat unstable overlap between ethics and economic advantage. Depending on societal attitudes and institutions, the degree of overlap may be more or less extensive at any given time. But it will never be perfect so long as human well-being, the ultimate concern of ethics, is thought to encompass more than economic considerations. Moreover, in a dynamic society, the relationship between these two domains will be constantly changing and the degree of overlap in constant flux, as suggested by Figure 3-4. Even a relatively settled equilibrium can easily be upset by changes in the environment—in attitudes, law, technology, circumstances, or ideas.

Returning to the tainted inventory case in our hypothetical society, we can see that any of a number of changes—a shift in attitudes, the introduction

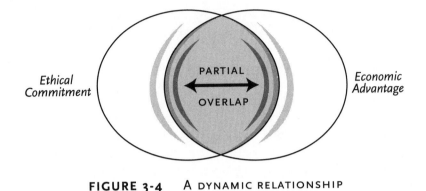

FIGURE 3-4   A DYNAMIC RELATIONSHIP

of competition, the development of a functioning legal system—could alter the relationship between ethics and financial self-interest. Just as changing laws and attitudes in the United States have strengthened the financial case for fair and nondiscriminatory hiring, similar changes in the hypothetical society could strengthen the financial case for product integrity and accurate labeling.

Not long ago, civil rights leader Jesse Jackson spoke to a group of Wall Street executives about hiring more minorities and African-Americans. Rather than appealing to ethical arguments about fairness, rights, or equality of opportunity, Jackson appealed to the executives' financial self-interest. He told them that discrimination was costing them money and that they could not afford to deprive themselves of the talent residing in the non-white population. Jackson's argument would have seemed ludicrous 50 years ago, but in today's economic, legal, and social environment, it rings very true. As a result of social and institutional changes, the ethical argument and the economic argument have become much better aligned.[40]

To take another example, the revolution in information technology has opened up new opportunities for profitable theft, deception, and invasions of personal privacy. It will take some time to close off these opportunities, but eventually laws and social attitudes are likely to evolve in that direction. At the same time, this technological development has had something of an opposite effect by heightening the visibility of much corporate behavior that was previously hidden from public view. In this aspect, it has contributed to strengthening the overlap of ethics and financial advantage by increasing the likelihood that both positive and negative behavior will be exposed to public view.

Of course, any equilibrium between ethics and economic advantage is equally vulnerable to destabilization from within. As we discussed in Chapter 2, respect for basic ethical norms builds social trust. Yet, paradoxically, an increase in trust creates new incentives for opportunism, for a trusting community is a thief's paradise.

In the end, we must acknowledge that the link between ethical commitment and economic advantage is both fragile and ever changing. Whether the relationship tends toward harmony or hostility reflects the financial and moral standards to which companies are held and the context in which they operate. But even under favorable conditions, the financial case for ethics goes only so far. Although the financial case is stronger than has often been thought, it does not fully explain the turn to values. For that something more is needed.

This chapter has suggested that the ethics boom of recent decades has less to do with any inherent connection between ethics and economic advantage than with changes in the business environment. As I argue in the next chapter, a deeper explanation lies in a fundamental change in what's expected of leading companies today.

4

The Corporation's
Evolving Personality

If the value shift we see in many companies around the world cannot be wholly explained in purely financial terms, can a better explanation be provided? A more satisfactory account begins with an appreciation for a subtle but striking development in what has sometimes been called the "personality" of the corporation—the pattern of attributes thought to define its essential nature. This change in the character of the corporation has affected how companies are thought about, what's expected of them, and how they are evaluated. Seen in broad historical context, this development is nothing short of revolutionary, though its gradual nature, unfolding across the last century, has somewhat obscured its significance.

This development, which has picked up momentum in recent decades, explains why the notion that ethics pays has gained plausibility in recent years—and also why this maxim is nonetheless an inadequate guide for companies that aspire to positions of leadership in today's world. Let me introduce this development with a brief anecdote.

In the mid-1990s, I traveled to Argentina on a research and speaking trip. As it happened, my visit occurred not long after IBM Argentina had been accused of paying off the directors of Argentina's state-owned Banco Nación to win a $250 million contract to supply the bank's information systems. The bribes, which were allegedly offered to the directors and others through a shell company whose only apparent purpose was to channel these payments, were at the time said to be some $37 million, or 15 percent of the contract's value. As I spoke with Argentine executives and business students, I discovered that many of them wanted to talk about the problem of corruption. Perhaps I should have expected as much, given the findings of public opinion polls at the time. Gallup polls showed that

Argentina's citizens consistently ranked corruption, along with unemployment and education, as the country's top three problems.

Whenever I asked about corporate values, the talk would eventually turn to the pervasiveness of corruption and the difficulty of avoiding it when doing business in Argentina. I was told that in many sectors bribery, kickbacks, and payoffs had come to be accepted as normal—simply the way things were done. The IBM example was naturally cited as a case in point. However, it was usually mentioned in a tone of surprise laced with a hint of disapproval that IBM would do such a thing! When I asked why they were surprised that IBM would do what they had just told me was commonplace, they would reply with a look of puzzlement. "Well, we expect more of a world-class company like IBM."

To anyone steeped in traditional thinking about the nature of the corporation, this response is quite remarkable. Within this tradition, it has long been an article of faith that companies are nothing more than convenient instruments for carrying out business activities—-that they are entirely amoral and thus lacking any capacity for ethical self-discipline or moral judgment. In this view, whether they are described as instruments of production or instruments of wealth creation makes little difference. From this traditional perspective, expecting a company to conform its activities to a set of ethical standards—let alone take the lead in addressing a societal problem like corruption—is entirely inappropriate. It would be like expecting an automobile, a mechanical device devoid of consciousness and incapable of moral judgment, to obey the rules of the road or to swerve to avoid a child who runs into the street.

Yet these Argentine executives and business students expected IBM to obey the law and to figure out how to go about its business without running afoul of ethical standards against payoffs. What's more, they expected IBM, as a global and presumably world-class company, to behave *better* than prevailing norms dictated and in this way contribute to solving one of the country's most pressing problems.

The people I spoke with in Argentina are not alone. According to the Millennium Poll on Corporate Social Responsibility, a 1999 survey of more than 25,000 individuals across 23 countries on six continents, two in three people say that companies should go beyond their traditional functions of making a profit, paying taxes, creating jobs, and obeying the law. In addition, respondents said, companies should also try to set a higher ethical standard and contribute to broader societal goals. In other words, companies should achieve profitability in ways that help build a better society. In all but three of the countries surveyed, 50 percent or more of those surveyed took this position. Among those who expressed this view, about half defined the corporation's role as "exceeding all laws, setting a higher ethical standard, and helping build a better society for all." The remainder of this subset said companies should operate "somewhere between" the traditional definition of the corporation's role and this more demanding one.[1]

Parallel but even more striking results emerged from an August 2000 survey in the United States.[2] Some 95 percent of these respondents said that companies should sometimes forgo some profit for the sake of making things better for their workers and communities. Although, as with almost any survey research, we could quibble about methodologies, response bias, and other issues, it is noteworthy that both groups of respondents evidently expect companies to exercise moral judgment in carrying out their activities.

A Glance at History

In attributing a capacity for moral judgment to the corporations, these respondents go against an orthodoxy whose lineage is both long and venerable. The doctrine of corporate amorality has ancient roots in corporate law, and it has played a central role in the thinking of many economists and management theorists up to this day. This doctrine found perhaps its most colorful expression in the comment of an eighteenth-century English jurist who railed at the corporation for lacking either "pants to kick" or "a soul to damn."[3]

Though forcefully put, the thought itself was not original. In a seminal legal case decided early in the preceding century, another eminent English jurist, Sir Edward Coke, had declared that corporations, because they had no souls, could neither commit treason nor be outlawed or excommunicated.[4] Coke was writing about a hospital, a charitable corporation, in an era when most business corporations, apart from trade guilds, were bodies set up under royal charters to develop foreign trade and colonies.[5] In fact, the corporate form came to be used extensively for business in England only in the latter part of the nineteenth century.

To Coke, and to many who came before him, it made no sense to attribute moral responsibility to a corporation. How could such a manifestly "artificial" and "intangible" entity be a moral agent? That it could not seemed self-evident. The logic had been spelled out almost four centuries earlier by Pope Innocent IV, to whom the "fiction theory" of the corporation is sometimes attributed.[6] After wrestling with the problem of punishment for ecclesiastical corporations, the Pope concluded that the exercise was more or less futile. Unlike a real person, he reasoned, a corporation has neither a body nor a soul to experience the pain of punishment. And therefore, as merely a "fictional person," a corporation was by its very nature an unsuitable subject for punishment or excommunication.[7]

The fiction theory, shorn of its overt religious origins, was carried forward and reaffirmed in 1819 by the U.S. Supreme Court in the well-known case of *Dartmouth College* v. *Woodward*.[8] Although this case concerned a charitable corporation, business corporations were by this time gaining popularity in the United States, where some 350 were established between 1783 and 1801.[9] Even so, the business corporation was thought of mainly as an agency of government chartered to build bridges, turnpikes, canals, and the like. In exchange for meeting such public needs, it was granted certain special privileges and immunities, the specific nature of which would change and evolve over time.

In *Dartmouth College*, Chief Justice John Marshall described the corporation as "an artificial being, invisible, intangible, and existing only in contemplation of law."[10] As such, he wrote, a corporation could possess only those properties conferred by its charter of creation. Among these were "immortality" and "individuality," as well as others necessary to carry out the purpose for which it was created. Needless to say, moral personality was not included—nor could it have been, given the "artificial" or "fictional" status ascribed to the corporation. By their very nature, fictional entities lack the attributes necessary for moral standing, or so it was reasoned. Indeed, Marshall declared in another case that, as an "invisible, intangible, and artificial being," a corporation, was "certainly not a citizen" under the Constitution.[11]

In the late nineteenth century, the fiction theory underwent a makeover reflecting the changing times. With the proliferation of "general incorporation statutes," beginning around midcentury, the government's role in forming corporations receded into the background. Under these statutes, corporations could be formed without a special charter from a state legislature.[12] By 1875, special charters had become largely a thing of the past, and virtually anyone could form a corporation simply by filing the appropriate forms and paying the required fee.[13] Many did so: The latter half of the century saw a phenomenal increase in the number of incorporations across the United States. A similar expansion occurred in England as freedom of incorporation took hold and the joint stock company, with the advantage of limited liability, became a form available as of common right.[14] These open policies on corporate formation lent credence to the new idea that the corporation was not, as Marshall had declared, a creature of the state with only those powers conferred by its charter, but a creature of private agreement.[15]

The new conception of the corporation as a fictional umbrella for a private association of shareholders strengthened the argument against government control over corporations and enlarged their sphere of authority. Nevertheless, the corporation's moral status, or lack thereof, remained unchanged. By reaffirming the corporation's fictional nature, the new approach negated the possibility that the corporation could have an identity separate from the identities of the individual shareholders comprising it. Nor could the corporation have either a moral personality or any responsibilities beyond those of its shareholders viewed as individuals. Besides, as a mere instrument, a corporation could hardly be evaluated in moral terms.

Of course, not everyone bought into the idea of the corporation as a fiction. By the dawn of the twentieth century, with the spectacular growth of corporations in the United States and Europe, academics on both sides of the Atlantic had begun to challenge this characterization. They insisted that the corporation was a "natural" or "real" entity, thereby drawing attention to the sociological fact of growing corporate power and influence as seen in the great railroad and manufacturing corporations as well as the immensely powerful oil trusts of the time.

The "natural entity" theory found an audience among both critics and supporters of the corporation's growing influence. Critics saw it as justifying their concerns about increasingly large concentrations of capital and its impact on community life. Supporters, on the other hand, saw it as legitimating new rights for corporations and enhancing the authority of officers and directors in relation to shareholders.

The theory squared neatly with a variety of legal doctrines being applied to corporations by the end of the nineteenth century. By that time, the corporation's capacity to sue and be sued, its freedom of contract, and its right to certain constitutional protections were well established in the United States. For legal purposes, the corporation had been declared a citizen, contrary to Justice Marshall's earlier insistence that this was not the case. Moreover, U.S. law had unequivocally embraced the doctrine of limited shareholder liability. Shareholders were now safely shielded from personal accountability for the corporation's debts and other liabilities incurred by corporations in carrying out their activities. At the same time, the law prohibited shareholders from managing the corporation's day-to-day affairs and precluded them from challenging the board of directors' business decisions except in cases involving willful misconduct.[16]

These developments, which strengthened the corporation's legal personality and diminished the role of shareholders, made it increasingly awkward to describe the corporation as a fiction or to think of it as a purely private contractual arrangement among a group of investors. Indeed, the very term "corporation" took on two usages, sometimes referring collectively to the body of shareholders and at other times referring to those with authority to act on the corporation's behalf.

Although the natural entity theory might have provided a platform for a distinctive idea of corporate, as opposed to individual, morality, it did not develop in that direction.[17] Instead, discussions of the corporation's personality trailed off into a morass of confusion over such abstruse matters as whether the corporate "person" was really a "person."[18] By the 1930s, legal academics had largely abandoned this line of thinking, and talk of the corporation's personality faded. However, the natural entity theory had by then done its practical work of legitimating large-scale enterprise in the eyes of the law.[19] The corporation had attained sufficient stature to be counted among the ranks of society's essential institutions. According to one leading authority on corporations writing at the time, "It was apparent to any thoughtful observer that the American corporation had ceased to be a private business device and had become an institution."[20]

The "institutional" view of the corporation thus moved into the mainstream and became the dominant framework for legal thinking. With this move came suggestions that the corporation, as such, had responsibilities not just to stockholders but to other parties as well—a position that would seem to imply a moral personality for the corporation. Noting a seeming shift in public opinion, a leading U.S. legal theorist speculated in 1932, ". . . a sense of social responsibility toward employees, consumers, and the general public [might someday] come to be regarded as the appropriate attitude to be adopted by those who are engaged in business."[21] However, it would take several more decades for this sense to become widespread. Even in 1958, an opponent of the social responsibility movement called it still "young and rather unassuming" but dangerous enough to portend trouble should it gain momentum.[22]

Meanwhile, the fiction theory of the corporation had not entirely died off. In certain economic circles, this old bottle was being filled with new wine. Rejecting ideas of corporate entities and seemingly oblivious to the legal developments noted earlier, these thinkers offered up a new blend of private contracts as the essence of the corporation. According to the model that eventually emerged, the corporation was not merely a private agreement among investors but a series of private agreements among providers of production inputs.[23] Injected with new vitality, the fiction theory was propelled into prominence again in the 1960s and 1970s.

Unlike the English jurist who had seen in the corporation's fictional nature a cause for frustration, the theory's new proponents viewed it as a shield against the period's increasingly strident calls for corporate responsibility.[24] "Only people can have responsibilities," wrote a leading economist in 1971, in a coolly reasoned argument against corporate social responsibility.[25] Because corporations are only "artificial persons," he postulated, they can have only "artificial responsibilities." According to this line of reasoning, advocates of corporate social responsibility are guilty of a grave mistake of metaphysics. By virtue of companies' very nature as legal fictions, they cannot have responsibilities to their employees, customers, or the communities in which they operate—or so the argument ran.

This argument, with its eerie echoes of Sir Edward Coke and even Pope Innocent IV, can only ring hollow to the contemporary ear. The size and influence of today's corporations far exceed anything even remotely imaginable to the authors and early proponents of the corporate fiction doctrine. Yet even today, some lawyers and economists insist that the corporation is merely a "legal fiction," implying that it is not a proper subject of moral assessment. They argue that companies are only amoral instruments of commerce, extensions of their shareholders' property rights. Echoing the centuries-old view, they argue that moral responsibilities can attach only to individual human beings and that it therefore makes no sense to speak of such things in relation to corporations.

Of course, such metaphysical niceties did not stop my Argentine interviewees from making moral judgments about IBM's behavior or prevent the survey respondents mentioned earlier from calling on companies to set a higher ethical standard. Nor have they stopped millions of employees, customers, investors, communities, and concerned citizens around the world from making moral judgments about the behavior of the companies they deal with.

Indeed, as the size and importance of corporations have increased, so has the general propensity to view their activities through a moral lens. We can hardly avoid asking such basic moral questions as: How do companies affect society, and in what ways are their activities beneficial or harmful? Are the benefits they provide sufficient to justify the rights and privileges they enjoy? Do companies respect the rights of others? Is their behavior consistent with basic ethical norms? Given the legal history just referred to, it may seem ironic that people today sometimes seem more inclined to focus their moral concerns on corporate behavior than on individual behavior in private life. The tendency, though, is understandable, given the extensive role played by companies in society today.

Theory versus Practice

While theorists build models of "fictional" companies operating in a world that is presumed to be morally inert, managers of real companies in the world as it is must deal with moral concerns on a regular basis. As the case examples in Chapter 1 showed, companies today are assumed to be moral agents with a capacity for moral judgment, and they are routinely dealt with, discussed, and judged as such. Recall how Salomon's constituencies reacted when management disclosed the bond traders' misdeeds—customers, creditors, investors, and employees alike began to separate themselves from the firm. As one CEO of a client company explained to a Salomon manager, "We know that you personally are ethical, but I can't go to the board and recommend Salomon. You understand that."[26]

Or consider the criticisms lodged against Shell. Unless a capacity for moral judgment is assumed, it makes no sense to take Shell to task for harming the environment or failing to promote human rights in Nigeria. Similarly, if corporations were entirely amoral, it would be absurd for employees to feel gratitude to Sealed Air for treating them fairly. The same goes for customers who would trust HDFC with their deposits on the basis of its past behavior. All these reactions—blaming, shunning, gratitude, trust—presuppose that companies are proper objects of moral assessment and concern.

The extent to which companies have come to be seen as moral actors is evident from the daily media. Moral controversies, allegations of misconduct, stories of moral leadership—these have all become as much a part of the daily business news as reports on profits, economic trends, and corporate mergers. The amount of such coverage varies, but hardly a day goes by that the front page of the *Wall Street Journal* doesn't include at least one such story.

On one presumably average news day in September 2000, for instance, the *Journal*'s left-hand lead article explored the fairness of the arbitration agreements that some mortgage companies were requiring their customers to sign.[27] Another lead article in the right-hand column examined safety concerns related to a McDonnell Douglas jet. Short summaries in the second and third columns pointed readers to other stories inside the paper about intellectual property piracy, antitrust issues in Europe, the safety of a new drug, a safety-driven tire recall, protests against unfair fuel prices in Europe, and the appointment of a new tobacco company executive. The summary noted that the new executive, unlike his predecessor, was well versed in regulatory matters and willing to discuss smoking safety with officials of the World Trade Organization. On that same day, the front page of the paper's second section featured one article about credit card scams in E-business and another about corporate espionage that focused on the rise in computer theft among high-tech rivals seeking competitive intelligence.

When innocent people are injured by corporate activities, moral questions are rarely far behind. Consider the controversy that began in August 2000 when Bridgestone/Firestone, the U.S. subsidiary of Japan's Bridgestone Corp., recalled some 6.5 million tires in the United States. Most had been mounted as original equipment on the Explorer, a popular sport utility vehicle made by Ford Motor Company. Faced with a growing number of accidents apparently triggered when the treads of certain tires pulled away from their rims, Ford and Bridgestone/Firestone together determined that a recall was the only way to prevent further incidents. At the time, tire-related accidents had been linked to 250 injuries and 88 deaths in the United States and at least 51 deaths in various countries in Latin America, the Middle East, and Southeast Asia.[28]

Issues of corporate responsibility moved to center stage and front pages almost overnight. How long had the companies known about the risks? Why hadn't they said anything earlier? Who was accountable for decisions that had been endangering the lives of unknown people around the world? How culpable were the companies? When subsequent disclosures revealed that both Ford and Bridgestone/Firestone officials had known about the risk of tread separation for some time prior to the recall, consumer trust in the Firestone brand weakened further. One study published less than a month after the recall began reported a drop in consumer trust of 39 percent in Asia-Pacific, 47 percent in South America, and 14 percent in Africa.[29] A *Newsweek* poll in early September found that more than 80 percent of U.S. respondents said that Bridgestone/Firestone was responsible, either principally or equally with Ford, for failing to warn consumers about the dangers of rollover accidents associated with the tires.[30]

These judgments took their toll on both companies. Sales of Ford Explorers stalled, and sales of Firestone tires plummeted as distributors and customers began defecting to other suppliers. Bridgestone's credit and investment ratings were downgraded. Injured parties lined up to sue. Congress called for public hearings, with the chairman of one Senate committee declaring that both Ford and Bridgestone/Firestone had breached their moral obligation to the public in failing to disclose the tire safety issues when they first learned about them. Both companies' stock took a pounding, but Bridgestone was particularly hard hit and fell by more than 50 percent in the month following the recall.[31]

The 2001 collapse of Enron described in Chapter 2 elicited similar reactions and sentiments. Wall Street analysts claimed to have been misled by the company, and employees who lost their jobs and life savings said they had been betrayed. A conservative political columnist declared that "indignation" was the proper attitude toward Enron's behavior. Other observers described the conduct of Enron and Arthur Andersen, the company's accountant, as "a serious breach in corporate integrity," "a pervasive breakdown in ethics and corporate governance," and a "failure to maintain the ethical standards . . . fundamental to the American economic system."[32]

What are we to make of this discrepancy between theory and practice? Are all these parties mistaken in treating companies as proper objects of moral assessment? Certainly the injured parties, the general public, government officials, and company executives all speak as if culpability, responsibility, and trust were relevant concepts. Have they not yet realized that a corporation is nothing more than a convenient instrument for conducting business, an "artificial entity" and, as such, inherently amoral? And what about the journalists and commentators at the *Wall Street Journal*, the *Financial Times*, *Business Week*, and other business publications that report on moral aspects of business activity? Perhaps they, too, are mistaken in applying the concepts and categories of moral discourse to companies and their conduct.

Some, like the economist mentioned earlier, have taken this point of view. Presented with moral criticisms of corporate behavior, they refer back to essentialist arguments rooted in traditional theories about the corporation's true nature. The imagery varies—machines, instruments, soulless persons—but the conclusions seldom do. "Corporations are machines. . . . Not being human, not having feelings, corporations do not have morals," says one commentator, adding, "To ask corporate executives to behave in a morally defensible manner is absurd. Corporations, and the people within them, are not subject to moral behavior."[33] Another states, ". . . the large organization is amoral. It is, perhaps, the most important technological invention of our time, but it is only a tool and it has no intent."[34] Still other writers assert, "[C]orporations have no concept of inherent right and wrong because they are exclusively goal-directed."[35]

But such essentialist arguments miss the point. Regardless of traditional thinking and practice, more and more people today are calling for something new. To someone wronged or injured by a company's behavior, the doctrine of corporate amorality is cold comfort. Rooted in medieval ideas about entities and ensoulment, it is a doctrine that has outlived its time. As so often happens in the practical and professional sciences, practice has outpaced theory. And this is the central point. While many theorists have devoted themselves to refining the traditional orthodoxies, the world has changed dramatically. In today's society, the doctrine of corporate amorality is no longer tenable.

A Pervasive Presence

As many have by now observed, corporations today are not just tools we use to organize economic activity. They have become the environment we live in.[36] Many of us spend the better part of our waking hours working either directly or indirectly on behalf of corporations. They are the basis of our livelihood, generating the salaries and investment income we need to live. Here I count not only those employed by corporations and their satellite organizations, but also those who provide companies with professional services—consultants, lawyers, accountants, investment bankers, and so on—as well as those involved in regulating them, writing about them, studying them, and opposing them.

Even when we aren't working, we spend much of our time interacting with corporations in the person of individuals who represent them or act on their behalf. Corporations supply us with most of the basic goods and services we need to run our households, but we also depend on them for transportation, communication, energy, and other essential utilities to maintain the fabric of our daily lives. Increasingly, many of us are turning to corporations for child care, elder care, health care, schooling, and other social services. Corporations also supply much of our entertainment and information—the movies we see, the books we read, the music we listen to. They bring us our news and our news analyses. And because our savings, pension funds, and other investments are for the most part ultimately in corporate hands, many of us depend on corporations for our financial security and independence in retirement. With the exception of taxes and charitable contributions, most of the income that flows into middle-class households ends up in corporate coffers.

But our dealings with corporations extend well beyond such discrete transactions. The visible hand of the corporation touches nearly every aspect of our lives. Through their marketing efforts, corporate persuaders try to tell us how to dress and how to behave. They advise us on matters of health and personal hygiene. Through their employment policies, corporate decision makers determine when we must work, when we may meet with our children's teachers, when we may visit a doctor. Through campaign donations, lobbying, and public relations efforts, corporate advocates shape our public policy and our public discourse. Corporate architects and planners configure our landscapes, cityscapes, and public spaces. Corporate designers set aesthetic standards and shape our aesthetic sensibilities. Increasingly, academic scientists and researchers depend on corporate funding to support their work. Through these contributions and through research and development partnerships with leading universities, corporate influence shapes the development of our shared knowledge base and our educational curricula.

By virtually any measure we choose, the corporation today is a pervasive presence in society. Of the $18 trillion in U.S. business revenues for 1997, about 88 percent went to corporations rather than to unincorporated businesses.[37] For the retail sector, the proportion was slightly higher.[38] According to 1992 census data, 87.9 percent of working Americans, or just over 79 million, were employed by corporations.[39] In 1998, about half the American population owned stock in publicly traded companies, either directly or indirectly through mutual funds or retirement accounts.[40] By contrast, only about 1 percent were shareholders in 1900. Even in 1970, the percentage was only about 15 percent.

The last century's enormous growth in economic activity owed much to corporations, whose role in society and position relative to noncorporate sectors of the economy were both thereby enhanced. In 1939, for instance, individual proprietorships and partnerships earned some 22 percent of that year's $2 trillion in U.S. business revenues (in 1999 dollars). By 1996, the share earned by noncorporate businesses had dropped to 11 percent. Between 1939 and 1996, a period during which the U.S. population doubled, revenues of individual proprietorships and partnerships grew threefold and sevenfold, respectively, while corporate revenues increased nearly tenfold.[41]

Patent grants are another indicator of the corporation's increasing importance. The proportion of patents for inventions issued in the United States to corporations, as compared to individuals and governments, rose to 84.1 percent in 1998 compared to 75.7 percent in 1980.[42] (Among the world's patent systems, the U.S. system is generally regarded as the most favorable to individuals because it awards patents on a "first to invent" rather than a "first to file" basis.)

A growing proportion of U.S. research and development is under corporate control or influence. Corporate R&D spending, as a percentage of total R&D spending by U.S. industry, government, universities, and nonprofits, rose from 44 percent in 1953 to 67 percent in 1999.[43] Business funding of R&D carried out in higher education settings remained a small portion of total funding in the mid-1990s, but still more than doubled from 2.5 percent in 1980 to 5.8 percent in 1996.[44] And in 1999 some schools derived as much as 10 percent of their research budgets from corporate underwriting. Between 1991 and 2000, the number of licensing or options agreements executed annually between universities and companies more than tripled, from about 1300 to more than 4000, according to data gathered by university licensing professionals.[45]

Although corporations are prohibited by law from making donations to federal election campaigns, they have nonetheless played an important role in campaign finance. Employee donations to corporate political action committees (PACs) as well as "soft-money" contributions from business sources accounted for more than 70 percent of total PAC and soft-money donations to campaigns in the 1998 election cycle.[46] An additional indication of corporate clout is seen in the pattern of federal income tax receipts: The proportion of federal income taxes paid by corporations, as a percentage of the total paid by individuals and corporations, dropped from 42 percent in 1954 to only 17 percent in 1999.[47]

Other figures, too, suggest just how big a role companies play in the life of the society. According to one 1996 study, occupational fraud and abuse—the deliberate misuse of an employing organization's resources—costs some $400 billion annually, while street crime such as robbery and burglary cost something on the order of $4 billion.[48]

The growing popularity of for-profit forms of organization has meant that more Americans are receiving essential services from corporate providers. As of 2000, for example, 63 percent of the enrollees in U.S. health maintenance organizations were signed up with for-profits.[49] In 1988, 12 years earlier, a majority had been enrolled with nonprofits.[50] Local governments, too, have been making more extensive use of private-sector providers to deliver services. The proportion of services contracted out by U.S. county governments rose from 24 percent to 35 percent between 1987 and 1992. And of the new services offered during this period, more than half were contracted out to private-sector suppliers.[51]

Other indicators point to the corporation's pervasive presence and growing influence around the globe. Although the data are scattered and impressionistic, they sketch an unmistakable picture of a world in which corporate concerns play an increasingly central role:

- Between 1980 and 1996, more than 2000 public enterprises were privatized in more than 80 countries, primarily developing ones.[52] In monetary terms, nearly a trillion dollars worth of state-owned enterprises were transferred to the private sector in the 1990s.[53]
- Outside the United States, privatized companies were generally among the largest firms in their home country's stock markets.[54] In a few smaller countries, the proceeds raised from privatizations in the 1990s amounted to as much as 15 percent to 25 percent of the nation's gross domestic product (GDP).[55]
- Between 1983 and 1999, total capitalization of the world's non-U.S. stock markets grew from $1.49 trillion to $18.36 trillion, a 12-fold increase of which an estimated 20 percent to 25 percent was due to privatizations. Including the United States, total world market capitalization grew from $3.38 trillion to $35.0 trillion during this period, and privatizations accounted for roughly 10 percent of the rise.[56]
- The total value of shares traded on stock markets in developing countries grew from $25 billion in 1983 to $2.32 trillion in 1999.[57]
- In developing countries, investment in infrastructure projects with private-sector participation grew from about $16 billion in 1990 to $95 billion in 1998.[58]
- Sales of the world's largest 200 corporations, totaling $8.3 trillion, were equivalent to 27.5 percent of world GDP in 1999, an increase from 25 percent in 1983.[59] A separate report found that, in 1999, the combined sales of the world's 2000 largest publicly held companies were $21.1 trillion.[60]
- In 1999, the world's five largest corporations each had sales larger than the GDPs of 182 countries.[61] General Motors, Wal-Mart, Exxon Mobil, Ford Motor, and DaimlerChrysler each had sales ranging from $160 to $177 billion.[62]
- In the 1990s, as compared with the 1980s, the corporate sector's contribution to R&D funding in the OECD countries increased relative to government and other funding sources.[63] In 1999, the private business sector contributed about 63 percent of the OECD countries' total R&D expenditures, compared with just over 51 percent in 1981. The government's share increased in only six countries during the 1990s.

When the doctrine of corporate amorality was conceived, the corporation was a rare and exotic form of life. Over the course of centuries, as society changed, the corporation evolved into a useful form for pooling capital and organizing business activity. Once the prerogative of the crown or the legislature, the corporate form was opened up to general usage with the enactment of free incorporation laws in the latter half of the nineteenth century.

Today, thanks to such attributes as legal standing, limited liability, and ease of incorporation, the corporation is still a convenient tool for conducting business. However, it has become much more than that. It has become society's dominant institution and its favored organizational form. Increasingly, for-profit corporations, rather than nonprofit, governmental, and noncorporate business organizations, are being relied on to carry out society's activities. At the same time, large multinational corporations have been growing larger and more influential.

Of course, corporations have not become all-powerful, as some commentators have argued. Companies generally operate in specific markets and lack the coercive powers of the state (though at times they have been implicated in attempts to overthrow states). They are also subject to various countervailing forces that we will discuss later. Nonetheless, their influence today is palpable all around the globe and in all aspects of life—more so than ever before. Even governments are being urged to mimic the practices of business and innovative entrepreneurs.

Given the corporation's extensive and important role in society today, the doctrine of corporate amorality has lost whatever validity it might have had in an earlier era. In granting corporations an exemption from morality, we would exempt 80 percent to 90 percent of what goes on in our lives today. And eventually, in black hole fashion, the exception would swallow the rule.

Those who argue that corporations are inherently amoral trade on an ambiguity between the corporation as an idea and the corporation as a going concern. If we think of the corporation as a legal form or an abstract idea, calling it "amoral" is harmless enough, though "pre-moral" might be more accurate. Considered in this way, the corporation is amoral in the same way that all abstractions are amoral. The moral question emerges only when the corporation is thought of as an agent peopled with directors, executives, and employees who are engaged in making decisions, bringing goods and services to market, and interacting with the rest of the world. As a going concern, a corporation can behave in an entirely amoral fashion, as has often been the case. Alternatively, it can behave as an actor that recognizes responsibilities, honors commitments, makes value judgments, and generally exhibits the traits attributed to moral agents. Contrary to the essentialist claim, however, there is nothing inherent in the *idea* of the corporation that necessitates corporate amorality in practice.

Given the world we live in, it is not surprising that more and more people have come to expect companies to behave as moral actors. As the corporation's role has expanded, it has taken over functions previously performed by individuals, governments, and unincorporated groups. In many cases, the moral standards applied to these noncorporate actors have been carried forward to their corporate replacements. Doctors, for example, are not excused from the Hippocratic oath just because they are employed by a corporation. Similarly, corporate providers of formerly public services have found that they are expected to pay heed to the public's concerns just as the former government provider was expected to do.[64]

The crucial point here, however, is the sheer pervasiveness of corporate activity. Given that the corporate sphere has become all-encompassing, life for most people would be exceedingly difficult and uncertain if the corporate sphere were permitted to operate outside the principles of morality.

We need only recall seventeenth-century philosopher Thomas Hobbes's memorable description of life in an amoral society: "poore, nasty, brutish, and short."[65] Such a society, which Hobbes equated with a "state of nature," would lack for industry, commerce, and agriculture, as well as knowledge, arts, and letters—and, worst of all, people would live in "continualle feare, and danger of violent death . . . ."[66]

Hobbes paints a depressing and perhaps exaggerated picture. Nonetheless, contemporary research lends support to his speculations. Several studies have found positive links between social trust and national prosperity suggesting that countries with higher levels of generalized social trust tend to do better economically than those with lower levels.[67]

Further endorsement of the Hobbesian vision comes from research on the relationship between corruption and national development. Documenting what lawmakers have long believed, researchers have shown that high levels of corruption inhibit investment, retard growth, hinder democratic institutions, and siphon off valuable public resources.[68] One recent study of the relationship between corruption and foreign direct investment likened corruption to a tax. Using a formula derived from analyses of investment data and various corruption indices, the author concluded that an increase in corruption from the low levels found in Singapore to the high levels found in Mexico would have the same negative effect on inward investment flows as an 18 percent to 50 percent increase in tax rates.[69] Another study concluded that corruption was as powerful as political instability in its negative effects on economic growth.[70] Of course, all those who live in societies plagued by terrorists, gangsters, and vandals know firsthand the costs that amorality imposes on every aspect of life.

Too often, we think of ethics as a set of rules whose rationale no one can quite remember. Relegated to the domain of "feeling" or "emotion," morality takes on an air of mystery or is thought to be a nice but nonessential embellishment to the day-to-day business of living. But, as this research suggests, a system of morality is at bottom a highly practical invention. By tapping into fundamental human instincts, it enables individuals and societies to function more effectively than would otherwise be the case.[71] Though different ethical systems have different strengths and weaknesses, they serve similar functions insofar as they endow human activity with meaning, prescribe standards of behavior, and establish expectations for how we should treat one another. Among other things, an ethical system facilitates trust among its adherents and thus creates the necessary foundation for cooperative endeavor.

In response to the growing influence of corporations and perhaps guided by an instinctual sense of the dangers of pervasive amorality, we have come to expect companies to exhibit a moral personality. To be sure, this personality can only be expressed and "embodied" through those who act on the corporation's behalf—its directors, executives, employees, and other representatives. But all groups act through their members, and companies are no different from teams, orchestras, legislatures, or any other collective endeavor in this regard. We need not postulate an ethereal "corporate conscience" to explain corporate morality, any more than we need to posit an ethereal "corporate mind" to account for corporate strategy or corporate learning.

In the end, whether we ascribe moral personality to the corporation is not a question of metaphysics but of pragmatics. As a purely pragmatic matter, a society cannot survive, let alone thrive, if it exempts its most influential and pervasive institutions from all notions of morality. This, more than anything, explains why society has, in effect, endowed the corporation with the moral personality that many theorists have long insisted it could not have.

A Gradual Evolution

This redefinition of the corporate personality has occurred slowly and largely unnoticed. In fact, few managers are even aware that this evolution has taken place. Rather than seeing changes in society's expectations for corporate behavior as part of a broad pattern, most have responded incrementally as if each new concern were a discrete issue. Thus, many companies have spawned a host of minibureaucracies, each focused on a specific topic such as quality, safety, the environment, discrimination, diversity, citizenship, bribery, legal compliance, ethics, values, culture, work and family, social responsibility, human rights, and so on. Similarly, advocacy groups for these different issues have seen themselves as distinct and often at odds with one another.

By taking a broader perspective, however, we can see that all of these differing "issues" are actually aspects of a single process by which a presumption of corporate moral agency has supplanted the doctrine of corporate amorality. Through this process, which we might term the "moralization" of the corporation, companies have come to be regarded, at least implicitly, as moral actors in their own right. As such, they are presumed to have not only technical functions, such as producing goods or generating profits, but also moral attributes, such as responsibilities, aims, values, and commitments. Seen in this light, a company's stance on quality, safety, the environment, and so on are but differing facets of its moral personality.

The process of moralizing the corporation has been a gradual one, whose origins can be traced to the nineteenth and early twentieth centuries. At least one "natural entity" theorist broached this idea in his writing at the turn of the last century.[72] And there were always exceptions to the "official" doctrine of corporate amorality, even in its heyday. In the 1860s, for instance, the U.S. company now called Armstrong World Industries took as its motto "Let the buyer have faith," apparently seeking to distance itself from the then-prevailing doctrine of *caveat emptor* ("Let the buyer beware").[73] Corporate philanthropy also began its emergence in the nineteenth century in such activities as the railroad companies' collaboration with the YMCA to provide community services in areas served by the railroads.[74] Like Levi Strauss, mentioned in Chapter 3, many companies can point to long traditions of philanthropy and civic contribution.

Early tendencies in this direction can also be seen in efforts to develop business codes of ethics in the 1920s and 1930s. One commentator writing in 1932 praised these codes as "the first attempts of a great and powerful social group to gain its own self-respect and the respect of other members of society."[75] Noting that business was "born in the ethical slums of lowly parents," he saw these codes as historically quite significant.[76] Although the majority of codes seem to have been industry rather than company efforts, they nonetheless bespoke a felt need to bring some sort of moral order into business affairs.[77]

Regardless of its standing in legal and economic theory, moreover, "the soulless company" never held much promise as a marketing theme. With the emergence of large-scale enterprise in the late nineteenth century came systematic company efforts to project an image of corporate humanity.[78] It was the mission of the early public relations function to combat the public's suspicions and distrust of companies whose size and scale had never before been seen. Numerous early corporations sought moral legitimacy and a place among society's recognized institutions through employee welfare programs, civic contributions, and image-building campaigns. Among the most celebrated was AT&T's campaign beginning in 1908 to humanize its public image and shed its reputation as a feared and hated monopoly.[79] An AT&T executive speaking in the 1930s characterized the campaign as an effort to transform the public image of a "soulless . . . corporation . . . of the trust-busting era" by clothing it in "the radiant raiment of . . . a service ideology."[80]

Such early steps in the direction of corporate morality had a distinctively unilateral quality. Companies that needed the favor of consumers and the general public strove to present themselves as humane and attentive to the public welfare. But such presentations would eventually give rise to expectations of corporate responsibility going well beyond companies' own chosen projects and public relations campaigns. Leanings in this direction were evident in the 1930s, for example, in the speculation of the legal theorist quoted earlier who anticipated a day when social responsibility would be the prevailing ethic in companies.

By the 1950s and 1960s, corporations were well established in the firmament of western societies' institutions. In a well-known 1953 case, the New Jersey Supreme Court captured a growing sentiment by upholding the legitimacy of corporate charitable contributions against the charge that they exceeded the corporation's authority. In its opinion affirming the corporation's authority to make "reasonable" donations in support of the public welfare, the court noted the increasing wealth under corporate control and pointed to "modern conditions" as requiring "that corporations acknowledge and discharge social as well as private responsibilities as members of the communities within which they operate."[81]

Although talk of the corporate soul had faded, calls for corporate responsibility were beginning to take on a new urgency in the face of new societal challenges such as urban decay and increasing pressure for civil rights alongside the continuing growth and influence of corporations. Several influential books highlighted the growing power of corporations,[82] and writings on corporate social responsibility became more prevalent as academics, executives, and journalists took up the subject.[83]

As already noted, some criticized such calls as misdirected. However, others saw a looming crisis that could only be averted by a greater sense of corporate responsibility. "As things stand now," wrote a leading corporate scholar in 1964, "these instrumentalities of tremendous power have the slenderest claim of legitimacy."[84] Observing that legitimacy, responsibility, and accountability were essential to any enduring power system, he declared further that corporations would have to find "some claim of legitimacy, which also means finding a field of responsibility and a field of accountability" to the broader society. Thirty years earlier, this same scholar had challenged the idea of corporate responsibilities to the public or to any constituency other than shareholders. But times had changed.[85]

Indeed, by the late 1960s and early 1970s, the view that corporations were moral actors with choices to make about a range of social concerns was much in evidence. Issues of corporate responsibility moved into the public sphere and many U.S. and multinational companies were taken to task for a host of alleged moral failings including neglecting consumer safety, ignoring civil rights, polluting the environment, bribing government officials, violating election laws, misleading investors, and even toppling governments in developing countries.[86]

Although a few academics in the then-nascent field of business ethics took up debate on the legitimacy of the moral-actor premise, their discussion was overtaken by events.[87] The Vietnam War, the oil crisis, inflation, racial tensions, emerging environmental concerns, and urban unrest resulted in a sharp decline in confidence in American institutions generally.[88] Corporations came under attack from a generation with new expectations, particularly in the wake of the overseas payments scandal in which more than 400 companies admitted to making illegal campaign contributions and bribing foreign government officials to win business overseas.

The shortcomings of adherence to a creed of amorality, and its potentially self-defeating consequences, became widely apparent. According to some estimates, U.S. business lost roughly 80 percent of its public goodwill during the period.[89] In 1977, only 15 percent of the public thought that business tried to strike a fair balance between profits and the public interest, compared with 70 percent in 1968.[90]

The payments scandal, beside giving rise to new legislation against such conduct, sparked a new level of concern about corporate responsibility.[91] During the 1970s, a few large companies took the innovative step of establishing board-level committees to address ethics, public issues, and social responsibility.[92]

The 1970s also saw the emergence of socially active shareholders, aided by a 1970 federal court ruling that cleared the way for shareholders to use the proxy process to raise issues of social concern.[93] Encouraged by the example of investors who had used the proxy process to bring social issues before the board at General Motors, other socially concerned shareholders followed suit at other companies. "Socially responsible" mutual funds also appeared on the scene in this decade.[94] Through these channels, shareholders began to express their views on a range of corporate issues from employment policy and product safety to investment overseas, particularly in South Africa, where apartheid was then still entrenched by force of law.[95]

By the late 1970s, many U.S. and multinational companies had begun to adopt at least the trappings of ethical self-discipline by drafting corporate codes of conduct. Codes, as noted earlier, were not entirely new, but they became more prevalent during this period. This trend continued and spread in the 1980s and 1990s.[96] In 1986, a group of 18 leading U.S. defense contractors went beyond the idea of a code and developed an "ethics program." The signatories to the Defense Industry Initiative on Business Ethics and Conduct agreed not only to develop a written code but also to train their employees in its requirements, to encourage the reporting of violations, and to provide for public accountability. Moreover, each signatory agreed to outside review of its adherence to the terms of the initiative. Under the rubric that "ethics programs are here to stay," the group also set in motion an annual industrywide best-practices forum.[97]

During roughly the same period, leaders of the U.S. and Canadian chemical industries launched efforts to improve chemical makers' health, safety, and environmental performance. The industry, already under attack for its seeming indifference to health and environmental concerns, "found itself awash in a sea of mistrust and misunderstanding" after 3000 local residents (but no employees) died of toxic leaks from Union Carbide's plant in Bhopal, India, in 1984. The eventual result was Responsible Care, a program that required industry association members to adhere to a set of agreed-on principles and to implement new codes of practice in areas such as emissions reduction, waste management, community responsiveness, and employee health and safety. Member companies were obligated to show progress toward satisfying legal requirements in these areas while also adopting state-of-the-art practices and addressing public concerns identified through industry association research.[98]

The 1970s marked a watershed in the evolution of the corporation's personality. In the three decades since, it has become common to speak of companies as having values, commitments, and responsibilities—attributes that can be ascribed only to moral actors. Terms like "corporate character" and "corporate culture," which before the 1970s could hardly be found in the literature, are now part of the business vernacular.[99] The articulation of a corporate purpose beyond the making of money has become an important management function.[100] Stakeholder theory, which focuses on companies' relations with their various constituencies, has gained a wide following.[101] Talk of the corporate "soul" has re-emerged, with at least a dozen recent book titles making reference to the phrase.[102] Trust, reputation, loyalty, and other such moral and quasi-moral topics have become subjects of business writing and research.[103]

Because these topics tend to be pursued in isolation from one another by specialists in different subfields of business study, the connections among them have rarely been noticed. However, they share a common but unarticulated premise insofar as they tacitly assume that companies may be viewed as moral actors with moral personalities that can and should be managed.

The assumption of moral personality has even begun to seep into the law. Consider these developments in the United States and the United Kingdom:

- The concept of "organizational culpability" appeared for the first time in new laws introduced in the United States in 1991. Under these laws, which provide courts with guidelines for sentencing organizations convicted of criminal wrongdoing, judges are instructed to consider a company's culpability when deciding on an appropriate sentence. Companies with programs to prevent and detect misconduct are entitled to a lesser finding of culpability—and to a lesser fine. Similarly, "moral credit," in the form of reduced fines, can be awarded to companies that voluntarily take responsibility for their misdeeds.[104]

- In 1994, after more than 14 years of discussion by leading U.S. scholars, lawyers, and judges, the American Law Institute published its principles of corporate governance, which stated that corporations were permitted to take ethical considerations into account in their decisions and to devote resources in reasonable amounts to public and humanitarian purposes.[105]

- In the 1990s, corporate ethics specialists began to appear on lists of expert witnesses to be called in litigation involving allegations of corporate misconduct.

- In 1989, a leading U.S. court held that preserving a "palpable, distinctive, and advantageous" corporate culture was a legitimate factor in corporate decision making.[106] The Delaware Court of Chancery, known for its expertise in corporate law, upheld a board

of directors' authority to rebuff a hostile takeover bid that was
favored by the majority of its shareholders. The board argued that
a previously arranged alliance would better maintain the company's
culture and ability to serve the public. While acknowledging that
the law would not always recognize an interest in preserving corporate culture, the court concluded that it was a legitimate concern
in the case at hand. In some cases, noted the court's opinion, "[t]he
mission of the firm is not seen by those involved with it as wholly
economic, nor the continued existence of its distinctive identity as
a matter of indifference."[107]

- By the late 1990s, some 31 U.S. states had enacted statutes allowing, and in one case requiring, corporate directors to take into
account the interests of constituencies other than shareholders in
making decisions on behalf of the corporation, particularly in takeover situations.[108]

- In the mid-1990s, the SEC backed away from efforts to narrow the
ability of shareholders to raise social concerns through the proxy
process. Faced in the early 1990s with many such proposals and
finding it difficult to make valid distinctions among those that corporations were required to include and those that could be excluded
as inappropriate, the SEC initially ruled the whole area of employee
relations off limits.[109] Setting aside its previous position requiring
the inclusion of proposals that raised important social issues, the
SEC reasoned that all proposals concerning employee relations per-
tained to "ordinary business operations," a recognized category of
permissible exclusions, and could therefore be omitted from a company's proxy materials regardless of their social importance. Although the SEC's position was upheld on appeal, pressure from
shareholders eventually led the agency to reverse its stance.[110] In
announcing its reversal, the SEC noted, "[W]e have gained a better
understanding of the depth of interest among shareholders in having an opportunity to express their views to company management
on employment-related proposals that raise sufficiently significant
social policy issues."[111]

- In 1998, the U.S. Labor Department issued an advisory opinion stating that pension-fund fiduciaries were permitted to use social criteria in selecting investment vehicles so long as financial returns were
comparable to other investments of similar risk.[112] Prior to the
announcement, many had argued that social investing was by defi-

nition a breach of pension managers' fiduciary obligation and therefore not permissible.

- Throughout the 1990s, various U.S. government agencies adopted
  and refined the organizational culpability concepts introduced by
  the organizational sentencing guidelines of 1991 referred to earlier
  in this section. For example, the Environmental Protection Agency's
  "Incentives for Self Policing," first announced in 1995, provided for
  reduced civil penalties and wiped out criminal sanctions altogether
  in certain cases involving companies with effective compliance and
  self-policing programs.[113] In 2001, the SEC said it would consider
  the effectiveness of a company's compliance program in deciding
  whether to bring charges of violating federal securities laws.[114]
- Under new U.K. pension laws that went into effect in 2000, trustees
  of all private-sector pension funds must disclose whether their
  investment strategies take environmental, social, and ethical considerations into account.[115] The change, according to a government
  official, reflected the government's desire "to encourage trustees to
  be fully aware of the entire range of factors which might affect the
  value of the investment."[116]
- New listing requirements for the London Stock Exchange that
  took effect in 2000 require listed companies to disclose their policies for managing significant risks, including not only financial and
  technological risks but also risks related to legal, health, safety, environmental, reputation, and "business probity" issues.[117]

In these developments, we see the corporation increasingly depicted as
a moral actor—as an agent having a distinctive identity, capable of considering others' interests, deserving of praise and blame, and capable of self-
evaluation, self-discipline, and self-correction. In other words, even the law,
which is usually a lagging social indicator, is beginning to incorporate a mor-
alized view of the corporation.

Of course, the traditional view of the corporation is still very much
alive. Even as the moral-actor premise has become more widely accepted,
some have continued to affirm the old orthodoxies. In March 2001, for
instance, a book reviewer writing in the *Wall Street Journal* took an author
to task for criticizing corporate involvement in the Holocaust on the
grounds that he had mistakenly applied moral judgment to a realm that is
inherently amoral.[118] Similarly, many business academics continue to rely
exclusively on models that assume moral indifference. The assumption of

amorality is still deeply embedded in most orthodox management theory as well as many organizations—a point we will come to later.

However, the inadequacy of management concepts based purely on amoral models of the corporation is becoming increasingly apparent. Take the concept of corporate "re-engineering," which was widely implemented in the 1990s. One leading proponent, commenting on the unanticipated negative impacts of some re-engineering initiatives, acknowledged in 1996, "I was reflecting my engineering background and was insufficiently appreciative of the human dimension. I've learned that's critical."[119]

This is not to say that an amoral view is never valid. The detached technical perspective we associate with the amoral view is often essential. Reasonable strategies, workable structures, efficient processes for transforming inputs into outputs—all of these depend on detailed technical understanding. In fact, managers who lack a firm grasp of their company's technical and financial functioning would scarcely be competent to guide its moral functioning, for it would be foolhardy to espouse a moral stance that an organization was technically or financially incapable of achieving. Clearly, a company cannot fulfill any responsibilities, to investors or any other group, unless it exists. And a company cannot exist for long—at least in a market economy—without high levels of technical competence and strong, sustained profitability. Thus, competence in traditional amoral modes of analysis is essential. However, these cannot substitute for an understanding of the corporation as a moral actor.

It is when amoral models are taken as complete and self-sufficient that problems arise. While people today expect companies to demonstrate technical excellence, to be efficient, and to create wealth, they also expect them to behave as moral actors exhibiting the range of competencies required of other moral actors. Among these are the ability to frame their own purposes, to conform their activities to basic ethical standards, to show consideration for others, to exercise moral judgment in conducting their affairs, to accept responsibility for their errors and misdeeds, and to contribute to the larger community to which they belong.

The moralization of the corporation provides the key to understanding the recent turn to values. The growing acceptance of the moral actor premise, implicit in the developments reviewed here, has affected how companies are expected to behave and has raised the bar for their performance. In the next chapter, we will look more closely at the evidence for these claims.

5

A Higher Standard

The corporate turn to values reflects the evolutionary process described in the previous chapter. As companies have become pervasive and powerful actors in the world, society has endowed them with a new kind of character. More and more, they are being evaluated as if they were responsible human beings whose functional tasks must be carried out within a moral framework. Accompanying this transformation has been the emergence of a new yardstick for assessing corporate performance. Instead of being measured only in financial terms, companies today are increasingly being held to a standard that has both moral and financial dimensions. The most outstanding performers are those that excel along both.

Evidence of this "ethico-nomic" standard is abundant. Corporate reputation studies, best-company rankings, employee commitment surveys, public opinion polls, stock price movements—these are a few of the more telling indicators. Like the survey respondents mentioned earlier, those who say that companies should set a higher ethical standard and contribute to broader societal goals in addition to performing their traditional functions, other constituencies are injecting moral criteria into their evaluations of corporations. We can see this in the expectations and concerns different groups bring to their dealings with companies. Whether they are deciding where to work, where to buy, where to invest, or what companies they want in their communities, significant numbers of people are including moral considerations with financial ones in their deliberations.

Constituency Expectations

A tour of the corporation from the vantage point of various constituency groups illustrates some ways in which both types of considerations come together to shape attitudes and judgments.

Employee Perspectives

Consider employees. Of course, employees want to be well paid. They expect compensation that is at least competitive, if not better than, market rates in terms of wage and salary levels, benefits, bonuses, and increasingly, stock. They also want the resources they need to do their jobs and do them well. And of course they will be concerned about their employer's long-term financial prospects, especially if they are asked to develop firm-specific skills that are not readily transferable to other work environments.

At the same time, though, they want to be respected, treated fairly, and recognized for their contributions. They prefer colleagues who are trustworthy and who can be counted on to keep their promises. Increasingly, employees expect to be informed about on-the-job hazards, and they appreciate consideration shown for their health, safety, and general well-being. Most value opportunities for learning, advancement, and personal growth. Many also want to use their talents to make a positive difference in the world and to be part of a company they can feel proud of. And most want time for their families and a life outside of work.

The importance of both financial and moral considerations as part of an employer's appeal is borne out in various surveys and studies. Consider *Fortune* magazine's annual review of the best companies to work for in the United States. Although the companies listed in the top 100 have varied from year to year since the review was launched in 1998, their defining attributes have changed little. The best workplaces have consistently been those that pay well, invest in their people, and treat employees with dignity and respect. At the favored companies, managers are seen as trustworthy, and employees have a high level of trust in one another. Employees are proud to work at these companies and proud to be associated with their products and services. These companies also foster a sense of camaraderie, and employees enjoy their time at work. The edge, *Fortune* concluded in its 2001 review, comes from having a culture where people are respected, treated as adults, and made to feel the company cares about them.[1]

A similar profile emerges from the 32-country study of employee commitment referred to in Chapter 2. According to this study, employee commitment is driven by six factors: fairness, including fair pay, fair policies, and fair practices; care and concern for employees; trust in employees; company reputation; work and job resources; and satisfaction with day-to-day activities. Around the world, employees who rated their companies highly on these factors were more inclined to stay with their organization, to recommend it to others, and to go the extra mile in doing their jobs.[2]

Other researchers have found that students gauge a prospective employer's attractiveness by its community relations, employee relations, and product quality.[3] Still others have found that corporate community involvement has a positive effect on many employees' sense of pride, loyalty, and commitment to their companies.[4]

Taken together, such studies bear out what the moral-actor premise would predict. As employees, many people make moral judgments about their corporate employer's activities, and many prefer to be associated with companies they judge to be morally as well as financially sound.

Customer Perspectives

Customers, too, bring both ethical and economic concerns to their dealings with companies. Of course, they want low prices and fair value for money. And, like employees, if they are contemplating a long-term relationship or will face high switching costs, they want assurances about the company's future as a going concern. At the same time, they want to deal with companies that are reliable, treat them fairly, and respect the confidentiality of personal and business information. They look for suppliers whose products and services meet their needs for quality and performance. Most customers want to know about health, safety, and environmental risks associated with what they buy. In some parts of the world, particularly more developed countries, consumers are paying more attention to the conditions under which a company's goods and services have been produced and preferring those made in accordance with certain social and environmental standards.

Again, several studies and surveys bear out these general observations. As we have already seen, customer loyalty depends as much on how customers are treated and the quality of what they buy as on the price they pay for goods and services.[5] Reputation experts have found that the companies held in highest repute by consumers are those that display excellence across a variety of dimensions—financial performance, workplace environment, products and services, vision and leadership, social responsibility, and general appeal.[6] Unsurprisingly, consumers base their judgments about these matters on their own personal experiences and those of their close acquaintances, although media coverage also plays a role.[7] And, as previously noted in Chapter 2, companies that do best in reputation studies are generally, according to a *Fortune* report on America's most-admired corporations, "good guys" in addition to being financial standouts.[8]

Other studies have found that consumers have more favorable impressions of companies that support causes they themselves are concerned about.[9] Consumers are also more disposed to buy from companies they perceive as ethical and socially responsible.[10] Marketing studies have found that consumers rank honesty, fairness, and trustworthiness as the principal attributes of the ideal company.[11]

Like employees, consumers appear to have two areas of ethical concern. One has to do with how their own immediate interests may be affected by a company's ethics. Will the company stand by its products, deal fairly, and so on? The second involves a company's stance toward third parties and the broader community. Is the company a good citizen, environmentally responsible, fair in dealings with its suppliers, and the like?

No study has compared consumers' sensitivity to these two areas, but both appear to play a role in decision making. Common sense would suggest that consumers might think more about the first area than the second and that concerns about the second area might vary from country to country. Indeed, one study found that French and German consumers were somewhat more inclined than Americans to take a company's stance toward the community into account in their shopping decisions.[12] Still, a recent survey of some 2500 Americans found that 36 percent claimed they seriously considered a company's corporate citizenship when deciding whether to buy its products.[13]

Although consumer concerns vary somewhat by locale, surveys indicate that consumers worldwide define "corporate ethics" and "corporate social responsibility" as encompassing a wide range of issues. In fact, consumers are apt to interpret these concepts rather more broadly than executives do, and to see ethical issues where executives see only technical ones.[14] Among the issues found in different surveys to be salient to consumers are truth in advertising, product safety, and environmental protection in the United States[15]; employment security in France and Germany[16]; and bribery, tax evasion, and counterfeiting in Hong Kong.[17]

Consumers are also willing to shun companies they disapprove of. A 1999 study of U.S. consumers found that nearly a quarter of those surveyed said they had boycotted a company's products or urged others to do so during the previous year because they disapproved of the company's policies or actions.[18] A 1998 study of British consumers revealed similar tendencies, with 28 percent saying they had boycotted a company's products on ethical grounds during the previous 12 months.[19] About the same proportion said they had chosen a product or service because of a company's ethical reputation. The Millennium Poll, the 23-country survey referred to in Chapter 4, found that about 23 percent of respondents said they had either rewarded or punished a company in the previous year based on their perceptions of its social performance. Consumers were more active in North America (51 percent) and Northern Europe (39 percent) than in Eastern Europe (15 percent) and Asia (14 percent).[20]

Community Perspectives

A similar picture emerges when we move to the community perspective. Communities, too, want companies to provide jobs and tax revenues, and they are often willing to offer up generous incentives to induce companies to bring these benefits to their locales. However, as we have seen, many expect companies to do more than just supply these basic economic goods. They also want enterprises to clean up their messes—and sometimes those of their predecessors—and to reduce or eliminate other negative impacts of their activities. In addition, they expect companies to obey local laws, protect the natural environment, and help solve community problems. Although the specific needs of communities vary widely around the world, public officials and civic leaders everywhere are looking to business to take up the slack left by a shrinking government sector.[21] At the same time, officials and civic leaders expect to be informed of company actions and even to be involved in making decisions that have a significant impact on the community.

The Millennium Poll found that respondents worldwide judged companies by a mix of financial and social factors. Asked to describe how they formed impressions of individual companies, half mentioned issues such as labor practices, business ethics, social responsibility, and environmental impacts. In 20 of the 23 countries surveyed, as noted earlier in Chapter 4, a majority said that companies should go beyond their historic role of making a profit, paying taxes, creating jobs, and obeying the laws. Among the issues of global concern were employee health and safety, fair treatment of employees, ending bribery and other forms of corruption, protecting the environment, and eliminating child labor. These findings are consistent with other public opinion polls indicating that people today expect companies to conduct themselves as citizens—moral actors with civic responsibilities—in all their countries of operation.[22] Besides paying taxes and obeying the law, this often means companies are now expected to take an active role in helping to address broader societal problems.

Further evidence regarding the public's expectations comes from a recent study of U.S. juries charged with deciding questions of corporate liability.[23] About half the jurors surveyed said that corporations should be held to exactly the *same* moral standard as individuals. A typical comment: "I feel that corporations have the same ethical, moral responsibilities that we individuals do, and I think they should be held to those standards."[24] Although this group felt it would be unfair to expect more of companies than of individuals, about 40 percent of the jurors said that corporations should be held to a *higher* moral standard than individuals. These more demanding jurors pointed to such considerations as corporations' greater resources, greater knowledge, greater size, greater impact, and special role in society.

Public opinion surveys and at least one mock jury study found even larger percentages favoring higher standards for corporations.[25] A 1996 study carried out in Washington, D.C., Tokyo, and Moscow, for example, found that majorities in all three cities agreed that corporations had a greater obligation than did individuals to avoid accidents. Majorities in all three also said they expected corporations to be more careful than individuals when making decisions.[26]

Investor Perspectives

And what about investors? Without question, shareholders are looking for competitive returns, if not something even better. But most also expect other things—transparency, timely information, reliable forecasting, fair treatment, opportunities to be heard. Also, whether large or small, investors generally expect to be treated with respect and their interests, financial and otherwise, to be taken seriously by knowledgeable and dedicated management teams whose loyalties are not compromised by conflicts of interest. Some shareholders are even beginning to pay attention to how the companies they invest in treat other parties.

The past several decades have seen growing investor interest in an everwidening set of corporate issues. As shareholders have become more numerous and more organized, they have also become more actively interested in the management of the companies in which they invest. Many investors today want information not just about traditional accounting and financial data but also about governance mechanisms, antitakeover measures, executive compensation, employment practices, and corporate policies on the environment, social responsibility, and human rights.[27]

As noted earlier, one vehicle for expressing investor concerns has been the shareholder proxy process enacted into U.S. law in 1942.[28] According to the Investor Responsibility Research Center, investors submitted some 820 proposals through the proxy process in 2000, including 242 proposals on social issues in more than 180 major U.S. companies.[29] As reflected in these proposals, investors' leading social concerns in 2000 were the environment, equal employment, and international labor and human rights issues, though a number of other issues were also raised. Investors in other nations have only recently begun to submit such proposals, and the rules for doing so vary enormously from country to country. However, one study of investor activity in non–U.S. companies counted 141 shareholder proposals in 2001, of which 49 dealt with social issues.[30] Of the 49, 42 targeted 8 Japanese companies, mostly in the power industry.

Investors are increasingly willing to voice social concerns informally as well. A study of U.K. occupational and local-authority pension funds conducted in 2000 found that 39 percent of the funds espoused a policy of engaging with management on social issues.[31] In 1999, U.S. institutions and funds claiming to be actively involved in social advocacy controlled some $922 billion in assets.[32] Many more large institutional investors, while not calling themselves social advocates, in fact engage with management on a range of issues.

The growth of social investing over the past three decades is another indicator of investors' broadening concerns. Although the use of moral as well as financial criteria in making investment decisions is not wholly new, it emerged, as noted in Chapter 4, as a defined investment strategy within the mutual fund industry only in the early 1970s.[33] Then viewed as a far-fetched idea doomed to financial failure, the social fund sector in 1999 claimed some 175 funds with total assets of $154 billion in the United States, up from $12 billion since 1995.[34] The United States has the largest number of such funds, variously called "social awareness funds," "principled investment funds," "ethical investment funds," and the like. However, they have also emerged in Canada, Europe, Australia, South Africa, and recently in Japan.[35] As of mid-2001, Europe was estimated to have some 250 such funds available to the public, representing about $12.8 billion in assets.[36]

If we consider not just mutual funds, but assets in all socially screened portfolios, the U.S. total was estimated at nearly $1.5 trillion at the end of 1999. While still only a small portion of the $16.3 trillion then under professional management, the sector grew at a compound annualized rate of 74 percent between 1995 and 1999, compared to a rate of 25 percent for all mutual fund assets during this period.[37] Many of the socially screened portfolios were heavily invested in technology stocks, and it is unclear how much of their growth should be attributed to this factor and how much to a widening investor base.

Perhaps more significant for most companies is evidence that some in the traditional financial community are also taking a broader view. New share indexes are one example. In 1999, Dow Jones joined forces with the SAM Sustainability Group to launch the Dow Jones Sustainability Group Indexes (DJSGI), a new set of share indexes that track companies whose strategies integrate environmental and social considerations with economic ones. Companies selected for this family of global and regional indexes must demonstrate commitment to their different stakeholders, including the communities in which they operate, while also showing sound financial returns and long-term economic growth. Based on the premise that more investors today are attracted to companies that create long-term shareholder value through attention to economic, environmental, and social developments, the indexes target companies that are setting best-practice standards while also maintaining superior financial performance.[38]

In 2001, the *Financial Times* and the London Stock Exchange launched a similar set of indexes. For inclusion in this set of "ethical share" indexes, called the FTSE4Good family, companies must satisfy criteria related to the environment, human rights, and social issues, including stakeholder relations.[39]

Throughout the 1990s, a number of mainstream brokerage firms launched funds and other products to appeal to this segment of the investing public. Among those starting their own social investment funds were major money management firms, including Merrill Lynch, Smith Barney, Vanguard, UBS, and Credit Suisse. A Europe-wide survey of 302 financial analysts and fund managers conducted in 2001 found that a third of the respondents offered products for the social investing market.[40] Observers have predicted continuing growth in this sector based, for example, on a recent U.K. survey of pension plan members, which found that almost two-thirds wanted their trustees to do social investing.[41]

Mainstream institutions have also launched new religion-based funds such as Islamic funds that invest only in companies whose practices are consistent with the ethical guidelines of Islam. A Merrill Lynch study has estimated the untapped worth of this market alone at $600 billion.[42]

Quite apart from such special funds, however, we have seen that investors frequently shy away from companies implicated in wrongdoing or injurious activities. The sell-offs after the Treasury auction crisis at Salomon, the tire controversy at Bridgestone/Firestone, and the revelations of financial misreporting and self-dealing at Enron are not unusual. As noted in the preceding chapters, some researchers have shown that misconduct, especially if high-level officials are implicated or the misbehavior is thought to be pervasive, can undermine investor confidence and lead to significant losses in market value.[43] Others have found that stock prices react favorably when companies win affirmative action awards and negatively when they settle employment-discrimination suits.[44] And many individual investors say they consider a company's ethics when deciding whether to invest in its stock. In one survey of U.S. investors, 72 percent claimed to do so.[45] In another, 26 percent said that a company's business practices and ethics were extremely important to their investment decisions.[46]

Such evidence suggests that, whether or not investors themselves are directly concerned about corporate conduct, they recognize that others' concerns can translate into financial consequences for the companies they invest in. Even if they have not yet come to fully appreciate the benefits of adhering to positive values, investors seem increasingly aware of the causal chains through which misconduct can lead to lost confidence, lost sales, hiring difficulties, legal problems, and credit downgrades that undermine a company's market value. Thus, as Shell and others have found, mainstream analysts are beginning to show interest in corporate policies on social, environmental, and other nonfinancial matters. And we find commentators in mainstream financial publications advising public and private fund managers to expand their risk assessment frameworks to include "national security, human rights and religious-freedom concerns."[47]

A New Performance Paradigm

As this survey of constituency expectations indicates, companies today must meet increasingly demanding specifications to be competitive in the markets for talent, customers, public support, and, increasingly, capital itself. Taken together, these specifications point to an emerging new standard of corporate performance that calls for excellence along both financial and moral dimensions. Often we think of a "performance paradigm" or "performance model" as having two elements that are roughly equivalent to the idea of ends and means. The "ends" element is a conception of the goals to be attained, while the "means" element is a theory of how best to attain them. As the moral-actor premise has taken hold, it has challenged both aspects of traditional performance models and invited us to rethink older conceptions of what corporate performance is as well as orthodoxies about how to achieve it.

Consistent with the traditional view of companies as amoral instruments of commerce, "corporate performance" has generally been thought of as synonymous with "financial results." Whether measured as profits, return on equity, return on average capital employed, economic value added, or any number of other financial metrics, the ultimate performance standard has been a purely financial one, at least in the capitalist world. In the communist world, the performance of enterprises has been measured differently, though no less instrumentally, in terms of production output. In either system, how the desired results are achieved has been treated principally as a technical issue and not as a matter of particular moral concern.

Within this frame of reference, everything else—people, communities, the natural environment—has mattered only as a means to this end. If the single-minded drive for financial results yielded benefits for consumers, employees, and other nonshareholders, so much the better. If not, damaging side effects were just that—damaging side effects. From the corporate perspective, any such effects were problems to be dealt with by other people such as governments, schools, families, churches, charities, or individuals. They were certainly not problems to be confused with issues of performance. Indeed, in almost 20 years as a business academic, I have rarely heard anyone question this conception of performance, so deeply is it embedded in conventional thinking.

Despite its pedigree, this view of corporate performance is increasingly out of step with practice. As moral judgment is being brought to bear on corporate activity, performance is no longer being equated solely with financial results, and heightened scrutiny is being given to the means used to achieve financial goals. In today's environment, a company that aspires to world-class status cannot simply dismiss damaging impacts on third parties as matters outside its jurisdiction. Nor can it wave away charges of infringing important values or destroying public goods merely by pointing to superior financial results. To put it differently, a high-performance company that competes unfairly, mistreats employees, or neglects its civic role is becoming a contradiction in terms.

This is not to suggest that financial results have become any less important. If anything, given the constituency expectations reviewed earlier, financial results are more important than ever. There is little evidence to support one author's recent declaration that shareholder value is nearing its end.[48] But no longer are companies judged by financial results alone. To be considered truly outstanding, companies today must do more than achieve superior financial results or meet impressive production targets. They must receive high marks not only from shareholders concerned with financial returns but also from other parties with whom they interact. And to do so, as we have seen, they must satisfy a mix of economic and ethical criteria.

Perhaps the clearest indication of this emerging new standard is seen in the "most admired" and "most respected" company surveys that have proliferated over the past decade. Sponsored by various business publications, these annual surveys provide a window on how executives, board members, and business experts define corporate excellence. They have been called a form of "peer review" for professional managers.

Even among this most business-oriented of audiences, the highest accolades go to companies that succeed in satisfying multiple constituencies. As shown in Figure 5-1, which summarizes the criteria used in some of the best-known surveys, corporate excellence is in every case a matter of doing several things well and, with only a few exceptions, addressing the concerns of employees, customers, and communities, as well as investors.

Although each survey has its own criteria, the differences among them are overshadowed by their similarities. The factors typically relied on in these surveys reveal the importance of both financial and nonfinancial criteria. Financial results are clearly a must, but alone are insufficient to earn top ratings from this demanding group of critics. Aspirants to the roster of "most admireds" must perform along several dimensions, as assessed by various criteria summarized here and detailed in Figure 5-1:

- **General functioning:** Criteria related to overall organizational effectiveness

- **Appeal to investors:** Criteria related to financial performance and potential

- **Appeal to employees:** Criteria related to attractiveness to employees

- **Appeal to customers:** Criteria related to customer concerns

- **Appeal to communities:** Criteria related to community concerns

In recent years, management experts, too, have begun promoting the measurement of nonfinancial performance. For some, the rationale for using a broader set of gauges is wholly financial. According to this school of thought, managers can produce more reliable financial results if they better

EXPLANATION OF RATINGS CRITERIA FROM FIGURE 5-1

1. *General Functioning*

   Assessed by criteria such as quality of management; innovativeness; strong, well-thought-out strategy; long-term orientation; ability to change; systemic approach; honest/ethical; organizational effectiveness; global.

2. *Appeal to Investors*

   Assessed by criteria such as financial health; profitability; investment potential; use of assets; growth potential.

3. *Appeal to Employees*

   Assessed by criteria such as ability to attract, develop, retain talent; work environment; encourages organizational and personal learning; good employer; robust and human corporate culture; employee well-being.

4. *Appeal to Customers*

   Assessed by criteria such as quality of customer service; quality of goods and services; customer loyalty; customer satisfaction; innovative in responding to customer needs; market development; customer focus.

5. *Appeal to Communities*

   Assessed by criteria such as good corporate citizen; community and environmental responsibility; environmental practices; contribution to society; contributes to local economy; regulatory/legal compliance.

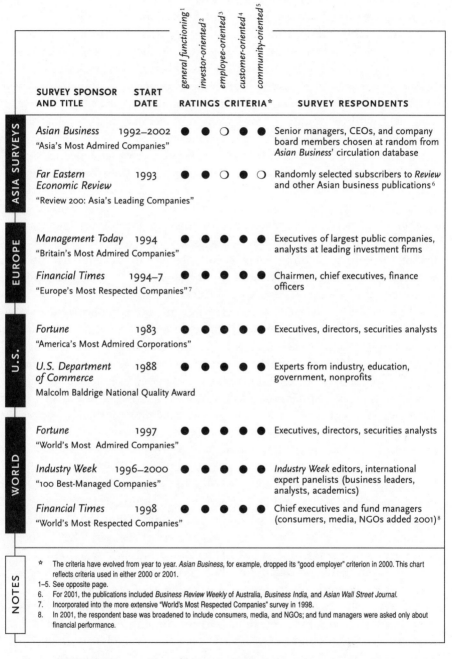

		general functioning[1]	investor-oriented[2]	employee-oriented[3]	customer-oriented[4]	community-oriented[5]	
SURVEY SPONSOR AND TITLE	**START DATE**			**RATINGS CRITERIA***			**SURVEY RESPONDENTS**
ASIA SURVEYS							
Asian Business "Asia's Most Admired Companies"	1992–2002	●	●	○	●	●	Senior managers, CEOs, and company board members chosen at random from *Asian Business*' circulation database
Far Eastern Economic Review "Review 200: Asia's Leading Companies"	1993	●	●	○	●	○	Randomly selected subscribers to *Review* and other Asian business publications[6]
EUROPE							
Management Today "Britain's Most Admired Companies"	1994	●	●	●	●	●	Executives of largest public companies, analysts at leading investment firms
Financial Times "Europe's Most Respected Companies"[7]	1994–7	●	●	●	●	●	Chairmen, chief executives, finance officers
U.S.							
Fortune "America's Most Admired Corporations"	1983	●	●	●	●	●	Executives, directors, securities analysts
U.S. Department of Commerce Malcolm Baldrige National Quality Award	1988	●	●	●	●	●	Experts from industry, education, government, nonprofits
WORLD							
Fortune "World's Most Admired Companies"	1997	●	●	●	●	●	Executives, directors, securities analysts
Industry Week "100 Best-Managed Companies"	1996–2000	●	●	●	●	●	*Industry Week* editors, international expert panelists (business leaders, analysts, academics)
Financial Times "World's Most Respected Companies"	1998	●	●	●	●	●	Chief executives and fund managers (consumers, media, NGOs added 2001)[8]

NOTES

* The criteria have evolved from year to year. *Asian Business*, for example, dropped its "good employer" criterion in 2000. This chart reflects criteria used in either 2000 or 2001.

1–5. See opposite page.

6. For 2001, the publications included *Business Review Weekly* of Australia, *Business India*, and *Asian Wall Street Journal*.

7. Incorporated into the more extensive "World's Most Respected Companies" survey in 1998.

8. In 2001, the respondent base was broadened to include consumers, media, and NGOs; and fund managers were asked only about financial performance.

FIGURE 5-1 EXECUTIVE PERSPECTIVES ON EXCELLENCE

understand and track the factors that drive it.[49] Many of these drivers, as we saw in Chapter 2, are nonfinancial. So, for example, in a business where customer loyalty is crucial for financial performance, managers would be advised to devise measures for assessing customer loyalty. Or in a business where employee turnover is costly, they would be urged to track employee satisfaction or even to go farther back in the causal chain to the motivators of employee satisfaction. This approach to nonfinancial variables is entirely congruent with the traditional performance model insofar as nonfinancial issues matter only as means to financial ends.

The evidence reviewed in this and the previous chapter, however, suggests that some nonfinancial variables are important on their own terms and may be critical success factors even if they are not causal drivers of financial results. Therefore, managers must care about them for the same reason they care about financial performance—because they are intrinsically important and part of what is expected of leading companies today. Matters such as honest accounting, treating employees with dignity, disclosing product risks, or being a good corporate citizen are not merely means to outstanding performance—they are increasingly part of its very definition.

This expanded conception of corporate performance is implicit in the calls for corporate accountability that have become commonplace in recent decades. As the moral-actor premise has taken hold, companies have been increasingly asked to answer not only for poor financial results but also for practices that offend or appear to offend against important human values. In some cases, they have even been asked to answer for the conduct of suppliers, distributors, or other business partners. These calls for accountability have taken various forms—media investigations, legal challenges, boycotts, and direct action by consumer, labor, civic, religious, and other nongovernmental organizations.

As we've seen, Shell was taken to task in the mid-1990s not only for its lackluster financial performance, but also for its environmental record, its stance on human rights, and its partnership with a brutal dictatorship in Nigeria. IKEA, Sweden's global home furnishings company, is another example. In 1994, IKEA's sourcing practices were challenged when a documentary—the one mentioned in Chapter 3—on child labor in the hand-woven carpet industry was aired on Swedish television. Named as a customer by a rug merchant depicted in the film, IKEA found itself a target of suspicion. True or not, the film gave the impression that the company was selling rugs made by child workers in South Asia. The children, some as young as six to eight years old, were shown hard at work and in some cases chained to their carpet looms by the factory owners who, following centuries-old practice, held the children in bondage as security for loans made to their families.[50]

Another well-known example is Nike, the U.S.-based footwear giant. Throughout much of the 1990s, Nike's sourcing practices were a subject of ongoing criticism and debate. Ignited mainly by labor groups, the campaign against Nike centered on the employment practices of its suppliers, all of whom were independent contractors operating in poorer countries of the world. The charges included inadequate pay, in some cases below the legal minimum; unsafe working conditions; abusive treatment by bosses, including physical abuse and sexual harassment; and hiring underage workers.

Note that many of the practices challenged in these cases are not new and, in fact, have been business as usual for many years. IKEA's sourcing practices were no different from so-called best practices in many other companies where cost, quality, and on-time delivery were the reigning criteria. In Nigeria, Shell was simply doing as it had always done, going back to the early 1970s, when the Nigerian government took a stake in what was then a two-way venture between Shell and British Petroleum (BP).

As for Nike, its practice of outsourcing athletic shoe production to low-cost factories overseas had earned the company kudos as a forerunner of the 1990s "virtual company." Far from being shameful or embarrassing, Nike's manufacturing strategy was for many years celebrated as a critical success factor in the company's rise to global prominence. This approach to manufacturing, which was highly innovative at the time of its adoption in the 1960s, was a cornerstone of founder Phil Knight's original concept for the company. It enabled Nike to drive its costs well below those of its competitors and to focus its attention on marketing—its other critical success factor. In the late 1980s, as Nike aggressively shifted production from country to country to take advantage of the cheapest producers, its earnings soared. The Nike swoosh became a symbol of success around the world. By the early 1990s, when the company's critics were beginning to gain visibility, the Nike brand was valued at some $3.5 billion and had risen 18 percent between 1992 and 1993 alone.[51]

Given this background, it is no wonder that companies targeted in such campaigns have often responded defensively or dismissed their critics as business illiterates. "It's not our responsibility" has been a common refrain, at least initially. (Not for IKEA, though, which responded to charges of benefiting from child labor by switching suppliers and initiating efforts to assist child workers.) When asked about labor conditions among suppliers in 1991, for example, a Nike manager responded, "It's not within our scope to investigate . . . I don't know that I need to know."[52]

These controversies crystallize the inevitable tensions between the old and the new. They show us the fault lines between the traditional view of the corporation as an amoral instrument of commerce and its more recent incarnation as a moral actor responsible for its actions and bound to respect the legitimate claims of others.

Proponents of the newer view have often been quite successful in mobilizing support for their concerns among the public, consumers, employees, and even some investors. Perhaps more telling than the sales losses and demonstrations following Shell's Brent Spar and Nigeria controversies were its own internal surveys, which found that many employees felt the company needed to take a clearer stand on human rights and the environment. Also, some Shell shareholders found the issues compelling enough to put forth a resolution asking management to implement and report on the company's environmental and corporate responsibility policies.[53] Although the resolution did not pass, it garnered 10.5 percent of the shares voted—enough that a *Times* (London) editorial called it "a huge blow to the company" and "a strong message to industry generally."[54] These events led Shell to begin including nonfinancial as well as financial information in its investor communications, in line with a perceived heightened interest among institutional investors in social responsibility.

As for Nike, by 1998 the company had shifted its position significantly. That year, its share of the U.S. footwear market dropped to 32.9 percent, compared to the previous year's 47 percent and following years of steady growth. Nike stock, which had generated enormous returns for shareholders over the previous five years, lost 20 percent of its value, bringing returns both below the S&P 500 and its industry competitors.[55] Even though analysts attributed these reversals to several factors, including product boredom, new competition, the Asian financial crisis, and to a lesser extent consumer backlash, Nike's stance on working conditions among its suppliers took a decidedly different turn that year.[56]

In what was widely regarded as an abrupt turnabout, Nike abandoned its earlier "not our responsibility" position and announced a six-point program aimed at improving its suppliers' working conditions, increasing support for its Asian microenterprise loan program, and improving university research on responsible business practices. The company shared its plans for a new environmental, health, and safety program that would give every Nike factory the tools and training needed to manage these issues. In announcing these initiatives, CEO Phil Knight talked about the company and its people as "passionate about sports" and "loving to compete," but also as "rooted in our responsibility to be good corporate citizens. . . . We are committed to improving working conditions for the 500,000 people who make our products."[57]

For managers used to thinking of corporate accountability exclusively in terms of accountability to shareholders for financial results, these developments may be difficult to accept. Besides meshing poorly with traditional frameworks, they also add significantly to the range of issues that demand managers' attention. The extent to which corporate accountability has expanded is depicted by the conceptual map shown in Figure 5-2.

As this figure shows, the moral-actor premise implies a domain of accountability that goes well beyond financial accountability to shareholders. The two axes, *accountability to whom* and *accountability for what*, mark out an area that is both more inclusive and more extensive than the traditional domain. That is, today's leading companies are expected to answer not only to shareholders, or even to core constituencies with whom they have a direct relationship. They're also expected to answer to third parties affected by their activities—or more precisely, to third parties injured by their activities (for so long as things are going well, questions of accountability tend to arise infrequently and mostly in the pleasant guise of who deserves praise for a job well done). Nor is it enough to satisfy these parties' legitimate financial claims. In addition, companies are expected to concern themselves with parties' legal rights as well as their extralegal claims based on such moral ideals as fairness, human rights, and civic responsibility.

The challenges are obvious. To stay abreast of each constituency's changing expectations, which, as a general rule, ratchet ever upward, com-

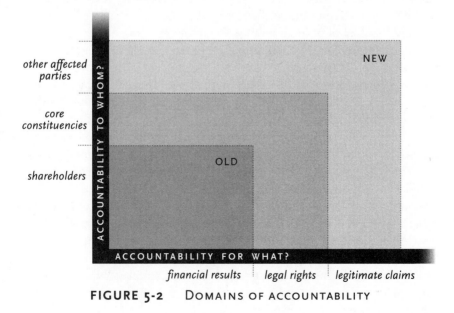

FIGURE 5-2   DOMAINS OF ACCOUNTABILITY

panies must monitor change on multiple fronts. In addition to changes in markets and technology, which have always been crucial, more attention must be paid to changes in society, politics, law, and culture. Managers must increasingly concern themselves not only with the financial implications of technological change but with the ethical and legal dimensions as well. This is especially true for those operating at the leading edge of technology, such as infotech or biotech. Few pioneering companies in these fields have escaped ethical or legal challenges. And it seems unlikely that sustainable business models will emerge unless these issues are incorporated into the model-building process—rather than being tacked on as an afterthought. As we will see in Chapter 8, for example, designing privacy controls into a new software product is far easier than retrofitting it after a public outcry.

Companies that operate in multiple businesses and varied social contexts face multiple challenges. The parties affected by their activities and even their core constituencies may vary from business to business or location to location— as may the parties' legitimate claims and concerns. In one business, customer safety may be a crucial issue, while in another, the dominant concern may be customer privacy. In some countries, employees expect their corporate employers to provide health insurance. In others, employees look to their government for this protection. In one region, environmental concerns may be paramount, while in another, citizens may be more concerned about education, unemployment, or fighting corruption. The framework sketched in Figure 5-2 implies that each business unit and location must carry out its own analysis.

The standard of accountability reflected in this framework may seem daunting. Note, however, that although the standard *is* more demanding in comparison to past practice, in another sense it is not particularly demanding at all. In essence, it simply asks companies to do what all moral actors are expected to do—namely, respect the legitimate claims of others as they go about their business.

What is "new" about the new standard is its application to companies and not just to individuals. Otherwise it is simply a restatement of a long-standing and widely endorsed principle of accountability whose proponents included Adam Smith, the eighteenth-century Scottish philosopher and forefather of modern economic thought. Although Smith is often credited with inventing the amoral view of the market, he also warned of the damaging effects of "malversation" or misconduct in corporate management.[58] And in *The Theory of Moral Sentiments*, his well-known book on moral philosophy, he argued that all violations of others' happiness, whether intentional or unintentional, required some form of atonement—a view quite compatible with the framework in Figure 5-2.[59]

Few companies, however, have been consciously designed to meet today's performance standard, and many lack the capabilities required to satisfy this more expansive definition of accountability. In later chapters, beginning with Chapter 7, we will consider what adjustments may be required and how managers can build the desired capabilities into their organizations.

Forces of Change

The emphasis on values seen in many companies today is both a reflection and a consequence of the emerging new performance standard described in this chapter. As the moral-actor conception of the corporation has gained acceptance, expectations for corporate performance have evolved accordingly. Companies, in turn, have responded to these new expectations with an array of initiatives and programs addressed to the various issues presented.

Thus, we see the many activities mentioned in Chapter 1: values initiatives, ethics programs, culture-building activities, stakeholder engagement efforts, citizenship initiatives, diversity initiatives, environmental programs, compliance programs, reputation management efforts, corporate identity efforts, business practices committees, supplier codes of conduct, and many others. Some companies, as noted earlier, have even begun to report publicly on their social and environmental performance. Also as noted earlier, whole new consulting niches, research institutes, and professional organizations have appeared to assist companies with these efforts.

The specifics of the new performance standard are still evolving, and numerous groups have come forth to offer ethical guidance for companies, often in the form of business principles, codes of conduct, and key performance indicators. By one count, the last decade saw almost 20 such initiatives by business groups, intergovernmental organizations, and nongovernmental organizations. And this does not include many less-publicized standard-setting efforts among industry associations, religious groups, and others.[60]

Some of these efforts have been linked with specific issues and concerns, such as corporate governance,[61] labor rights,[62] corrupt practices,[63] and the environment,[64] while others have offered comprehensive standards for corporate behavior. Among the best-known and more comprehensive statements to emerge in recent decades have been:

- **United Nations Global Compact:** Nine principles covering human rights, labor, and the environment announced in 1999[65]
- **Caux Round Table Principles for Business:** A comprehensive set of principles for world business developed by business leaders from Europe, Japan, and the United States and announced in 1994[66]

- **OECD Guidelines for Multinational Enterprises:** Guidelines for multinational corporations developed by the Organisation for Economic Co-operation and Development in 1976 and revised in 2000[67]
- **Global Reporting Initiative:** A comprehensive set of guidelines for reporting on environmental, social, and economic performance begun in 1997 by a coalition of environmental groups, companies, other NGOs, and academics[68]
- **World Business Council for Sustainable Development:** A general statement on the concept and implementation of corporate social responsibility begun in 1998 and issued in 2000[69]

In these documents and others currently being produced, such as the Asia Pacific Economic Cooperation forum code of conduct, we see an emerging set of "generally accepted ethical principles" for companies. Much as "generally accepted accounting principles" emerged earlier in the century as investors called for improved financial accountability, today's efforts to articulate ethical principles reflect the calls for new kinds of accountability. To be sure, differences and tensions exist among the various proposals, just as with financial accounting standards. The rights to free association and to collective bargaining, for example, are just one area. There are also glaring discrepancies between the espoused principles and actual practices. But the dominant impression is of an emerging consensus around certain core principles.

I have argued that the corporation's growing power and influence have played a major role in reshaping the standard used to assess its performance. However, that growth is itself the product of other forces that swept the globe during the twentieth century. In the absence of this particular confluence of forces, it is unlikely that society's expectations for corporate performance would have evolved as they did or that companies today would feel pressed to respond to the forces of change illustrated in Figure 5-3. After all, if corporations were all-powerful, they could ignore these pressures.

Although cause and effect are difficult to disentangle, the spread of democracy and the liberalization of societies around the world have been crucial to shaping the new standard of corporate performance. By liberalization, I mean the move toward privatization during the last two decades as well as the whole array of developments throughout the twentieth century that tended to strengthen the role of the individual in society. Among these are the decline of communism, freer markets, freer flows of information, and stronger property rights, as well as the extension of civil rights and economic opportunity to many members of previously excluded groups such as women and racial minorities.

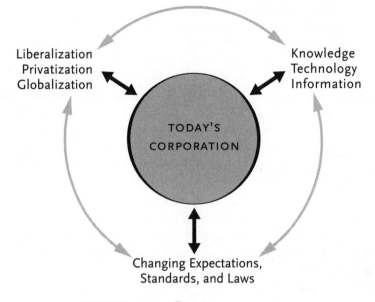

Liberalization
Privatization
Globalization

Knowledge
Technology
Information

TODAY'S
CORPORATION

Changing Expectations,
Standards, and Laws

FIGURE 5-3   FORCES OF CHANGE

Clearly, we still have a long way to go to achieve opportunity for all. Some regions have hardly been touched by these developments, and an estimated 1.2 billion people live on less than a dollar a day.[70] But opportunity is certainly more widely available at the start of the twenty-first century than it was 100 or even 50 years ago. Increasingly, men and women of all backgrounds aspire to economic self-sufficiency, either from necessity or personal choice. According to one estimate, in 2000 the world had 119 countries out of 192 that could be classified as democratic by the standard of universal suffrage and competitive multiparty elections, compared to only 22 in 1950 and none in 1900.[71] Another study put the number of "liberal democracies" at 61 in 1990, compared to 36 in 1960 and 13 in 1900.[72] Although the counts vary due to differences in the criteria used, the overall trend is unmistakable.

For managers, these changes have altered the landscape in various and sometimes contradictory ways. On the one hand, privatization has resulted in a massive transfer of power and authority from governments to the private commercial sector. Since the early 1980s, at least 100 national governments have engaged in some degree of privatization, including selling off government assets, issuing shares in state-owned enterprises, opening up competition in state-run sectors, or contracting out the provision of public services.[73] In this new environment, enterprise leaders have far more discretion to chart their own course and to succeed or fail by their own devices. Although every country is unique, managers in countries as diverse as Russia, Argentina, and Japan face similar challenges. Entrepreneurs can now be found all around the globe.

At the same time, as companies have become less answerable to government authorities, they have had to become more responsive to other parties, particularly the investors, customers, and employees on whom they now depend. Thus, while liberalization has reduced government's role in business, it has increased the role of competition in most sectors and given investors, customers, and employees a much greater say as arbiters of company success. In the marketplace and the civic arena alike, individuals today are more able to mobilize around their concerns and to make themselves heard. Companies that ignore these concerns do so at considerable risk. Even the global giants must take care lest more responsive competitors emerge or dissatisfied constituents withdraw their support or mobilize against them. After all, as we have seen, sustainable success requires a critical mass of willing investors, customers, and employees.

Renewed government intervention remains an ever-present possibility, for re-regulation or even nationalization could reemerge as solutions should companies be perceived as abusing their power or otherwise doing their jobs poorly. Although many would like to believe that liberalism has triumphed, it is really too early to tell. Free markets are no more "natural" than the tightly controlled and planned economies they replaced. Both depend on a government-supported framework and ultimately on the consent of the governed for their legitimacy. And neither can function effectively in the absence of a sound ethical framework. The future will depend on liberalism's ability to deliver on the promises made in its name.

Recent advances in information and communications technologies, too, have greatly affected the new expectations for corporate performance. These technologies have increased companies' efficiency and at the same time made them more transparent. Today, any interested party, whether inside or outside the company, anytime and anyplace, can get reams of information about a company's activities. Corporate critics, disappointed customers, and dissatisfied employees can readily broadcast their complaints to a worldwide audience as well. From time to time, I myself receive unsolicited E-mails from unhappy employees complaining about their companies' practices and policies. Recently, an Australian employee wrote about harassament and humiliation in her workplace. In another case, a frustrated agribusiness employee detailed his failed efforts to get his company to address serious health and safety issues in the plant where he worked.

Just as information technology supports the globalization of companies, it also supports the globalization of corporate constituencies and advocacy groups that monitor corporate behavior. Environmentalists, human rights advocates, consumer groups, labor organizations, class-action lawyers—all are using technology to inform and mobilize their forces worldwide. The traditional media—newspapers, television, and radio—stand ready to further disseminate reports of corporate misdeeds. For the first time ever, corporate constituencies and watchdogs around the world can readily engage in debate and discussion on issues of common concern.

As a result, many companies find themselves operating in a virtual fishbowl, with their every move on record and potentially subject to wider scrutiny. This transparency heightens competition and amplifies the potential benefits for companies with something positive to offer. It also increases the risk that controversial or questionable activities will be revealed and disclosed to a wider audience. The popular "newspaper test" advocated by many executives as a screen for unacceptable behavior—consider whether you would be embarrassed to read about your actions on the front page of your local newspaper—has become less an exercise in counterfactual "what if" thinking, and more a matter of realistically projecting the future. The safest assumption for any company today is that everything will eventually become known.

The growing importance of knowledge and ideas in virtually all sectors of the economy has also given added impetus to the new standard. In industries all across the spectrum from traditional manufacturing to high technology, the need for intelligence, creativity, and sheer brainpower has never been greater. To move up the knowledge ladder and bring higher levels of value to their customers, companies must seek out employees who can develop new ideas and apply them creatively to solve customers' problems.

But to attract and retain the talent they need, companies must build organizations that employees want to join and offer work environments that will nurture intelligence and creativity. As we saw earlier in this chapter, many employees today are looking to join companies they can be proud of, where they are respected, well-compensated, treated fairly, and encouraged to develop new skills and knowledge. We also saw in Chapter 2 that commitment, cooperation, and creativity are higher when companies adhere to basic human values.

Compared to a century ago, today's employees are far more highly educated and their jobs are more knowledge-intensive. In 1910, for instance, only 3 percent of the U.S. population 25 and older had graduated from college, compared to 24 percent in 1998.[74] During roughly the same period, the proportion of male workers employed in tertiary occupations such as professional, managerial, and service jobs tripled from 21 percent to 58 percent.[75] The very qualities that make these employees desirable—knowledge, intelligence, creativity—also tend to make them critical and demanding of their corporate employers. In fact, compared to their industrial-era counterparts, everyone today expects more from corporations. After all, to say that a society is knowledge-driven or information-rich is just another way of saying that more people are knowledgeable and informed. Consequently, they are apt to be more critical and more demanding.

The doctrine of corporate amorality was always a parasitic idea. It presupposed that society's moral order would be tended and maintained by families, schools, churches, governments, and other civic organizations. So long as the rest of society looked after that moral framework, corporations could be treated as an exception. But we are now seeing what happens when the balance shifts—when corporations are no longer the exception but the rule, and when their influence on society surpasses that of governments, schools, and civic organizations.

Just as liberalization has shifted the boundaries between business and government, it has broken down old distinctions between for-profit and not-for-profit organizations. In the United States, for example, health- and child-care services that were once the domain of charitable and noncorporate providers are becoming increasingly commercialized and corporatized. Between 1982 and 1997, the proportion of child-care dollars going to for-profit providers in the United States rose from 48 percent to 59 percent.[76] Between 1988 and 1994, memberships in for-profit health maintenance organizations grew by 92 percent while memberships in their nonprofit counterparts grew by only 25 percent.[77] As previously noted, by 2000 for-profit HMOs had garnered 63 percent of the enrollee base, whereas nonprofit HMOs had enrolled a majority (53 percent) 12 years earlier.[78] Though less pronounced, the trend to for-profit care can also be seen among community hospitals, where the percentage of for-profit beds rose to 13.5 percent in 1998, compared to 7.7 percent in 1975.[79]

Liberalization has also blurred familiar boundaries between home and work. The walls that separated the sphere of domesticity from the sphere of commerce have crumbled as women have entered the corporate world and men and women alike have sought to combine work and family. The proportion of married women in the U.S. workforce, for example, grew from 6 percent in 1900 to 61 percent in 1998.[80] A 1998 report on U.S. companies found that 9 percent of companies with 100 or more employees provided child care at or near work sites.[81] These and other trends such as the spread of telecommuting have undermined the clear differentiation between work and home necessary to sustain the corporate amorality doctrine.[82] Without this underpinning, the doctrine loses much of its intellectual coherence as well as its practical viability, for it becomes increasingly difficult to determine when moral judgment is appropriate and when it is not.

In the past, it might have been possible to think of business as a separate realm exempt from the ethics of hearth, home, and community. As late as 1968, a consultant writing in the *Harvard Business Review* defended business practices that were of "questionable morality" if judged by "ordinary standards" on the grounds that business had its own "rules of the game." He advised executives, moreover, that failure to draw a sharp distinction between the ethical systems of the home and those of the office could be deleterious to their health.[83]

Today, such an argument cannot stand. So intertwined is business with every aspect of life that it has become impossible to distinguish, let alone disentangle, these different threads. Corporations are routinely judged by ordinary standards of morality. No one expects saintliness, but the use of potentially harmful ingredients in a company's products—one of the practices defended by the author cited above—would be roundly condemned if it came to the public's attention today.

In view of these forces—the rise of the corporation, liberalization around the globe, advances in knowledge and technology—the emergence of a new and more demanding standard of corporate performance was perhaps inevitable. That, however, does not mean that companies have fully grasped the new standard or that meeting it is easy. As one journalist observed in an article on sweatshops and global retailers, "Consumers want clothes made in decent factories offering decent pay, but they also want cheap goods. It's hard to give them both."[84] For many, the very idea will require a radical shift in mindset—not to mention fundamental changes in management practice. Before turning to the practical implications of the new standard, though, let's tie up a few loose ends and consider some of the likely objections to what has been said so far.

6

The New Value Proposition

A couple of years ago my assistant came to me with an "urgent" message. A representative from a company that was about to go to press with its new code of conduct had called to ask if I'd be willing to supply a blurb for the document—just a sentence or two to reinforce the message that ethics pays. For reasons that may now be clear, I was unable to oblige. In today's environment, companies that aspire to excellence will want to take a more affirmative stance on values—one that regards them as an integral part of superior performance and not just a means to it. Those who see values as only a financial strategy are misreading the new value proposition, but this is not the only reason to be careful with "ethics pays."

As we have already discussed, this appealing slogan is an overgeneralization. Einstein once warned that "things should be made as simple as possible—but not simpler." Unfortunately, "ethics pays" asserts rather more than the facts can bear. To be sure, the facts can bear quite a lot. As we saw in Chapter 2, the links between ethics and economic advantage are stronger and more extensive than has often been thought. In many ways and in many contexts, values *do* enhance financial performance. And the economic benefits have only increased with the spread of liberalization and democratic institutions. Still, ethics and economic advantage coincide only partially and somewhat imperfectly. Sometimes they can diverge quite sharply. By suggesting an invariant link between what's right and what's profitable, "ethics pays" claims too much. Anyone tempted to say it's "close enough" might reflect on what happens when a navigator's compass or surveyor's transit is off by just a few minutes.

What's more, in portraying the link as automatic or naturally occurring, it ignores the importance of effort in forging the connection. To the extent that "ethics pays" accurately describes reality, it is largely because effort has been devoted to creating the conditions that make it true. Building a shared ethical framework, an open society, an educated populace, a free market, and an effective legal system do not happen automatically. But, as we saw in Chapter 3, they are necessary to effect the close convergence between values and financial success implied by "ethics pays."

When these conditions are absent or weak, the challenge for management can be daunting. Secrecy, corruption, ignorance, and lawlessness render the link between values and financial success highly tenuous. Even when the necessary conditions are reasonably well established, charting a workable strategy that is both morally and financially sustainable requires intelligence and imagination, as well as sheer hard work. It may also require engagement with parties outside the organization, industrywide coordination, or collaboration with governmental and nongovernmental agencies. In many cases, the question is not whether ethics does or does not pay, but whether it can be made to pay.[1]

"Ethics pays" also sends a confusing and potentially self-defeating message. In the future, high-performing companies will increasingly need ethical competencies to match the economic and technical competencies they have historically sought to cultivate. They will need, for instance, to be as skilled in moral reasoning as they are in economic reasoning. They will also need a motivational structure that enables them to achieve demanding financial targets while at the same time presenting themselves to the world as moral actors. In a subtle way, "ethics pays" undercuts both these requirements. If a slogan is necessary, "ethics counts" is more to the point.

A Winning Combination

Executives who appeal to financial arguments for values usually do so in the belief that they are strengthening their case. In fact, they are sending a somewhat more ambiguous message. Contained within their confident insistence that "ethics pays" is the nagging question, "What if it didn't?" Speeches that laud the financial benefits of ethics are a natural invitation to such inconvenient questions as . . .

- What if we *could* improve sales by making misleading claims about our products, spreading false rumors about our competitors, or agreeing with rivals to fix prices?
- What if we *could* cut costs by signing up suppliers who use child labor, dumping our waste in the public water supply, or paying off the tax authorities?

- What if we *could* improve margins by refusing to serve low-income clients?
- What if we *could* secure commercial funding more easily by falsifying our financial records?
- What if we *could* protect our stock price by recording next year's anticipated sales as this year's revenues, or using questionable accounting techniques to remove debt from our balance sheet?
- What if we *could* increase profits by partnering with a brutal dictator, selling a product made with bogus ingredients, or providing entertainment that undermines important social values?

In some situations, as we've seen, any of these activities could be quite lucrative—and, historically, some of them have been. Even taking into account the risks of litigation, negative publicity, employee alienation, and other potential costs, the gamble may be financially worthwhile. In such cases, should values simply be set aside? If "ethics pays" is the governing philosophy, the answer would seem to be "yes." In fact, if values are nothing more than financial rules of thumb, the smart policy would be to follow them in just those cases where economically sensible and otherwise to suspend them.[2]

But how smart is such a policy in a world that wants both moral and financial excellence from its companies? To the extent that values such as honesty, fairness, or citizenship are viewed as independent factors of excellence, they are more than financial rules of thumb. They are not just causal drivers of excellence but internal components of the very idea. They have become part of excellence itself, to the point that a company simply cannot be world class without embracing them. As noted earlier, to describe a company as a "superior performer" when it competes unfairly, treats employees badly, or neglects the environment is increasingly a contradiction in terms. Even if financially beneficial, these activities are incompatible with the higher standard expected of leading companies today.

Here we come to the root of the difficulty. On the surface, "ethics pays" seems to endorse values. At a deeper level, it is doing just the opposite. It is a back-handed compliment that takes away as much as it gives. Managers who base their appeal solely on the financial benefits of ethical commitment are only reinforcing the patterns of reasoning and justification that make it difficult for people to take moral considerations seriously. These are the same patterns that blur the moral aspects of managers' decisions and undermine the motivations that drive superior performance. Rather than recognizing ethics as a legitimate discipline and values as inherently important, "ethics pays" actually says that values are important only insofar as they serve financial aims. The subtle message is that, in the end, economic considerations are still the only legitimate basis for management decisions and financial performance is still the only thing that really counts.

However, as we saw in the previous chapter, companies today are increasingly judged by a composite "ethico-nomic" yardstick that combines both moral and financial criteria, and superior performance requires excellence along both dimensions. In Chinese thought, a "superior" person has sometimes been defined as someone who brings out the best in other people. That is just what superior companies must do—bring out the best in people, and in every sense—technical, intellectual, and moral. Nothing less will do if the aim is to excel against the new standard.[3]

Superior performance appears in the upper-right quadrant of the graphic shown in Figure 6-1. This area represents companies that have achieved outstanding financial results while at the same time excelling along the moral dimension.

But how do we assess performance along each of these dimensions? The measurement of financial performance is a highly developed art, with a wide variety of accepted indicators and measures to choose from. As

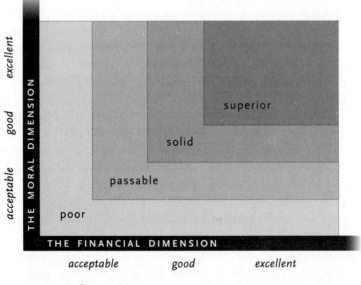

FIGURE 6-1   MAPPING CORPORATE PERFORMANCE

noted in Chapter 2, a recent study identified some 70 measures of corporate financial performance, market based as well as accounting based, used
by scholars testing for correlations between companies' financial and social
performance. Though experts disagree about which metrics are preferable
and vie with one another to introduce new and better ones, it is not difficult to think of methods for evaluating companies along this dimension.[4]

Assessing performance on the moral dimension is inherently more difficult, and the search for useful indicators in this regard is in its infancy.
Several groups, such as the Global Reporting Initiative mentioned earlier,
have begun to test possible standardized measures. Some companies have
created their own assessment tools, customized to their own distinctive values. Johnson & Johnson, for example, has for many years conducted an
annual survey to evaluate adherence to the tenets of its corporate credo.
Royal Dutch/Shell has been exploring various indicators of nonfinancial
performance since it began reporting publicly on its social and environmental results in 1998.[5]

In the absence of more developed tools, we might recall the commitment ladder discussed in Chapter 3, and conceive of the moral dimension
by analogy with the levels of membership in a typical civic association.

- At the first level ("acceptable") are the dues payers who do the minimum required to remain in good standing. These companies practice an ethic of compliance by adhering to the law and avoiding the
  kinds of gross wrongdoing that we earlier characterized as offenses
  against basic justice.
- At the next level ("good") are the sustaining members who practice
  an ethic of consideration based on positive reciprocity. These companies comply with the law, but beyond that also observe the norms
  of fairness and responsibility expressed in what we have called "generally accepted ethical principles." In their dealings with others, they
  are conscious seekers of mutual gain.
- At level three ("excellent") are the benefactors or sponsoring members who practice an ethic of contribution. These companies give
  more than they get and give beyond their "fair share." Like dues payers and sustaining members, they comply with the law and show
  consideration in their dealings with others, but they also seek out
  opportunities to make additional contributions, for example, by
  addressing problems they did not create or assisting those to whom
  they are not indebted.

- Not shown because they are unacceptable are the "free riders," mentioned in Chapter 2, who seek to enjoy the benefits of membership without bearing any of its burdens, and the even more problematic "subversives," who exploit the benefits of membership but undermine the conditions that make them possible. Along with illicit companies that operate outside the law, these might be arrayed along a downward extension of the vertical axis indicating the levels of unacceptable behavior.

As this ladder suggests, companies that aspire to higher levels of performance must develop capabilities that have not traditionally been viewed as critical to corporate success. To behave as moral actors, they will need to

- actively manage their own values and identity, practicing self-governance, self-evaluation, self-correction, and self-improvement
- conform their activities to generally accepted ethical principles
- bring moral judgment to bear in their planning and decision making
- accept responsibility for their deeds and misdeeds
- seek opportunities to contribute to the communities in which they operate

In order to do these things, companies will need to supplement the economic logic embedded in "ethics pays" with other ways of perceiving, understanding, reasoning, and engaging with the world. For a start, they will need to employ the skills of moral reasoning and analysis. Companies that cannot reason from the moral point of view will find it difficult to display any of the attributes expected of a moral actor or to anticipate the moral judgments that others are likely to make about their behavior.

A Better Slogan

Consider the IBM Argentina case again. As mentioned in Chapter 4, IBM's Argentina subsidiary was accused in the mid-1990s of paying off directors of the state-owned Banco Nación to win a $250 million contract to supply the bank's information systems. What actually occurred is impossible to say—in 2000 IBM settled related charges brought by the SEC in the United States without admitting or denying the SEC's findings—but from a purely financial point of view, a well-placed bribe would surely have been an attractive option. In view of Argentina's apparently high tolerance for corruption as evidenced, for example, in the public opinion polls mentioned earlier, company officials might reasonably have assumed that rivals were considering similar gratuities, and the possibility of discovery and punishment would have seemed very remote. The large size of the contract and the certainty of securing it would have more than offset the small risk of incurring punishment. Seen through the lens of economic logic, deciding to offer a payoff would have been a very rational course of action under the circumstances.[6]

From an ethical point of view, however, a payoff would have been clearly irrational for, among other reasons, it would have violated well-grounded norms of behavior that were unambiguously applicable to the situation. Prohibitions against bribery are found in most codes of business conduct and in the laws of most countries including Argentina and the United States. Such prohibitions are essential to the effective functioning of societal institutions because they help assure that public and private fiduciaries—those entrusted with authority to act on others' behalf—exercise independent, unbiased judgment in carrying out the responsibilities of office. To the extent that these norms have been enacted into law through legitimate democratic processes, their applicability is also grounded in an obligation to obey the law. If rationality is defined in terms of consistency with sound principles of conduct, the payoff decision would have failed several basic tests.[7]

This analysis points to the danger in relying exclusively on economic logic. In a company that recognizes only economic rationality, it can be difficult to mount a persuasive case against many practices that are ethically problematic, if not plainly wrong. What can one say, for example, to a proposed bribe in the circumstances just described or to the "inconvenient" questions mentioned at the beginning of this chapter?

We might wish to answer these questions by appealing to values such as truth, dignity, fair play, or good citizenship, but such ideas are not readily accommodated within the logic and language of economics. Terms like "responsibility," "dignity," or "citizenship" have no obvious correlates in the discipline that deals with "revenues," "costs," "margins," and "profits." When the usual criteria for evaluating proposals are NPV (net present value), ROI (return on investment), or EVA (economic value added), analysis in terms of fairness, transparency, duty, or social impact is perhaps as useful as trying to speak your native language in a foreign country.

These inconvenient questions call for concepts and reasoning patterns that lie outside what is thought to be properly part of economics. Such questions have historically been pursued within the humanistic disciplines, particularly within the field of ethics or moral science. While economics has taken as its focal point the problems of wealth creation and efficient resource use, ethics has taken its direction from the problems of human development, well-being, and fulfillment in their broadest sense. Starting from these distinctive motivating concerns, these disciplines have naturally developed rather different repertoires of concepts and methodologies that are not readily translatable from one to the other.[8] Figure 6-2 depicts a number of these differences.

People schooled in these different disciplines and their adjuncts often see and describe the world quite differently. When economists scan the world, they see markets and investment opportunities. When humanists scan the world, they see communities and cultures. When investors hear about a helicopter crash in an oil field, they think about production losses. When social-service providers hear the same news, they think about safety and security. From an economic point of view, a payoff to win a contract is just the cost of acquiring a customer. From an ethical point of view, it is a corrupt act of bribery. What managers at Wall Street's former E. F. Hutton called a "draw-down formula" for efficient cash management, the lawyers who eventually prosecuted the company saw as an unethical and illegal "check-kiting scheme."[9]

In order to meet the new performance standard, companies will need to engage both these points of view. In the final analysis, ethics cannot be collapsed into economics. Yet, the human ideal encompasses justice and humanity just as much as efficiency and prosperity. Any company that fails to acknowledge that values such as truth, fair play, dignity, and citizenship can be legitimate reasons for action—quite independently of their financial benefits—will find it difficult to present a moral face to the world or even to answer those who pose the questions presented above. Like the "anti-

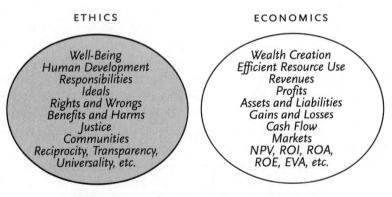

ETHICS

ECONOMICS

Well-Being
Human Development
Responsibilities
Ideals
Rights and Wrongs
Benefits and Harms
Justice
Communities
Reciprocity, Transparency,
Universality, etc.

Wealth Creation
Efficient Resource Use
Revenues
Profits
Assets and Liabilities
Gains and Losses
Cash Flow
Markets
NPV, ROI, ROA,
ROE, EVA, etc.

FIGURE 6-2   COMPLEMENTARY DISCIPLINES

ethics" executive with whom I once shared a podium, such companies will simply have to go silent when asked whether they would use bonded child labor if it gave them a cost advantage and could be hidden from public view.

"Ethics pays" is a comfortable way to embrace values while staying within a familiar frame of reference. But confidence in this familiar frame of reference is misplaced. The new performance paradigm calls for an enriched repertoire of reasoning skills. Expected to behave as moral actors and subject to the moral judgment of others, companies will need to perceive, reason, and decide as moral actors. They will need to incorporate the moral point of view into their outlook and operations and learn to speak the language of ethics as fluently as they speak the language of economics. They will need to bring moral discipline to bear on their activities to the same extent they bring financial discipline to bear. In staking the case for values on financial self-interest, executives run the risk of undermining the very capabilities that their organizations will need for success within the new performance paradigm.

For this reason, among others, "ethics counts" is a better slogan. Unlike "ethics pays," which casts ethical commitment as a footman to financial interest, "ethics counts" embraces values as a full partner in the quest for outstanding performance. When we talk about an "ethics counts" philosophy, we are talking about an approach that recognizes the intrinsic worth of values and takes moral considerations seriously in their own right. "Ethics counts" appreciates the synergies and linkages explored in Chapter 2 while recognizing the tensions and discrepancies discussed in Chapter 3. Above all, it recognizes that corporate strategies must make both moral and financial sense. Ethics counts—and so does strong, sustained profitability.

Acknowledging that ethical considerations have standing in their own right opens up the possibility of conflicts between moral and financial points of view. There can be no general across-the-board resolution to such conflicts—only an effort to use one's best judgment and imagination in charting a pathway through the competing considerations. However, a structured approach to deliberation can be useful, and in a later chapter, I present a framework to guide this process. Although requiring tough choices, an honest confrontation between the two perspectives is likely to force clearer trade-offs when trade-offs are necessary. It can also spark hard thinking and creative solutions to vexing problems, as we will see later in Chapter 9. In any case, such conflicts are bound to occur even if they are not acknowledged and dealt with as such. An "economics-only" approach may theoretically "solve" the problem of conflict by making all choices commensurable on a common scale. In practice, this is not much of a solution, since many moral goods have no obvious monetary equivalent.

Paradoxically, an "ethics counts" approach has economic advantages as well. This brings us back to the issue of motivation, which is crucial to the link between values and financial results. As we saw in Chapter 2, fairness, honesty, respect and consideration for others often pay off handsomely in economic terms. Why? In part because they spark feelings of trust, loyalty, gratitude, and reciprocal respect on the part of those on the receiving end. Why are people more apt to "go the extra mile" for a considerate employer? Why are work groups more creative when they are dealt with fairly and honestly? Why are people more loyal to companies that are trustworthy and reliable? Of course, tangible benefits may accrue in that consideration may mean flexible hours, honesty may convey needed information, and fairness may mean a pay raise. But the perceived motivation for providing these tangible goods frequently has an energizing effect that far exceeds the value of the goods themselves.

This "value added" comes from the authentic human-to-human connection that occurs when values are respected. When people recognize one another as moral actors—capable of responsibility and creativity, deserving of respect and consideration—the by-product is energy. In this sense, values beget value. Much like the spark that occurs when opposing electrical charges encounter one another, the human encounter produces human energy. This dynamic represents a kind of value creation that cannot be measured in monetary terms and is usually ignored in economic studies. Yet it has a palpable effect that often results in strengthened bonds, enhanced effort, and an elevated sense of purpose and commitment.

Authenticity is the crucial element. If perceived as inauthentic—as self-serving, manipulative, or expedient—honesty, fairness, consideration, and even great beneficence lose much of their energizing effect and bonding power. Take the example of honesty. As we've discussed, many of the economic benefits that flow from honesty depend on its ability to generate trust. Because most people prefer to do business with people they trust, honesty can often be a competitive advantage. We do not, however, regard people as honest or trustworthy if we perceive them to be truthful only when it's in their financial self-interest. In fact, these are precisely the people we do not trust. We view them as opportunists who will abandon truth and us whenever it becomes inconvenient.

To secure the economic benefits of honesty, one must be perceived as being *committed* to honesty, which means viewing truth as something intrinsically good and not subject to reevaluation on a case-by-case basis.

This is not an absolutist position. Certainly there are cases in which a commitment to truth can be overridden by other considerations and commitments. One needn't, for example, tell a terrorist the truth about the whereabouts of his victim, to update a classic question debated by moralists. At the same time, authentic belief is rather different from believing in honesty as a financial rule of thumb with exceptions to be exploited as opportunity permits.[10]

It is not always easy to tell the difference between these two attitudes. That is why we are reluctant to describe someone as honest or truthful if we do not know the individual well. It also helps to see how a person deals with difficult situations that pit honesty against economic self-interest. It's precisely when honesty is shown to be valued for its own sake that it generates trust and becomes economically beneficial. Thus, paradoxically, to secure the economic benefits of honesty, it's necessary to convey the impression that they don't really matter—to behave as if ethics actually counts. Recall the old Groucho Marx quip: "The secret of life is honesty and fair dealing. If you can fake that, you've got it made."[11]

The same dynamic applies to other attributes. If I perceive that your concern for my welfare is motivated only by your need for my cooperation, I may well go along with your scheme for the benefits I stand to gain, but your concern will not earn my gratitude, trust, or loyalty. It will not spark that extra energy above and beyond the terms of our exchange. In fact, if you couch your proposal as concern for my welfare when I perceive it as manipulation, it is likely to generate my suspicion and distrust—even to the point of putting me off the deal.

This dynamic comes into play at the corporate level as well. Much of the acclaim accorded to Johnson & Johnson for its handling of the Tylenol crisis, for instance, was due to the motivations attributed to the company. Johnson & Johnson was widely perceived to have acted out of concern for the public and to avoid further deaths associated with its product. In the weeks following the crisis, thousands of articles praising the company's conduct appeared in newspapers across the United States. The titles are telling: "Bravo J&J," "Public Safety Came First," "A Company with a Human Heart." Wrote one journalist, "Johnson & Johnson is in business to make money. It has done that very well. But when the going gets tough, the corporation gets human, and that makes it something special in the bloodless business world." For FDA officials, the experience of working with such a public-spirited company at a time of crisis was particularly gratifying. Dr. Mark Novitch, then FDA Deputy Commissioner, called it the most memorable experience of his public service. Had Johnson & Johnson's motives been perceived as entirely self-serving or purely monetary, the reputational effects, and therefore, the ensuing financial consequences, of its actions would have been quite different.[12]

Similarly, the reputational benefits that flow from acts of corporate citizenship depend on their being perceived as genuine acts of citizenship motivated at least in part by a sense of civic commitment. Purely altruistic motivation is not required, but the public is impatient with marketing dressed up as citizenship. Civic activities undertaken to distract the public from damage being done elsewhere are quickly seen through. Likewise, if employees perceive a call to values as a litigation-protection program for senior management or the board of directors, it is unlikely to stimulate creativity, energy, commitment, or any of the other positive effects we explored earlier in Chapter 2.[13]

These considerations suggest that it is exceedingly difficult to realize the economic benefits of an ethical orientation without actually having an ethical orientation. Because the economic benefits of moral action depend on the perception of moral motivation, an instrumental "ethics pays" attitude is apt to be self-defeating. Even from a purely financial point of view, then, it makes sense to recognize the intrinsic value of values.

Learning from the Critics

As companies have turned to values, their efforts have often met with mixed reactions—enthusiasm from some and skepticism from others. In some circles, the idea that managers should concern themselves with ethics remains deeply counterintuitive, if not subversive or vaguely threatening.

A certain degree of skepticism is always healthy but, in this arena, hardly surprising in view of the corporate history outlined earlier. The doctrine of corporate amorality has left a legacy that is not easily erased, and most mainstream management theory remains squarely within this tradition. In keeping with the ethos of industrial era managers like Henry Ford who wanted "pairs of hands" and not whole "human beings" in his workplace, employees have for many years been instructed to leave their values at home. To anyone accustomed to working within this tradition, talk of values in the corporate context is bound to sound peculiar and unrealistic.[14]

Moreover, ethics itself has historically been thought of as a purely personal or individual matter, rather than an organizational concern. Concepts like "corporate values," "corporate ethics," "corporate responsibility" are all of relatively recent vintage, originating, as we have seen, in the needs of modern industrialized societies. For obvious reasons, these concepts are not to be found in classic writings on ethics. As a consequence, talk of values at work is often interpreted in purely personal rather than organizational terms.

Although most people who have been brought up within an ethical tradition have an intuitive grasp of what it requires of them, few have been exposed to ethics as a discipline in the way they have been exposed, say, to economics. Each year, some 1.4 million U.S. college students take introductory economics courses where they learn the basic concepts and tools of economic analysis and imbibe the classic view of markets as amoral. The number who take introductory ethics courses is not tracked, but it is safe to assume that far fewer learn the basic concepts and tools of ethical analysis each year. Even in high school, most students learn something about the strengths and weaknesses of different economic systems, but receive no comparable exposure to the strengths and weaknesses of different ethical systems.[15]

Much of the skepticism about corporate efforts to present a moral face to the world can be traced to management failures to articulate a clear and compelling rationale for such efforts. What should be positioned as a company-wide effort focused on the company as a whole too often comes across as a litigation-protection program for top management, a new marketing campaign, or even an attack on people's personal values.

Here we come to a crucial distinction, often missed by proponents and critics alike, between the values of the corporation, understood as an actor in society, and the values of the individuals who carry out the corporation's activities. Because a company can act only through its people, the two can never be entirely separated in theory or in practice. Nonetheless, it is crucial not to confuse them. A company, as a moral actor in society, has commitments, values, and responsibilities, such as duties to its lenders or contractual obligations to its customers, that are distinct from those of its individual members. These corporate responsibilities survive even when a company's individual members and agents change. At the same time, a company's members and agents all have personal commitments and responsibilities outside of work as well as personal values that they need not share with one another or with their corporate employer. Failure to observe this distinction is a theme running through some of the most frequently heard criticisms of the corporate turn to values.

No social change, especially of the magnitude described here, occurs smoothly and uniformly across the affected population, or without controversy and debate. Before turning to the practical challenges of meeting the new performance standard, let's look in detail at a few of the most common counterarguments and criticisms. Even though none survives careful scrutiny, each contains an instructive kernel of truth from which we can learn something important.

Sentimental Psychology: "It's too late"

Some critics of corporate efforts to promote values question their worth in an adult environment. Believing that ethics is learned in childhood or not at all, these skeptics wonder whether such activities aren't a waste of time and resources. If values are learned "at mother's knee"—as it's sometimes sentimentally put, management efforts to address these matters are simply too late—a waste of time and resources. They are bound to fail, so what's the point? Or so goes this line of thinking.[16]

This objection gains initial plausibility from the truth that childhood experiences do exert a powerful influence on adult attitudes and values. Moreover, adult attitudes and habits are notoriously hard to change. Still, in taking the goal of corporate values programs to be employees' moral reform, this objection is somewhat tangential to the central issue posed by the new performance standard. For companies aiming to align their activities with generally accepted ethical standards, the challenge is not so much to reform employees' values as to legitimate in the workplace values that have long been recognized outside it as applying to civilized relations among moral actors.

Nonetheless, this objection is not totally irrelevant. If developing the new corporate personality requires that some people learn to respect and apply values and standards other than those they learned in childhood, which it surely does, then this objection has direct bearing on the topic at hand. Indeed, if moral development ceased in early childhood, as this objection seems to imply, it would pose a serious problem for many corporate programs and development efforts.

The "it's too late" position, however, is premised on an overly pessimistic theory of moral development. Even though early childhood experiences unquestionably exert a powerful and sometimes difficult-to-reverse influence on adult attitudes, a considerable body of research shows that moral development continues well past childhood and is indeed a lifelong enterprise. Researchers have shown that most individuals go through several stages of development and attain genuine personal integrity, a state of moral and psychological wholeness, only in the final stages of life. Some have found distinctive phases of moral growth, typically a progression from a self-centered, to a conventional, to a principle-driven sense of morality.

Moreover, studies consistently indicate that moral education programs effect more change among adult participants than among younger people.[17]

Individual moral development in the corporate context has not been widely studied. However, nearly half the respondents (49 percent) to a 1994 survey of 4000 U.S. workers said that their business ethics had improved over the course of their careers. This belief was strongest among those who worked in companies with comprehensive corporate ethics programs, and almost 20 percent of the respondents whose companies had such programs said that their personal ethics had improved *because of* their ethics at work.[18]

Most of us know from our own experiences that moral development does not end in childhood. As we watch our children grow, we see their values evolve and a mature sense of responsibility emerge. Many of us have also lived through and witnessed major changes in social attitudes, such as the gradual shift from overt segregation and racism to more egalitarian values. Such changes could not have occurred within such a short time period without some evolution in adult values. In this book, we have already met individuals, like Shell's Phil Watts, whose on-the-job experiences led them to think in new ways about corporate responsibility and their individual responsibilities as corporate executives.

The experiences and transitions recounted by Bill Sells, a former executive of Manville Corporation and today an ardent advocate for product stewardship, are particularly compelling. Sells retired from Manville in the early 1990s after nearly 30 years with the company that shocked the business world in 1982 by becoming the largest U.S. industrial corporation ever to file for bankruptcy protection. (In 1997, the company reverted to its original name, Johns Manville.) Formerly among the world's leading suppliers of asbestos fiber, Manville by 1982 had become mired in a seemingly endless string of lawsuits over asbestos-related deaths and diseases.[19]

Despite knowing for decades about the dangers of asbestos, the company had been slow to acknowledge and publicize them. As early as the 1930s, research linking asbestos and cancer had begun to reach Manville's medical department, but company and department personnel actively suppressed the information and concealed it from affected workers. Not until the 1960s did Manville begin putting warning labels on its products and, even then, it took seven years to get labels on all products containing asbestos.

When juries in the 1970s learned of the company's earlier efforts to suppress information about the hazards of asbestos, they began returning larger and larger verdicts for the plaintiffs whose claims arose from much earlier exposure due to the 40-year latency period for asbestos-related diseases. At one trial, a lawyer testified to a conversation he'd had with the company's corporate counsel some 40 years before. When the lawyer had asked about Manville's policy of concealing chest X-ray results from company employees, the corporate counsel had reportedly replied that keeping employees working until they died saved the company a lot of money. When eventually it appeared that Manville's projected legal liabilities would exceed its assets, the company took the then-novel step of filing for Chapter 11 protection.[20]

For Sells, Manville's legal and financial troubles were challenging, but they could not compare with what preceded them. In a sense, the asbestos litigation and bankruptcy were only the public face of a personal experience that he called "the most powerful" of his life. In the late 1960s, when he was a young manager and Manville was just beginning to acknowledge the dangers of asbestos, Sells had been appointed general manager of a poorly performing plant where asbestos-cement pipe had been made for many years. His assignment was to increase the plant's productivity. By the time he arrived, however, longtime workers had already begun to die from asbestos-related causes, and mesothelioma, an invariably fatal and particularly painful disease, was making its first appearance.

As more and more workers were stricken, Sells soon found himself a regular visitor at the local hospital. At the same time that the death toll from asbestos was mounting, the plant's viability was coming under increasing pressure. With nearby plants marked for closure, still-healthy workers grew increasingly afraid of losing their jobs. As Sells traveled from plant to hospital and back again, he soon realized that, though people dreaded the possibility of dying, "they also dreaded the possibility of losing the very jobs that put them at risk." He realized that it was his responsibility as the plant manager to protect them from both outcomes. It was not a question of profits versus health or shareholders versus workers—it had to be both.[21]

Sells eventually watched every member of his administrative staff die from asbestos-related cancer. He emerged from that experience an impassioned advocate for product stewardship, which he defines as "product responsibility extending through the entire stream of commerce."[22] It is a philosophy that rests on candor about risks, attention to human health and safety, and respect for the natural environment. More than anything, he says, his experiences taught him that responsibility must be active, overt, and farsighted. "No one, till the day I die," says Sells, "can take from me the belief I have in industry's need for product stewardship."[23]

Although Sells's insights came to him through a set of dramatic and painful experiences, moral development sometimes occurs slowly and imperceptibly, as in the case of Carol Sheehan, a purchasing manager at Wetherill Associates, Inc. (WAI). A supplier of electrical parts to automotive rebuilders and remanufacturers, WAI was founded in 1978 with the express purpose of demonstrating the practicality of doing business honestly. Since then, it has operated according to a creed of "right behavior," defined as behavior that is "logically right, expediently right, and morally right for all concerned." Employees are encouraged to "fill the needs of the situation in the highest possible manner—with absolute honesty and integrity."[24]

When she joined WAI, Sheehan was more than a little bit skeptical. In her previous company, deception had been an accepted practice, especially in the purchasing department where she worked. To get information on competitors, for example, her group would telephone suppliers using a rival's name and, on the pretense of having changed to a new fax number, ask the supplier to fax its pricing information. When Sheehan was told in her job interview about WAI's philosophy and that she would be fired for lying or backstabbing, she responded, "Lying? I'm a buyer. I lie for a living!" As she tells it, she knew from the beginning that the WAI people were serious, but she didn't believe it could be done. Besides, it went against everything she had learned from her former employer. Over time, though, as the company prospered and she learned to work in the new way, she bought in. The process, as she put it, was a bit "like osmosis. You absorb it. After a while you start acting that way."

Like lawyers, doctors, and other professionals, business people have special responsibilities that go with their distinctive roles in society. These responsibilities can only be grasped after people have attained a certain level of intellectual and moral maturity. Although children do learn important values at their parents' knees—and many of these *do* carry over into corporate life—the special responsibilities of executives or the challenges of dealing with the complex moral problems that often present themselves to managers are unlikely to be among those lessons. So far, I have yet to meet even one manager who learned at "mother's knee" about fiduciary duties, conflicts of interest, or product stewardship. We might speculate on why this sentimental view of moral development is so popular, but in the end it has little to do with the realities of human growth or corporate ethics.

Comforting Self-Delusions: "We don't need it"

A related objection comes from critics who, believing the corporation to be nothing more than an aggregate of individuals, question whether it's necessary to focus on *corporate* values per se. "We're all decent people," say these skeptics, "so what's the point?" As long as companies hire only good people, they believe, corporate ethics shouldn't be an issue.

Like the first objection, this one borrows its initial plausibility from an obvious truth: that corporate excellence starts with individual excellence. Without decent, well-intentioned, and competent people, a company cannot hope to achieve superior performance. Thus, hiring is indeed an important part of any effort to build a strong corporate value system. But, as we've discussed, forging a moral personality for a company requires much more than merely assembling a group of decent, well-intentioned individuals. To meet the new performance standard, a company's people must function together in a way that projects to the world a moral personality for the organization as a whole. Through the coordinated actions of its people, the company must present itself as a moral actor fulfilling its responsibilities as an organization.

Without a well-defined conception of the corporation's responsibilities, decent people who are doing their level best can find themselves uncomfortably at odds with the expectations of the broader society. This danger is illustrated clearly in a 1977 study of corporate decision making by Scott Armstrong, a professor at the Wharton School. Armstrong and his colleagues asked 57 groups of executives and business students from eight countries to play the role of an imaginary pharmaceutical company's board of directors. Each group was given a hypothetical scenario and asked to decide what to do on learning that one of their company's leading drugs was causing an estimated 14 to 22 "unnecessary" deaths a year and would likely be banned by regulators in the company's home country. The drug in question accounted for some 12 percent of the imaginary company's sales and a larger percentage of its profits.[25] In the scenario, a rival was offering an alternative medication that had the same benefits at the same price but without the serious side effects.

More than 80 percent of the corporate "boards" decided to continue marketing the product both domestically and overseas, and to take legal, political, and other necessary actions to prevent the authorities from banning it. Of the remaining 20 percent, some said they would continue marketing the drug until regulators actually banned it, while others said they would cut back on production or market only to doctors who requested it. No group decided to recall the product and the study revealed no significant differences among the groups by age or nationality.

When Armstrong asked another set of 71 individuals, captive audiences of business students, managers, and faculty members, for their personal assessment of the decision to continue shipping the drug, 97 percent said the decision was "socially irresponsible." These individuals, none of whom were involved in the role playing exercise, were given a description of the scenario and told of the company's decision to continue selling the product and to take legal and political action to prevent its removal from the market. Thus, 80 percent of the participants acting in a corporate capacity made a decision that 97 percent of those acting in a personal capacity judged to be morally unacceptable. This startling discrepancy suggests how powerfully—and subtly—corporate roles can influence behavior.

By mistakenly collapsing the issue of corporate ethics into an issue of employees' individual ethics, the "we don't need it" objection sidesteps another crucial question: What happens when moral people are placed in an amoral context? Put more generally, do decent people do better in a context of moral indifference or a context of moral involvement?

To make this question more concrete, consider the following scenario, which I've used with many management groups. The scenario is fictional but based on a real incident. "Dale" is an auto mechanic with a national chain of repair centers whose job includes inspecting cars, recommending repairs, and performing repair work. The chain's management has instructed Dale and its other mechanics to sell a certain number of alignments, springs, shock absorbers, and brake jobs during every eight-hour shift. If the mechanics fail to meet these quotas, they can be transferred or have their work hours cut back. In addition, for every hour of work performed beyond a specified minimum, the mechanics can earn special incentive pay. Dale suspects that other mechanics are recommending and performing unnecessary repairs to meet their targets and earn extra pay. Dale knows for a fact that some mechanics have told customers that their cars' struts are "blown out and leaking" when they aren't.[26]

When I've asked managers to consider this situation from an ethical point of view, virtually all of them say that it would be unacceptable for Dale to do what the other mechanics are doing. Why? Three rationales are typically given: It would be dishonest, it would breach an implicit agreement with the customer, and it would be a violation of customers' trust. However, when asked to predict what Dale is likely to do, two-thirds to three-quarters predict that Dale will lie to customers just as other mechanics do. In other words, most managers predict that Dale will do what everyone says is ethically unacceptable, even though they have no reason to believe that Dale is anything but a decent human being. When the managers defend their prediction, most cite the quota and incentive system set up by management—not Dale's character.

Occasionally, a manager will question Dale's personal ethics, usually by way of a joke about auto mechanics. I usually follow Dale's story with another scenario, also fictional but based on a real situation. "Pat" is a surgeon with a large hospital system. Pat's contract outlines a "production budget" that calls for 52 surgeries and 150 office visits per month. By increasing production to 78 surgeries a month, Pat can earn a bonus of 30 percent of the pretax earnings generated by the additional operations. Pat and other physicians who fail to meet their budgets are denied valuable professional opportunities and reminded that their practices could be sold if their performance does not improve. It turns out that managers' predictions about Pat's behavior vary little from those about Dale's. Surgeon or auto mechanic—the behavioral forces are pretty much the same.

As these predictions indicate, we instinctively know that placing people in an amoral context tends to erode their values. As one employee explained to me, "You lose your bearings and your ability to distinguish right from wrong." The amount of the erosion may vary, but the risk is real, even for people who are otherwise considerate and conscientious. People who are treated as cogs in an amoral machine often tend to behave like cogs in an amoral machine. Perhaps this is one reason why ethical traditions in both the East and the West warn against treating people as instruments or merely as means. Of course, we are all useful to one another in various ways, and the market mechanism capitalizes on this very potential. The problem comes when we take this positive feature of social life to extremes and treat ourselves and other people *only* as means and not also as moral actors.[27]

Many executives who are quick to take credit for creating cultures that motivate sales or productivity improvements are equally quick to deny responsibility for cultures that encourage misconduct. They see ethics in the traditional way—as a purely personal matter that has nothing to do with the organizational context created by management. Yet, corporate misconduct has been repeatedly traced to organizational factors such as unrealistic performance pressures, perverse incentive systems, careless hiring practices, inadequate training, and leadership failures; and organizational culture has been found to be a major contributor to corporate crime. Even legal scholars are beginning to recognize that social norms are at least as powerful as formal legal norms in shaping people's behavior. Incidentally, as we will see in the next chapter, both Dale's company and Pat's hospital system eventually faced legal charges stemming from fraud and overselling.[28]

The "not necessary" objection rests on a too-simple view of human behavior. It assumes that bad deeds are the work of bad people and that decent, well-intentioned people will automatically do what's best, independently of the context in which they find themselves. Research, however, has consistently discredited this view. The well-known Milgram experiments, carried out in the early 1960s by Yale University social psychologist Stanley Milgram, demonstrated how readily people follow orders given by an authority figure even if it means doing harm to others. Milgram's research subjects, volunteers for an ostensible study of memory and learning, showed themselves willing to administer what they had been told were painful electrical shocks to anonymous "learners" when instructed to do so by an experimenter. Many were not deterred even when they could hear the cries of the "learner" being subjected to the painful process. When asked afterward why they had administered the shocks, many replied, "I wouldn't have done it by myself. I was just doing what I was told."[29]

More recent research on "bystander behavior" shows how powerfully people's behavior is affected by the example of others. Intrigued by a series of tragic cases in which large groups of people stood by passively as helpless individuals were beaten to horrific deaths, Princeton University social psychologist John Darley sought to better understand the effects of peer behavior on people's responsiveness to strangers in distress. In one set of experiments research subjects were working alone on an assigned task in a computer room when they heard cries from next door. In a second set of experiments, the research subjects were individuals working in a small group of strangers when they heard the cries. Group members other than the subject had been instructed not to respond to the cries. Researchers found that 80 percent of those working alone got up from their work to check on the individual calling for help. By contrast, only 20 percent of those working in the groups did so. When interviewed after the experiment, those who had not responded explained that they had looked to the others to see what to do.[30]

These findings show the extent to which people take their behavioral cues from others—and cast doubt on any simple correlation between good deeds and good people or bad deeds and bad people. This is not to deny the existence of good and bad people. We've all known both kinds. It's easy enough to find people who are malicious, devious, and hateful. However, the central point is that bad people do not have a monopoly on bad deeds. Countless examples of misconduct, both corporate and individual, illustrate the myriad ways in which decent, well-intentioned people can find themselves doing things that violate their own ethical standards, and that they themselves disapprove of.

Through a lapse in judgment or simple inattention, people can quickly find themselves drawn into questionable activities. Perhaps they've over-looked a crucial issue or failed to give due weight to an important consider-ation. Or maybe they've acted in haste, under pressure, or with insufficient information. In some cases, it's a matter of avoiding embarrassment or sav-ing face. In others, it's due to an excess of zeal or to overconfidence. Some-times it's due to ignorance—people don't understand their responsibilities, the situation, or the technology they're working with. In some cases, it's a deliberate misdeed done to benefit the company or for some other "good cause," or even for the sheer excitement of breaking the rules and getting away with it. And some lapses—even in retrospect—are just inexplicable.[31]

Building a company that performs to the new standard requires some-thing more realistic than "We're all decent people." Even good people are fallible, and the risk of moral error multiplies exponentially in an environ-ment of moral indifference. Most of us are far more susceptible than we think to the influences and opinions of those around us, and more willing than we may realize to leave difficult moral judgments to others. In the absence of an active effort to build and maintain a set of organizational val-ues, the values of individuals are left to the corrosive forces of indifference. In any case, for the organization as a whole to present itself as a moral actor requires a coordinated effort among its individual members.

Misleading Creation Myths: "It's beyond our authority"

The moral-actor standard, as we've seen, requires a company to respect the legitimate claims of other parties as it goes about its business. But some have questioned management's right to do this. "Isn't management bound by its fiduciary duty to maximize financial gain for shareholders?" asks this group. By what authority can managers recognize the claims of third par-ties? To these skeptics, corporate ethics sounds a little bit unethical, espe-cially if it means incurring costs or foregoing opportunities for profit.

This objection—let's call it the "fiduciary objection"—has often been used to rebut moral claims advanced on behalf of nonshareholder con-stituencies. Several years ago in an academic forum, I argued that produc-ers of hazardous agricultural chemicals had a moral obligation to reduce the health and environmental risks associated with the products they were marketing in poor countries around the world. At the time, these products, some of which had been banned in industrialized countries, were being marketed without educational support or even warnings to people who lacked knowledge of the risks and trade-offs involved in using them. The results included serious environmental problems and thousands of deaths and illnesses each year.[32]

These marketing activities, it should be noted, were completely lawful. In many exporting countries, laws governing the safety of agricultural chemicals did not apply to chemicals made for export. And in many of the importing countries, mostly developing or poor countries, relevant regulations were at the time either nonexistent or ineffective. In addition, widespread illiteracy and ignorance about the health and environmental effects of excessive dependence on agricultural chemicals meant a wide-open market for products known to have complex risk-benefit profiles.

A respected business academic countered my analysis with the argument that voluntarily incurring costs to combat the health and environmental problems associated with these chemicals would violate managers' fiduciary obligation to shareholders. As fiduciaries, he claimed, managers have one obligation—to maximize shareholder's wealth within the law. Therefore, it would be wrong for managers to take steps to prevent injuries to third parties if doing so would reduce sales, raise costs, or otherwise have a negative effect on profitability.

This argument can only be understood as a vestige of the corporate amorality doctrine. It is plausible only if we assume that companies are amoral entities and that managers, in their role as company agents, can therefore ignore the moral aspects of what they do. Otherwise, it is difficult to construct a coherent line of reasoning that could justify the resulting conclusion. In fact, applying the standard assumptions of morality to companies or to their managers leads in just the opposite direction—toward an obligation to avoid injuring innocent customers, users, or other third parties.

If companies are deemed moral actors, this alternative conclusion follows as a straightforward application of the principle of noninjury. Some such restraints against harming and destroying innocent life have been among the basic ethical norms of virtually all communities, so far as we are aware. In some situations, it is true that other considerations can sometimes override this principle: the consent of the injured, the greater good of the injured, or in some cases the greater good of other parties. But the prospect of financial gain for the perpetrator has never been regarded as sufficient justification for inflicting harm on innocent others without their consent. And it is hard to imagine how a society could remain viable for very long if it were.[33]

Purely for the sake of their effective and sustainable functioning, societies need their members to observe something like the principle of noninjury, at least among themselves. Recall the emphasis placed on this principle by Adam Smith, who insisted that even unintentional violations of others' "happiness" required some form of "atonement." If managers are deemed agents of the corporation and the corporation deemed subject to this principle, it follows that managers are responsible for assuring that the corporation's activities do not injure innocent parties and to make appropriate recompense if they do. Certainly this is the stance taken in many recent codes of business conduct.[34]

Even if we view managers as agents of shareholders rather than agents of the corporation, they would still be subject to the general social obligation to refrain from injuring innocent third parties. This obligation, which attaches to all members of the community, persists even when individuals take on special obligations through contracts, promises, or other forms of commitment. Becoming an agent for shareholders does not cancel out this general obligation any more than, for example, becoming a parent does. Just because parents are obliged to protect and promote their children's interests, they are not therefore relieved of the usual duties of citizenship or permitted to wrong others.

This result follows from the basic logic of obligation. Except under exigent circumstances, an obligation to one party cannot normally be unilaterally extinguished by taking on an obligation to another. By the same token, general obligations to the community at large—to refrain from fraud, avoid injury, respect others' rights, obey the law—cannot be extinguished simply by taking on special obligations to particular individuals. In other words, if it is wrong to steal to enrich oneself, it does not become right to steal to enrich someone else.

Just as an agency relationship with shareholders does not cancel out managers' preexisting obligations, it does not insulate shareholders from responsibilities they would otherwise have if managing their capital themselves. If individuals have duties to use their property in ways that respect the legitimate claims of others, they do not escape these duties by hiring someone else to manage their property for them. For example, if it is wrong to use my property in ways that damage my neighbor's environment, it is equally wrong when my agent does it for me. This was apparently what U.S. Supreme Court Justice Louis D. Brandeis had in mind when he declared to Congress in 1911 that shareholders were responsible for seeing that their representatives followed policies that were consistent with the public welfare.[35]

The view that managers have a single obligation—to serve shareholders—is often coupled with the view that shareholders have a single interest—to make as much money as possible regardless of how it is done. Certainly there are investors of this type. However, as we have seen, growing numbers of shareholders are taking a broader view. As shareholding has become more widespread, the interests and concerns of investors have become more diverse. More investors recognize that they cannot totally divorce their interests as shareholders from their interests as customers, employees, creditors, or suppliers. At the same time, investors are also citizens and members of families. In all these capacities, they have an interest in a stable and well-functioning society. Thus, even if we view managers only as agents for shareholders, we cannot conclude that management's job entails the narrow pursuit of a single objective. As traditionally understood, the fiduciary's obligation is to serve the interests of the principal, whatever those interests may be. As it turns out, many investors today have multiple interests, including an interest in having companies observe the principles of common decency in their dealings with their people and the rest of the world.

Whether managers are agents for shareholders or agents for the corporation has been much debated, but for purposes of meeting the fiduciary objection it is unnecessary to resolve this debate. As my analysis has shown, both views lead to the conclusion that managers should attend to the moral aspects of their decisions and respect the legitimate claims of the parties affected. Nonetheless, I suggest that managers are best thought of as agents for the corporation. Not only is this view more consistent with how companies are perceived and with their role as moral actors in society today, but also it more readily accommodates the multiple responsibilities whose fulfillment, as we saw in Chapter 5, is necessary for corporate success. As a purely practical matter, it is thus a more useful frame of reference for managers seeking to build high-performing companies.

Proponents of the single-duty interpretation of fiduciary obligation sometimes point to the law for support. But contemporary jurisprudence, at least in the United States, offers scant justification for this narrow interpretation. Whatever the law of fiduciary obligation may have said in the past, it does not in general today require executives to ignore the moral claims of third parties. As mentioned in Chapter 4, corporate decision makers are legally permitted to take into account "ethical considerations that are reasonably regarded as appropriate to the responsible conduct of business" even if "corporate profit and shareholder gain are not thereby enhanced." They are also permitted to "devote a reasonable amount of resources to public welfare, humanitarian, educational, and philanthropic purposes."[36]

Only in a narrow class of cases—when a corporation's sale or breakup is "inevitable"—have courts said that taking nonshareholder interests into account is inappropriate. If a board has decided to sell, break up, or effect a transfer of corporate control, then it is obligated to go for the deal "that offers the best value reasonably available to the stockholders." Otherwise, courts have recognized that corporate decision makers may take into consideration a variety of factors, including a transaction's effect on the company, its impact on shareholders, and its impact on other constituencies.[37]

Normally, under the "business judgment rule," courts decline to second-guess corporate decision makers so long as they have acted on an informed basis, in good faith, and in the honest belief that their decisions served the company's best interests. And, as noted in Chapter 4, some 31 U.S. states have enacted legislation that tempers the court-made prohibition on considering nonshareholder interests in change-of-control and takeover situations. These so-called "other constituency" statutes permit boards to take nonshareholder constituencies into account even in this class of cases.[38]

Taken literally, the fiduciary objection does not stand up to analysis, but it should not be dismissed too summarily. Though poorly expressed, it serves as a useful reminder that respect for third-party claims does not excuse poor financial performance. Nor does it justify inattention to shareholders. When shareholders entrust their capital to managers, they do so with the implicit expectation of financial gain, and they are entitled to expect management's best efforts to protect and increase their investment. For shareholders' sake and for the sake of the company's other constituencies, managers have a moral obligation to achieve strong, sustained profitability.

To continue this logic, obligations to third parties no more cancel out duties to shareholders than duties to shareholders cancel out obligations to third parties. Reasoning from either direction leads to the inescapable conclusion that managers have multiple obligations and, thus, an overarching responsibility to incorporate these obligations into their company's strategic and operating processes. All efforts to fix a once-and-for-all ranking of constituencies—whether shareholders, customers, employees, or the community at large—are doomed to failure because it is impossible to say in advance and in the abstract whose claims should take priority in particular cases of irreconcilable conflict. Such trade-offs can only be made through a process of moral deliberation, that takes into account the nature of the conflicting interests, the facts of the situation, and the likely consequences of alternative choices.

Of course, as a general proposition, we can say that honoring basic human rights takes priority over promoting financial self-interest, that compliance with basic principles takes priority over charitable contributions, and that cleaning up one's own messes takes priority over cleaning up messes made by others. Still, reasonable people may disagree about the nature and scope of managers' obligations in any given situation, just as they debate the market potential for a proposed new product or the economic merits of a proposed merger. Nonetheless, in a world in which companies are expected to behave as moral actors, it is part and parcel of the managers' job to reconcile competing obligations and to make value judgments under conditions of uncertainty. These tasks cannot be avoided by invoking simplistic conceptions of the fiduciary role.

Many who are attracted to the single-duty interpretation of managers' fiduciary obligation envision a late-nineteenth-century story of the corporation's origins. As we saw in Chapter 4, this is a story about owners of capital getting together, agreeing among themselves to form a corporation, putting some funds into a common pool, and hiring someone to manage the pooled capital on their behalf. In this version, the starring role is given to the owner of capital. It is from the "capitalist" or investor that managers derive their authority via the board of directors, and it is the investor to whom managers are accountable. In this account, the corporation owes its existence to the investors who are its "members" and whose property comprises the "corpus" to be managed. The investors' authority itself derives from their power as owners of property.

Recall that in an earlier period, the corporation was depicted as a creature of the state, brought into existence by charter and endowed with the authority conferred on it by the sovereign. In this older account, investors play an important role but only a supporting one. The protagonist and source of management's authority is the sovereign, and it is the sovereign to whom the corporation owes its existence and to whom management is ultimately accountable. The sovereign's authority, in turn, flows from its role as protector of the public welfare and its monopoly on coercion.

A creation story for today would star neither the capitalist nor the sovereign, but the entrepreneur. In this account, the corporation is a creature of entrepreneurial initiative that originates from the entrepreneur's energy and skill in transforming a business idea into a going concern. Notice that the entrepreneur's authority derives not from a monopoly on coercion (like the state) or the ownership of capital (like the investor), but from practical knowledge in marshaling and coordinating the people and resources needed for the company's successful functioning. Managerial authority thus derives ultimately, not from a single source such as the sovereign or a group of investors, but from all those on whom the company depends for its continuing existence.

In modern liberal societies, most corporations owe their existence, or what is sometimes called their "license to operate," to several basic groups. Although companies' situations vary somewhat, most have a set of constituencies including some or all of the following:

- the governments whose laws and policies recognize them as actors in society and grant them privileges such as limited liability and bankruptcy protection as incentives for their formation
- the investors, both shareholders and lenders, who provide the capital necessary to finance their activities
- the employees who provide the skills, knowledge, and human energy necessary to carry out their activities
- the suppliers who provide the raw materials, components, specialized knowledge, and other resources necessary to carry out their activities
- the customers who purchase their goods and services, the income from which is necessary to compensate investors, employees, and suppliers for their contributions and to pay the taxes due to governments
- the general public from whom the other parties are drawn and whose tolerance is necessary for the corporation's continuing existence

All of these groups are important for success, and losing the support of any one can sometimes prove fatal. A government investigation, an investor sell-off, an inability to retain employees, a failure to attract customers, a loss of suppliers, or public shaming by an NGO are all excellent ways for managers to lose their ability to lead. We have already seen some cases of how this works. Recall, for instance, what happened when Salomon disclosed its Treasury desk misdeeds. As various constituencies distanced themselves from the company, its top executives were forced to resign.

Without the goodwill and voluntary cooperation of its diverse constituencies, a company can go only so far. And it is difficult to see how a company could secure this goodwill and cooperation, at least in a modern democratic society, without embracing a moral stance in its dealings and respecting the legitimate claims of those affected by its activities. That managers' obligation to create value for shareholders should permit—let alone require—companies to ignore injuries caused by their activities is, at best, a legacy of a creation myth that has outlived its time.

A Tragic *Non Sequitur*: "It will harm the world's poor and powerless"

As the turn to values has gained momentum, yet another group of critics has begun to speak out about the dangers they see in this development.

According to this set of critics, ideas such as corporate ethics and corporate social responsibility are potentially damaging not only to companies but also to the poor and powerless of the world. Like the previous group of doubters, these skeptics find the idea of corporate ethics a little bit unethical. However, they base their argument not on fiduciary obligation but on the alleged harmful effects of these new ideas, which they attribute to misguided NGOs and too-eager-to-please multinationals. Although some of these purported dangers are a bit far-fetched, others do raise legitimate concerns that deserve to be addressed.

Some in this camp have argued that, by embracing values, companies invite governments to impose costly regulations on their activities. This argument, which was also made by critics of corporate social responsibility in the 1970s, is among the more far-fetched. Cases in which government regulation was introduced *because* companies were acting responsibly are the exception rather than the rule, if they exist at all. At least in the United States, as noted in Chapter 2, the history of government regulation is largely a story of government efforts to correct social indifference, misconduct, and overreaching by business. Antitrust laws, food and safety laws, advertising regulations, securities regulations, consumer protection, environmental protection, anticorruption laws, equal employment laws, and workplace-safety standards are just a few examples of legislation triggered by corporate indifference to social concerns. Judging from the historical record, an ethical stance would appear to lessen the likelihood of government regulation rather than to increase it, as these critics suggest.[39]

Indeed, one deliberate goal of the U.S. defense industry's initiative on business ethics discussed earlier was to stave off government regulation. Recall that in 1986, the industry was under severe attack for a series of alleged and actual misdeeds referred to collectively as "fraud, waste, and abuse." Faced with the prospect of extensive and even more restrictive government regulation, the industry vowed to do a better job of governing itself and organized the initiative in an effort to do so. The government, which was brought on board early in the process, accepted the effort and shelved many of the proposed regulations. In light of the broad historical record and instances like this one, warnings about the "regulatory danger" of corporate social responsibility seem highly exaggerated.

Less far-fetched but something of a red herring are the alleged harmful effects of higher standards on the world's powerless, especially the poor and the politically disenfranchised. Those who make this argument tend to focus principally on two issues—labor practices, particularly child labor, and environmental protection. Reasoning that safe workplaces, adult workers, and clean technology are generally more expensive than their opposites (unsafe workplaces, child workers, and dirty technology), these critics argue that values are costly. Poorer companies, therefore, may be unable to compete if they are expected to meet exacting standards in these areas. Moreover, people who need jobs, particularly women and children, may be thrown out of work altogether. Curiously, these critics do not show the same concern when multinationals adopt costly new technologies that their poor-country counterparts cannot afford, though precisely the same logic would apply.[40]

These critics like to point out that refusing to deal with suppliers who use child workers may result in further harm by forcing children into prostitution, the illicit drug trade, and so on. The consequences of the Harkin bill are often cited as an example. The bill, which was introduced in the U.S. Congress in 1992, and called for a ban on imports produced by illegal child labor, had yet to be passed 10 years later, but garment makers in Bangladesh promptly dismissed 50,000 to 70,000 underage children who had been working in the apparel industry. With no alternative provisions made for their welfare, the effect was devastating. Some children found their way into even more hazardous situations such as unsafe jobs, where they were paid even less, or prostitution.[41]

But what are we to conclude from this incident? That companies should forget about values? That they should ignore workplace safety, child workers, environmental degradation, fair wages, and other ethical issues? This would be a tragic *non sequitur*. Surely, the logical conclusion is not to abandon values but to seek a better solution. Just as the child advocates, labor groups, and apparel makers joined forces to rethink the child labor problem after the disaster in Bangladesh, the moral-actor standard requires corrective action when errors are made.

Without question, it would have been better not to make the errors in the first place, and they might have been avoided had more thought been given to the likely consequences of proposing an import ban. Perhaps protective measures could have been put in place simultaneously with the ban, or educational support combined with work opportunities. In any case, however, the International Labour Organisation (ILO), the U.N. Children's Fund, and the garment makers reached an understanding in 1995 that, among other things, provided schooling for affected children and income support for their families. The program is far from perfect, but it is a reasonable start to resolving a complex and urgent problem.[42]

Cognizant of the risks to children, other companies have approached the child labor problem with greater circumspection. Some, like Levi Strauss and IKEA, have provided educational programs for child workers. Others have set up welfare and educational programs for disadvantaged children in the regions where they operate, or lent support to governments and NGOs working to eliminate child labor through such projects as offering mobile education units for child workers, training their families in income-generating activities, providing transportation to secondary schools, and various other cooperative efforts.[43]

Although costs are certainly a factor, we should not forget that even small contributions can have a significant impact in this area. Not long ago, I was leading a discussion about the child labor problem with a group of aspiring young managers. As the group began to grapple with the situation of a small company that sourced many of its products from regions known to have significant numbers of very young child workers, the point was soon made that child labor was not the company's doing. However dismal the bonding of children might be—and all agreed that it was grossly inhumane—the company had not caused it. After a lengthy discussion of the reasons it made no sense for the company to address the problem—too costly, too big, a violation of fiduciary obligation—one of the previously silent members of the group put up her hand to be recognized.

She began by expressing deep disappointment at the tenor of the discussion, and then proceeded to tell the story of her own family's struggle out of poverty. In the account she gave, the pivotal actor was the owner of the factory where her grandmother had worked as a child. The owner had arranged for a tutor to come into the factory for two hours each day to teach the children who labored there. As a result, many of them learned to read—their ticket to hope and a better future. The young woman, who had been educated at some of the world's leading universities, was a living example of the power of seemingly small contributions. Her story had a palpable impact on the discussion and unleashed a burst of creative solutions that could make both ethical and economic sense.

In the end, the critique of corporate ethics that claims to speak for the poor and powerless rings hollow. In cautioning against knee-jerk solutions, this critique provides a useful service. But insofar as it aims to discredit the turn to values, it misses its mark and only underscores the importance of intelligence, imagination, and courage in finding and implementing solutions that work. Whatever the issue, whether child labor, the environment, corruption, or any other, the solutions must be ethically sound and economically viable. Like technical progress, moral progress occurs gradually through continuous effort punctuated by occasional bursts of insight and creativity. The inevitable mistakes and dead ends are not, as these critics seem to suggest, reasons to abandon the effort.

The picture invoked by this group of critics—of an ethics movement foisted on large multinationals by misguided NGOs—is quite misleading. As we have seen, the turn to values is rooted in an evolutionary process whose roots go back more than a century. And it is being driven by a confluence of forces such as liberalization, privatization, and advances in knowledge and technology that have given rise to new expectations for corporate performance. Although consumers in rich countries have played a role through boycotts and buying patterns, so have many other influential groups. If NGOs have been effective in raising the profile of certain labor and environmental issues, it is only because the ground has already been laid for their efforts.

Moreover, a concern with civic responsibility is not exclusive to large, multinational corporations. It can be seen in small companies as well as large ones and in all parts of the world, as the Siam Cement Group's environmental protection efforts and HDFC's mortgage programs for India's very poor both attest.

Some skeptics object to corporate responsibility as a dangerous extension of corporate power and influence. They maintain that companies should confine themselves to economic activities and leave social matters to others. They also warn against large concentrations of power and the effects of commercializing and corporatizing every aspect of life on the grounds that evolution favors a diversity of social institutions. It is better to maintain a strict separation between institutions that serve economic purposes and those that serve social purposes, and, to the extent that corporate social responsibility blurs this distinction, it represents a danger to society at large. Or so these critics say.

Insofar as these critics stress the dangers of too much corporate power, they have a good point. Excessive corporate power is a real danger. The question, however, is what to do about it, given that corporations are already involved in every aspect of life. While it might be appealing to confine economic activity to its own sphere outside the framework of society and community, what could this possibly mean in practice today? As noted earlier, the intermixing of work life and family life, the blurring of boundaries between for-profit and not-for-profit activities, and the corporation's pervasive influence on society's functioning all make it for practical purposes impossible to build a wall between the economic and social realms.

To be sure, concentrations of power, whether in corporate, government, or private hands, are dangerous. But even more dangerous is power wielded amorally. Today's calls for social responsibility are not so much calls for companies to take on new functions as calls for them to carry out their existing functions in new ways. Corporations already deliver social services, educational materials, news, and entertainment. They are already in the business of cloning people, mapping genomes, and charting the progress of science and technology. They already shape public discourse, public policy, and public space. Given these realities, the argument that corporate social responsibility represents a new and harmful incursion of social concerns into the economic sphere seems bizarre, to say the least. Still, these critics are right to stress the importance of countervailing centers of power and to caution against corporate hubris.

A full response to skeptics who cite the harmful effects of corporate ethics would require empirical studies well beyond anything that has been attempted to date. For the time being, we can only evaluate these warnings in light of history, logic, and the experiences of companies that are making serious efforts to incorporate values into their daily operations. From this vantage point, the question is whether the world's people—as customers, employees, investors, citizens—are likely to be better off or worse off if companies embrace the moral-actor standard. The evidence to date, viewed from either a moral or a financial perspective, strongly favors the turn to values.

To put it another way, what is the most likely future: a world in which companies are expected to behave as moral actors, or a return to the corporate amorality doctrine? For all the reasons covered in the previous six chapters, the latter seems highly unlikely. Far more likely is a future in which companies are expected to show a moral face to the world while at the same time fulfilling their functions as wealth creators, producers, and employers. The challenge, for many, will be to build the capabilities required to meet this standard. Let's now turn to that topic.

7

Performing at a Higher Level

Wwhat will it take to meet the new performance standard? Although many managers have been paying more attention to values, relatively few, in my experience, have recognized the full significance of the moralization process described earlier or its profound implications for companies and how they are managed. Many of the activities undertaken in response to the new expectations have the quality of decorative add-ons, rather like a baseball team trying to improve its performance by hiring a new vocalist to sing the National Anthem. Such efforts may be all to the good, but they're unlikely to generate the desired result.

Consider an E-mail query I received asking for my advice on implementing a set of company values. Perhaps spurred by legal and public relations difficulties the company was then facing, someone in the communications department had decided that values were needed. A list of values had been generated, management had given its approval, and the question now was implementation—how to "roll out" the values across the organization. The process, it was assumed, could be carried out smoothly, efficiently, and without disruption to the company's normal ongoing activities. And ideally, it could be done in a matter of weeks.

Absurd though it may seem, this scenario is not that unusual. As companies have become aware of the higher standard they're expected to meet today, more than a few seem to believe that "having values" means having a list of values and that "implementing" values is a discrete staff activity unrelated to actual line management. Innumerable companies have spawned minibureaucracies to administer various special programs—for ethics, diversity, compliance, the environment, and so on—as they have experienced pressures for improvement in these areas. Far too many of these programs are basically peripheral and largely self-contained activities with little connection to the company's main operating systems.

The issue is not the sincerity and dedication of the people involved in these efforts. Having known many of them, I don't doubt their capabilities or intentions for a moment. However, success in meeting the new performance standard will require something much more comprehensive and fundamental. Taken seriously, the moral-actor standard has implications for how companies are governed and for every aspect of management, from the choice of company structure and strategy to the measurement and reporting of performance. Let me draw on some examples to explain.

An Unsettling Experience

Consider the experience of Sears, Roebuck and Co. In 1990, the longtime leader of the U.S. retailing industry was in serious trouble. That year, earnings in the company's merchandising division—its department stores, appliance business, and auto centers—were down 60 percent from the previous year to $257 million, and investors were clamoring for improvement. While rivals Wal-Mart and Kmart had grown smartly in the 1980s, Sears had seen its own market share decline. By 1990, the company had slipped to number three among U.S. retailers.[1] In an effort to cut costs and spur performance, management announced a plan to eliminate some 48,000 jobs and instituted a series of changes in the company's compensation systems.[2]

The plan included a revised compensation system for personnel in the company's auto repair centers, which in 1991 contributed $2.8 billion to the merchandising division's $31.4 billion in revenues. Instead of a straight salary, all service advisers—those responsible for inspecting cars and advising customers on needed parts and repairs—were switched to a combined salary and commission system. Besides receiving a commission on what they sold, service advisers were expected to sell a certain dollar volume of goods and services, as well as a certain number of specific items such as brake jobs, alignments, and so on, in each eight-hour shift.

The company's auto mechanics faced similar changes. The program for the mechanics who actually repaired the 20 million cars serviced by Sears in 1991 included tighter production quotas and new productivity incentives. Instead of receiving only an hourly wage, mechanics would be paid a reduced hourly wage plus a specific dollar amount tied to the quantity of work they completed. The new system operated much like a piecework system, but the net effect was to increase the demands on mechanics. They would have to do almost 60 percent more work to earn an amount equal to their previous hourly wage, but they could also earn more than their previous wage by doing more work.

By the summer of 1992, things had only gotten worse. Customer complaints against Sears's auto repair business—at the time, the largest company-owned automotive service organization in the United States—were spiraling out of control, and Sears had become the target of misconduct charges by officials in 44 states. Employees and former employees were coming forward with stories about the "pressure, pressure, pressure to get the dollars" and about the practices employed to do so.[3] Across the country, 18 class action suits were pending against the company. The charges covered a host of alleged misdeeds including misleading customers, selling unnecessary repairs, charging for unauthorized work, issuing false invoices, carrying out negligent repair work, and violating various laws and regulations governing the auto repair business.

The allegations had surfaced initially in California, where rising customer complaints had triggered an investigation by state consumer affairs officials. After failing to reach a settlement, state officials initiated an action to revoke the licenses of the company's 72 repair centers in California, and the troubles at Sears hit the newswires. Within a few days, similar allegations had emerged in Florida and New Jersey. A week later, auto repair revenues were down 20 percent in California and 15 percent nationwide. The company's stock price had slipped by 9 percent. Things were so bad that Sears became the butt of late-night television jokes, with comedian David Letterman offering audiences his "Top 10 repair jobs recommended by the Sears automotive department." Number 10 was "grease the ashtrays"; number one was "add a redwood deck."[4] By the end of the summer, evidence of misdeeds had emerged in 41 more states.

What went wrong? How did Sears, a company that traditionally regarded itself a leading U.S. retailer, manage to fall so far short of today's expectations? The answer lies in a mismatch between the new performance standard and the systems that management had put in place to guide the company's activities. Had those systems been better geared to Sears's responsibilities to customers, employees, investors, and the public, the company might well have avoided the missteps that attracted national attention in the summer of 1992. Perhaps most problematic was the performance improvement plan initiated in 1991. Even if no one intended the ethical violations that ensued, they were a natural and predictable outcome of the new compensation and quota systems given the context in which they were implemented.

The problem with these systems becomes evident on closer examination. As discussed in the previous chapter, I have frequently asked groups of managers to consider the case of Dale, the auto mechanic. As may now be evident, the scenario was based on the Sears case. In my experience, most say that the fictional Dale will mislead customers about their cars' condition if necessary to meet his (or her) quotas. Even though they know nothing about Dale's character, background, age, or skill level, the majority predict that he will pursue a course of action that virtually everyone agrees is ethically unacceptable. When asked to explain their prediction, audiences invariably point to the quota and compensation system put in place by management.

This analysis stands to reason. The compensation system emphasized only one thing—meeting the assigned quotas. So far as we know, staff at the auto centers had no ethical guidelines and no training in values and standards relevant to their work, nor did Sears have effective processes for assuring customer satisfaction, tracking customer complaints, or monitoring adherence to governing laws and trade standards. The performance of mechanics was judged solely by their success in meeting the assigned targets.

In a system like the one Sears put in place, what happens if fewer than eight customers during a particular shift actually need a brake job? For some employees, this is not a problem. In keeping with traditional ideology, they simply set aside any personal scruples they might have and do whatever is needed—lie, exaggerate, scare the customer—to meet their quota. Others, however, are likely to experience conflict between their personal values and what the company expects of them. If their quotas are unrealistic, the extra-conscientious ones may find themselves in a more or less continuous state of moral turmoil. Like one Sears mechanic quoted in the press, they will feel "torn between moral integrity, losing my job, and trying to figure out how to work all this out."[5] Some will follow the lead of their more flexible colleagues, if only to keep their jobs.

In a difficult environment like the one Sears was facing, the latter outcome is all the more likely. At the time, Sears was facing growing competition from car dealerships and muffler specialists who had moved into auto repairs to compensate for diminishing profits in other parts of their businesses. Between 1983 and 1990, car dealerships saw the percentage of profits from auto repairs rise from 11 percent to 86 percent. With the repair industry generally in a slump and the heightened pressure from new competitors, the quotas set by Sears's management were perhaps simply unrealistic. Finding it impossible to meet their quotas by providing services actually needed and authorized by customers, enterprising mechanics and advisers understandably turned to other methods.

Certainly, opportunities for the practices alleged against Sears were plentiful. The market does a poor job of policing seller misbehavior in businesses where expert advice is a significant component of what the customer is buying. As in their dealings with doctors, lawyers, financial advisers, and other vendors of expert judgment, many customers are at the mercy of their service advisers and mechanics for guidance on what repairs their cars may need. For many types of repairs, customers will also be unable to determine whether the work has been done well or poorly. The potential for profitable fraud in this situation—a classic case of information asymmetry—is well known and documented. When *Reader's Digest* magazine studied the auto repair business back in 1941, it found that 63 percent of the garages asked to repair a minor defect either misrepresented the nature of the problem or the work they did to correct it. While honest mechanics charged 25 cents or less, others charged $4.00 on average, and some charged as much as $25.[6]

Despite the obvious pressures and opportunities for deception and overreaching, the managers at Sears did little to guard against it. If anything, the performance measurement and compensation system they put in place only exacerbated these pressures. Then, when accusations of misconduct began to emerge, management stumbled again. More than six months before the charges became public, Sears's CEO was notified of the allegations in a personal letter from a senior official in the California attorney general's office. The letter cited a rising number of complaints against Sears, described what the state had done to investigate, and presented the resulting allegations. Sears vigorously challenged the state's investigative techniques but apparently did not do its own internal investigation. Instead, after an initial round of discussions, the company delegated the matter to an outside law firm known for its trial work.[7]

After several more months of discussions and negotiations, the parties eventually agreed on a set of standards to govern auto repairs. But they were unable to reach a financial settlement, and state officials finally decided to take legal action instead. To be sure, the delays in reaching a settlement were not the only factor in that decision. At the time, the California legislature was threatening the consumer protection agency with substantial funding cuts, and agency officials no doubt welcomed the opportunity presented by the stalled negotiations to go public with the results of their investigation.

When news of the legal charges broke, Sears's first response was a cacophony of denials and assurances from different parts of the organization. However, to their credit, once Sears's managers grasped the magnitude of the situation, they acted swiftly to settle the legal charges and took bold steps to stem the erosion of customer confidence. Their program included $46.6 million in customer coupons and refunds for anyone who had been charged more than $50 for unneeded repairs. The compensation and goal-setting system for service advisers was scrapped and replaced with a reward system based on customer satisfaction. Sears also stepped up efforts to monitor the provision of services with internal checks and external audits by unidentified "shoppers." In addition, the company funded an industry-consumer-government effort to develop standards for auto repair practices and later launched a company values initiative.

Rethinking Alignment

Although Sears did its best to salvage the situation, the questions remain. Why did these practices occur in the first place? Why wasn't the company better equipped to deal with the charges when they began to emerge? As suggested earlier, the answer lies in a failure to establish organizational guidance systems that would have allowed the company to meet the responsibilities inherent in the new performance standard. By organizational guidance systems, I mean the whole array of structures, systems, and processes that managers put in place to guide a company's functioning, both day-to-day and longer term. At Sears, these systems were so focused on meeting investor demands for better financial performance that they neglected the company's responsibilities to other parties—most prominently, its customers, but also its employees and the public—as well as its non-financial responsibilities to investors. Indeed, the systems intended to spur financial performance not only undermined the company's ability to fulfill these other responsibilities, but also, as with many examples we have seen, ultimately failed in financial terms as well.

In retrospect, the mistakes made at Sears may seem obvious, but we should keep in mind that the management team was only doing as many experts and consultants have advised in recent years. The compensation systems they introduced were designed to tighten the alignment between employees' financial interests and the financial interests of shareholders. The company used typical incentives—money and work assignments—to do so. By selling more repair services, advisers and mechanics could increase their own earnings and at the same time presumably boost earnings for shareholders as well. This approach, we often hear, is the way to drive outstanding performance.

On the face of it, this logic has a certain appeal. But that logic depends on another crucial assumption—that superior performance is only about financial results. If, as I have argued, superior performance means something more complex, then lockstep alignment of financial interests across the organization may be an impediment rather than an impetus to excellence. In fact, tightening up financial alignment to the point of driving out all other considerations is apt to heighten a company's vulnerability to precisely what happened at Sears.

It's certainly a path that other companies have pursued with similar results. Compare the incentives adopted by Columbia/HCA Healthcare Corp., the Tennessee-based health-care giant that rose to prominence in the 1990s. To spur growth and earnings, management put in place high-powered financial incentives for both physicians and hospital administrators. Like the service advisers and mechanics at Sears, many of Columbia/HCA's doctors were given "production budgets" of so many surgeries per month. For surgeries in excess of the targeted number, they collected bonuses tied to the earnings they generated. (The example of "Pat" mentioned in the previous chapter was based on the Columbia/HCA case.) Some physicians earned substantial amounts in extra pay for boosting hospital admissions. Others held shares in the facilities where they worked—shares that rose in value as the hospitals' earnings climbed.[8] Moreover, the company's administrators took home substantial bonuses for meeting aggressive profitability and growth targets. According to a consulting study, a quarter of Columbia/HCA's administrators won bonuses of at least 80 percent of their salary.[9]

The strategy was largely successful in driving growth and earnings. Known for its aggressive acquisitions, relentless cost cutting, and hardball negotiating tactics, Columbia/HCA became the world's largest for-profit hospital chain in less than a decade. A two-hospital operation in 1988, the company by 1996 boasted facilities in 37 states and annual revenues of nearly $20 billion.[10]

Meanwhile, however, Columbia/HCA's business practices had attracted the attention of various state and federal authorities. In 1997, the U.S. Justice Department launched the largest criminal probe ever undertaken against a health-care provider. Based on evidence that the company had submitted fraudulent cost reports, miscoded patient illnesses to obtain higher reimbursements, and rewarded physicians for funneling patients into its hospitals, among other things, the government brought a series of charges against Columbia/HCA and its executives. In 2000, the company (later renamed HCA, Inc.) paid a record $840 million in criminal fines, civil penalties, and damages in partial settlement of charges that it had overbilled government health insurance programs. Two company subsidiaries agreed to plead guilty to several counts of criminal misconduct.

We should note that, like Sears, Columbia/HCA took aggressive corrective action to repair its image and its practices in the wake of the public disclosures. In July 1997, the board of directors installed a new management team headed by Thomas Frist, Jr., the board vice chairman and largest noninstitutional shareholder, as CEO. Frist, a physician who had built and run Hospital Corporation of America (HCA) before it was bought by Columbia Hospital Corp. in 1994, proceeded to ban performance-tied bonuses and physician investments. He also hired the former coordinator of the U.S. defense industry's business ethics initiative to head up an ethics makeover for the company.[11]

Or consider the example of Sunbeam Corporation, whose CEO for a short period in the mid-1990s, Albert J. Dunlap, was notorious for the frequent insistence that shareholders were the only constituency he was concerned about.[12] Brought in to rescue a floundering Sunbeam in 1996, Dunlap slashed the workforce and established ambitious financial targets backed with significant stock option grants to top executives.[13] To meet the goals, Sunbeam would have had to increase sales five times faster than its rivals and improve profitability more than twelvefold in one year. Widely regarded as unrealistic, the targets were nonetheless pushed hard and managers' careers depended on their hitting the numbers.

Within two years, Sunbeam was under investigation by the SEC for accounting irregularities. Auditors uncovered a variety of dubious techniques that had been used during Dunlap's tenure to boost sales and inflate earnings. In one quarter alone, Sunbeam managed to add $50 million in revenues by such methods as booking sales for products that customers had not agreed to accept and deleting records to conceal customer returns. Weakened by accounting irregularities and hobbled by debt, Sunbeam filed for bankruptcy protection in February 2001. The company settled civil fraud charges brought by the SEC three months later.[14]

A similar dynamic appears to have been in play at Enron. High-powered financial incentives for achieving financial targets, lockstep alignment of financial interests among executives and directors, inadequate checks and balances, inattention to nonfinancial responsibilities such as truthful accounting—the same volatile combination led rather predictably to earnings inflation and financial misreporting. In November 2001, only a month before declaring bankruptcy, Enron filed earnings restatements that reduced its reported profits by nearly $600 million for the previous four years.

The problems we see in these cases derive not from the concepts of alignment or performance-based incentives, but from how these concepts are applied. These examples force us to confront the underlying assumptions: "Alignment with *what?*" "Incentives for *what?*" "What is the 'performance' for which pay is being awarded?" If companies are viewed as moral actors and expected to fulfill responsibilities to their various constituencies, they must align their guidance systems with this requirement. They cannot operate as if hitting their financial targets or, in some of these cases, appearing to hit their financial targets were the only thing that mattered. Yet that seems to be precisely the assumption embedded in the management systems adopted by these companies.

The issue is not just incentive and compensation systems but the whole set of structures, systems, and processes referred to earlier in this chapter as organizational guidance systems. Depending on how they are designed, compensation and reward systems can be powerful guidance mechanisms. But many other processes play equally important roles in shaping and channeling behavior. Among the most crucial are processes for marshaling and allocating resources, hiring and developing personnel, planning and coordinating work, gathering and disseminating information, formulating and communicating standards, controlling and auditing operations, researching and developing new opportunities, measuring and reporting on performance, and so on. And, of course, the direction and example set by a company's leaders, which may be the most powerful guidance mechanism of all.

Taken together, these guidance systems must support the kinds of thinking and behavior that will enable the company as a whole to behave as a moral actor exercising considered judgment and fulfilling its responsibilities to its various constituencies. To meet this standard, managers cannot limit their thinking to incentives for financial results or to alignment with shareholders' financial interests. Financial results are crucial, of course, but the challenge lies in creating systems that give due regard not just to financial concerns but also to nonfinancial aspects of performance and to the legitimate claims of nonshareholder constituencies. Put differently, the challenge is to design a set of systems that will align the organization's functioning with the new performance standard.

"Alignment" is not an ideal term for this idea. Besides having many uses that are easily confused—financial alignment, goal alignment, systems alignment—it has mechanistic connotations that evoke images of efficient machines and masses of people acting in unison. Managers sometimes imagine alignment as the synchronous activity of expert rowers in a large boat. This image effectively conveys the idea of coordinated effort, but the image is also misleading in some respects. Any complex performance—an orchestral concert, a Balanchine ballet, a championship football match, or a successful military campaign—involves many kinds of coordination. Checks and balances, contrasts and counterpoints, and even planned dissonance are just as important as coordination mechanisms aimed at producing uniformity. Although participants must share an overarching aim, they will necessarily have diverse and sometimes competing intermediate objectives. A brilliant performance will thus display verve, tension, excitement, and excellence along multiple dimensions.

Still, in the absence of a better term, "alignment" will have to do. If we remember that alignment need not imply uniformity, it conveys the essential idea we are looking for—that of fit or correspondence between a company's guidance systems taken as a whole and the expectations inherent in the new performance standard.

The Organizational Infrastructure

The Sears example shows that companies do not spontaneously arrange themselves in a way that makes it easy or even feasible to demonstrate the competencies expected of a moral actor. Instead, companies must be designed, managed, and led in a way that makes this possible. A company's ability to conform its activities to a set of ethical principles, to make sound judgments when values conflict, or to engage in self-scrutiny and self-correction all presuppose a suitably designed and effectively functioning organizational infrastructure.

Even a relatively simple competency such as the ability to keep promises depends on certain organizational prerequisites. For a start, the organization must have some method for gauging its capabilities. Because promise-keepers are by definition careful not to make commitments they cannot keep, the organization must have some parameters for deciding what commitments are reasonably within its capabilities. Then, of course, the organization needs a process for keeping track of the promises made on its behalf as well as channels for communicating this information to the appropriate parties inside and outside the organization. It must also have methods for securing the cooperation of the parties needed if it is to deliver on its promises, for coordinating their activities over time, and for dealing with the many contingencies that may occur at any stage in the delivery process.

Moreover, everyone involved in this chain of activities must, as individuals, be promise-keepers. That is, they must be actively committed to keeping their promises to one another and to parties outside the organization. They must view "I promised" and "I agreed" as compelling reasons for action. So the company also needs processes for communicating this value and assuring that all members accept and respect it, individually and collectively. Assurance mechanisms, feedback loops, and systems for rectifying errors are thus essential.

Some might question whether it's really necessary to affirm the importance of keeping promises. Isn't that obvious—something learned at "mother's knee"—to recall our earlier discussion? In many organizations, however, people have been told for years to leave their values at home, and for all the reasons we've already discussed, many still think of work as an amoral, ethics-free zone. Moreover, what constitutes a promise and how important it is varies across cultures and even from individual to individual. "I'll try to get it to you early next week" may mean "I'll have it in your hands on Monday morning" or "You'll hear from me no later than next Friday"—or something else. For some, a promise is less a firm commitment than a starting point for further negotiations.

Even such generally accepted ethical principles as keeping promises need to be validated as organizational principles, not just as personal commitments. Individuals must know these principles are relevant at work and that others know it, too. Otherwise, some may mistakenly think they are alone in their beliefs and set these values aside in misguided deference to others. Of course, simply stating a principle is not sufficient to validate it. Validation occurs through practice and over time as the principle is seen to be an integral and operative force in the organization's activities.

Weakness in any part of this supporting infrastructure can lead to broken promises. Think about what happens if production planners lack timely information about promises made by the sales force, or the marketing team makes promises that are beyond the logistics department's capabilities, or managers lack the resources required to secure the cooperation of key parties. Suppose some members of the activity chain regard promises as "no big deal" and fail to deliver at the appointed time, or a materials shortage develops and the company has no backup plan for securing essential supplies. Sometimes a simple communication failure may be to blame. For example, one department makes a commitment without informing another department whose involvement is necessary to implement it.

As this one example suggests, building a company that can keep promises is as much about organizational design and functioning as about individual attitudes and beliefs. Other moral competencies present a similar challenge. Consider what's required for a company to be responsive when its activities cause injury to others. Here again, having safety-minded executives is only part of the equation. If those executive beliefs are to be translated into corporate action, the organizational prerequisites must be firmly in place. Just as important as the right incentives is ready access to relevant information.

The crucial role of information flows is evident in the events that led up to the Bridgestone/Firestone tire recall in August 2000.[15] As noted in Chapter 4, the U.S. recall involved some 6.5 million tires, most of which were mounted as original equipment on Ford Explorers, a popular sport-utility vehicle made by Ford Motor Co. The recall marked the culmination of an investigation launched in May 2000 by federal auto safety officials in response to consumer and insurance company reports about possible tread separation problems with the tires. For reasons that were not entirely clear, the rubber treads of certain tires—the ATX, ATX II, and Wilderness AT brands—would sometimes separate from their steel belts, causing drivers to lose control of their vehicles and leading in some cases to fatal rollover accidents.

Both Ford and Bridgestone/Firestone (BFS), the U.S. subsidiary of Japan's Bridgestone Corp., agreed to cooperate with the government inquiry, and in July BFS turned over its confidential warranty claims data to the government and also to Ford. By early August, government data had implicated the tires in some 270 accidents in the United States—17 percent of them fatal and most involving Explorers.[16] Meanwhile, Ford and BFS had been carrying out their own investigation. Working around the clock in a "war room" at Ford's Michigan headquarters in late July and early August, teams of analysts pored over Firestone's tire warranty data and concluded that a recall was the only way to prevent further accidents, limit the companies' legal liability, and protect two of the world's leading brands.[17]

On the surface, the two companies initially appeared to be deserving of praise for acting swiftly to protect public safety despite a significant cost to themselves. At the time, the cost to each was estimated to be about $500 million. By late 2001, the amount had risen to more than $2 billion for Bridgestone, and Ford had set aside another $3 billion to cover the cost of replacing 13 million more BFS tires on its vehicles because of tread separation risks revealed by Ford's testing.[18] However, subsequent disclosures revealed that both companies had known about the tread separation and rollover problems for quite some time. Or, to be more precise, various individuals and departments in each company had received information about these problems long before federal auto safety officials initiated their investigation.

Perhaps the first indicators of potential problems with the tires came in the form of warranty claims and lawsuits filed in the early 1990s. The number of tread separation claims, however, was small and apparently did not attract the attention of BFS attorneys or claims administrators. By the mid-1990s, the number of claims was rising, and in 1996, the company's engineers learned from state officials in Arizona that tires on state vehicles were losing their treads in hot weather.[19] As early as 1997, insurance company officials alerted BFS to the unusually high rate of accidents involving Firestone tires.[20] That same year, BFS finance officials discussed the rising costs of claims and lawsuits involving the ATX tire at their quarterly financial meetings, but the issue evidently did not go beyond the finance area.

By the late 1990s, various BFS personnel were aware of tread separation problems on tires sold in parts of the Middle East, Latin America, Southeast Asia, and the United States, and in 1999 and 2000 Ford actually replaced the Firestone tires on Explorers sold in some 16 countries.[21] BFS had declined to participate in these "customer satisfaction programs," however, citing poor road conditions and driver error rather than tire defects as the cause of accidents. By the end of 1998, according to a report by a safety research and litigation coordination firm, BFS, and, in some instances, Ford as well, had been sued in cases involving 22 deaths and 69 serious injuries allegedly from tire-related auto accidents.[22] As disclosed in 2000, BFS's own records showed more than 1500 legal claims relating to failures of the tires being recalled as well as rising numbers of requests to replace tires under warranty.[23]

So why did BFS and Ford wait until July 2000 to examine the full scope and seriousness of the tread separation and rollover accidents? According to BFS executive vice president Gary Crigger, who announced the recall, customer safety was a paramount concern for his company. "Nothing is more important to us than the safety of our customers," he stated.[24] Similarly, Ford's CEO had been declaring for some time that safety and customer service were corporate priorities. Indeed, in May of 2000, the same month that government officials began their investigation, Ford issued its first corporate citizenship report which emphasized the company's dedication to customers and detailed its efforts to be a leader in auto safety.

To understand the delayed response, we must look more deeply into the two organizations. Both BFS and Ford were handicapped by, among other things, information and communication systems that had not yet caught up to their espoused values. Although BFS possessed abundant information about the tread separation problems, much of it was scattered across the organization in various regional and functional pockets—the warranty claims department, the legal department, the engineering department, the customer relations department, the marketing department, the quality control department, the finance department.

Although a number of executives clearly knew something of the problems, the public record suggests that this information was never assembled and analyzed in a systematic way from a safety perspective. As Crigger said of the claims and lawsuits, "They are considered to be individual cases that occur for a variety of reasons. So they have never been part of performance evaluation."[25] Speaking from Tokyo after the recall, Bridgestone's CEO acknowledged that the flow of information from the BFS subsidiary had been unsatisfactory.[26] He claimed that, apart from an incident report forwarded to him in 1996 when the widow of a Houston reporter sued BFS, he had received his first summary of the accident situation in May 2000 when U.S. safety officials launched their investigation.[27]

At Ford, the situation was apparently similar. A memo of September 15, 1999, from Ford's group vice president for purchasing indicated that he was aware of tread separation problems with a small number of Explorers driven for long periods at high speeds in Saudi Arabia, Oman, Qatar, and Venezuela. However, he mistakenly believed these to be the only examples of this problem. "No known instances have occurred in other markets," he wrote. At the time the memo was written, however, Ford's general counsel and its chief safety official would have known about cases in other jurisdictions—but neither was on the distribution list for the memo which was addressed to Ford's CEO, its vice president for international operations, and six vice presidents.[28]

The tire replacement programs initiated by Ford in Saudi Arabia, Venezuela, Thailand, and other countries show clearly that a number of company officials were well aware of the tread separation problems. However, Ford did not keep systematic data on tire performance, nor did it have ready access to data on tire warranty claims, because tires are customarily warranted by their makers rather than by car companies. Tire suppliers, moreover, tend to regard claims data as highly confidential. So it was not until the summer of 2000, after Ford learned of the government's investigation and negotiated access to Firestone's claims and warranty data, that the company was in a position to carry out a systematic search for evidence of tread separation problems.[29]

We cannot know whether the gaps in the companies' information systems would have been corrected had the recall crisis not intervened. But among the first acts of John Lampe, who was appointed CEO of BFS only two months after the recall, was to announce plans to "break down the castle walls" between departments that might have hindered the flow of information about the tire failures.[30] He proceeded to reorganize the company's 16 tire operations into four groups and to establish a quality committee reporting directly to him that would review safety data and track the performance of tires on vehicles sold overseas.[31] In Japan, Bridgestone set up new mechanisms to assure that claims information would reach Tokyo and also appointed new personnel to assure adherence to strict production standards.[32]

Of course, information and communication flows are not the whole story. A complete account would go back to Bridgestone's acquisition of Firestone in 1988, the labor disputes that plagued the company from 1994 through 1996, and the variations in quality standards across different manufacturing lines. Still, a company's ability to meet the new performance standard depends crucially on its decision makers having access to the needed information. Getting the incentives right, as we saw in the Sears example and others discussed earlier in this chapter, is important, but it is only part of the puzzle. Even if people are motivated to meet the new standard, their ability to do so is constrained by the resources and information they have at their disposal. Given limited time and attention, managers cannot address everything they know about—much less things they don't know about.

The recall crisis at Bridgestone/Firestone underscores again the more general point of this chapter—that meeting the new performance standard is as much about organizational design and functioning as about individual attitudes and beliefs. Many of the problems I have seen in companies over the years can be attributed to what might be called, at least from the perspective of today's performance standard, organizational design defects. In many instances, a failure of corporate responsibility occurs because a company's guidance systems are poorly aligned with today's expectations. The incentives are skewed, the controls are inadequate, the information base is too narrow, and so on.

Considering that few companies have been designed with today's performance standard in mind, such misalignments are perhaps not surprising. In fact, as mentioned in earlier chapters, much of the accepted wisdom on management and organizations remains rooted in traditional thinking about the corporation as a legal fiction—an amoral instrument for carrying out economic activities. If we require companies to behave as moral actors, however, we must rethink conventional ideas about management and organizations. We cannot simply assume that old models will work to meet the new standard.

A Comprehensive Approach

By now, my pessimism about many current values initiatives—and the reasons for that pessimism—may be evident. To effect a shift in values, it is not enough to merely roll out a values statement, distribute a code of conduct, or exhort people to higher standards. However much executives may talk about values, the practical question must eventually come down to what companies do. And that depends as much on how they are organized and managed as on their executives' convictions. In other words, management and organization are the vehicles through which beliefs, values, and convictions are transformed into corporate action.

In a company designed to meet the new performance standard, we would expect to see a moral perspective woven into day-to-day activities. Its guidance systems would be aligned with today's accountabilities, and ethical concerns would be as integral to management's thinking as concerns about markets and profitability. Its people would use their moral faculties to the same degree as their technical skills, and they would bring the power of their intellect to bear on difficult moral questions in the same way they tackle complex questions of finance, technology, or logistics.

How might this work? Several of the profiles in Chapter 1 suggested some possibilities. There we saw, for instance, how Sealed Air integrated values into the training of its sales force and how values guided HDFC's business practices as the company developed. The experience of AES, the independent power producer first mentioned in Chapter 2, provides another instructive example. Even though AES has not yet achieved a fully satisfactory model, its approach provides some useful insights on integrating values into corporate functioning.[33]

AES founders Roger Sant and Dennis Bakke aimed explicitly at creating what they saw as a new form of business enterprise that would be socially responsible as well as profitable. Their business plan for AES was much more than a set of strategic objectives and financial forecasts for the power company they wanted to build. It also laid out their philosophies on business, hierarchies, and the role of employment in people's lives. It was as much a moral vision as a financial one, but, as noted in Chapter 2, the founders disavowed the notion of an instrumental relation between the two. Although they did not use the specific framework of this book, their approach shared its central premise—that superior performance in today's world has both a moral and a financial dimension.

By the time the two business school graduates began circulating their plan, they had already spent several years working together on energy issues in Washington, D.C. Following a stint at the U.S. Federal Energy Administration, where Sant headed the Ford administration's conservation efforts and Bakke served as his chief aide, they spent four years doing energy research at a think tank associated with Carnegie-Mellon University. Over this period, Sant and Bakke had become convinced that power companies needed to do more to protect the environment and to integrate environmental concerns into their business models. They believed it imperative that companies approach social responsibility in an integrative way rather than tacking it on "at the end of their thinking."[34]

They were also convinced that work should be a place where people could develop as individuals and flourish in the use of their talents. Besides providing a livelihood, it should be a way for people to develop their capabilities, engage with others, and contribute to society. Sant and Bakke rejected the "economic man" of theoretical lore—autonomous, rational, self-interested, opportunistic, and guileful.[35] Instead, they saw people as moral, intelligent, socially inclined but individually unique and, at the same time, quite capable of error. They imagined a company where all people would be treated as "adults," defined in their terms as:

1. Thinking, creative, and capable of making hard decisions
2. Willing and able to assume accountability and responsibility
3. Unique and deserving of special treatment
4. Positively disposed to work in groups
5. Eager to make a contribution or join a cause
6. Fallible, even intentionally so at times

Both Sant and Bakke took corporate citizenship as a given, and they saw companies as having civic responsibilities just as individual citizens do. For them, however, social responsibility was about much more than civic duty or corporate largesse. It encompassed their whole philosophy of business, from their view of people as "social individuals" to the very purpose of a corporation, which they described as "stewarding resources to meet a need in society."

They recognized the crucial importance of strong financial performance, but they nevertheless saw it as a by-product of fulfilling a legitimate corporate purpose rather than as the purpose itself. Bakke likened profitability to breathing—unquestionably necessary, but hardly an ultimate goal. Within their framework, a company had responsibilities to each of its stakeholder groups—employees, customers, shareholders, suppliers, governments, and communities. Although the relative importance of each group might vary from time to time as circumstances changed, none was more important than the others in any absolute sense. Each and all deserved to be recognized and treated fairly. To be successful, a company would have to honor commitments to each group.

When the U.S. power sector was deregulated in 1978, Sant and Bakke recognized an opportunity to create an enterprise that embodied their beliefs. They put together a business plan for the company and defined its purpose as "meeting society's need for electrical power in a way that was safe, clean, reliable, cost-efficient, and fun." In 1981, with $1 million in venture capital funding, they launched what they both viewed as a bold experiment. By early 2002 the AES experiment, though still very much in progress, had become the world's largest independent power producer, with more than $9 billion in revenues for 2001 and a generating capacity of some 64,000 megawatts spread across more than 180 plants in 31 countries.[36]

To guide AES's people in carrying out the company's purpose, Sant and Bakke early on crystallized their core beliefs into a set of principles. As noted in Chapter 2, these were included in the prospectus for the company's initial public offering in 1991. "These values," they wrote, "are goals and aspirations to guide the efforts of the people of AES as they carry out the business purposes of the company":

- **Integrity**, which they defined as wholeness, honoring commitments, and adhering to truth and consistency. "The company seeks to honor its commitments," they wrote. "[T]he things AES people say and do in all parts of the Company should fit together with truth and consistency."
- **Fairness**, which they defined only partially, leaving it to decision makers "to routinely question the relative fairness of alternative courses of action." They stated, however, that AES desires " . . . to treat fairly its people, its customers, its suppliers, its stockholders, governments, and the communities in which it operates." Over time fairness came to be defined as "justice," with each stakeholder or person receiving a reward proportionate to that party's respective contribution.
- **Fun**, which they defined as creating "an environment where each person can flourish in using his or her gifts and skills and thereby enjoy the time spent at AES . . . AES desires that people employed by the Company and those people with whom the Company interacts have fun in their work."
- **Social responsibility**, which they defined as being "involved in projects that provide social benefits such as lower costs to customers, a high degree of safety and reliability, increased employment, and a cleaner environment." Social responsibility came to be understood as doing a good job in accomplishing the company's purpose— delivering safe, clean, reliable, reasonably priced electricity and

other services—as well as doing something extra for the betterment of society.

These aspirations have served as a moral center that has guided the company's development over the past 20 years. Their meaning and interpretation have in turn been influenced by the course of that development. Early in their venture, Sant and Bakke concluded that their ideas about work could not be easily realized in a traditional hierarchical organization. It was simply not possible for people to develop their talents and skills in a steep multilevel hierarchy with rigid job descriptions and narrowly defined responsibilities. As a result, the concept of having fun came to be associated with employees having enough authority to be real decision makers.

In this spirit, AES has sought to keep the organization relatively flat and to resist the creation of a large centralized staff at headquarters. The company has tended toward leaner-than-average staffing in the field as well. According to an AES plant manager based in Eastern Europe, it all comes back to the company's guiding principles. Running lean, he said, "is consistent with the 'fun principle'—you are more responsible, you have more room to learn more things and make more of a contribution. It's more rewarding. If there are four people doing one person's job, what kind of responsibility do you have?"

Even though the company had grown from about 500 people in 1991 when it went public to more than 37,000—actually, some 55,000 counting employees of affiliated companies—by the end of 2001, the number of staff at AES's headquarters in Arlington, Virginia, remained steady at about 75. Activities such as hiring and purchasing, which are centralized in many traditional organizations, have been carried out on a decentralized basis at AES, often at the level of plant and project teams. Instead of creating a cadre of specialists to handle environmental permitting or the contracting involved in building a new power plant, AES has typically relied on teams of enterprising individuals, often novices, to take on these tasks. Learning is part of the job, and a new team's first responsibility is to tap into the knowledge and experience of colleagues across the company.

The practice of entrusting specialized work to people who lack specialized training flows directly from the founders' belief in people's inherent capabilities. If people want to learn new things and take on new responsibilities, and if they have the ability to do so, why limit them to doing what they already know how to do? The company's heavy reliance on small, project-oriented work groups, has meant that people have had many opportunities to take on new challenges. In this way, they have not only learned new skills and developed new competencies, but they have also acquired the overall sense of responsibility and business understanding essential to "thinking like a CEO," something expected of everyone at AES.

In keeping with this "all adult, all responsible" philosophy, members of the company are generally referred to as "AES people" rather than "employees." This same line of reasoning has led AES to minimize traditional employment distinctions such as "hourly employees" versus "salaried employees" and "maintenance workers" versus "operators." Where legally permitted, hourly employees have the option of receiving the same compensation package as others, including salary, bonus, and stock options or profit sharing. By 2001, 90 percent of the people in businesses owned by AES for at least three years were paid on a salary basis, with eligibility for bonus and profit sharing, compared to only 10 percent in 1995.

Just as values have helped to shape AES's structure, they have also been woven into the processes and systems that guide its functioning, starting with the definition and measurement of performance. Consider the following:

Performance Measurement

Across the board, AES's performance criteria have reflected the company's ethical commitments as well as its financial ones. This is true for individuals, teams, plants, and the company as a whole. Plant performance, for example, is measured against a combination of factors that include power availability, safety, environmental emissions, budget, and the values survey. Conducted annually, this survey asks employees across the company to evaluate AES against its espoused principles. Questions probe different aspects of each principle and invite scaled as well as open-ended responses. The results, charted across locations and over time, are used for both evaluation and learning purposes.

AES's broad conception of performance is evident in its annual report. Along with the expected company financials, the report typically includes discussion of the values survey, the year's safety and environmental performance, issues in stakeholder relationships, new business development, and commitments for the year ahead. In some years, breaches of company principles have been discussed prominently, as have financial difficulties or other setbacks. The report typically covers a mix of financial concerns such as income, cash flow, and new businesses intermixed with such nonfinancial matters as living AES principles, improving safety, and making everyone a business person.[37]

AES executives, up to and including the CEO, are similarly evaluated on multidimensional criteria. For each executive, the board of directors considers the individual's contributions as well as companywide results in the two areas of corporate values and business responsibilities.[38] To evaluate performance on the values dimension, the directors use quantitative measures such as the values survey, safety data, and environmental data in combination with a qualitative assessment of the individual's efforts to promote understanding and adherence to AES's principles. Similarly, when evaluating individuals' performance on the business responsibilities dimension, the board looks at factors such as margin improvements, operating reliability, and earnings per share contributions as well as the development of new business, community relations, and effective planning.

Compensation and Rewards

The compensation package offered to AES people around the world varies somewhat, due mainly to cultural, historical, and legal differences. The preferred package, however, consists of three elements: salary and benefits, a performance-based bonus, and a component related to the company's overall financial results. The performance-based component is generally tied to both individual and group performance as measured on the dimensions described earlier. Employees share in the company's financial results through profit sharing and stock ownership.

Here again, the approach both reflects and reinforces the AES belief that everyone should be—and be treated as—a responsible businessperson. Just as AES has sought to eliminate the distinction between hourly and salaried workers, it has also sought to extend share ownership more broadly across the company. When AES was much smaller and operating principally in the United States, virtually all employees participated in the stock option plan. In 2001, about half the AES people located in the United States were participating, but only about 3 percent worldwide. The company has been actively exploring ways to extend share ownership more broadly, especially in countries where the practice is uncommon.

Bonuses for executives are tied to performance, as they are for all AES people. Poor financial performance can reduce a bonus, and so can poor performance on other dimensions. In 1998, when the company had four fatal accidents—three involving contractors and one, a civilian—the AES executive team took a 10 percent bonus cut in recognition of these tragedies. AES's chairman estimates that about half of the average AES person's compensation depends on technical factors such as financial, safety, and environmental performance, and about half on how well individuals and groups understand and adhere to the company's values.[39]

Hiring and Orientation

Because AES is highly decentralized, the hiring process can vary considerably from locale to locale. However, a key aim in all hiring is to identify the candidates most likely to support and fit the company's value system. Apart from employees who join through acquisitions, job candidates participate in a lengthy interview process designed to facilitate mutual discovery but especially to help potential candidates learn as much as possible about AES before joining.

Once on the job, new people participate in an orientation designed to deepen their understanding of AES's guiding principles. For many years, all orientation sessions were held at corporate headquarters. New employees and their spouses were flown to Virginia to meet and talk personally with the founders and other AES leaders. With the company's rapid growth in the 1990s, division heads and plant managers around the world have taken on much of the responsibility for orienting new people. Still, each year a substantial number of newcomers and their spouses attend orientations in Arlington.

Information and Communication

From the beginning, Sant and Bakke recognized that intense communication and access to information would be crucial for enabling people to make sound decisions consistent with AES's values. Thus, early on, the company began to gather and disseminate information about plant operating characteristics such as environmental performance, safety, and adherence to values as well as traditional data about energy availability, costs, and efficiency.

Although all performance data, both financial and nonfinancial, are available to anyone on an "as wanted" basis, much important information travels through informal channels. According to Sant and Bakke, a paradoxical result of eliminating layers of approval has been to intensify the amount of information gathering and advice seeking. In putting together an acquisition proposal, for instance, a project team begins by seeking out others' experiences across the company. Working from that base, the team then develops its own approach, taking into account the particulars of the local situation as well as AES's values and general operating parameters. The advice process includes input from group heads, corporate officers, and board members, but the ultimate decision to proceed rests with the proposal's proponents.

Planning and Coordination

Planning and coordination take place in various structured and unstructured settings at all levels of the company. In yearly strategic planning sessions, managers from around the company discuss priorities, trade-offs, and how to strengthen both profitability and company values. For AES managers, whether to pursue a growth opportunity is not only a matter of risk-adjusted return. It's also a question of whether the company can live its principles. As one project director explained, "We're looking for places where we can make a difference. We're prepared to tackle tough markets if it makes sense from the financial point of view and if it's in keeping with our values."

At bimonthly divisional planning meetings, time is routinely set aside for discussion of values issues. These sessions make it easy for division managers and project leaders to canvass their colleagues on matters of current concern, large or small. At a recent meeting of the company's European division, for instance, a project leader sought her colleagues' advice on how to respond to a request from a company that was bidding on a contract to build a new AES plant. The bidder had called after the deadline for final offers and asked if it could lower its bid. After the group discussion, the project leader and chief engineer together decided not to allow the bidder to revise its submission.

New Project Development

Much of AES's expansion around the globe has been carried out through project teams that manage new plant development and competitive bidding on privatizations as well as negotiated acquisitions. Consistent with the company's philosophy of decentralization, these teams handle virtually all aspects of a new project, from financing and contract negotiations to the choice of technology and community contributions. Like the India team mentioned in Chapter 3, each project group must reconcile AES's values with the conditions and cultures in which they may be operating.

As AES has expanded, it has enlarged its repertoire of civic contributions beyond the environmental activities for which it won early acclaim. When global warming emerged as a public concern in the mid-1980s, the company initiated an innovative tree planting and forest protection program to offset carbon dioxide emissions from its plants. Conceived in collaboration with the World Resources Institute and implemented through various governments and NGOs, the program became a standard part of AES power projects. As the company moved into developing countries, however, many felt that carbon dioxide offsets were not the best use of funds set aside for civic activities. In many communities, other needs such as water treatment plants, medical clinics, and schools were far more pressing. Project teams therefore began working with local officials to decide on the most appropriate use of the company's public responsibility funds.[40] AES has assiduously avoided "strategic philanthropy"—the practice of selecting philanthropic projects on the basis of their benefits to the company—instead seeking to channel its contributions to the most urgent needs in communities where it operates.

Acquisitions and Restructuring

As AES has acquired facilities around the globe, it has frequently faced the challenge of restructuring plant and company workforces to improve profitability. Here, again, AES's moral commitments have shaped its approach. Although the company favors lean staffing, it has tried to avoid the kinds of mass firings that have accompanied many privatizations and instead to handle downsizing in more humane and dignified ways. Even though each case is unique, restructing has typically been dealt with using a high degree of openness about staffing and profitability requirements, intensive education and communication about the unfolding situation, involvement of local plant and union personnel in developing new staffing plans, and generous voluntary termination packages.

Besides garnering goodwill, this approach has even helped AES win some bidding contests, such as a bid to purchase a Hungarian utility in 1996, The utility's four facilities were heavily overstaffed, and government officials, though eager for privatization, were concerned about the social costs involved in halving the workforce, especially given the high rates of unemployment in the surrounding area. To address their concerns, AES hosted "study visits" to a previously restructured plant in Northern Ireland. There, the Hungarian officials spoke directly with the plant manager and others to learn what AES had done and how it had worked. The AES project team also launched preliminary discussions with plant and union personnel at the Hungarian facilities, and then put together a comprehensive plan tailored to the Hungarian situation and informed by the downsizing experiences at other AES plants.

As part of its voluntary termination package, AES proposed, among other things, to provide funds for retraining and relocating workers to areas with higher employment, to create opportunities in spin-off businesses, and to establish a venture capital pool to fund departing employees' ideas for self-employment. AES's bid trumped its competitor's, which was estimated to be some 30 percent higher but lacked any plan to address the social impact of restructuring. Although AES's social commitments added costs to its proposal, the government appeared satisfied that AES's total package of financial and social terms was the better option. The plan, moreover, was so successful in achieving its staffing targets that in some departments the severance program was oversubscribed.[41]

Category Confusion

As noted earlier, AES's enterprise model is still evolving. In the wake of financial difficulties that began to present themselves in 2001, the company launched a review of its operations to identify ways to improve its economic performance, strengthen its values, and tighten its accountability mechanisms. But perhaps the description above is adequate to suggest how a company might align its guidance systems with the new performance standard. In AES, we see a company that is seeking to merge social and financial imperatives into a workable business model that performs for all its constituencies. And we see what it might mean to tap into people's moral capabilities along with their technical skills and intellectual competencies. At each step of the way, people would be encouraged to consider value factors as well as technical factors while helping the company carry out its purpose in a way that satisfies responsibilities to investors, customers, employees, and communities.

I have noted that many companies have responded to their constituencies' changing expectations in a piecemeal way by adding one program after another—an ethics program, an environmental initiative, diversity initiative, a quality initiative, a legal compliance program, a community involvement initiative, an empowerment initiative, and maybe even a values initiative, too—as each concern has arisen. Unfortunately, the net result of all this activity is often little more than initiative-fatigue and confusion—or cynicism. Despite the best efforts of hard-working staff, these programs remain detached from one another and from the lifeblood of the organization. They are like the add-on orbits concocted by Ptolemy, the second-century astronomer, in order to explain away the inadequacies of his earth-centered cosmology. Each program has its own internal logic and rationale, but its relation to the others and to the underlying system remains obscure.

A company like AES suggests the possibility of a very different and much simpler approach. AES has no ethics program, no environmental initiative, no empowerment program, no diversity initiative, no community involvement initiative. It's not that AES considers these issues unimportant. Quite the opposite. But instead of being pursued through a series of discrete programs, these concerns are embedded in the company's basic management systems and processes. They are integral to its day-to-day activities and outlook. Rather than epicycles of ethical concern welded onto a morally indifferent engine of commerce, they are a natural and logical expression of the premises on which the company is based.

Starting from the moral-actor premise makes all the difference. Like the Copernican shift from an earth-centered model of the universe to a sun-centered one, the shift from amoral mechanism to moral actor simplifies and makes intelligible what was previously complex and puzzling. Trust, fair employment, environmental responsibility, human dignity, corporate citizenship—to anyone who thinks of a company as an amoral mechanism for carrying out economic activities, these can only seem to be irrelevant distractions. Strictly speaking, inanimate "mechanisms" cannot have such concerns. For that matter, they can't have values, commitments, or responsibilities either, since these are currencies used only among moral beings. However, if we accept that companies are moral actors, the picture changes. Instead of being irrelevancies thrust onto managers by other parties, issues such as trust, responsibility, and the like become an inherent part of management's job.

To acknowledge that a company is a moral actor is not to deny its economic functions. If anything, by transforming these *functions* into *responsibilities*, the moral-actor standard renders them weightier and more important than they would otherwise be. To frame economic functions as economic responsibilities is to make clear that managers are accountable for and must answer for their economic performance. At the same time, though, the moral-actor standard sets companies' economic responsibilities in the context of their other responsibilities as moral actors and members of society. In a company designed to this standard, we would expect to see these responsibilities attended to in the board room, in the executive suite, and in the company's day-to-day operations.

For all their talk about values, however, many companies have yet to internalize this simple, yet fundamental idea. While espousing values and issuing ethical codes, their managers nonetheless operate on the premise that a company is essentially amoral. This premise is deeply embedded in the psyches of their managers, who tend to think of systems, processes, and structures as ethically inert or value neutral. Unwittingly, they promulgate high-minded codes of conduct and values statements alongside pay schemes and performance metrics that virtually assure these ethical commitments will be ignored.

Seeking to understand this discrepancy, I have sometimes asked executives what their compensation experts have told them about the ethics of various pay schemes. So far, I have yet to find a single executive whose compensation adviser has discussed this matter. To some, the question itself is puzzling. Along the same lines, I once asked a group of about 50 corporate ethics officers to whom I was speaking whether they had participated in discussions of their company's compensation scheme. Only two or three hands went up.

Many people think of values as occupying the blank spaces surrounding a company's formal processes and systems. Or they imagine values as a special kind of management tool—like an audit system or information system, only somewhat more ethereal. Thus, they assume that they can implement a "value system" without disturbing any of their company's other systems or processes, or that they can address the question of "values" separately from the question of how the company is structured or its processes worked out. I've seen more than a few change initiatives designed in just this way—first comes structure, then come processes, and then, when everything else is in place, the company turns to values. But this logic is both backwards and highly impractical. Values should be the starting point, not the finishing touch.

Terms like "value system" make it easy enough to slide into this way of thinking. "Value system," "audit system," "compensation system"—"system" makes them all sound comparable. This view, however, reflects what is sometimes called a "category mistake"—treating things of fundamentally different types as if they were members of the same category.[42] Values are not a "management tool" or a special type of management system that runs parallel to a company's audit or compensation system. Nor are they bits of ethereal matter hovering in the space unoccupied by formal systems and structures. When we speak of company "values" and "value systems" we are talking about the beliefs, aims, and assumptions that undergird the enterprise and guide its management in developing strategies, structures, processes, and policies. They constitute an organizational "intrastructure" that gives a company its distinctive character and ethos—its moral personality.

Moreover, executives and entrepreneurs who are serious about the new performance standard cannot view "values implementation" as a task that they can delegate to others. In fact, it may be one of the few jobs that are both impossible to delegate and impossible to do alone. Whether by design or default, managers define and shape company values through virtually everything they do. At the same time, values implementation is something done by everyone in a company every day. If the aim is to build a company capable of meeting the new performance standard on a sustained basis, the approach must be comprehensive, management led, and oriented toward a moral center that recognizes both social and economic responsibilities.

By a moral center, I don't mean just a code of conduct or list of aphorisms inscribed on a Lucite plaque, but rather a set of answers to the fundamental questions every moral actor, whether an individual or a company, must come to terms with. For companies, the questions can be framed around four main themes:

- **Purpose** What is the company's purpose? Besides creating wealth and using resources efficiently, what is the company's contribution to society? How do its products and services add value to people's lives?
- **Principles** What are the company's guiding principles? What precepts guide the conduct of its people in carrying out its purpose? What are its nonnegotiable standards? Its ideals and aspirations?
- **People** What is the company's concept of the person? Who counts as a member of its moral community? Whose interests are considered in its decision making?
- **Power** What is the scope of the company's power and authority? To whom and for what is the company accountable? How is decision-making authority to be allocated within the organization?

Busy executives sometimes dismiss questions like these as "philosophical," meaning "of no practical importance." As numerous examples have shown, however, a guiding philosophy is perhaps one of the most practical things a company can have. In the case of AES, for instance, we saw how a company's value system translated into a set of organizational strategies, structures, and processes aimed at building a company that was both profitable and socially responsible.

To what extent has AES succeeded in this endeavor? Without more complete information about the company's performance along both social and financial dimensions, an objective assessment is impossible. Moreover, the analysis is made more difficult by economic and social trends that boosted many companies' financial performance during the 1990s and then hammered their shares in 2001 and 2002. Nonetheless, during the period from 1992 through 2000, AES's first eight years as a public company, a number of indicators were quite positive. Company revenues grew at a rate of 42 percent compounded annually; earnings grew at a rate of 36 percent; and annual returns to shareholders averaged 38 percent. At the same time, AES consistently achieved safety levels above U.S. industry averages, emissions 40 percent to 60 percent below the levels allowable by law, and plant reliability rates above U.S. industry levels. The company has typically devoted some 4 percent to 5 percent of after-tax net income to civic activities, including matches for individual contributions and company-sponsored projects.

During this same period, however, AES also had its share of controversies and setbacks, including some ethical lapses such as environmental misreporting at an Oklahoma plant in 1992. An assistant plant manager discovered that employees in the water treatment area were diluting waste-water discharge samples and filing false discharge reports rather than seeking help to correct a water quality problem. The company promptly reported the matter to the Environmental Protection Agency (EPA), paid a fine, addressed the water quality issue, and strengthened environmental compliance training and oversight.[43] Another public controversy arose in California, where AES acquired three facilities in 1998. In 2000, the company found itself caught in the cross fire between environmentalists seeking cleaner air and water and energy regulators seeking to ameliorate an impending energy shortage. The state called on AES to step up electricity production, but doing so meant stretching the capacity of old boilers previously slated for refurbishment and thereby exceeding permissible emissions limits. The result was an embarrassing—for a company dedicated to environmentalism—$17 million fine.[44]

Until better measures are devised for assessing both aspects of corporate performance, evaluations will remain something of a hit-or-miss business. Based on my interactions with the company over the past decade, however, my guess is that AES would rate very highly in any objective assessment for this period. A telling indicator is the uncommon level of satisfaction AES people report deriving from their work. However, a credible judgment can only be based on a thorough review of the facts as they relate to the company's social and financial performance around the world. For that, more information would have to be culled and analyzed.

In the absence of its value system, would AES have done as well financially during the 1990s? It's hard to say. As we know, the company has never tried to justify its values on the basis of their economic benefits. And much of the company's financial success in the 1990s was due to the wealth of opportunities opened up by the worldwide movement to privatization. Another factor was AES's heavy reliance on nonrecourse project financing which enabled it to borrow heavily to finance its many ventures without risk to the parent company.

Nonetheless, some analysts think the value system was an important ingredient. When AES stock was approaching an all-time high in 2000, a Salomon Smith Barney analysis commented, "Some mock AES's corporate culture as hokey or forced. However, we believe . . . AES's dedication to its core values is a major driver of its success."[45] The report then detailed how AES management had fostered an "environment wherein its people are given unheard levels of responsibility and respect" and sketched out the ways in which the company's values had contributed to its financial performance. Like the findings discussed earlier in Chapter 2, the report noted the company's superior ability to handle risk; its high levels of productivity, innovation, and operating efficiency; its excellent environmental performance; its ability to grow with comparable ease; its excellent community relations; and so on. The analysts' financial bottom line: continued growth and stock performance.

As it turned out, the analysts were wrong about the last point, at least in the short term. In 2001, AES made several missteps and faced a series of difficulties related to currency weaknesses in South America, declining energy prices in the U.K. market, an ill-fated attempt to purchase a Venezuelan telecom company, as well as continuing controversy in California. That September, AES missed its earnings estimates for the first time since going public. The company's stock plummeted to 1998 levels. As with previous setbacks, AES reacted quickly and in accordance with its values. Vowing to refocus the business, 26 top managers voluntarily accepted salary reductions and agreed to take a large portion of their 2002 salary in the form of stock options. But in early 2002, as the aftershocks of Enron's collapse surged across the energy industry, AES stock suffered another blow. The company's shares slid even further, back to the lows of 1992. The company's stock was pummeled again in April 2002, when a short-lived coup temporarily unseated the Venezuelan government.

In June 2002, under pressure from investors, Bakke relinquished his role as CEO to Paul Hanrahan, a 15-year veteran of AES and one of its four chief operating officers. Bakke, who took a seat on the board chaired by

Sant, acknowledged his responsibility as CEO for the previous year's terrible economic performance and underscored the need for new leadership. Shortly thereafter, AES informed the World Bank that it had discovered evidence of past corruption by its prime contractor on a controversial power project in Uganda, thus indefinitely postponing further action on the project. The Bank had already approved $175 million of financing and was about to approve another $195 million in risk guarantees. In announcing the delay, AES officials stated that "the company will proceed only when it is completely satisfied that all aspects of the project fully comply with all legal and ethical standards."[46]

Some might say that, under these circumstances, AES should set its values aside and forget about its ethical commitments. This would be like telling Johnson & Johnson to abandon its credo during the Tylenol crisis. Only in hindsight did the Tylenol episode come to symbolize organizational strength and resilience. At the time, the prospects for recovery appeared bleak indeed. The public had stopped buying Tylenol products, and experts were predicting the brand's demise. No one knew how the capsules had been adulterated or who, in the end, might be shown to be responsible. Inside the company, as Johnson & Johnson CEO Jim Burke would later recall, "we were all scared to death." But thanks in large measure to a deeply embedded value system, the company weathered the storm and emerged as an even stronger organization.

Several years ago, Jim Burke visited Harvard Business School to talk to MBA students about the Tylenol crisis. In the course of his discussion, and almost incidentally, he offered yet another reason why values are crucial for leading companies today. "Without a moral center," he told the students, "you can swim in chaos." If a moral framework is vital for superior performance when conditions are benign, it is even more essential in times of turbulence and stress.[47]

8

A Compass for Decision Making

The previous chapter explored the implications of the new performance standard for organizational design. There we saw how ethical considerations might be woven into an organization's functioning through the design of its guiding systems for planning, execution, and performance assessment.

At the end of the day, however, a company's success in meeting the new standard comes down to the quality of its decision making. A company's incentives, information systems, and performance measures may be impeccably designed, and its business principles, codes of conduct, and values statements beautifully articulated—but if its people do not actually bring a moral perspective to bear in their thinking and decision making, these efforts will count for little.

Consider again the Bridgestone/Firestone example. There's no question that faulty information flows contributed to the tread separation crisis, as did the lack of consistent quality and safety standards around the globe. But the testimony of executives who appeared at congressional hearings held in the aftermath of the recall revealed something even more fundamental. At one point in the proceedings, a member of the hearing subcommittee began to probe why BFS had not acted sooner and, citing the company's own 1997 data on the rising costs of tread separation claims, eventually asked BFS executive vice president Gary Crigger how the claims data had actually been used. The committee member, clearly frustrated by Crigger's vague reference to its being used in "an accounting sense," tersely interrupted, "So you looked at it from a financial point of view but not a consumer safety point of view?" Crigger replied, "I'm sorry to say that I believe that is the case."[1]

A similar failure to engage the moral perspective appears to have been a factor at Enron. In an August 2001 letter to the company's chairman and

CEO Kenneth Lay, an employee concerned about the company's accounting practices noted that "it sure looks to the layman on the street that we are hiding losses." But the lawyers appointed to investigate the matter concluded that the company's accounting methods were not "inappropriate from a technical standpoint." Although they acknowledged that certain transactions could "be portrayed very poorly if subjected to a *Wall Street Journal* exposé," the lawyers nonetheless found nothing "that was not reasonable from Enron's standpoint or that was contrary to Enron's best interests."[2]

In the coming years, the level of moral scrutiny given to corporate behavior by employees, customers, investors, communities, and governments is only likely to increase. Even as pressures for financial performance continue to mount, companies will also be expected to operate within a moral framework given the evolutionary path we have charted and the needs of the world's people. Inside companies, this trend means that individuals and groups at every level—frontline employees, functional managers, business unit managers, executive leaders, boards of directors—must become more sensitive to the moral aspects of their dealings with one another and with external parties. They will need to become more skilled at identifying ethical issues, engaging in moral deliberation, and making decisions that stand up to moral as well as financial tests of rationality.

As things now stand, moral analysis is rarely a defined part of management decision making, and ethical issues are generally managed by exception. To the extent that moral concerns have come into corporate decision making, they have typically taken the form of "smell tests," "sleep tests," and "newspaper tests": Does it smell okay? Will it keep me awake at night? How would it look on the front page of the newspaper? Like corporate strategy before the days of competitive analysis, moral assessment has been more a matter of instinct or gut feel than a considered and informed thought process.

Although instinct is an important guide to moral judgment—I would rarely advise anyone to ignore it—it is often incomplete, certainly inarticulate, and sometimes mistaken. Few people, even experienced managers of impeccable personal character, have such well-honed instincts that they can intuitively and single-handedly grasp the moral questions raised by a new product proposal or a financial restructuring plan, let alone form a sound judgment about them or a plan for addressing them. Furthermore, the moral questions at the frontiers of technology, where leading companies must increasingly operate, are dauntingly complex. Although instinct may work well enough for simple questions of right and wrong that arise in familiar situations, its reliability diminishes rapidly in novel or complex situations.

Nor is instinct much help when it comes to moral dilemmas—conflicts among values or competing responsibilities—or when members of a group have different moral instincts.

What's more, moral concerns are outside the purview of most common frameworks for management decision making. Just as a doctor using diagnostics for detecting cardiac problems might fail to see symptoms of breast cancer, a manager using the tools of competitive or financial analysis might easily fail to see important moral issues. Thus, a proposal may pass rate-of-return hurdles and competitive analysis screens while at the same time failing even basic moral tests. In fact, crucial issues may not even come to management's attention until after a moral challenge has been issued—and at that point it may be too late for an effective response.

What's needed is a method for integrating the moral point of view into the management decision process. A structured process for identifying and evaluating moral concerns can correct for the blind spots inherent in many conventional frameworks and help decision makers more effectively link the values they espouse with the choices they actually make. In this chapter, I will suggest such a process based on a framework that has grown out of my teaching and research. This framework is not a moral algorithm or a theory of right action so much as a prompt to focus managers' attention on the moral aspects of their decision making.[3]

Ask, Don't Tell

This framework exploits the power of questions to engage people's moral faculties. For many, the idea of ethics is strongly associated with codes of conduct, values statements, or lists of moral imperatives. Certainly, history has given us a long tradition of such "to do" and "not to do" lists as sources of moral guidance. However, another classic approach to moral insight has less to do with answers and more to do with the kinds of questioning and discussion used by two of the great practical moralists of all times—Socrates in ancient Greece and Confucius in ancient China. These thinkers sought to guide behavior not by issuing directives but by engaging their listeners in a collaborative process of discussion and deliberation. Socrates, in particular, relied on an incisive process of questioning and probing that came to bear his name—the "Socratic method." Confucius depended more on illustrative examples and stories to bring out important points, but again in the context of discussion and mutual exploration.

These masters knew that moral insight is more apt to come from live interchange among informed and inquiring minds than from lists of abstract principles. Or put differently, principles and codes are nothing until brought to life in the context of human activity. Anyone who's looked at a typical code of conduct or statement of business principles knows how hard such documents are to read, let alone understand and retain. It's only when they are connected with actual concerns in the context of real situations that they engage the mind and the will. Codes and principles are neither self-applying nor self-interpreting. In the end, they derive whatever force they have from people's decisions to follow them, and they must be interpreted in light of facts and circumstances that themselves may be open to interpretation.

Few decisions of substance have only one moral aspect. More often, two or more important values conflict, as when a duty of confidentiality to one party conflicts with a duty of candor to another. Often a course of action that meets the needs of one group will create hardship for another. Codes, values statements, and the like help to identify and frame the issues in such cases, but they cannot resolve moral conflicts or create a practical path of action. For that, the only answer is informed judgment based on thoughtful consideration of competing claims and differing perspectives. Working through a situation to arrive at a reasonable course of action calls for imagination as much as analysis and may even require in-depth research. Given the inherent variability of circumstances, a set of questions is likely to prove far more useful than a set of prepackaged answers.

The power of questions can be seen in many management activities. Consider strategy formulation. A company's strategy is not dictated by a set of abstract principles, useful though such principles may be. Formulating a sound strategy requires a careful process of analysis that takes into account a number of potentially competing considerations. Reasonable people can and do disagree; they bring to the process different facts, different interpretations of the facts, and different beliefs about the likely future, as well as different aims and priorities. It is by sifting through the relevant considerations, deliberating about the merits of available alternatives, and imagining likely futures that decision makers arrive at what looks to be the most promising course. Of course, solutions sometimes come in a flash, but they more typically emerge through a shared process of thought that can be aided with a structured set of questions and analytic techniques: What opportunities are presented? What are our capabilities? Who are our existing and potential competitors? And so on.

Another example: When managers evaluate a potential investment or proposed new product from an economic point of view, they do so with certain characteristic questions in mind. How big is the market? How attractive are the profit margins? How much investment is required? What's the likely return on this investment? How long will it take to realize this return? And so on. Any serious project proposal will address such questions even before they are asked because the proponent knows that sooner or later they will be. Only by answering the whole set of such questions is it possible to determine whether the proposal makes any economic sense. Even so, it may be difficult to form a sound judgment without some experience base.

Business neophytes usually have to learn these questions—through the experience of being asked and perhaps not having answers, or through formal training, although formal training will decay quickly unless put to use on the job. At first, learners may have to work through the questions somewhat laboriously by following a detailed checklist of important considerations. But eventually the questions become internalized as "second nature," the need to answer them becomes ingrained, and answers are sought more or less by instinct. In simple, recurrent situations, even the answers themselves may be instinctual, but more complex cases that involve high stakes will usually require thorough analysis based on in-depth research. Here, again, a structured process can be helpful.

What questions, then, might help to inject the moral point of view into decision making?

The core question of ethics, the question at the root of the discipline, is the classic, "How should we live?"[4] Although this overarching question—perhaps mankind's most fundamental—might seem a bit unwieldy for our purposes, it quickly unfolds into several subsidiary questions that look and feel more manageable: "What should we aim for?" "How should we conduct ourselves?" "What do we owe others?" "What rights do we have?"

Such subsidiary questions, each of which can be broken down further into subcomponents, suggest four modes of moral analysis that can be quite useful in making decisions. Each mode is associated with a distinctive form of practical reasoning and a tradition of ethical thought whose motivating concerns are directly related to the four themes presented at the end of Chapter 7. Let me provide a thumbnail sketch of the four modes before showing how they might be used in a corporate decision context.

Purpose—Will This Action Serve a Worthwhile Purpose?

This mode of analysis has to do with the ethics of ends and means, or "pragmatic analysis." "Pragmatic" is sometimes used to mean "expedient rather than moral," but I am using the term in its more general sense to mean "goal-directed" or "purposeful." Pragmatic analysis examines the quality of our goals and the suitability of the means we choose for attaining them.

This mode of analysis thus calls for clarity about both ends and means, but the ends must be judged worthwhile and the means found to be effective as well as efficient.[5]

The central question is whether a proposed course of action will serve a worthwhile purpose. But an answer to this question will normally require answers to a cluster of subsidiary questions calling for facts as well as judgment:

- What are we trying to accomplish? What are our short- and long-term goals?
- Are these goals worthwhile? How do they contribute to people's lives?
- Will the course of action we're considering contribute to achieving these goals?
- Compared to the possible alternatives, how effectively and efficiently will it do so?
- If this is not the most effective and efficient course, do we have a sound basis for pursuing the proposed path?

Principle—Is This Action Consistent with Relevant Principles?

A second mode of analysis examines actions from the standpoint of applicable principles and standards. Its roots lie in the ethics of duty and ideals. Let's call it "normative analysis" since it references various norms of behavior, those entailed by self-imposed ideals and aspirations as well as those found in bodies of standards such as law, industry codes, company codes, and the emerging body of generally accepted ethical principles for business. In contrast to pragmatic analysis, which uses instrumental or means-end reasoning, normative analysis relies on reasoning from general principles to specific instances—what has sometimes been called "formal reasoning."

The central question is whether a proposed course of action is consistent with the relevant principles. Among these may be principles that express duties or obligations whose fulfillment is required as well as principles that express ideals or voluntary standards associated with good practice. Normative analysis involves subsidiary questions such as:

- What norms of conduct are relevant to this situation—including those found in law, customary practice, industry codes, company guidelines, or the emerging body of generally accepted ethical principles?
- What are our duties under these standards?
- What are best practices under these standards?
- Does the proposed action honor the applicable standards?

- If not, do we have a sound basis for departing from those standards?
- Is the proposed action consistent with our own espoused standards and ideals?

People—Does This Action Respect the Legitimate Claims of the People Likely to Be Affected?

A third mode of analysis focuses on the expected consequences of a proposed course of action for the people likely to be affected by it. Will they be injured? Will they benefit? Will their rights be violated or infringed? This mode of analysis is sometimes called "stakeholder analysis" or "stakeholder impact analysis" because it takes the vantage point of those with a stake in the outcome. The central question is whether a proposed course of action respects the legitimate claims of the parties affected by it.[6]

Stakeholder analysis is useful for identifying opportunities to mitigate harms as well as to pursue mutual gains. Skill in social reasoning is essential for carrying out this kind of analysis, since understanding others' perspectives and circumstances is the starting point for evaluating their concerns, interests, and expectations. However, formal reasoning is also involved insofar as norms play a role in assessing the claims presented. Key questions in stakeholder analysis include:

- Who is likely to be affected, both directly and indirectly, by the proposed action?
- How will these parties be affected?
- What are these parties' rights, interests, expectations, and concerns as derived from law, agreement, custom, past practice, explicit norms, or other sources?
- Does our plan respect the legitimate claims of the affected parties?
- If not, what are we doing to compensate for this infringement?
- Have we mitigated unnecessary harms?
- Are there alternatives that would be less harmful or more beneficial on balance?
- Have we taken full advantage of opportunities for mutual benefit?

Power—Do We Have the Power to Take This Action?

A fourth mode of analysis stems from the ethics of power. In a sense, this is the most fundamental question because it concerns the actor's authority and ability to act. Unless a proposed action is within the scope of the actor's legitimate authority and unless the actor actually has the ability—the skills, resources, clout, energy—to carry out the proposed plan, all the previous questions are moot. Following the ancient dictum that "ought implies can," this analysis might be termed a "capacities" or "wherewithal" analysis. It examines both the actor's moral right and his material resources to act. From this perspective, then, the central question is whether the proposed action is within the actor's legitimate power. This question leads to the following subsidiary inquiries:

- What is the scope of our legitimate authority in view of relevant laws, agreements, understandings, and stakeholder expectations?
- Are we within our rights to pursue the proposed course of action?
- If not, have we secured the necessary approvals or consent from the relevant authorities?
- Do we have the resources, including knowledge and skills as well as tangible resources, required to carry out the proposed action?
- If not, do we have the ability to marshal the needed resources?

These questions are not a set of moral precepts or standards of behavior in any conventional sense but rather a set of analytical frames or moral "lenses." Each lens is associated with a characteristic cluster of questions that can help managers "see" more clearly ethical issues that an economic perspective might obscure or relegate to the background. Like the varied lenses used by a photographer, each one brings into focus different features of the situation so that they can be more readily inspected and compared with other features. Of course, the aim here is not just to identify these features but also to evaluate their importance and then to address them, perhaps by modifying a plan or taking further action if that's what the situation calls for.

The importance of "merely" recognizing an issue, however, should not be underestimated. The long tradition of corporate amorality has meant that many managers are habituated to a kind of moral disengagement at work and can find themselves in an ethical minefield without even realizing it. Many leaders of corporate ethics programs say that the vast majority of the problems they must deal with originate with decision makers who simply didn't see the issues, or didn't see them early enough. Think about the Bridgestone/Firestone executives who looked at the increase in claims only from a financial point of view and not from a consumer safety point of view. Researchers have documented among managers a phenomenon they have called "moral muteness," or the inability to engage with or speak about moral questions in the workplace.[7]

From time to time I have experienced the symptoms of this phenomenon. A few years back, in connection with an ethics seminar I agreed to present for a company's leadership development program, I was to spend a day at corporate headquarters interviewing key executives to identify any special issues or concerns the seminar should cover. I was stunned when my agenda for the day indicated that each interview was set for only 20 minutes. When I asked about the time slots, the coordinating manager explained that he'd set up short meetings because he couldn't imagine what people would talk about in a longer period. (In the end, the company decided to forgo the background interviews and instead asked me to present a general seminar addressing issues in the industry.)

On the other hand, I have also found it quite easy to engage managers in discussing moral concerns. If asked the right questions in the right way, most managers have plenty to say on the topic, and many welcome an opportunity for thoughtful discussion of issues they don't normally talk about at work. In the classroom, I have found that the course of discussion can be radically altered by asking a simple question such as, "What would be the most responsible thing to do here?" or "Are there any ethical issues here?" or "We've got a pretty good plan of action. Do you think this would be the right thing to do?" Even such broad general questions can open up a field of exploration that otherwise might never come up.

The lenses in this framework, however, go beyond simply identifying issues. Each lens suggests an overarching criterion of evaluation—contribution to a worthwhile purpose, consistency with governing principles, respect for the claims of others, and consistency with legitimate authority. While leaving much to interpretation, these lenses nonetheless highlight the central ethical questions that managers are likely to encounter and provide a basis for robust consideration of these issues in a decision-making context. The framework is most useful in the context of a fully developed company philosophy along the lines sketched in Chapter 7, where decision makers have clear touchstones for each set of questions: the company's purpose, its guiding principles, its key stakeholders, and how its power structure works.

Notice that the lenses are not independent of one another. Rather than offering mutually exclusive and unique perspectives, they present a series of related but different angles for viewing and sizing up issues. Take, for instance, a simple question such as whether to disclose a workplace hazard to employees. A normative analysis might reveal an obligation to disclose, based perhaps on law or company standards. A stakeholder analysis would focus on employees' right to know. Because rights and duties often mirror one another, we are in effect looking at two sides of the same coin in this case. In a sense, the lenses provide a 360-degree moral assessment tool.

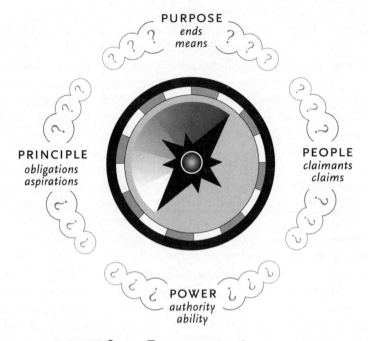

FIGURE 8-1   THE MANAGER'S COMPASS

These four lenses, taken together, create the metaphorical "manager's compass" shown in Figure 8-1. Unlike a code of conduct that offers specific directives, the manager's compass is more of a navigational device designed to help chart a reasonable course through what can sometimes be a sea of conflicting demands. Unlike a magnetic compass or gyrocompass, this metaphorical compass is not oriented to any one direction, nor does it function independently of its user. Rather, it can be thought of as an orienting device or a tool for determining an appropriate direction.

The process of working through the questions associated with each cardinal point can do more than simply help decision makers to avoid gaffes and missteps. It can also spark creative thinking and help them to refine and strengthen proposed plans of action. The sequence in which the perspectives are considered is unimportant. In some cases, it will be necessary to revisit each one several times to forge a satisfactory proposal. In others, the analysis may elicit only one or two main issues. What's important is that the thought process include each perspective. Ideally, a chosen course of action will in the end satisfy all four criteria.

Putting the Compass to Work

To see how this framework can work in practice, consider the experience of Lotus Development Corp. and Equifax, Inc., two U.S. information companies that teamed up in the early 1990s to introduce an innovative new software product for small businesses. At the time, Lotus was a premier software developer known widely for its spreadsheet program, Lotus 1-2-3. Equifax was one of the three leading U.S. consumer credit bureaus and top ranked among *Fortune's* 100 diversified service companies for the previous decade. Both companies saw themselves as technology leaders committed to responsible information practices. Still, after three years of development work, they ended up having to cancel plans to ship the new product.[8]

Arguably, this outcome could have been avoided had the executives in charge of evaluating proposals for new products asked the questions suggested by our framework. Indeed, Equifax executives later said that this experience taught them the importance of considering the ethical issues early in the product development process.

Both parties had been enthusiastic about their joint undertaking. For Lotus, which had just been surpassed by Microsoft as the market leader in personal computer software, the venture represented an opportunity to extend its product offerings and reduce its reliance on 1-2-3. For 90-year-old Equifax, an alliance with a young, fast-paced company like Lotus meshed well with its goal of transforming itself into an information leader. With this aim in mind, Equifax executives had launched a number of initiatives to establish effective standards for responsible information handling. These included bringing in a leading privacy expert to audit its information practices, publishing its own statement of fair information practices, and commissioning a national study of consumer attitudes on information privacy.

The new product idea was in many ways brilliant. Called Lotus Marketplace: Households, it was a compact disc (CD) database and software package conceived of as part of a family of tools designed to help small businesses target potential customers. Small businesses would be able to draw from a database of information on 80 million U.S. households—out of some 93 million households in total—to do market analyses and generate targeted mailing lists from their desktop computers. Rather than having to buy one-time mailing lists from list brokers at the then-going rate of 8 cents per name, small businesses would purchase a set number of names and records, which they would then own and use as frequently as desired. The cost for an initial purchase of 5000 names and records, selected to meet the purchasers' specified criteria, was $695.

In making their initial selection of names, purchasers could create customized lists of prospects using a series of data fields that included name, address, age, gender, marital status, estimated household income, lifestyle (this field had 50 categories such as "inner-city singles," "accumulated wealth," etc.), and buying propensities for more than 100 specific products ranging from cloth diapers to luxury cars to frozen dinners. All the information on the CD was generated from data already gathered by Equifax for use in its credit reporting and marketing information businesses. The data came from a wide variety of sources, both public and private. Among the private-sector sources were banks and other credit grantors as well as companies such as mail-order retailers. Public sources included the U.S. Postal Service, voter registration records, drivers' license records, and census data.

For small businesses and nonprofit organizations, Marketplace promised a cost-effective way to compete with larger rivals who could afford to pay significant amounts for sophisticated market analyses and direct-mail marketing lists. In fact, Equifax had developed a growing business in selling mailing lists generated from its credit files. With Marketplace, small businesses would have equivalent capabilities at their fingertips. They would have the ability to analyze lists and sales territories, to print labels, and to export mailing lists and certain aggregate data into other software packages such as word processing, presentation, and database management software.

For both Lotus and Equifax, Marketplace looked like a real winner. As an incremental business that relied on already-gathered data, it offered attractive profit margins estimated by some analysts to be in the neighborhood of 40 percent. As the first product of its type, Marketplace enjoyed certain first-mover advantages, including a clear field for reaching both the estimated 5.2 million small businesses in the United States at the time and the almost 80,000 nonprofit organizations nationwide with revenues over $100,000. Even if the two companies captured only a small segment of this potential market, significant improvements in their respective bottom lines could result. Although, given the product's revolutionary nature, a payback timetable was hard to predict, everyone involved was optimistic about its ultimate success and confident that the resources and three years of effort by the 40 people on the project would prove to have been well spent.

But this optimism began to fade almost immediately after Lotus and Equifax announced the new product to the public in April 1990. Instead of accolades for the cutting-edge venture, the announcement prompted a barrage of concerns and criticisms. One strain of criticism had to do with the data subjects—the people whose names and records would be included on the CD. Had they consented to having their incomes, lifestyles, and buying habits made available to the world? By what mechanism could they have their names removed? Another criticism had to do with potential misuse of the product. Had any precautions been taken to prevent its falling into the hands of criminal elements who might, for instance, have a strong interest in identifying all the unmarried upper-income women living alone in affluent communities around the country? Then there were concerns about accuracy. By its very nature, the information included on the CD would become quickly outdated. How did the product's makers intend to guard against problems stemming from having so much misinformation in general circulation? Finally, there was the problem of data security. How strong were the built-in technical protections against possible data theft?

Lotus and Equifax arranged for a review of the Marketplace situation by the Direct Marketing Association, the trade group that represents mailing-list companies and users of mailing lists. The review team, which included the director of the association's ethics and consumer affairs committee, came back with three problems that for the most part echoed the concerns of the general public. The DMA group felt that data subjects needed a more effective way to opt out of inclusion on the CD and that a strict mechanism for screening buyers was called for. They also expressed concern about consumer perceptions and about how Lotus and Equifax planned to educate the public about Marketplace. For example, focus groups revealed that people mistakenly believed that the disc contained detailed records of the data subjects' actual purchases and payments, when in fact it included only general buying propensities inferred from the actual purchase records.

Based on the DMA group's findings, the Marketplace development team changed some product features and added more privacy controls to protect against data theft and product misuse. Data subjects would be able to remove their names by contacting either Lotus, Equifax, or the DMA and supplying their social security number. The companies also vowed to screen purchasers and to sell only to legitimate companies—no individuals—that would purchase Marketplace directly from Lotus. The purchase agreement was tightened, and buyers would agree not to use the data to generate mailings for misleading offers, pornographic materials, or speculative real estate investments. Moreover, Equifax invited consumers to contact its office of consumer affairs with their concerns and complaints.

However, the changes were too little and too late. By the summer of 1990, concerns about Marketplace were up for discussion on Capitol Hill and in the news media. Privacy advocates began a coordinated effort to oppose Marketplace on the grounds that it involved secondary use of personal information without the consent of the data subject. They also challenged the name-removal system as inadequate. After all, how would subjects even know that their names were included on the CD? How would they know how to contact the proposed name removal service? And would people's privacy concerns be assuaged by having to supply the company with their social security number? Critics continued to emphasize the risks of unauthorized use and misuse of freely available information about individual consumers. They aroused public fears by citing cautionary examples such as a then-recent attack on a Hollywood actress by an obsessed fan who had tracked down his victim by using information obtained through a casual inquiry at the California Department of Motor Vehicles.

By November 1990, some eight months after Marketplace had been announced to the public, Lotus had received nearly 30,000 communications opposing the product. One widely posted E-mail addressed to the company's CEO put it bluntly: "If you market this product, it is my sincere hope that you are sued by every person for whom your data is false, with the eventual result that your company goes bankrupt." Equifax, for its part, was growing concerned about how the controversy might damage its main business of credit reporting. Although representatives from both companies had met directly with several privacy groups and the Marketplace development team had made yet another round of adaptations to the product, the situation grew worse. As consumer opposition mobilized over the Internet or on public computer networks, bulletin boards, and conferences, the number of people asking to remove their names increased. Each removal cost the project another $1.[9]

Marketplace had been scheduled for shipment in spring 1991, but in December 1990 executives from both companies met to review their product strategy in light of the privacy and other ethical issues that remained unresolved. Though opinions on these issues differed, a consensus emerged that it would be impossible at that point to address the issues raised in a cost-effective manner. Too many people were asking to have their names removed from the disc. Even if further changes were made to the product, it would be difficult to cut through the misinformation and horror stories to educate the market about the improvements. In any case, the cost of a massive education effort would likely be prohibitive, given the speculative nature of the product. Finally, there were concerns that further controls would lessen the attractiveness of Marketplace to its intended users.

Lotus and Equifax decided to cancel their plans to begin shipping Marketplace. Later that year, Equifax discontinued sales of direct-mail marketing lists generated from its credit files. After the Marketplace controversy, executives at Equifax concluded that using credit data to generate such lists was inconsistent with the company's stance on social responsibility. The

Federal Trade Commission later agreed, as did a federal court when, a year or so later, it upheld an FTC order stopping Equifax competitor Trans Union from using credit data in this way.[10]

Looking back, we can clearly see how the manager's compass could well have helped avert this costly outcome. If the top managers at Lotus and Equifax had asked Marketplace's proponents the simple questions posed by the compass, many of the issues that eventually erupted would have surfaced early in the process. Perhaps Marketplace could have been designed differently from the beginning, perhaps it could have been marketed differently, perhaps the companies would have decided not to pursue it at all. At the very least, they might have been better prepared for the onslaught of criticism.

The issues surface first with the normative analysis. A review of the pertinent bodies of standards would have pointed to several principles that raised red flags concerning duties of fairness, accuracy, and confidentiality that should have been considered in the early stages of the product design. Although none of these principles alone is definitive, taken together they point strongly toward a duty to inform consumers of their inclusion in the database and to at least offer them an opportunity to have their names removed, if not to seek their explicit prior consent to inclusion. The relevant principles and bodies of standards included:

- Equifax's own statement of fair information practices, which included at least two, and arguably three, relevant principles. The company itself had declared that "every person has a right to know what information has been reported on him/her so that its accuracy can be assured, corrected or explained as needed in fairness to all involved." Also relevant were the company's statements on privacy, which asserted that "every person has a right to personal privacy consistent with the demands and requests he or she makes of business" and that "every person is entitled to have this privacy safeguarded through the secure storage and careful transmittal of information." Notice that Equifax's principles were stated in the form of individual rights and thus might also have arisen in the course of a stakeholder analysis assessing the claims of affected parties.
- The industry trade group's guidelines for ethical business practices, which included at least two relevant principles. First, the DMA's ethics handbook advised that customers whose data might be rented, sold, or exchanged for direct-marketing purposes should periodically be informed of this potential and that marketers should offer customers an opportunity to have their names deleted or suppressed on request.

The DMA further advised that mailing lists and selection criteria should not be based on information that consumers might reasonably expect to be kept confidential.

- The legal framework established by the U.S. Fair Credit Reporting Act, which invoked several ethical principles and laid out specific directives for the proper use of credit and other consumer information. The act called on credit bureaus to meet the information needs of commerce in a way that is "fair and equitable to the consumer, with regard to the confidentiality, accuracy, relevancy, and proper utilization of such information. . . ." Specifically, it required credit bureaus to seek consumers' written authorization to share information with any party other than one with a "legitimate business need for the information in connection with a business transaction involving the consumer." Had the team looked at legal developments in other jurisdictions, they would have found that the European Commission was then considering legislation to give data subjects control over sensitive personal information.[11]

- Consideration of what we have called "generally accepted ethical principles," which would have raised many of the same issues. In addition to questions of individual privacy, this situation also presents issues of basic trustworthiness. Arguably, information entrusted to Equifax for purposes of credit evaluation is covered by an implied agreement of confidentiality, either with the consumers who have sought credit or with the banks and other credit grantors who have extended it. In some instances, information might even have been covered by explicit confidentiality agreements. In either case, whether that information was protected explicitly or implicitly, using it to create Marketplace would appear to have violated the trust of many who gave information to their credit grantors assuming it would be held in confidence.

A stakeholder analysis would also have yielded valuable input into the process by directing the team's attention not only to the small business customers for whom the product was designed but also to other parties with important interests at stake. A useful way to identify potentially affected parties is by thinking in terms of tiers. Like the ripples from the proverbial pebble tossed into a pond, the effects of any action tend to diminish with time and distance. The greatest impact is likely to be felt by the parties closest at hand.

- The first tier, of parties with specific interests at stake and with whom the product's makers had a direct commercial relationship, would include credit grantors and other data sources as well as prospective customers, employees, and investors. These are sometimes called core constituencies or core stakeholders.

- A second tier, of parties with specific interests likely to be directly affected but with whom there is no direct commercial relationship, would include most prominently the data subjects, individual members of 80 million households, whose names and records were included in the database.

- A third tier, of parties with a general interest in the situation and some claim to authority in its handling, would encompass such groups as government regulators, industry self-regulation authorities, and the U.S. Congress, as well as other lawmaking and standard-setting bodies.

- Finally, a fourth tier, of parties with a general interest in the situation and special knowledge or expertise relating to it, would have included various public advocacy and nongovernmental organizations such as Computer Professionals for Corporate Responsibility and the ACLU Project on Privacy and Technology. Indeed, these two groups eventually spearheaded the campaign against Marketplace.

Through a process of identifying these parties and gaining an understanding of their interests and concerns, the Marketplace team would likely have had the benefit of early awareness of the emerging debate over "information privacy"—the U.S. term—or "data protection," as it is called in Europe. They would have learned that 64 percent of the American public had as early as 1978 expressed concern about threats to their personal privacy. The team would have had to face up to the claim being asserted in many forums that individuals should have a right to control the use of personal information generated by their activities, particularly the use of sensitive data concerning their health or finances. The team would certainly have had to confront increasing calls for a principle of "no secondary use without consent" to govern the use of this information.

A wherewithal or capacities analysis would have flagged many of these same issues. It would have prompted questions about the team's authority to use the data gleaned from the various public as well as private-sector sources Marketplace relied on. From this perspective, the question is whether the Marketplace team had a right to use this information, or was it, in a sense, trading in stolen property? Of course, the issue is still controversial in part because the system of rights that govern such information has yet to be clearly defined. As frequently happens, legal and ethical norms lag well behind our technological capabilities. The Marketplace team certainly had the technological ability to use the information Equifax had gathered and analyzed, but the authority to do so—and without paying for it or seeking the prior consent of the data subjects—was highly contested.

On the one hand, authorizing companies to buy, sell, and use such data freely would arguably make for greater efficiency, less "junk mail," and lower prices on consumer goods. In theory, companies would be able to target their marketing only to interested customers, thus reducing their marketing costs and their prices, while also saving customers the nuisance of dealing with unwanted solicitations. On the other, these benefits would unquestionably come at a cost to individuals' sense of privacy and security. That information is power can hardly be denied, and power can always be used for good or ill. A glance at the past provides a useful reminder of the vast potential for manipulation available to those who control information. Instances such as marketing high-priced credit to the financially distressed, pushing high-fat foods to the diet conscious, and purchasing the names of Jewish singles registered with a "confidential" dating service—all real reported examples—only scratch the surface of possibilities.[12]

Some measure of the ambivalence and perhaps confusion felt by many Americans regarding this trade-off is reflected in opinion surveys commissioned by Equifax and released at about the same time Marketplace was announced. This survey found that 79 percent of Americans were concerned about threats to personal privacy, up from the 64 percent in the 1978 survey mentioned earlier. However, when asked specifically about direct marketers' use of mailing lists based on consumer characteristics, responses varied dramatically depending on how the question was phrased. Asked whether it was a "good thing" or a "bad thing" that marketers could buy information about their consumer characteristics such as income level, residential area, or credit-card use, 69 percent thought it was a "bad thing," and 86 percent said they were somewhat or very concerned about it. On the other hand, 67 percent said it was "acceptable" for companies to buy names and addresses of people in certain age groups, estimated income groups, and residential areas with certain shopping patterns so they could target their mailings to those most likely to be interested in what they were selling. The percentage who found this practice acceptable rose to 88 percent if those who didn't want to receive mailings could have their names excluded from the lists.

These findings were not available to the Marketplace team in the early phases of its product development work. If they had been, perhaps the team would have noted this public ambivalence about the use of consumer data to create mailing lists in general and its skittishness about the buying and selling of individual credit-card data in particular. And, given the apparent importance to the public of being able to request removal from lists, the team might have tried to devise a more acceptable and workable option for removing data subjects.

In short, the analyses suggested by the manager's compass might have revealed that Lotus and Equifax were venturing into strong ethical cross-currents with their new product idea. And it might have helped the development team devise a product design and marketing strategy capable of negotiating those currents. Of course, we cannot know where the process would have led, but the analysis strongly suggests several promising avenues whose exploration would be unlikely in the absense of a framework like the manager's compass.

Correcting for Blind Spots

The Marketplace experience illustrates the value of a systematic process of moral analysis. Recall how attractive the product looked when we asked the standard questions: How big is the market? What's the likely demand? What's the profit potential? Viewed solely in terms of the usual economic categories—margins, competitive advantage, profit potential, learning opportunities, investment returns—the project was a strong positive. Once the ethical considerations were brought to light and factored into the picture, however, things looked much different. And, as a result, the economics changed as well. For example, to be realistic, the cost structure would have to include mechanisms for workable consent or name removal. It could no longer presume free access to the names and records included in the database.

Without a framework like the manager's compass to inject the moral point of view into their deliberations, decision makers are vulnerable to the blind spots and biases inherent in many commonly used frameworks. Competitive analysis, for instance, is a powerful aid in strategy formulation, but it does not ask managers to think about stakeholder impact, social contribution, or conformity with legal and ethical norms. Cost-benefit analysis is another such ubiquitous framework. Based on the sensible and obvious idea that the benefits of an action should exceed its costs, this methodology has many valid uses. But what is a benefit? And what is a cost? And for whom? Here difficulties can arise unless we are careful.

Although cost-benefit analysis might in theory do a reasonable job of accommodating ethical considerations, in practice it frequently fails to do so. Because the method tends to focus on *monetary* costs and benefits, gains and losses that are not readily priced can be easily overlooked. And because the emphasis is generally on costs and benefits *for the decision maker,* effects on other parties are not taken as seriously as they should be. Going back to an earlier example, IBM's alleged payoff to Banco Nación officials would have been perfectly reasonable for IBM from a cost-benefit perspective, even though seriously flawed from an ethical point of view.

Part of the difficulty lies in the method's insistence on monetizing all costs and benefits. Standard valuation and accounting techniques help little when it comes to costing out the loss of privacy associated with the unfettered gathering and exchange of consumer information in our previous example. And by what logic can we place a monetary value on moral injuries such as the loss of trust caused by dishonesty, the degradation of the personality caused by abusive work practices, or the heightened risk of cancer associated with a new product? These are just a few examples where cost-benefit analysis comes up wanting.

Economists and lawyers have tried to develop monetary equivalents for such injuries, particularly in the area of health and safety risks. To the non-economist, however, these efforts are less than convincing. From a moral point of view, for example, it is problematic to value the health of a male executive more than that of a young mother just because the executive has greater earning potential or would be willing to pay more to avoid injury. Yet, that is the effect when such measures are used to monetize injuries and risks to safety. The exercise is no more convincing on the benefit side. Heightened trust, personal growth, strengthened community—these have no obvious or convincing monetary equivalents to plug into the analysis.

An equally vexing problem is deciding what to count as a "cost" and what as a "benefit." In the absence of a moral framework, this simple categorization is not always so clear as one might think. An earthquake, for instance, produces human tragedy on a grand scale. At the same time, it can be a financial boon to engineers, builders, and construction finance companies.

In the summer of 2001, Philip Morris, the U.S.-based tobacco, beer, and food giant, was taken to task for a cost-benefit analysis in which cost savings to society from smokers' early deaths were counted as a "positive effect" of tobacco usage. The analysis, commissioned by company officials in the Czech Republic, was done in an attempt to counter claims that cigarette sales were a drain on the country's economy and to make the case against proposed excise tax increases. The study concluded that smoking yielded the Czech government a net gain of $147.1 million in 1999, largely because of savings on health care, pensions, and housing due to smokers' premature deaths.[13]

Public reaction was swift and to the moral point. Although the analysis apparently neglected to consider the costs and benefits of alternatives to tobacco usage, this technical limitation attracted little notice. What captured attention was the bizarre and seemingly callous decision to treat cost savings from premature deaths as a "benefit" of tobacco usage. If a government's first duty is to protect and promote the welfare of its citizens, then surely anything that brings about their premature death should be counted as a cost, not a benefit. In the wake of the outcry, Philip Morris's CEO acknowledged that funding the study "exhibited terrible judgment as well as a complete and unacceptable disregard of basic human values."[14]

He might have also noted that disregard for basic human values has been a recurrent problem with the cost-benefit method. Like many other decision guides used in business, cost-benefit analysis tends to blur distinctions that from a moral point of view are highly material. There's a world of difference, morally speaking, between cost savings that result from product-related deaths versus savings that result from product-related gains in efficiency. But this difference is easily lost if the focus is only on the amount of the savings. A similar point applies to other morally significant distinctions—between harms and wrongs, rights and interests, duties and desires.

Compare a company that harms competitors by improving its product with one that harms them with false claims of improvement. Even if the monetary loss to rivals is the same in the two cases, they merit very different moral assessments. The first company has caused harm but done nothing wrong. In fact, it has done just what it is supposed to do within a competitive system. The second, on the other hand, has both harmed its rivals and wronged them. It has also wronged its customers and society at large by offending against a basic principle of justice. The distinction between harms and wrongs is morally elemental. As former U.S. Supreme Court justice Oliver Wendell Holmes, Jr., once pointed out, even a dog knows the difference between being kicked and being tripped over.[15]

Equally basic is the distinction between rights and interests. Morally speaking, rights-based claims generally take priority over claims based only on interests or desires. Rights, it is sometimes said, "trump" interests. So, in a case of conflict, a consumer's right to the truth about a product's contents trumps a sales rep's interest in making more sales. An employee's right to the minimum wage trumps an employer's desire to lower costs. And, to return to the Marketplace example, if consumers have rights over certain types of personal information, then these rights trump companies' interests in unfettered access. Such priorities, however, are difficult to capture in a simple monetary calculus of costs and benefits.[16]

Interpersonal trade-offs between monetary and nonmonetary goods have been notoriously resistant to the traditional tools of economic analysis. Trying to compare, say, risks to your life with benefits to my bank balance is the ultimate in mixing "apples and oranges." Perhaps the best-known example of the problems inherent in such calculations dates back to the beleaguered Ford Pinto, a subcompact car introduced to the U.S. market in 1970. Designed to compete with the smaller Japanese cars increasingly popular with American motorists at the time, the Pinto was developed under a foreshortened time frame and within strict parameters—no more than 2000 pounds in weight and $2000 in cost.

The Pinto, however, seemed destined for trouble. With flawed pollution control equipment and a fuel system said to be particularly prone to damage, the Pinto soon became the center of controversy. An increase in small-car accident rates, including some spectacular fires involving Pintos, led government regulators to propose new regulations aimed at reducing the incidence of fuel-fed fires.[17]

Ford thought the regulations unnecessary and chose to oppose them on the basis of a cost-benefit analysis that put the costs of compliance well in excess of its benefits. Ford calculated that compliance with the proposed regulations, which could be met by installing an $11 safety valve on each vehicle, would cost the company some $137 million. However, this step would achieve benefits to consumers worth only $49 million—the estimated value of saving 180 lives, avoiding 180 serious burn cases, and preventing the loss of 2100 vehicles. Meanwhile, in addition to opposing the regulations, Ford did nothing about the Pinto's safety problems, on the grounds that evidence showed the Pinto to be no more hazardous than other subcompacts. Ford, we should note, was not alone in its enthusiasm for cost-benefit analysis or its conundrum over fuel-tank safety, for, as a 1999 *Wall Street Journal* story revealed 26 years after the fact, General Motors was doing similar calculations at the same time to determine the costs of fuel-fed fire-related fatalities.[18]

When Ford's cost-benefit analysis later came to light, the company was criticized for what many called "putting a dollar value on life." In Ford's defense, its figure of $200,000 per life was the same one being used by the National Highway Traffic Safety Administration at the time—and the same one used by GM in some of its calculations. Setting aside the problem of monetizing the nonmonetizable—a problem, no doubt, but one we've already discussed—the Ford example shows up another blind spot in this type of analysis. The lives at stake were not just any lives taken by indiscriminate forces somewhere on the planet. At issue was Ford's own product, and in many cases, the lives and property of its own customers. But where is the customer's perspective? And what about Ford's relationship with buyers of its products?

Whatever claims injured parties might have had against Ford derived from a set of causal and social relationships. What we expect of others is shaped in large measure by the relationship we have with them and by the norms that govern relationships of that type. Yet such factors play no role in a standard cost-benefit analysis. Even though consumers should surely have been counted among the core stakeholders in this situation, with certain expectations and important rights at issue, their perspective was nowhere evident. The analysis, instead, purported to take an omniscient perspective that compared the costs to Ford with the benefits to society at large.

Consider what the result might have been if the analysis had been done from other perspectives. What might consumers have said if asked to compare the estimated $11-per-vehicle cost of the special safety valve with the reduced risk of a fiery death in an automobile accident? Or what if the analysis had been done from a purely Ford perspective, comparing the costs of compliance for Ford with the benefits of compliance for Ford?

Ford was eventually hit with class action suits by Pinto owners in two states as well as with a spate of wrongful death and personal injury claims. In one case, a California jury awarded the plaintiffs $125 million in punitive damages, in addition to actual damages, in a wrongful death action involving a fuel tank explosion. Though the amount was reduced to $3.5 million on appeal, the case prompted Ford to settle many of the pending legal claims. Meanwhile, government regulators made a formal finding of fuel system defects that led Ford to recall some 1.5 million Pintos for repair at an estimated cost of some $20 million. Pinto sales languished in the wake of these events and the negative publicity surrounding them.

Based on publicly available information, it's hard to say precisely how much the Pinto problems cost Ford in the end. But a retrospective cost-benefit analysis from Ford's perspective suggests that accepting the government's proposed safety regulations at the outset would probably have been a bargain, even at $137 million. We might note that in 1999 GM was ordered to pay $1.2 billion in punitive damages in a court case that involved an older vehicle with fuel tank problems similar to the Pinto's.[19]

For all its aura of objectivity and precision, cost-benefit analysis is highly vulnerable to distortions and biases that cloud the moral issues. Results can vary dramatically depending on what perspective is taken, what effects are included, and what economic values are attached to the components of the analysis. Much of the clouding is due to the illusion of precision that comes from monetizing expected outcomes. That we can "objectify" such moral goods as trust, community, or life itself by attaching monetary values to them is self-delusion of the highest order. We only compound the error by then calling ourselves rational for, say, trading off "consumer trust worth $500 million" for an increase of $800 million in shareholder value. What's needed is an analytical model that takes the claims of others seriously in their own right and that reveals, rather than obscures, the moral texture of the relationships within which every company must operate.

Some readers might question whether attention to stakeholder relationships really makes any difference. In this regard, it is worth coming back to the Scott Armstrong research on corporate decision making mentioned in Chapter 6. As readers may recall, groups were asked to play the role of board members for a hypothetical pharmaceutical company and, in this role, to decide what to do upon learning that one of their company's leading drugs was causing an estimated 14 to 22 unnecessary deaths annually and would likely be banned by regulators. Earlier, I described the discrepancy Armstrong found when he compared the decision made by most of these "boards" with the judgments made by individuals asked to evalute this decision. Another part of Armstrong's study sought to determine whether different types of boards would act differently when faced with this same scenario and, in particular, where there were differences between stockholder-oriented boards and stakeholder-oriented boards.[20]

Armstrong found a striking difference in how the two kinds of boards dealt with the scenario. Boards that had been instructed that their role was to maximize returns to stockholders were much more likely to recommend that the company continue marketing the drug and fight the proposed ban. About 76 percent of the 41 stockholder boards made this recommendation. In contrast, only 23 percent of 57 boards that had been instructed to consider the impact on stakeholders, including stockholders, customers, and employees, made this recommendation. These boards instead tended to recommend halting production, limiting drug promotions, or withdrawing the drug from the market and deferring to regulators' judgment on the ban. As these findings indicate, how corporate decision makers conceive of their role and what factors they consider in making decisions can have a profound influence on what they do.

Center-Driven Decision Making

For both moral and financial reasons, today's companies need a methodology for integrating the moral point of view into their decision making. Even those who aspire only to an "acceptable" level of performance need some way to test their decisions against basic norms of law and ethics early on rather than waiting for challenges and complaints to arise later. By bringing a moral perspective to bear in their decision-making processes, companies will also be better equipped to assess the economics of their choices.

As we have seen, the ethical and economic aspects of corporate decisions are often tightly and intricately interwoven. In Chapter 2, we discussed at length the causal mechanisms that link values with economic outcomes. In many cases, the ethical questions raised by a policy or strategy decision such as a financial restructuring or a change in pension policy, cannot be properly understood without a grasp of the economics involved. Conversely, the economic consequences cannot be understood unless the ethical dimensions are appreciated. Marketplace and the Ford Pinto case just discussed are good examples.

In a world that expects companies to create wealth while conducting themselves as moral actors, managers will need to practice what might be termed "center-driven" decision making. This term refers to the area of overlap between ethics and economics shown in the diagram already presented in Chapter 3 and depicted here in Figure 8-2. If managers are to target this area, which might be termed the "zone of acceptability," they will need skill in making decisions that stand up to the various forms of ethical analysis discussed here as well as the more familiar tests of financial attractiveness. Put simply, they will need to marry NPV (net present value) with MPV (moral point of view) analyses.

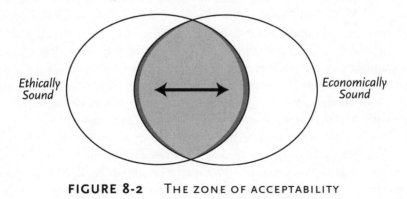

FIGURE 8-2   THE ZONE OF ACCEPTABILITY

This area of overlap might also be called the zone of "sustainability," as suggested by my colleague Tom Piper, since actions that fall outside it will often be unsustainable over the longer term. Activities outside the zone are apt to be challenged by injured parties, declared unlawful, or regulated out of existence on the one hand. Or they may be so resource intensive that they become financially infeasible on the other. As we saw in Chapter 3, the extent to which actions outside this zone are in fact sustainable has much to do with the social and institutional context in which they occur.

To locate this zone, managers cannot rely only on the tools and concepts of economic analysis. For all the reasons we have discussed, they will need a repertoire of ethical concepts and moral reasoning skills as well. This is where the manager's compass comes into play. Through the questions it poses, the compass provides a structured process for bringing the moral point of view to bear in making decisions and linking espoused values to actual choices.

Everyone knows companies whose professed values, as found in their mission statements, values statements, business principles, codes of conduct, credos, and the like, seem to have no bearing whatsoever on what they actually do. Recall the "never-been-read" Enron codes of conduct on offer through eBay after the company's collapse. Somehow espoused principle and actual practice fail to engage with one another. In the previous chapter, we saw how organizational design factors contribute to this disjunction. In this chapter, we have seen the role played by decision processes in companies whose tacit and explicit frameworks used for making decisions did not readily incorporate ethical considerations. Unless these decision frameworks can be opened up and made receptive, any attempt to instill values into the organization will most certainly fail.

Although the compass framework has grown out of my research and teaching, its deeper roots are found in various traditions of moral thought. Anyone familiar with these traditions will see traces of such philosophies as pragmatism, utilitarianism, liberalism, Confucianism, virtue ethics, and so on. To academic experts in these different schools of thought, this mixing of traditions and doctrines is heresy, but for practicing managers this mixing of traditions is a plus. By harnessing key insights from contending schools of thought, the compass provides a more powerful framework— one with diverse perspectives and built-in checks and balances.

The process of working through the different lenses is useful not only for identifying crucial issues, as in the Marketplace example, but also for mapping areas of disagreement, generating new options, and, perhaps most important, evaluating possible choices. Sometimes a judgment emerges quickly and easily. The analyses converge, and a course of action meets, or fails, all the implicit criteria. At other times, the process will raise more questions than it answers. It may elicit conflicting principles or contested claims of right, as in the Marketplace example. In those cases, further analysis or in-depth research may be required. When existing standards conflict or fail to cover the case at hand, extended deliberations may be needed to formulate a new principle or determine the best trade-off between competing values.

The work involved in using the framework, especially in complex cases, may dismay those who think that ethics should be easy. Executives who would never expect a lawyer or consultant to evaluate a proposed strategic move in a 10-minute conversation will often expect an ethics specialist to do just that. Yet ethical analysis, if done conscientiously, can be just as demanding as other, more familiar forms of evaluation.

Consider again the legendary Tylenol recall decision. Many people think of that decision as having sprung spontaneously from CEO Jim Burke's mind in a flash of goodness or genius. Others believe it was somehow dictated by the company's credo. What really happened was less romantic and less clear cut.

The decision, in fact, emerged over the course of several days as Johnson & Johnson engaged in extensive information gathering and deliberation about how best to respond to the situation. Market researchers and others sought information about the concerns of customers, regulators, and other affected parties. "We researched every act we made," recalled Burke. "In order to decide what to do, we wanted to know what impact it would have." Meanwhile, two independent teams were assigned the task of wrestling with the decisions presented by the crisis. Working in parallel, the two teams considered more than 150 possible scenarios before the executive group decided to withdraw Tylenol from the market.[21]

So what did the company credo have to do with it? The credo certainly did not ordain a recall in the event of product tampering. In fact, the credo said nothing at all about recalls. It simply outlined the company's responsibilities to its various stakeholders. But the role it played was crucial. Much like the manager's compass, it injected the moral point of view into the decision-making process and gave the decision makers a structured way to link the company's espoused values with its actions at a highly charged juncture in its history.

Of course, time does not always allow for in-depth analysis, and some cases *are* simple. We come back to the "newspaper tests," "smell tests," and "sleep tests," with which the chapter began. These and other moral rules of thumb—"reciprocity tests," "generality tests," "legacy tests," "mirror tests," and "trusted friend tests"—may be likened to the "quick ratios" and "acid tests" of financial analysis. They are no substitute for thorough assessment in complex cases, but they do serve a very useful function. Sometimes, they may be all one has to go on.

Looking back, some observers today wonder why the Tylenol decision created such a stir. Given that it turned out to have been so profitable for the company, they question the need to bring values into the explanation. In retrospect, the decision reads easily as a pure financial play. At the time, however, the financial impact was much less clear, and, as noted previously, many experts predicted that the Tylenol brand would not survive. "A flat prediction I'll make," said a leading marketing consultant, "is that you will not see the name Tylenol in any form within a year. . . . I don't think they can ever sell another product under that name." What those experts failed to anticipate was the public reaction to what was perceived as a deliberate act of corporate responsibility that was beautifully executed and skillfully followed up with a well-designed recovery plan.[22]

In a restless sea of moral and financial expectations, managers cannot navigate with financial perspectives alone. To meet the new financial, legal, and ethical accountabilities, companies will need to integrate the moral point of view into their decision making. The manager's compass is one framework for doing this. Undoubtedly there are others that could work just as well, or perhaps even better, so long as they raise the core questions highlighted in this chapter. Just as important as the framework is the care and rigor with which it is applied. What's essential is to have some way of engaging the moral perspective at the moment of decision. Otherwise, companies will find it very difficult to meet the new standard of perform-ance on a sustained basis.

9

The Center-Driven Company

The new standard of performance is likely to remain in effect for the foreseeable future. Whether we anticipate prosperity or recession, peace or war, it is hard to imagine the corporation's importance to society diminishing or its functions being transferred to other institutions. In the years ahead, we are thus likely to see continuing calls for companies to be more efficient and more profitable, and at the same time more responsive to their constituencies, more accountable for the impact of their activities, and more respectful of law and generally accepted ethical standards. In this environment, we can also expect many more companies to recognize the benefits of honoring human values and presenting a moral face to the world as they carry out their business.

The corporation is one of mankind's great inventions. It has enabled human beings to establish cooperative endeavors that overcome barriers of time and space while also reducing the costs that individuals acting alone would incur in organizing such efforts. Without the corporation, or some such comparable structure, complex enterprises of the scale and scope seen in the world today would be unimaginable. The corporation has been equally crucial in fostering entrepreneurial activity, technological innovation, and new businesses. It has created wealth and economic prosperity for many. In fact, the corporation's utility has made it the organizational form of choice for more and more people and purposes over time.

As its role has changed and expanded, however, the corporation itself has had to evolve. At various points in history, it has taken on new attributes that reflect society's changing ideas about what companies should do and how they should be managed. Some of these societal changes have necessitated only incremental modifications. Others, like the shift from corporate chartering to general incorporation statutes in the nineteenth century, have been revolutionary in their impact.

Today, the corporation is undergoing another revolutionary change. The moralization of the corporation represents a radical departure from the amoral, mechanistic conception that has dominated previous thinking. Like the legal changes that prompted the shift from charter-driven to finance-driven companies, the attribution of moral personality to the corporation necessitates fundamental changes in its internal structure and management.

This shift, in turn, has implications for corporate leadership. To build the organizational capabilities needed for success in the new era, companies will need leaders with the skills and commitments required to meld a high moral standard with outstanding financial results. They will need leaders with new ways of thinking about the tasks of management and the challenges that face companies today. A summary of the organization model that has emerged from the discussion so far will suggest what I mean.

Center-Driven Leadership

To integrate the ideas developed in the previous two chapters, we can say that many of today's companies will need to become more "center-driven" if they wish to thrive in the new era. The term "center-driven" recalls the earlier diagram of ethics and economics as partially intersecting sets and it signifies a mode of operating that recognizes both moral and financial imperatives as binding. At the center of the diagram is the area of overlap we have termed the zone of acceptability. It represents actions that are both morally and financially sound. Activities outside this zone may be feasible for a time, but they cannot be the basis of superior performance, and they will often be unsustainable over the longer term.

The center-driven company targets its efforts toward this central area. Its people bring a dual perspective to their decisions, which must pass tests of both ethical and economic rationality. Its guidance systems are aligned with the accountabilities that flow from these imperatives. Its dealings with parties inside and outside the organization reflect this distinctive ethos. Its performance measures track effectiveness in both social and financial terms. Its leaders recognize that corporate performance has moral as well as financial aspects and that the pursuit of excellence requires attention to both. And they hold themselves accountable for the company's performance along both dimensions.

Although few companies have as yet succeeded in wholly integrating a moral perspective into their operations, many have made minor adjustments in the form of the initiatives and add-on programs that we have discussed. Eventually, others are likely to realize that something more fundamental and comprehensive is required. Like Royal Dutch/Shell, for example, other companies will recognize a need to rethink their management systems from top to bottom and better align their business processes with the new accountabilities.[1]

The effort underway at Shell, initiated in the aftermath of the events described in Chapter 1, encompasses a multitrack, multiyear set of activities aimed at integrating social and environmental accountabilities into the company's operating systems. These activities, which began in 1998 and were mapped out through 2004 in Shell's performance report of 2000, are intended to lead the company to a fully unified approach that combines social, environmental, and economic excellence. Thus, the company is developing new management frameworks and decision tools, as well as setting new operating standards, modifying key business processes, identifying new performance measures, and extending the scope of its public reporting to include social and environmental as well as financial data each year.

Although thoroughly researched and carefully planned, Shell's effort is very much a matter of "learning by doing." It could hardly be otherwise. As one Shell executive observed, "We have 300 years of experience with financial accounting, 30 years with environmental accounting, and virtually none with social accounting." In 1996, however, Shell's executive team decided that the time had come to bring more attention and rigor to these previously neglected areas. When Shell's leaders looked at their research inside and outside the company and reviewed the state of public opinion worldwide, they saw sweeping changes in social attitudes toward multinational corporations. Trust in corporate judgment was diminishing, and concerns about the impact of corporate activities on society and the environment were growing. In what the team dubbed the emerging "show-me" world, companies like Shell would need to become far more open and far more attentive to the environmental and social aspects of their business. From these conclusions, it was only a short step to the organizational transformation effort launched in 1998.

Inspired by the concept of sustainable development, Shell's new organization and management model has been dubbed a "sustainability model." However, to the extent that it has the following attributes, Shell's model is an example of what I mean by a center-driven company:

- Its people are committed to excellence in both moral and financial terms.

- Its guidance systems are aligned with its financial and nonfinancial accountabilities.
- Its people use decision frameworks that integrate social and financial considerations.
- Its people assess its performance along both moral and financial dimensions.
- Its people engage with one another and with external parties as moral actors.
- The company as a whole displays the competencies expected of a moral actor.

In the previous two chapters, I sketched out what a center-driven company might look like in practice. Through various examples, I tried to show what it means to integrate the moral point of view into decision making and how a company might align its guidance systems with the accountabilities inherent in the moral-actor standard. Even if examples have put some flesh on the bones of these abstract ideas, it should be clear that the model is still evolving. We have many examples of companies that are turning to values and seeking to improve their performance relative to today's expectations, but we do not yet have tested templates for success or tested models for transitioning to the center-driven model.

It should also be clear that the model allows much room for variation. There is no one right way to build a center-driven company. Although all companies have certain standing constituency groups such as investors, employees, customers, and the community, their actual constituency profiles and the particular claims of each constituency vary widely from company to company and industry to industry. Different companies may organize themselves and their guidance systems quite differently while still achieving the necessary alignment with the new accountabilities. As discussed in Chapter 7, however, the approach needs to be comprehensive and responsibilities to each group attended to.

Given that the capacity for choice is the defining feature of a moral actor, we should also expect to find considerable variation in companies' moral personalities. Adherence to legal and generally accepted ethical standards leaves plenty of room for the distinctive aims and commitments that differentiate companies from one another. Within this broad framework, every company must choose a set of purposes and commitments that define its unique moral identity. The products and services it elects to offer are perhaps the most visible aspect of this identity. Through its offerings, a company conveys a sense of what it holds to be worthwhile and also reveals the level of care and effort its people bring to their work. But, as we have discussed, a company's moral personality is reflected in everything it does—how its people interact with one another, how they interact with others, the accountabilities to which they hold themselves, and the decisions they make on a daily basis.

Even though much work is yet to be done to develop the center-driven model more fully, one thing is quite clear from the organizational attributes sketched above. This new type of company will require a distinctive type of leadership and management. It will need leaders with a breadth of vision and a repertoire of skills that go well beyond the traditional tools of management and financial analysis.

Among other things, these leaders will need an appreciation for the role of business in the wider social system and a capacity to work with leaders from other sectors of society. Instead of the value-neutrality once cultivated as the hallmark of scientific management, they will need a mature moral sense as well as skill in making value judgments and reconciling conflicting responsibilities. They will need to know about different ethical systems and how they work. They will need insight into the whole human being and not just the abstraction known as "economic man." Above all, they will need an understanding of the corporation as a moral actor with financial and non-financial responsibilities to each of its constituencies and to the community at large.

In this book, we have already met many such individuals. Through positive efforts, often in difficult circumstances, the managers described here, and many others, are showing how center-driven leadership translates into concrete organizational strategies and actions. They are proving that a center-driven approach is not only workable but also a catalyst for innovative ideas. Even in such thorny areas as workforce restructuring, product safety, supply chain management, and corruption control, these individuals are showing that moral commitment backed with skill and intelligence can spark novel approaches to vexing problems.

Innovations in Workforce Restructuring

Consider first Marianne Nivert, innovator in workforce restructuring. In 1995, when she was head of human resources for Sweden's Telia Group, the Nordic region's leading provider of Internet and communications services was anticipating having to lay off some 5000 to 7000 employees in the coming three years. Not only was the former state-run telecom company heavily overstaffed, but also many employees lacked the skills needed to compete in a world of rapidly changing technologies and new customer demands. To remain at the forefront of the industry, which by then included more than 70 competitors, Telia would have to reduce its existing workforce substantially, while, at the same time, doing extensive recruiting for personnel with the needed expertise.

Recognizing the limitations of a traditional approach to restructuring and remembering the painful downsizing process the company had gone through in 1992 just before it was privatized, Nivert and her team came up with a novel proposal. Instead of taking the conventional path of laying off excess employees and hiring a new cohort of more highly skilled replacements, the company decided to experiment with a redeployment program that would help existing employees upgrade their skills for possible reemployment by Telia. Besides cushioning the negative social impact of restructuring, the program would enable the group to function more smoothly and without losing the valuable and company-specific knowledge possessed by these employees.

Under Nivert's leadership, a newly created redeployment team clarified its objectives and gained the cooperation of the trade unions. Telia agreed to forgo layoffs while the project was in progress and began working closely with the unions to provide training, vocational guidance, study grants, and business support to surplus employees. The team also developed a collection of redeployment "tools" that included partnerships with business units, employment agencies, and suppliers. Through these collaborations, the team helped employees to build new skills and find new positions both within and outside the Telia Group.

As a consequence of the redeployment program, about 2800 of the employees originally slated for redundancy were brought back into Telia and given new positions. The remainder either secured employment elsewhere, started their own businesses, went back to school, or retired. Fewer than 1.5 percent were given notice. Beyond these specific outcomes, the experiment generated a fundamentally new and more flexible approach to the experienced workforce. Instead of traditional early-retirement programs, longtime employees were offered guaranteed employment provided they would be willing to take temporary assignments and accept reduced salaries if they were not actually working. For many mature employees, such continued employment on a flexible basis was preferable to retiring and collecting a pension.

In the end, the redeployment effort worked not only to the benefit of the affected employees and the Swedish government but also to Telia itself. According to researchers at Stockholm University, the redeployment program saved the Swedish government an estimated $135 million and the affected employees some $85 million, while benefiting Telia to the tune of some $310 million. Moreover, 95 percent of the employees affected said they preferred the new approach to the traditional one. For its part, Telia also gained the competencies needed to address the environment of the late 1990s, the goodwill of some key constituencies, and greater flexibility in adapting to an ever-changing competitive landscape.[2]

Telia's example has inspired other companies to reexamine their ways of handling redundancies. Invited to discuss its restructuring project at the European Commission's 1998 meeting on labor market issues, Telia's redeployment group soon found itself inundated with queries from companies in other parts of Europe as well as Asia and South America, along with other Swedish organizations. Some have even taken Telia's approach as a model for their own efforts. Within Telia, meanwhile, the ideas that emerged with the initial redeployment project have continued to evolve as the company has had to further shrink its employee base. Nivert, by the way, was appointed Telia's CEO in 2001, following a stint as acting president and CEO.

Innovations in Managing Safety

Consider Bill Sells, innovator in risk management, whose experiences with the asbestos crisis at Colorado-based Manville Corp. (renamed Johns Manville in 1997) were discussed in Chapter 6. In 1986, as head of Manville's Fiber Glass Products Group, Sells was stunned to learn that scientists studying fiberglass safety had found a small, but statistically significant, excess in cancers at plants that produced glass wool, a type of fiberglass. When this finding was announced at a research conference in Europe, the study was only partially complete, and its authors cautioned that further work was needed to determine the factors associated with the risk. Nonetheless, the news was disturbing to researchers and fiberglass makers alike.[3]

Sells quickly mobilized his Manville colleagues who all agreed that the company was facing a crisis. Fiberglass had replaced asbestos as Manville's lead product following the product liability disaster that, as noted in Chapter 6, had led the company to declare bankruptcy four years earlier under the weight of $2 billion in legal claims. In 1986, fiberglass accounted for 42 percent of Manville's nearly $2 billion in sales and about 75 percent of its profits. Virtually everyone viewed fiberglass as the future of the struggling company. As the pressures and uncertainties surrounding fiberglass safety mounted, Sells wondered whether fiberglass was going to be the next asbestos. "The parallels were frightening," he recalled.

The executive team immediately began a series of intensive meetings that went on for several weeks as they brought in experts to review the scientific evidence and to assess the potential economic, legal, and social impacts that the new research would have on the company's leading division. They anticipated tremendous concern among all stakeholders—employees, unions, distributors, insurers, stockholders, and customers, not to mention government regulators and scientists who would now scrutinize fiberglass much more carefully. Still, management wasted no time in getting out word of the study. Within six hours of receiving the news, notices were posted on bulletin boards at headquarters and at every Manville plant in the world. The essential question the executive group would have to decide, however, was what to do in view of the news. On the table were options ranging from "do nothing" to "exit the fiberglass business."

As a result of their initial review process and subsequent additional rounds of meetings with a long list of interested parties, the executive team decided on an aggressive communications and relabeling campaign to disclose the potential cancer risk to employees, distributors, and customers and provide them with fiberglass safety information. Even though relabeling was not required by any law or regulation, team members were well aware that the International Agency for Research on Cancer, an agency of the World Health Organization, had classified fiberglass as a "possible" carcinogen, though not a "probable" one, based on studies of laboratory animals. Many of the company's lawyers, along with its competitors, advised against the campaign on the grounds that it might stir up unnecessary fear and repercussions that could lead to litigation and lost business. But the executive team concluded that it was best to meet the challenge head on. Team members had satisfied themselves that the product was safe, but they also believed that those exposed to fiberglass had a right to make their own decisions about fiberglass safety based on the available information. Should fiberglass be later proven to be carcinogenic, the company would also be protected both legally and ethically.

To reduce the risk of losing business, however, they came up with an innovative program to indemnify the company's customers against settlements, court judgments, and legal costs associated with any claims for fiberglass-related injuries that should arise from end-users. In other words, Manville would foot the bill for such claims. The indemnification program, which won Manville wide and positive publicity, was a bold demonstration of the company's confidence in its products and served to neutralize much of the misinformation that was floating around at the time. The program also assured that Manville would be in control of any fiberglass litigation that might arise in the future.

In the end, the projections of lost business and lawsuits proved much overblown. Although Manville did lose some business because of the re-labeling, the loss was temporary because the company's competitors also eventually decided to relabel. On the other hand, the company's proactive stance and skillfully executed campaign also won it business as well as goodwill from customers who praised its candor and consideration. "I especially appreciate your offer of indemnity," wrote the president of one customer firm. "The best way to meet the fiberglass problem was quickly, openly, and head-on. You have certainly accomplished those goals . . . . Thank you for the consideration you have shown to us."

In later commenting on the decision, Tom Stephens, Manville's CEO from 1986 to 1996, spoke of the courage required to make the right decision in the face of pressures to look the other way. Perhaps that was to be expected from a company that had barely survived the asbestos crisis, termed by Manville's medical director "the worst occupational health disaster ever known to any company in the free world." However, both experiences—asbestos and fiberglass—lent credence to the management team's guiding conviction that "the prosperity of a business is dependent on being in step with the values of the society in which it operates."

Innovations in Supply Chain Management

Consider Jacques Zwahlen, innovator in supply chain management. Shortly after being appointed CEO of Charles Veillon, Switzerland's largest mail-order company, Zwahlen faced the first real test of his leadership. One morning in 1994, as he was reading the newspaper and having a cup of coffee, a radio broadcast in the background caught his attention. The reporter was speaking about a recently-aired documentary film on child labor in the South Asian handwoven carpet industry. In fact, the film was the documentary referred to in Chapters 3 and 5. The program, which also included an interview with a child labor expert, discussed the plight of the estimated 120 million to 250 million working children worldwide, including bonded child workers in the carpet industry. Zwahlen was immediately concerned.[4]

Only a few months earlier, just prior to becoming CEO, he had been part of the team that decided to add a line of handwoven carpets to the company's line of home furnishings. With the industry consolidating, competition intensifying, and the Swiss economy expected to remain stagnant, the team had approved the move as part of a plan to improve Veillon's overall market position and profitability. By diversifying the company's product offerings, they hoped to increase the size of the orders placed by customers, principally working women between the ages of 25 and 35. The team had given no thought at all to the carpet makers' working conditions and had planned to source the carpets through European suppliers who, in turn, would most probably work through middlemen.

Zwahlen immediately contacted Veillon's carpet buyer and asked him to find out whether the carpets the company was planning to sell were made by child workers. When three of the company's four suppliers declined to provide information about their sources, Zwahlen decided to search for alternative suppliers. Recognizing that simply boycotting goods produced by child workers might ultimately drive children into even more hazardous occupations, as discussed in Chapter 6, he was not content with simply distancing Veillon from the problem. Instead, he turned to a child welfare organization to learn of constructive ways that his company could contribute to improving the lot of child workers and others working under inhumane conditions in the regions where Veillon sourced its goods.

Zwahlen's inquiries and further deliberations among the company's buyers and the members of its executive council led Veillon eventually to revise its sourcing standards to include an assessment of workplace conditions in the supplier evaluation and selection process. The revised criteria also included employment and environmental considerations as well as the more usual quality, price, and delivery factors. In addition, Veillon redirected some of its charitable spending to an experimental program to combine work and education for children in the carpet industry. Well aware that "disinvestment pure and simple" could "destroy the local economy without providing alternative solutions," Zwahlen saw support for child development as an essential part of the company's response.[5]

Considered remarkable at the time, Veillon's stance attracted attention in many parts of Europe and in the United States. Zwahlen was invited to appear on "La Marche du Siècle," a well-known public affairs program aired on French television, and to present his ideas at the Institut Universitaire d'Etudes du Développement in Geneva where he had earned a diploma in development studies 10 years earlier. He was even invited to testify before a committee of the U.S. Congress.

For his part, Zwahlen did not see what was so extraordinary about the steps Veillon had taken. "We monitor the quality of our products, why not the working conditions of the people who manufacture them?" he asked somewhat rhetorically. Given that Veillon was trying to "base its development on values that respect the human person," it seemed only natural to Zwahlen that the company should decline to participate in a practice like forced labor that is so destructive of human dignity and potential.

Although sales following the spate of attention rose a few percentage points over the previous period and compared favorably to those of competitors, Veillon personnel did not attribute the uptick to the child labor initiative. The company chose to make little of it in its merchandising and marketing materials, and instead invited interested customers to write for more information in a notice placed in its catalogues. For Veillon's director of strategic planning, the company's response was no more, and no less, than what the business environment demanded. "Anyone who underestimates the importance of the 'social compatibility' of its products," he commented, "doesn't understand the business environment of the late 1990s."

Innovations in Battling Corruption

Consider Fola Adeola, who in 1989 set out to build an organization that he hoped could serve as a "role model" for Nigerian society. Fed up with the corruption that plagued the Nigerian banking industry where he worked, Adeola sensed an opportunity to do something about it. At the time, many of the large international banks had left the country, creating a void that enterprising Nigerians were rushing to fill. Adeola approached his long-time friend and colleague Tayo Aderinokun with the idea of starting a new bank. What the two had in mind, however, was radically different from what they saw around them. Indeed, many of the banks then being licensed were not really banks at all so much as vehicles for their founders' private investment activities.[6]

What Adeola and Aderinokun envisioned was not only a genuine bank but a special kind of bank that would be known for outstanding customer service, superior financial results, and exemplary corporate citizenship. Professionally run and committed to high standards in all its activities, it would operate on the basis of talent and effort rather than privilege and political connections, as was the norm in Nigerian business. They imagined a corps of dedicated employees with a shared interest in the enterprise, all contributing their best efforts, working together in a collegial manner, and sharing in the rewards of the endeavor. For Adeola and Aderinokun, this was more than a banking opportunity. It was an opportunity to build a lasting institution, and they were not shy about saying they wanted it to be an ethical one.

Adeola and Aderinokun had no illusions about the difficulty of their undertaking. They had seen many Nigerian banks fail, brought down by the corrosive effects of corruption, self-dealing, and reckless lending nourished by a virulent strain of egoism that left no room for cooperative endeavor. In previous jobs, Adeola had seen lending officers willingly make loans that they knew would never be repaid just to collect the commissions. He had seen how the flow of information dried up when commission-hungry employees competed with one another to bring in new accounts. And he had seen the effects of bribery, which he called an insidious "cancer" that bred distrust among staff and customers alike. And once started, the cycle became unstoppable. As with lying, said Adeola, "once you start . . . you have to tell more lies to cover up the lies you told at the beginning."

He and Aderinokun had few financial resources—enough to secure a banking license but little more. And they faced a daunting environment of intense competition, political uncertainty, and hostility, at least on the surface, to the value system they hoped to introduce. Nigeria, reputed to be among the world's most corrupt countries, was scarcely the most promising venue for Adeola's and Aderinokun's undertaking. Both men knew all too well the pervasive role of political favoritism and corruption in fueling the nation's business. A crucial concern, as they contemplated their plan, was how to shield, or at least buffer, themselves and their bank from these hostile forces.

This concern led them to an unusual approach to raising venture capital. Rather than opportunistically signing up any investors they could find or indiscriminately canvassing all potential backers, they decided to target investors who shared their values. From a list of 150 prominent Nigerians whom they identified as potential investors, they narrowed the field to 43 based on their perceived quality of character. They wanted to deal only with investors who themselves could understand and appreciate the ideas of professionalism, integrity, and citizenship on which they wanted to build the bank—an unheard-of strategy in an environment where political influence and financial clout were the presumed drivers of business. Of the 43 prospects Adeola and Aderinokun approached, 42 decided to invest. Many, recalled Adeola, were pleasantly surprised to find "that real bankers were coming to them to invest in a [real] bank."

In early 1991, Guaranty Trust Bank (GTB) opened its doors in Lagos. It was one of Nigeria's 120 banks and 400 finance companies, a dramatic increase over the country's mere 36 banks only five years earlier when the country had launched a program of extensive deregulation and liberalization. Shortly after the opening, Adeola and Aderinokun faced the first real test of their aspirations. It was the end of the fiscal year and the bank was not yet making money. The question was whether to report a first-six-month loss or to bury it in what everyone hoped would be the following year's profits.

Although some board members favored nondisclosure, Adeola and Aderinokun felt strongly that the loss should be published because it was truthful and would signal GTB's trustworthiness to the market. They convinced the board to support them, and then proceeded, with some trepidation, to announce the loss. "We were the first bank to ever publish a loss like that in this environment," said Adeola, who was both surprised and relieved that nothing bad happened as a result of their unprecedented candor. "For me," he recalled, "that was a major sign . . . that doing the right thing doesn't mean that you'll necessarily get punished."

Not all of the founders' ideals were so well received, however. Although employees were proud of GTB's stance on corporate citizenship, which included, among other things, paying appropriate corporate income taxes, many were loathe to pay their own personal taxes. Most employees insisted on submitting false income estimates that the bank was then responsible for verifying to the authorities. "Why pay?" reasoned many who not only partook of the notion that tax evasion was something of a national sport, but also pointed, with some justification, to the many corrupt officials in the government who would only embezzle the funds or appropriate them for their own personal use.

Adeola's arguments about good citizenship and building the country fell on deaf ears, and he did not insist for fear that he would undermine the morale of valuable employees who were otherwise on board with GTB's distinctive values. He reasoned that it was more important to keep the bank functioning effectively and moving in the direction of better practice than to risk failure at the early stage by refusing to compromise on this point, important though he thought it was. The matter, he told himself, could be dealt with later, and indeed it was, though not as he had hoped.

The issue came to a head in 1997, following a tax audit that revealed the shortfall in employees' past tax payments. GTB paid the amounts due and established a policy requiring accurate tax declarations and proper withholding, but Adeola decided that rather than simply writing off the experience as many urged, he would ask employees to reimburse the bank for the amounts paid on their behalf. For Adeola, it was a matter of principle. However, his insistence that employees repay the bank, even with five-year interest-free loans to help cover the indebtedness, angered many. Some employees left, and morale plummeted. For a time, Adeola wondered whether he was destroying all that he had created.

The crisis prompted Adeola to initiate a bank-wide self-examination. "We took a look at the whole bank—our values and ethics and goals—from top to bottom," he said. "Everyone got involved." The result was a reaffirmation of the original vision for GTB and a recommitment to the ideals he and Aderinokun had originally articulated. The tax evasion episode became part of the course Adeola taught to new recruits to introduce them to the bank's mission, operations, and culture.

By 1996, five years after its founding, GTB had emerged from the dense pack of competitors as Nigeria's fastest-growing bank. Regarded by many analysts at that point as the country's best indigenous bank, it was one of only two commercial banks to receive a top risk rating in 1996—the other was a subsidiary of Citibank—and it ranked fourth among all banks in terms of profit after taxes. In that year, GTB was listed on the Nigerian stock exchange, and, soon afterwards, the exchange conferred on GTB its President's Merit Award "for promoting corporate governance and encouraging healthy competition among quoted companies." GTB won the award again in 1999. Although industry competition has indeed increased, GTB was still, as of 2002, considered one of Nigeria's leading banks.[7]

GTB's early success owed as much to the founders' careful execution of their start-up plan as to their original inspiration. At each step as they mobilized resources and built the relationships and skills necessary to launch their venture, they were attentive to the moral profile they envisioned. By the time their license was approved in 1990, they had already hired and begun working with the more than 80 people needed to open the bank. They drew on outside speakers and training programs as well as self-designed courses to prepare their recruits. In some sessions, employees learned about the technicalities of accounting and banking operations. In others, they worked on forging a set of guiding principles—"how we wanted to live our lives here."

From these sessions emerged agreed-on tenets for behavior that were in many cases radical departures from the Nigerian business norm. For instance, employees agreed that everyone would follow the same rules. Managing directors would carry their own briefcases and park their own cars. Everyone would eat in the same dining room. Hierarchy in the organization would be kept to a minimum, and employees would call each other by their first names. To assure that everyone had contact with customers and with one another, all would serve as a teller at least one day a month.

Excellence in customer service was a key value, and much of the initial training focused on customer-related issues. Before opening, researchers conducted customer surveys to learn more about customer needs and expectations. At the same time, GTB signaled its values to the marketplace through nontraditional advertising and the nontraditional design of its head office. Instead of putting tellers in "cages," the banking hall was designed on an open plan. Prior to launch, GTB used the architectural plans for its unusual building as the centerpiece of its advertising. The first ad was titled "May we share our plans with you?" Then, every other week, the company offered a new ad updating readers on the building's progress. Moreover, in keeping with the openness and transparency Adeola and Aderinokun wanted to foster, GTB investors received monthly newsletters and progress reports throughout this period.

Gradually, the founders' vision took substance, and the bank itself took on a moral personality that was unique in the Nigerian context. "Guaranty Trust Bank—for all of us, no exceptions—was totally different," said one early employee with experience in the industry. "What was good about it was that we *all* consciously decided to go this route because we felt and believed that there was going to be real gain at the end of the day rather than going the old route of not caring about customers or each other."[8] The company has also shown that it cares about the broader community through its program of civic activities. Commented Adeola, who was scheduled to retire as GTB's chairman and CEO in August 2002, "We believe that when you make money in an environment, you should give some of it back—especially to benefit very, very poor people."

Breakthrough Thinking

The success of efforts such as these four may seem unremarkable or even inevitable and preordained. In retrospect, they seem like no more than common sense. After all, why would any company not want to do what these managers did, especially if it turns out to be profitable, or at least without cost? Recall what these four companies were aiming for in each case:

- to minimize the impact of a mass layoff on employees and the community
- to protect employees and customers from product-related health risks
- to work with suppliers who treated people decently and paid a decent wage
- to build a company known for outstanding customer service, superior financial results, and exemplary corporate citizenship

But this after-the-fact vantage point misses a crucial issue. Before the fact, the leaders of these efforts had to wage an uphill battle against the status quo and against received thinking. Many of the ideas that these companies successfully implemented simply would either not have occurred to managers steeped in orthodox management thought, or would have been rejected as "not our business," "too costly," or "unworkable." Recall Nike's early insistence that supplier labor practices were none of its business, or consider how many executives have reasoned that acceding to bribery is the only way they can compete.

Getting from orthodox assumptions to the "common-sense" initiatives undertaken by these managers is a tricky business. From the vantage point of conventional management thinking, these individuals were concerned about all the "wrong" things:

- Nivert and her colleagues wanted to minimize the proposed restructuring's negative effects on employees and the community. Orthodoxy teaches that these are "externalities" best dealt with by governments, families, and communities.
- Sells and his colleagues believed that employees and customers had a moral right to know about potential health risks even if the law did not require disclosure and even if disclosure might result in lost business. Orthodoxy teaches that putting the interests of other constituencies ahead of shareholders is a breach of managers' fiduciary obligation.
- Zwahlen was concerned about the labor and environmental practices of his company's suppliers. Orthodoxy teaches that the "invisible hand," Adam Smith's eighteenth-century metaphor to explain how markets transform individual self-interest into societal well-being, will eventually release child workers from bondage, clean up the environment, and assure that society's welfare is maximized—and that, to make this system work, managers should focus on maximizing their company's financial performance.
- Adeola wanted to build a lasting institution known for professionalism, outstanding customer service, superior financial results, and exemplary corporate citizenship. Orthodoxy teaches that the purpose of a corporation is to maximize shareholder wealth and that all the rest, if important at all, is important only as a means to this end.

From an orthodox perspective, all these individuals were behaving "irrationally," to the extent that their aspirations encompassed more than financial self-interest. For "rational economic actors," as that term is widely used, we must look to Adeola's competitors—those who were setting up banks to function as their personal investment vehicles—or to the Enron and other executives who skewed their companies' accounting to boost the value of their personal stock options.

From a center-driven outlook, however, the concerns of these four managers are not "irrational," nor are they "wrong" or "misguided." They are quite normal, acceptable, and rational. Because center-driven management starts with the premise that a company is a moral actor, it is simply a given that an excellent company will be concerned about the consequences of its actions, the rights of its constituencies, and its contribution to the broader community. The challenge is thus to figure out a practical path of action that will enable the company to remain competitive while respecting the rights of others and minimizing the collateral harms caused by its activities. Put in visual terms, the challenge is to enlarge the zone of overlap as shown in Figure 9-1 by bringing into the zone activities previously thought to lie outside it.

If a company is successful in charting a path that is sound both economically and ethically, the result will satisfy the orthodox, even though the orthodox might never have envisioned the path or experienced the concerns that led to it. Of course, not all efforts will be successful, but there is no *a priori* reason to rule out the possibility. As these four examples suggest, much can be achieved when intelligence, imagination, and application are brought to bear on the questions at hand.

Center-driven management is less a technique or a collection of "best practices" than a philosophy of management that is grounded in a distinctive set of assumptions about the nature of people, companies, and the role of business in society. Although these assumptions lead to certain characteristic ways of seeing and doing things, the resulting practices can be puzzling if divorced from the underlying beliefs and assumptions that drive them. Most of these assumptions have been discussed at length in earlier parts of the book, so here I will only summarize the most important ones. But notice that each one challenges a key tenet of management orthodoxy.

- **Corporate personality.** The corporate personality premise holds that companies are moral actors, rather than amoral and purely functional devices as has been traditionally held. As such, companies not only carry out important functions such as producing goods and services, creating wealth, creating employment, innovating, and developing new

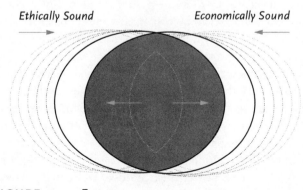

Ethically Sound   *Economically Sound*

FIGURE 9-1 EXPANDING THE ZONE OF ACCEPTABILITY

ideas, but they also make choices, have distinctive personalities, and interact with other moral actors in society. As moral actors, they may be expected, at a minimum, to pay their dues to society by adhering to the law and to basic principles of justice. Ideally, however, they will embrace a higher standard by conforming their activities to generally accepted ethical principles, taking responsibility for their errors and misdeeds, showing consideration for others in conducting their affairs, and contributing to the communities of which they are part.

- **Corporate performance.** The corporate performance premise holds that superior performance consists of excellence along both moral and financial dimensions, not just financial performance alone. By definition, a company cannot be an outstanding performer if it fails to conform its activities to generally accepted ethical principles, even if its financial performance is outstanding when viewed in isolation. Although precise standards of excellence may vary from context to context, the minimum requirements are defined by the need for profitability as well as the need for basic justice as embodied in legitimate systems of law.

- **Corporate accountability.** The corporate accountability premise holds that accountability extends well beyond the traditional view of accountability to shareholders for financial results. As moral actors, companies are also answerable for injuries that their activities cause to other parties such as customers, employees, partners, and lenders as well as to third parties and communities in which they operate. They are accountable for fulfilling both financial and non-financial responsibilities to each of their constituencies.

- **Corporate conduct.** A corporation's conduct consists of all actions taken by its members or representatives on its behalf, including actions by executives, managers, or employees acting alone as well as actions carried out by multiple parties working jointly. Thus, the corporation as a whole can be responsible for actions that are attributable to no single individual, and actions taken by a single individual can constitute corporate conduct. In other words, the corporation is not a fiction, as orthodoxy holds, but a social reality with a distinctive personality that is expressed through the conduct of its members and representatives. How a company's people treat one another or the company's customers is as much a matter of corporate ethics as how the manufacturing department deals with waste.

- **Human behavior.** Human behavior is multifaceted. No one factor—pursuit of money, power, justice, love, truth, self-interest or any other single thing—can fully explain what drives people. By and large, most people have mixed motives and varied aspirations. And, although they have financial needs, they also have physical, intellectual, and moral needs and capabilities as well. As a moral actor, a modern company interacts with people not just as "economic actors" or "factors of production," but in all these aspects—financial, physical, intellectual, and moral.

- **Rationality.** Rationality means using reason to enhance life. It can therefore be rational to assist others, to contribute to one's community, and to do one's fair share even if free riding on the efforts of others is possible. It is also rational to honor valid legal and ethical standards even when doing so will not directly advance one's own immediate self-interest. To the extent that definitions of rationality as "profit-maximizing" or "self-interest maximizing" deem such behavior "irrational," they are too narrow. The benefits of living in a well-ordered society are enjoyed by all, and actions that strengthen others generally contribute in some way to the actor's well-being. Moreover, the key to a satisfying life lies not in maximizing a single good to the exclusion of all others, but in finding a suitable mix that addresses the diversity of human needs.

- **Progress.** Progress is not inevitable. Whatever is good in a way of life must be constantly protected, and improvements rarely occur in the absence of leaders who can envision something better and are committed to showing the way. Although people's first responsibility is to provide for themselves, the "invisible hand" alone cannot be counted on to assure an efficient use of society's resources or the well-being of the world's people. The unalloyed pursuit of financial self-interest leads not to societal well-being but to societal distrust and decay. For a company or society to be strong, each individual must pursue self-interest in a way that respects other people and maintains the social fabric of the community. The market is a wonderful mechanism, but its effective functioning depends on a sense of responsibility among its participants.

The examples of innovative practices sketched earlier in this chapter show many of these beliefs in action. They show managers who recognize that their companies are moral actors with both financial and nonfinancial responsibilities to their constituencies and the broader community. They show people who are highly skilled and highly practical in their efforts to achieve both moral and financial excellence. Without being moralistic, they are comfortable bringing values into discussions of strategy, policy, and practice. And they are straightforward in addressing moral dilemmas and value conflicts. All are profoundly aware of human limitations, yet, recognizing that the "invisible hand" of the market works best when it has a visible support system, they remain undeterred in their effort to look for better ways to do things.

To meet the new standard, companies will increasingly need leaders who can break through the thought system embedded in old orthodoxies. By now, it should be clear that we are not talking about individual personality traits or "good people" versus "bad people." We are talking about different ways of thinking and viewing the world. The competencies required to lead the center-driven corporation are qualitatively different from those required to lead the amoral finance-driven corporation or its predecessor, the charter-driven corporation. What's needed are competent leaders who take a broader view of their role—one that is commensurate with the corporation's role as it is in society today and is likely to be in the future, and not as it was 100 years ago.

At the core of this new role definition is an enlarged sense of accountability. Today's executives must stand ready to answer for their decisions not only to their company's shareholders, but also to other constituencies. And they must be able to "give an account" that can survive moral as well as financial scrutiny. In other words, they must be "multilogical" strategists who are proficient in modes of ethical as well as economic reasoning and sensitive to moral as well as market considerations.

Looking to the future, companies will need to cultivate more leaders who understand these broader accountabilities and who are excited by the challenges they present. Given the corporation's role in society today, business leadership must be understood as a high calling that requires the finest efforts of intelligent men and women around the world. Through their activities as decision makers, organization builders, and societal leaders, they have the power to make the world not only more prosperous, but also more just and more humane. What could be a more worthy endeavor?

Limitless Opportunity

Some have said that a concern with corporate morality is characteristic of rich countries, or a particular religious heritage, or even a distinctively American preoccupation. Others have asserted that an ethical orientation is feasible only for large companies, or for small companies, or in certain types of industries. I have also heard it claimed that ethics is relevant mainly in regulated industries, or unregulated industries, or high-tech companies, or low-tech companies.

Judging from the examples considered in this book, all of these claims would appear to be false. The examples here have been drawn from many parts of the world, from a wide mix of industries, and from a broad array of company types and sizes. The managers mentioned in the text come from varied religious and cultural backgrounds—Christian, Buddhist, Muslim, Chinese, Hindu, humanist, and undoubtedly others of which I am not aware. As this rich base of examples indicates, the ideas presented here apply broadly to companies across the board and are not limited to any particular industry, country, or type of company.

Readers who have followed the argument this far may be wondering what the new standard implies for them. They may be thinking about companies they manage, companies they plan to start, or companies they advise. Some may be reflecting on companies they might work for or companies they are considering as potential investments. Of course, the specific implications for a given company will depend on its particular situation. However, the questions below outline a process that can be used to identify areas of strength, concern, and opportunity. To assess the readiness of a company or other business unit to meet the new standard, you may wish to consider the following questions:

PERSONALITY TYPE How would you characterize your company's moral personality?

- Which of the following descriptions strikes you as most accurate: indifferent, dues payer, sustaining member, sponsoring member? (See Chapter 6.)
- Which description would others be most apt to choose? Consider other employees as well as customers, investors, partners, contractors, regulators, and public officials. Think about current members of these groups as well as past members.

PERSONALITY PROFILE How would you describe the core beliefs that comprise your company's value system or "intrastructure"?

- How would you characterize the company's purpose, its guiding principles, its assumptions about people, the interests considered in its decision making, and its prevailing assumptions about power and accountability? (See Chapter 7.)

- How might others characterize the company along these dimensions?
- How do the profiles drawn by different parties compare?
- How do the beliefs reflected in the company's behavior compare with the beliefs espoused in its literature?

STANDARDS ASSESSMENT How would you rate your company's performance against the emerging body of "generally accepted ethical principles" for business? (See Chapter 5.)

- To what extent does your company adhere to the Caux Round Table Principles for Business? (See Appendix.)
- To what extent does your company adhere to the Principles of the U.N. Global Compact? (See Appendix.)
- To what extent does your company adhere to other bodies of standards that may be relevant to its activities? Consider, for example, the OECD Guidelines for Multinational Enterprises, codes of conduct for your industry, and legal standards of the various jurisdictions in which your company operates.
- In what areas is your company most at risk of violating these principles? Consider this question in relation to your company's functional areas (finance, accounting, marketing, etc.); its key constituencies (customers, investors, employees, suppliers, the public, etc.); its geographic divisions or locations; its business divisions or product lines.

CAPABILITIES ASSESSMENT How strong are your company's capabilities in the following areas?

- What is its capacity for self-governance, including self-discipline, self-evaluation, self-correction, and self-improvement?
- What is its capacity for adapting to changing laws and ethical standards, including the ability to anticipate changes and make appropriate operating adjustments?
- What is its capacity for moral reasoning and judgment, including the ability to reconcile conflicting claims and responsibilities?
- What is its capacity for moral responsiveness, including the ability to recognize and address ethical issues in each quadrant of the commitment matrix? (See Chapter 3.)

SYSTEMS ASSESSMENT How well are your company's guidance and operating systems aligned with the new expectations?

- What does your company owe its key constituencies, including its investors, customers, employees, the public, and any other relevant parties?
- What do your key constituencies expect from the company?
- To what extent are your company's guidance systems aligned with these accountabilities and expectations? Consider your company's systems and processes for such key activities as governance and oversight, planning and resource allocation, hiring and developing people, performance evaluation and compensation, gathering and disseminating information, controlling and auditing operations, identifying and developing new opportunities, measuring and reporting on the company's performance. (See Chapter 7.)
- How well aligned are your company's processes for day-to-day operations such as securing and managing funds, sourcing inputs and supplies, production, distribution, logistics, marketing and advertising, sales and service, and accounting and record keeping?

DECISION-MAKING METHODS To what extent do your company's decision frameworks and processes incorporate a moral perspective?

- To what extent do the analytic techniques used in making decisions include an ethical assessment of the type described in Chapter 8?
- To what extent do the criteria used in making both strategic and tactical decisions include moral considerations?
- To what extent are decision-making bodies constituted with the explicit aim of including members who are equipped to provide an informed moral perspective?

LEADERSHIP CAPABILITIES How well equipped are your company's leaders for the challenges presented by the new performance standard?

- Are your company's leaders aware of the changing expectations for corporate performance?
- Has their training prepared them to deal with the issues raised by this development in their various capacities as organization builders, decision makers, role models, and representatives of the company to its constituencies and the world?
- If the heads of your company's business units were asked to present an ethical assessment of their business, would they know what to do?

- If the managers of your company's business units were asked to provide an ethical analysis of an important business decision, would they know how to proceed?
- If members of the leadership team were asked to identify some ethical issues the company should be working on, would they be able to do so?
- If members of the leadership team received credible evidence of corporate misconduct, would they know what to do?

OPPORTUNITIES ASSESSMENT   What opportunities does your company have to improve its performance relative to the new standard?

- How would you assess your company's projected performance this year relative to the expectations of its key constituencies?
- What do your constituencies say about areas in which your company's performance could improve?
- Given your company's current and projected activities, what are your constituencies likely to say about the company's performance 3, 5, and 10 years from now?
- What do your answers to all the previous questions suggest about areas for improvement?

As you go through these questions, you may find that your answers suggest the need for far-reaching changes on the scale of the organizational transformation that Royal Dutch/Shell set in motion. Or, you may decide that only modest adjustments are called for. Change of any magnitude, however, will require the leadership of committed individuals who embrace the ideas of center-driven management. As we consider what the corporation has been and what it might become, the prospects for companies that can successfully merge social and financial imperatives are highly favorable. Indeed, in a world in which few people achieve their true potential, in which many are in great need, and in which society's trust in business seems to be diminishing daily, the opportunities would appear to be limitless.

Appendix

Emerging Standards

1 The United Nations Global Compact

At the World Economic Forum, Davos, on 31 January 1999, U.N. Secretary-General Kofi A. Annan challenged world business leaders to "embrace and enact" the Global Compact, both in their individual corporate practices and by supporting appropriate public policies. These principles cover topics in human rights, labour, and environment:

The Secretary-General asked world business to: | **HUMAN RIGHTS**

Principle 1: support and respect the protection of international human rights within their sphere of influence; and

Principle 2: make sure their own corporations are not complicit in human rights abuses.

The Secretary-General asked world business to uphold: | **LABOUR**

Principle 3: freedom of association and the effective recognition of the right to collective bargaining;

Principle 4: the elimination of all forms of forced and compulsory labour;

Principle 5: the effective abolition of child labour; and

Principle 6: the elimination of discrimination in respect of employment and occupation.

The Secretary-General asked world business to: | **ENVIRONMENT**

Principle 7: support a precautionary approach to environmental challenges;

Principle 8: undertake initiatives to promote greater environmental responsibility; and

Principle 9: encourage the development and diffusion of environmentally friendly technologies.

2 Business Principles Assessment

This checklist is based on the Caux Round Table *Principles for Business* developed in 1994 by a group of European, Japanese, and U.S. executives. Their aim was to express a world standard for business behavior. As you look over the checklist, imagine that you are an independent but fair and informed observer. Circle the number that best reflects your company's track record in adhering to each principle. If you disagree with the principle or do not consider it relevant, please circle the X. At the end of the form, please add any important items not covered by the checklist.

	PRINCIPLES	1. poor	2. fair	3. good	4. excellent	5. outstanding	not relevant
		LEVEL OF ADHERENCE					
GENERAL PRINCIPLES	creates value for all stakeholders	1	2	3	4	5	N/R
	contributes to economic and social development	1	2	3	4	5	N/R
	uses resources prudently and effectively	1	2	3	4	5	N/R
	conducts business with candor and truthfulness	1	2	3	4	5	N/R
	keeps promises	1	2	3	4	5	N/R
	adheres to international and domestic laws	1	2	3	4	5	N/R
	supports multilateral trade system	1	2	3	4	5	N/R
	protects and improves environment	1	2	3	4	5	N/R
	avoids and seeks to eliminate corrupt practices such as bribery, money laundering, other illicit activities	1	2	3	4	5	N/R
CUSTOMERS	provides quality that meets customer requirements	1	2	3	4	5	N/R
	treats customers fairly	1	2	3	4	5	N/R
	addresses customer complaints	1	2	3	4	5	N/R
	minimizes adverse health and safety impacts and discloses them to customers if appropriate	1	2	3	4	5	N/R
	produces goods and services that maintain or enhance the quality of the environment	1	2	3	4	5	N/R
	respects human dignity in products, marketing, advertising	1	2	3	4	5	N/R
	respects integrity of customers' cultures	1	2	3	4	5	N/R

continued

Prepared by Lynn Sharp Paine based on *Principles for Business* (Caux, Switzerland: Caux Round Table, 1994)

PRINCIPLES	1. poor	2. fair	3. good	4. excellent	5. outstanding	not relevant
	LEVEL OF ADHERENCE					

EMPLOYEES

Principle	1	2	3	4	5	N/R
provides jobs and compensation that improve living conditions	1	2	3	4	5	N/R
protects employees' health and dignity	1	2	3	4	5	N/R
communicates as honestly and candidly as possible	1	2	3	4	5	N/R
listens to and addresses employee suggestions	1	2	3	4	5	N/R
deals with conflicts in good faith	1	2	3	4	5	N/R
affords equal treatment and opportunity without regard to gender, race, religion	1	2	3	4	5	N/R
provides useful employment to differently abled people	1	2	3	4	5	N/R
has eliminated avoidable workplace illness and injury	1	2	3	4	5	N/R
encourages and assists employees in developing skills and knowledge	1	2	3	4	5	N/R
addresses problems of unemployment and dislocation associated with business decisions	1	2	3	4	5	N/R

OWNERS/INVESTORS

Principle	1	2	3	4	5	N/R
provides investors with a fair and competitive return	1	2	3	4	5	N/R
provides investors with accurate, relevant information	1	2	3	4	5	N/R
protects and increases investors' assets	1	2	3	4	5	N/R
respects investors' input (suggestions, complaints)	1	2	3	4	5	N/R
uses company assets for company purposes, not personal purposes	1	2	3	4	5	N/R

SUPPLIERS

Principle	1	2	3	4	5	N/R
behaves truthfully and fairly in all activities, including pricing, licensing, rights to sell	1	2	3	4	5	N/R
does not engage in coercion and unnecessary litigation	1	2	3	4	5	N/R
fosters long-term relationships in exchange for supplier value, quality, competitiveness, reliability	1	2	3	4	5	N/R
gives suppliers timely information and integrates them into the planning process	1	2	3	4	5	N/R
pays suppliers on time according to agreed terms	1	2	3	4	5	N/R
gives preference to suppliers whose employment practices respect human dignity	1	2	3	4	5	N/R

PRINCIPLES	1. poor	2. fair	3. good	4. excellent	5. outstanding	not relevant
LEVEL OF ADHERENCE						

COMPETITORS

does not collude with competitors	1	2	3	4	5	N/R
supports open markets for trade and investment	1	2	3	4	5	N/R
competitive behavior shows respect for competitors	1	2	3	4	5	N/R
does not use questionable payments or favors to secure competitive advantage	1	2	3	4	5	N/R
respects property rights – tangible and intellectual	1	2	3	4	5	N/R
acquires commercial information honestly and ethically, and not by espionage or unethical means	1	2	3	4	5	N/R

COMMUNITIES

avoids improper relations with government officials	1	2	3	4	5	N/R
addresses social or environmental harm caused by company activities	1	2	3	4	5	N/R
promotes human rights and democratic institutions	1	2	3	4	5	N/R
supports public policies that promote human development	1	2	3	4	5	N/R
collaborates with community groups to improve health, education, workplace safety, the economy	1	2	3	4	5	N/R
supports peace, security, diversity, and social integration	1	2	3	4	5	N/R
respects integrity of local cultures	1	2	3	4	5	N/R
contributes to charity, education, culture, and employee participation in civic affairs	1	2	3	4	5	N/R

OTHER

_____	1	2	3	4	5	N/R
_____	1	2	3	4	5	N/R
_____	1	2	3	4	5	N/R
_____	1	2	3	4	5	N/R

Copies of the Caux Round Table *Principles for Business* can be found at www.cauxroundtable.org or ordered (in multiple languages) from Caux Institute for Global Responsibility, Inc., RR2, Box 239, Waterville, Minnesota, 56096, Tel. +1 (507) 362-4916, Fax +1 (507) 362-4820; Email CauxRT@aol.com.

Notes

Chapter 1   The Turn to Values

1. See, e.g., James C. Collins and Jerry I. Porras, *Built to Last: Successful Habits of Visionary Companies* (New York, N.Y.: HarperBusiness, 1994).

2. For data from the survey of U.S. employees, see Joshua Joseph, *2000 National Business Ethics Survey Volume I: How Employees Perceive Ethics at Work* (Washington, D.C.: Ethics Resource Center, 2000), pp. 6–7.

3. Data on corporate board involvement in setting ethical standards comes from Ronald E. Berenbeim, *Global Corporate Ethics Practices: A Developing Consensus* (New York, N.Y.: The Conference Board, Research Report 1243-99-RR, 1999). For data on the prevalence of codes, credos, and values statements among the *Forbes* 500, see Patrick E. Murphy, "Corporate Ethics Statements: Current Status and Future Prospects," *Journal of Business Ethics*, vol. 14 (1995), pp. 727–740.

4. Data on corporate ethics officers comes from the Ethics Officer Association, see <http://www.eoa.org> (February 14, 2002).

5. On the ethics consulting business, see Mike France, Peter Elstrom, and Mark Maremont, "Ethics for Hire," *Business Week*, July 15, 1996, p. 26. Among the best known U.S. nonprofits doing research, information gathering, or consulting in these areas are the New York-based Conference Board; the Washington, D.C.-based Ethics Resource Center; and the California-based Business for Social Responsibility, whose corporate membership has grown from 45 in 1992 to 1400 in 2002. See Business for Social Responsibility website <http://www.bsr.org> (February 14, 2002).

6. This quote and a full account of the Martin Marietta experience can be found in Lynn Sharp Paine, "Martin Marietta: Managing Corporate Ethics (A)," HBS Case No. 9-393-016 (Boston, Mass.: Harvard Business School Publishing, 1992).

7. This quote is from Prompilai Khunaphante and Lynn Sharp Paine, "The Siam Cement Group: Corporate Philosophy (B)," HBS Case No. 9-398-019 (Boston, Mass.: Harvard Business School Publishing, 1997), p. 2. For a fuller account of

the company's philosophy, see also the (A) case: Prompilai Khunaphante and Lynn Sharp Paine, "The Siam Cement Group: Corporate Philosophy (A)," HBS Case No. 9-398-018 (Boston, Mass.: Harvard Business School Publishing, 1997).

8. This quote and a description of Wipro's value system can be found in Lynn Sharp Paine, "Wipro Technologies (A)," HBS Case No. 9-301-403 (Boston, Mass.: Harvard Business School Publishing, 2001), p. 2.

9. Scott Cook, "The Ethics of Bootstrapping," *Inc.*, September 1992, p. 95.

10. For a full account, see Lynn Sharp Paine, "Merck Sharp & Dohme Argentina, Inc. (A)," HBS Case No. 9-398-033 (Boston, Mass.: Harvard Business School Publishing, 1997).

11. Data on the cost of individual misconduct comes from Association of Certified Fraud Examiners, "Report to the Nation on Occupational Fraud and Abuse," 1996 <http://www.cfenet.com/media/report/reportsection4.asp> (October 26, 2001). For retailers' losses from employee theft, see Calmetta Coleman, "As Thievery by Insiders Overtakes Shoplifting, Retailers Crack Down," *Wall Street Journal*, September 8, 2000, p. A1.

12. Companies that follow the recommendations for preventing misconduct set forth by the U.S. Sentencing Commission in the Federal Sentencing Guidelines for Organizations can benefit from reduced fines should they be found guilty of a criminal offense covered by the program. For the requirements, see the United States Sentencing Commission, *Guidelines Manual* (Washington, D.C.: USSC, 2001), Ch. 8, section 8C2, pp. 423–439. Enactment of the guidelines, which took effect in 1991, has contributed to the spread of corporate ethics programs in the United States.

13. This account is based on Lynn Sharp Paine and Michael A. Santoro, "Forging the New Salomon," HBS Case No. 9-395-046 (Boston, Mass.: Harvard Business School Publishing, 1994). Unless otherwise indicated, this case study is the source of any quotations or quoted terminology found in this section. In the spring of 2001, Citigroup announced that it planned to stop using the Salomon name for its investment banking and brokerage operations. See Paul Beckett, "So Long, Poker Players: Salomon is History," *Wall Street Journal*, May 23, 2001, p. C18.

14. Robert E. Denham, "Remarks Before the 20th Annual Securities Regulation Institute," Coronado, California, January 21, 1993 (unpublished speech on file with the author).

15. Quoted in Anita Raghaven, "Salomon's Decision to Sell Out to Travelers Group May Be Traced to 1991 Treasury-Bond Scandal," *Wall Street Journal*, September 25, 1997, p. C1.

16. This account is based on Lynn Sharp Paine and Karen Hopper Wruck, "Sealed Air Corporation: Globalization and Corporate Culture (A), (B)," HBS Case Nos. 9-398-096, 9-398-097 (Boston, Mass.: Harvard Business School Publishing, 1998). Unless otherwise indicated, this case study is the source of any quotations or quoted terminology found in this section.

17. This account is based on Lynn Sharp Paine, "The Haier Group (A), (B), (C)," HBS Case Nos. 9-398-101, 9-398-102, 9-398-162 (Boston, Mass.: Harvard Business School Publishing, 1998); and Lynn Sharp Paine, "Haier Hefei Electronics Co. (A), (B)," HBS Case Nos. 9-300-070, 9-300-071 (Boston,

Mass.: Harvard Business School Publishing, 1999). Unless otherwise indicated, these case studies are the source of any quotations or quoted terminology found in this section.

18. Data on Haier's share of the U.S. refrigerator market comes from "Haier Ambitions," *AsiaWeek*, October 5, 2001, and Dan Biers, "Taking the Fight to the Enemy: China's Top Appliance Maker, Haier, Breaks into the U.S. Market Using a Combination of Quality, Price and Local Manufacturing," *Far Eastern Economic Review*, March 29, 2001, p. 52. On Haier's international presence, see Haier Group, "On an Innovative Way to a World-Famous Brand—A Brief Introduction of the Haier Group," Haier Web page, February 2001, <http://www.haier.com/english/about/index.html> (March 6, 2002). For the 1998 *Financial Times* survey, see "General Electric Takes Top Honours in First Financial Times PriceWaterhouseCoopers World's Most Respected Companies Survey," Table 18, "Asia-Pacific's Most Respected Companies," *Business Wire*, November 30, 1998. Haier's showing in the online poll of China's most respected companies was reported in "Hai'er Elected Best Listed Company," *China Online*, February 6, 2002 available from Dow Jones Interactive Publications Library, <http://www.library.hbs.edu/dji.htm> (March 7, 2002).

19. This material is based on Lynn Sharp Paine, "Royal Dutch/Shell in Transition (A), (B)," HBS Case Nos. 9-300-039, 9-300-040 (Boston, Mass.: Harvard Business School Publishing, 1999); and Lynn Sharp Paine and Mihnea Moldoveanu, "Royal Dutch/Shell in Nigeria (A), (B)," HBS Case Nos. 9-399-126, 9-300-127 (Boston, Mass.: Harvard Business School Publishing, 1999). Unless otherwise indicated, these case studies are the source of any quotations or quoted terminology found in this section.

20. This account is based on Joshua Hammer, "Nigeria Crude," *Harper's Magazine*, June 1996, as well as Paine and Moldoveanu, "Royal Dutch/Shell in Nigeria," op. cit.

21. Material in this section is based on Lynn Sharp Paine, "HDFC (A)," HBS Case No. 9-301-093 (Boston, Mass.: Harvard Business School Publishing, 2000). Unless otherwise indicated, this case study is the source of any quotations or quoted terminology found in this section.

22. Remarks by Deepak Parekh before the Indian Merchants Chamber in accepting its "Enhancing Business Community Image Award," April 26, 1999.

Chapter 2   Does Ethics Pay?

1. For a complete description, see Lynn Sharp Paine, "AES Honeycomb (A)," HBS Case No. 9-395-132 (Boston, Mass.: Harvard Business School Publishing, 1994).

2. From the Watergate tapes as excerpted in Frances Cullen, William Maakestad, and Gray Cavender, *The Ford Pinto Case* (Albany, N.Y.: State University of New York Press, 1994), pp. 266–271.

3. I owe the CFO quote to Professor Constance Bagley. It is from Bill Birchard, "How Many Masters Can You Serve?" *CFO*, July 1995, p. 54. The statement from the OECD advisory group is found in Organisation for Economic Co-operation and Development, *Corporate Governance: Improving Competitive-*

ness and Access to Capital in Global Markets, A Report to the OECD by the Business Sector Advisory Group on Corporate Governance (Paris: OECD, April 1998), p. 67. The report does go on to acknowledge that trade-offs may be necessary in the short term. For the Business Roundtable's view, see The Business Roundtable, *Statement on Corporate Governance: A White Paper from The Business Roundtable* (Washington, D.C., September 1997), at p. 3: "The Business Roundtable does not view these two positions [shareholder and stakeholder] as being in conflict . . ."

4. This account is based largely on the facts as recounted in two sources: Richard S. Tedlow, "James Burke: A Career in American Business," HBS Case No. 9-389-177 (Boston, Mass.: Harvard Business School Publishing, 1989); John Deighton, "McNeil Consumer Products Company: Tylenol" (Hanover, N.H.: Amos Tuck School, Dartmouth College, 1983).

5. This quote is from the video that accompanies Tedlow, "James Burke: A Career in American Business," HBS No. 9-389-177.

6. This chapter draws on several of my previous publications, principally the following: Lynn Sharp Paine, "Does Ethics Pay?" *Business Ethics Quarterly*, vol. 10, no. 1 (January 2000), pp. 319–330; Lynn Sharp Paine, *Cases in Leadership, Ethics, and Organizational Integrity: A Strategic Perspective* (Burr Ridge, Ill.: Richard D. Irwin, 1997).

7. Maughan quote from Seth Faison, Jr., "Salomon's Renovation Enters New Phase," *New York Times*, February 11, 1992, p. D1.

8. Unless otherwise indicated, all information and quotations in this section are from Lynn Sharp Paine and Michael A. Santoro, "Forging the New Salomon," HBS Case No. 9-395-046 (Boston, Mass.: Harvard Business School Publishing, 1994).

9. For a study of the longer-term financial effects of corporate illegality, see Melissa S. Baucus and David A. Baucus, "Paying the Piper: An Empirical Examination of Longer-Term Financial Consequences of Illegal Corporate Behavior," *Academy of Management Journal*, vol. 40, no. 1 (1997), pp. 129–151.

10. The facts of the Enron story can be found in many sources. For the account presented by the Enron Board of Directors, see William C. Powers, Jr., Raymond S. Troubh, Herbert S. Winokur, Jr., "Report of Investigation by the Special Investigative Committee of the Board of Directors of Enron Corp.," February 1, 2002. The facts as recounted here are taken from this report and also rely on the following sources: William Bradley, "Enron's End," *American Prospect*, January 1, 2001, p. 30; John R. Emshwiller, "Documents Track Enron's Partnerships," *Wall Street Journal*, January 2, 2002, p. A3; Daniel Fisher, "Shell Game: How Enron Concealed Losses, Inflated Earnings—and Hid Secret Deals," *Forbes*, January 7, 2002, p. 52; Susan Lee, "The Dismal Science: Enron's Success Story," *Wall Street Journal*, December: 26, 2001, p. A11; Bethany McLean, "Why Enron Went Bust," *Fortune*, December 24, 2001, p. 58; Peter Speigel, "Enron Collapse: The Fastow Factor—The Architect of Enron's Downfall," *Financial Times*, May 21, 2002, p. 32.

11. Quote from U.S. attorney Otto G. Obermaier is from Robert J. McCartney and David S. Hilzenrath, "Salomon, .S. Settle Bond Case; Wall Street Brokerage to Pay $290 Million," *Washington Post*, May 21, 1992, p. A1.

12. The emergence of regulations to curb business irresponsibility is traced in James Willard Hurst, *The Legitimacy of the Business Corporation in the Law of the United States 1780–1970* (Charlottesville, Va.: The University Press of Virginia, 1970). For post-Enron reform proposals, see, e.g., Amy Borrus, Mike McNamee, Paula Dwyer, Marcia Vickers, David Henry, "What Cleanup? As Washington Dithers, Financial Reform is Going Nowhere Fast," *Business Week*, June 17, 2002, p. 26; Scott Bernard Nelson, "Healing the Accounting Industry," *Boston Sunday Globe*, June 23, 2002, p. C1.

13. On the importance of such factors, see, for example, David Garvin, *Learning in Action: A Guide to Putting the Learning Organization to Work* (Boston, Mass.: Harvard Business School Press, 2000); Peter M. Senge, *The Fifth Discipline: The Art and Practice of the Learning Organization* (New York, N.Y.: Doubleday & Company, Inc., 1994).

14. Teresa M. Amabile, "How to Kill Creativity," *Harvard Business Review* (September–October 1998), pp. 77–87; "Mobilizing Creativity in Organizations," *California Management Review*, vol. 40, no. 1 (Fall 1997), pp. 39–58.

15. W. Chan Kim and Renée A. Mauborgne, "Making Global Strategies Work," *Sloan Management Review* (Spring 1993), pp. 11–27.

16. Robert H. Moorman, "Relationship Between Organizational Justice and Organizational Citizenship Behaviors: Do Fairness Perceptions Influence Employee Citizenship?" *Journal of Applied Psychology*, vol. 76, no. 6 (1991), pp. 845–855. See also Dennis W. Organ and Mary Konovsky, "Cognitive Versus Affective Determinants of Organizational Citizenship Behavior," *Journal of Applied Psychology*, vol. 74, no. 1 (1989), pp. 157–164.

17. James M. Kouzes and Barry Z. Posner, *The Leadership Challenge* (San Francisco, Ca: Jossey-Bass Publishers, 1987), pp. 16–19.

18. The research of Charles O'Reilly as cited in Kouzes and Posner, *The Leadership Challenge*, pp. 22–23.

19. See Anil K. Gupta and Vijay Govindarajan, "Knowledge Management's Social Dimension: Lessons from Nucor Steel," *Sloan Management Review* (Fall 2000), pp. 71–80, esp. p. 76.

20. David W. De Long and Liam Fahey, "Diagnosing Cultural Barriers to Knowledge Management," *Academy of Management Executive*, vol. 14, no. 4 (2000), pp. 113–127, esp. p. 119.

21. Rensis Likert, "A Motivational Approach to a Modified Theory of Organization and Management," in *Modern Organization Theory*, ed. Mason Haire (New York, N.Y.: John Wiley & Sons, 1959), pp. 184–217.

22. This study covered 1500 manufacturer-retailer relationships. Nirmalya Kumar, "The Power of Trust in Manufacturer-Retailer Relationships," *Harvard Business Review* (November-December 1996), pp. 92–106.

23. All quotes are from Lynn Sharp Paine and Karen Hopper Wruck, "Sealed Air Corporation: Globalization and Corporate Culture (B)," HBS Case No. 9-398-097 (Boston, Mass.: Harvard Business School Publishing, 1998).

24. The two surveys referred to in this paragraph were both conducted jointly by Walker Information and Hudson Institute. For the study linking loyalty and perceptions of company ethics, see "Integrity in the Workplace: The 1999 Business Ethics Study," Indianapolis, Indiana, May 31, 2000. For the 32-country

study of employee commitment, see Walker Information Global Network and Hudson Institute, "Commitment in the Workplace: The 2000 Global Employee Relationship Report," Indianapolis, Indiana, October 18, 2000.

25. The link between trust and quality is noted in W. Edwards Deming, Foreword to John O. Whitney, *The Trust Factor: Liberating Profits and Restoring Corporate Vitality* (New York, N.Y.: McGraw-Hill, 1994), pp. vii, viii.

26. For research on service management companies, see James L. Heskett, W. Earl Sasser, Jr., and Christopher W. L. Hart, *Service Breakthroughs: Challenging the Rules of the Game* (New York, N.Y.: The Free Press, 1990). For research on loyalty, see, e.g., Frederick F. Reichheld, *The Loyalty Effect: The Hidden Force Behind Growth, Profits, and Lasting Value* (Boston, Mass.: Harvard Business School Press, 1996).

27. The employee caught in a dubious sales scheme is quoted in Julia Flynn, Christina Del Valle, and Russell Mitchell, "Did Sears Take Other Customers for a Ride?" *Business Week*, August 3, 1992, p. 25. The Enron example comes from Elliot Spagat, "Employees, Angry and Broke, Offer Enron's Secrets for Sale on the Web," *Wall Street Journal Online*, January 22, 2002, <http://online.wsj.com> (February 25, 2002).

28. The intelligence gatherer who turned on his employer is described in Robert Johnson, "Inside Job: The Case of Marc Feith Shows Corporate Spies Aren't Just High-Tech," *Wall Street Journal*, January 9, 1987 <http://global.factiva.com> (June 14, 2002). The Salomon quote is from Paine and Santoro, "Forging the New Salomon," HBS Case No. 9-395-046, p. 10.

29. The research of Jonathan Haidt at the University of Virginia is discussed in Gareth Cook, "Seeing How the Spirit Moves Us," *Boston Globe*, December 6, 2000, p. A1.

30. Robert Axelrod, *The Evolution of Cooperation* (New York, N.Y.: Basic Books, 1984).

31. Quoted in Laurie P. Cohen, Michael Siconolfi, Kevin G. Salwen, "SEC Probes Collusion by Traders," *Wall Street Journal*, August 27, 1991, p. C1.

32. The attributes associated with a good reputation are discussed in Charles J. Fombrun, *Reputation: Realizing Value from the Corporate Image* (Boston, Mass.: Harvard Business School Press, 1996). See also Grahame Dowling, *Creating Corporate Reputations: Identity, Image, and Performance* (Oxford, U.K.: Oxford University Press, 2001).

33. See, e.g., Fombrun, *Reputation*, at p. 6; Dowling, *Creating Corporate Reputations*, pp. 49–63.

34. Jennifer Reese, "America's Most Admired Corporations," *Fortune*, February 8, 1993, pp. 44 ff.

35. In general, for the payoffs of a good reputation, see Fombrun, *Reputation*. For research on the beneficial effects of a good reputation for contractual outcomes, see Abhijit V. Banerjee and Esther Duflo, "Reputation Effects and the Limits of Contracting: A Study of the Indian Software Industry," *Quarterly Journal of Economics*, vol. 115, no. 3 (August 2000), pp. 989–1017.

36. See Todd Saxton, "The Effects of Partner and Relationship Characteristics on Alliance Outcomes," *Academy of Management Review*, vol. 40, no. 2 (1997), pp. 443–461.

37. Quoted in Peter Janssen, "Boom Time for Thai Cement," *Asian Business,* August 1990, p. 76.

38. Jonathan M. Karpoff and John R. Lott, Jr., "The Reputational Penalty Firms Bear from Committing Criminal Fraud," *Journal of Law and Economics,* vol. 36 (October 1993), pp. 757–802.

39. Video accompanying Richard S. Tedlow, "James Burke: A Career in American Business," HBS Case No. 9-389-177.

40. Jean-Noël Kapferer, *Strategic Brand Management: Creating and Sustaining Brand Equity Long Term,* 2d ed. (London: Kogan Page, 1997), pp. 29–31.

41. See also, e.g., David A. Aker, "Building a Brand: The Saturn Story," *California Management Review* (Winter 1994), pp. 114–133.

42. See John P. Kotter and James L. Heskett, *Corporate Culture and Performance* (New York, N.Y.: The Free Press, 1992).

43. For this study, which covered 81 publicly held companies during the period 1978 through 1983, see Donald K. Clifford, Jr., and Richard E. Cavanagh, *The Winning Performance: How America's High-Growth Midsize Companies Succeed* (New York, N.Y.: Bantam Books, 1985).

44. See James C. Collins and Jerry I. Porras, *Built to Last: Successful Habits of Visionary Companies* (New York, N.Y.: HarperBusiness, 1994).

45. See Curtis C. Verschoor, "Principles Build Profits," *Management Accounting* (October 1997), pp. 42–46.

46. Joshua Daniel Margolis and James Patrick Walsh, *People and Profits? The Search for a Link Between a Company's Social and Financial Performance* (Mahwah, N.J.: Lawrence Erlbaum Associates, 2001).

Chapter 3   Time for a Reality Check

1. The quoted material is excerpted from a letter written by a trader to his wife in Boston. See Margaret C.S. Christman, *Adventurous Pursuits: Americans and the China Trade 1784–1844* (Washington, D.C.: Smithsonian Press, 1984), p. 117.

2. For a chilling account of the ivory trade, see Adam Hochschild, *King Leopold's Ghost: A Story of Greed, Terror, and Heroism in Colonial Africa* (Boston, Mass.: Houghton Mifflin Company, 1998). The National Cash Register example is from Richard S. Tedlow, *Giants of Enterprise: Seven Business Innovators and the Empires They Built* (New York, N.Y.: HarperBusiness, 2001), p. 192.

3. Parts of this chapter are based on my article, "Does Ethics Pay?" *Business Ethics Quarterly,* vol. 10, no. 1 (January 2000), pp. 319–330.

4. Joshua Joseph, *2000 National Business Ethics Survey Volume I: How Employees Perceive Ethics at Work* (Washington, D.C.: Ethics Resource Center, 2000), pp. xi, 12. This survey was conducted by telephone, and the interviewees were randomly selected employees from the for-profit, nonprofit, and governmental sectors.

5. KPMG, Integrity Management Services, "2000 Organizational Integrity Survey: A Summary," KPMG US Web page, 2000, <http://www.us.kpmg. com/RutUS_prod/Documents/12/IMSrvy_.pdf> (March 6, 2002). This survey was based on a questionnaire sent to the homes of prequalified working adults in selected industries. The highest incidence of observed misconduct was found to be in consumer-related industries.

6. Arthur P. Brief, Janet M. Dukerich, Paul R. Brown, Joan F. Brett, "What's Wrong with the Treadway Commission Report? Experimental Analyses of the Effects of Personal Values and Codes of Conduct on Fraudulent Financial Reporting," *Journal of Business Ethics*, vol. 15 (1996), pp. 183–198, at 190.

7. "Press Conference with Attorney General Janet Reno and Joel Klein, Assistant Attorney General," *Federal News Service*, May 20, 1999.

8. As seen in "The Carpet," by Magnus Bergmar/Bergmar Produktion (Mariefred, Sweden, 1994), aired on Swedish television, March 1994.

9. Ellen Barry, "Games Feared as Violent Youths' Basic Training," *Boston Globe*, April 29, 1999, p. A1; Derek Donovan, "A Culture of Overkill: Music, Movies & Mayhem Game Over . . . Violence Takes Video Games to a Higher Level of Angst," *Kansas City Star*, April 24, 1999, p. E1.

10. For accounts of the Colorado and Kentucky school killings, see, in order, Evan Gahr, "Gore for Sale: Computer Games at a Store Near You . . . Be Afraid, Be Very Afraid," *Wall Street Journal*, April 30, 1999, p. W13; Gary Chapman, "Video Killers," *Texas Monthly*, January 2001, p. 61; Frank Main, "Move to Limit Violent-Game Sales," *Chicago Sun-Times*, October 20, 2000, p. 16. Police investigating the Erfurt, Germany, school killing of 18 in April 2002 found violent computer games and videos in the 19-year-old perpetrator's home. See Peter Finn and Erik Schelzig, "Students Recount Teen Killer's Methodical Path," *Boston Sunday Globe*, April 28, 2002, p. A21.

11. Lt. Col. Dave Grossman, *On Killing: The Psychological Cost of Learning to Kill in War and Society* (Boston, Mass.: Little, Brown and Company, 1995); Lt. Col. Dave Grossman and Gloria Degaetano, *Stop Teaching Our Kids to Kill: A Call to Action Against TV, Movie and Video Game Violence* (New York, N.Y.: Crown Publishing Group, 1999).

12. Donovan, "A Culture of Overkill."

13. Quoted in John F. Harris and Sharon Waxman, "FTC to Probe Entertainment Ads," *Boston Globe*, June 2, 1999, p. A3.

14. Quoted in Evan Thomas, "The King of Gore: Doom Creator John Romero Has Mayhem on His Mind," *Newsweek*, April 27, 1998, pp. 76–77.

15. Quoted in Gahr, "Gore for Sale."

16. For an interesting collection of requests for payment, including this one, see Lynn Sharp Paine, "Becton Dickinson: Ethics and Business Practices (A)," HBS Case No. 9-399-055 (Boston, Mass.: Harvard Business School Publishing, 1998), p. 9.

17. The idea of depicting this relationship using Venn diagrams comes from my colleague Professor Thomas R. Piper.

18. For a full account, see Lynn Sharp Paine, "AES Global Values," HBS Case No. 9-399-136 (Boston, Mass.: Harvard Business School Publishing, 1999). For a similar dilemma that arose for AES in California, see Kathryn Kranhold, "Balancing Act: 'Surf City' Power Plant Brings Hope for Crisis, Fear for Environment," *Wall Street Journal*, April 18, 2001, p. A1.

19. See Globe Spotlight Team, "Home Builder Leaves Trail of Bitter Buyers," *Boston Sunday Globe*, April 29, 2001, p. A1; Sacha Pfeiffer, "Efficient Practices a Hit with Wall Street," *Boston Sunday Globe*, April 29, 2001, p. A26.

20. See John Maynard Keynes, *A Tract on Monetary Reform* (London: Macmillan, 1924), Chapter 3. He went on to say that "Economists set themselves too easy,

too useless a task if in tempestuous seasons they can only tell us that when the storm is long past the ocean is flat again."

21. See Lynn Sharp Paine, "The Cherkizovsky Group (A)," HBS Case No. 9-399-119 (Boston, Mass.: Harvard Business School Publishing, 1999).

22. I owe this example to my colleague Professor Bruce Scott. See *South African Banking Review* (South Africa: The Banking Council), December 31, 1998, pp. 15–18, 24.

23. Charles Gasparino, "Wall Street Has Less and Less Time for Small Investors," *Wall Street Journal*, October 5, 1999, p. C1.

24. See Michael Wang, "S Africa's Nedcor Turns Hostile to Seize Standard Bank," *Dow Jones Newswires*, November 11, 1999; "S Africa Standard Bk Says Nedcor Merger Plan Unacceptable," *Dow Jones Newswires*, October 26, 1999.

25. Greta Steyn, "South Africa's Finance Minister Blocks Standard Bank Investment Corporation Takeover," *Financial Times*, June 22, 2000, p. 32.

26. For a full account, see Lynn Sharp Paine, "Levi Strauss & Co.: Global Sourcing (A), (B)," Harvard Business School Case Nos. 9-395-127, 9-395-128 (Boston, Mass.: Harvard Business School Publishing, 1994).

27. The account in this paragraph is based on the following sources: Ralph T. King, Jr., "Jeans Therapy: Levi's Factory Workers Are Assigned to Teams, and Morale Takes a Hit," *Wall Street Journal*, May 20, 1998, pp. A1, A3; Frank Swoboda, "An American Emblem's Presence Fades," *Washington Post*, February 23, 1999, p. A1; Louise Lee, "Can Levi's Be Cool Again?" *Business Week*, March 13, 2000, p. 144; Michael A. Verespej, "How to Manage Adversity: Why Do So Many Companies Do It So Poorly?" *Industry Week*, January 19, 1998, p. 24.

28. Disciples of Confucius are said to have compiled his thoughts around 400 B.C., some 75 years after his death. See, e.g., *The Analects of Confucius*, trans. by Simon Leys (New York, N.Y.: W.W. Norton & Company, 1997), p. xix, 175. See also, Roger T. Ames, Henry Rosemont, Jr., *The Analects of Confucius: A Philosophical Translation* (New York, N.Y.: Ballantine Books, 1998), p. 51 (discussing *li*). Although there is support for my interpretation in the literature, some scholars of Chinese thought would likely dispute it.

29. *The Analects of Confucius*, trans. by Leys, pp. 130–131; Ames and Rosemont, *The Analects of Confucius*, p. 49 (discussing *ren*).

30. See, e.g., James D. Wallace, *Virtues and Vices* (Ithaca, N.Y.: Cornell University Press, 1978).

31. The best-known source for this distinction is Carol Gilligan, *In a Different Voice: Psychological Theory and Women's Development* (Cambridge, Mass.: Harvard University Press, 1982). Gilligan relates this distinction to gender, but this seems dubious in light of the distinction's long history and embrace by male authorities. In the first century B.C., Cicero wrote of justice and generosity (also called kindliness or beneficence) as the two parts of the principle that holds human society together. See Cicero, *De Officiis/On Duties*, Book One, trans. by Harry G. Edinger (New York, N.Y.: The Bobbs-Merrill Company, Inc., 1974), p. 12 ff.

32. Quoted in Lynn Sharp Paine and Michael Santoro, "Forging the New Salomon," HBS Case No. 9-395-046 (Boston, Mass.: Harvard Business School Publishing, 1994), p. 6.

33. The account of Timberland comes mainly from James E. Austin, "The Invisible Side of Leadership," *Leader to Leader*, no. 8 (Spring 1998), pp. 38–46 at 41.

34. Lynn Sharp Paine, "Managing for Organizational Integrity," *Harvard Business Review* (March–April 1994).

35. The quotation is from *United States v. Beech-Nut Nutrition Corporation*, 871 F.2nd 1181 (2nd Cir. 1989) at 1186–1187.

36. Unless otherwise indicated, information in this paragraph comes from Sissela Bok, *Common Values* (Columbia, Mo.: University of Missouri Press, 1995), p. 15.

37. H.L.A. Hart, *The Concept of Law* (London: Oxford University Press, 1961), pp. 167, 176.

38. For a review of what leading Western philosophers have had to say about deceit, see Sissela Bok, *Lying: Moral Choice in Public and Private Life* (New York, N.Y.: Pantheon Books, 1978).

39. See Caux Round Table, "Principles for Business," Principle 3, Caux Round Table Web page, 1994, <http://www.cauxroundtable.org> (March 4, 2002); "An Interfaith Declaration: A Code of Ethics on International Business for Christians, Muslims and Jews," *Global Virtue Ethics Review*, vol. 1, no. 2 (1999), Principle 4, p. 126, first published 1993, available from Southern Public Administration Education Foundation Web page, <http://www.spaef.com/GVER_PUB> (March 6, 2002); Organisation for Economic Co-operation and Development, "The OECD Guidelines for Multinational Enterprises," part 1, section 7 (4), "Consumer Interests," p. 25, OECD online, revised in 2000 (created 1976), <http://www.oecd.org/daf/investment/guidelines/mnetext.htm> (March 4, 2002).

40. Jesse Jackson, quoted in "Wall Street: The Colour (and Sex) of Money," *Economist*, June 19, 1999, p. 78.

Chapter 4   The Corporation's Evolving Personality

1. "The Millennium Poll on Corporate Social Responsibility," executive briefing, conducted by Environics International, Ltd., in cooperation with the Prince of Wales Business Leaders Forum and the Conference Board, 1999, <http://www.environicsinternational.com/news_archives/MPExecBrief.pdf> (March 5, 2002).

2. Aaron Bernstein, "Too Much Corporate Power?" *Business Week*, September 11, 2000, p. 149.

3. As quoted in Christopher D. Stone, *Where the Law Ends: The Social Control of Corporate Behavior*, 2d ed. (New York, N.Y.: Harper & Row Publishers, 1975), p. 3. A slightly different version is quoted and attributed to Edward, First Baron Thurlow (1731–1806), Lord Chancellor of England, in John C. Coffee, Jr., " 'No Soul to Damn: No Body to Kick': An Unscandalized Inquiry into the Problem of Corporate Punishment," *Michigan Law Review*, vol. 79 (January 1981), p. 386: "Did you ever expect a corporation to have a conscience, when it has no soul to be damned, and no body to be kicked?"

4. In *The Case of Sutton's Hospital*, Sir Edward Coke (1552–1634) wrote, "They [corporations] cannot commit treason, nor be outlawed nor excommunicate,

for they have no souls." 10 Coke Report 1a, 77 Eng. Rep. 937 (Exchequer Chamber, 1613).

5. See generally Bishop Carleton Hunt, *The Development of the Business Corporation in England, 1800–1867* (Cambridge, Mass.: Harvard University Press, 1936).

6. See John Dewey, "The Historic Background of Corporate Legal Personality," *Yale Law Journal*, vol. XXXV, no. 6 (April 1926), pp. 655–673, at 665. For challenges to this attribution, see sources cited in William W. Bratton, Jr., "The New Economic Theory of the Firm: Critical Perspectives from History," *Stanford Law Review*, vol. 41 (July 1989), pp. 1471–1527 at note 151.

7. On the Pope's logic, see Coffee, "No Soul to Damn."

8. *Trustees of Dartmouth College v. Woodward*, 17 U.S. (4 Wheat.) 518, 636 (1819).

9. Joseph S. Davis, *Essays in the Earlier History of American Corporations* (Cambridge, Mass.: Harvard University Press, 1917), II, 8, 22, quoted in Oscar Handlin and Mary F. Handlin, "Origins of the American Business Corporation," *Journal of Economic History*, vol. 5, no. 1 (May 1945), pp. 1–23 at p. 4. Another historian puts the number of special charters creating corporations in the states during the period 1780–1801 at 317, 96 percent of which were of the public-interest variety. See James Willard Hurst, *The Legitimacy of the Business Corporation in the Law of the United States, 1780–1970* (Charlottesville, Va.: The University Press of Virginia, 1970), p. 17.

10. By the end of the nineteenth century, limited liability had come to be seen as an essential attribute of the corporate form. On the origins of limited liability, see Handlin and Handlin, "Origins of the American Business Corporation," pp. 8–17.

11. *Bank of the United States v. Deveaux*, 9 U.S. (5 Cranch) 61 at 86 (1809). This case was subsequently overruled and the corporation deemed in law a citizen of the state that created it. See *Louisville, Cincinnati & Charleston Railroad v. Letson*, 43 U.S. (2 How.) 497 at 557–558 (1844). For discussion of this development, see Herbert Hovenkamp, "The Classical Corporation in American Legal Thought," 76 *Georgetown Law Journal* 1593 (June 1988) at 1598–1599.

12. For a detailed discussion and analysis, see Morton J. Horwitz, "*Santa Clara* Revisited: The Development of Corporate Theory," Chap. 3 in *The Transformation of American Law 1870–1960* (New York, N.Y.: Oxford University Press, 1992), pp. 65–107. For the story of the parallel development in England, see Hunt, *Development of the Business Corporation in England*.

13. See George Heberton Evans, Jr., *Business Incorporations in the United States 1800–1943* (New York, N.Y.: National Bureau of Economic Research, 1948), pp. 3, 10.

14. Ibid., p. 35. See also Hunt, *Development of the Business Corporation in England*.

15. For a full account of the evolving concept of the corporation, see Hovenkamp, "Classical Corporation in American Legal Thought."

16. For description and analysis of these legal developments, see Hovenkamp, "Classical Corporation in American Legal Thought."

17. The subject of the corporation's moral personality is broached in a 1903 lecture by Frederic William Maitland, "Moral Personality and Legal Personality,"

which appears in *The Collected Papers of Frederic William Maitland*, vol. III, ed. H. A. L. Fisher (Buffalo, N.Y.: William S. Hein & Company, 1981), pp. 304–320.

18. For an effort to sort out the morass, see Dewey, "Historic Background of Corporate Legal Personality," pp. 655–673. See also Max Radin, "The Endless Problem of Corporate Personality," *Columbia Law Review*, vol. 32 (1932), pp. 643–667.

19. See Horwitz, *Transformation of American Law*, pp. 100–105.

20. A. A. Berle, Jr., Preface to Adolf A. Berle, Jr., and Gardiner C. Means, *The Modern Corporation and Private Property* (New York, N.Y.: Commerce Clearing House, Inc., 1932), p. v.

21. For this suggestion, see E. Merrick Dodd, "For Whom Are Corporate-Managers Trustees?" *Harvard Law Review*, vol. XVL, no. 7 (May 8, 1932), pp. 1145–1163 at 1160.

22. See Theodore Levitt, "The Dangers of Social Responsibility," *Harvard Business Review* (September-October 1958), pp. 41–50.

23. For a thorough account of the evolving concepts of the corporation in the United States, see Bratton, "The New Economic Theory of the Firm."

24. For an account of the corporate responsibility debate of the 1970s, see Fred D. Baldwin, *Conflicting Interests: Corporate-Governance Controversies* (Lexington, Mass.: D.C. Heath and Company, 1984).

25. Milton Friedman, "The Social Responsibility of Business Is to Increase Its Profits," *New York Times Magazine*, September 13, 1970, p. 33.

26. Quote from Lynn Sharp Paine and Michael A. Santoro, "Forging the New Salomon," HBS Case No. 9-395-046 (Boston, Mass.: Harvard Business School Publishing, 1994), p. 11.

27. *Wall Street Journal*, September 19, 2000, p. A1.

28. See Lynn Sharp Paine and Michael Watkins, "Recall 2000: Bridgestone Corp. (A)," HBS Case No. 9-302-013 (Boston, Mass.: Harvard Business School Publishing, 2001).

29. Margaret McKegney, "Ford, Firestone Woes Extend Beyond the U.S.," *Ad Age Global*, September 1, 2000.

30. *Newsweek* poll, conducted by Princeton Survey Research Associates, September 7–8, 2000, <http://www.pollingreport.com/business.htm> (March 5, 2002).

31. The reference is to Senator Richard C. Shelby (Republican, Alabama). See "U.S. Senate Committee on Appropriations, Subcommittee on Transportation Holds Hearing on Firestone Tire Recall," *Political Transcripts by Federal Document Clearing House*, September 6, 2000. Available from Factiva, <http://www.library.hbs.edu/hbs/factiva.htm> (June 17, 2002).

32. The quoted material is from the following sources: George Will, "From Evasion to Outrage about Enron," *Boston Globe*, January 16, 2002, p. A13 (calling for "indignation" toward Enron's behavior); Jim Landers and Christopher Lee, "House Panel Takes Auditors to Task over Shredding of Enron Documents: Senate Committee Says Enron's Collapse Indicates Crisis in Ethics," *Dallas Morning News*, January 25, 2002, p. 1A (Michigan Democratic Congressman John D. Dingell calls Andersen's shredding of doc-

uments "a serious breach in corporate integrity"); Judith Burns, "Business Group Urges Cautious Response to Enron Debacle," *Dow Jones News Service*, February 11, 2002 (Business Roundtable says the report on Enron by board member William Powers describes "'a pervasive breakdown' in ethics and corporate governance"); Felix Rohatyn, "The Betrayal of Capitalism," *New York Review of Books*, February 28, 2002, p. 8 ("part of a general failure to maintain the ethical standards . . . fundamental to the American economic system"). See also Elliot Spagat, "Employees, Angry and Broke, Offer Enron's Secrets for Sale on the Web," *Wall Street Journal Online*, January 22, 2002 <http://online. wsj.com> (February 25, 2002).

33. Jerry Mander, "The Myth of Corporate Conscience," *Business and Society Review*, vol. 81 (Spring 1992), pp. 56, 63.

34. Joseph L. Bower, "On the Amoral Organization," in *The Corporate Society*, ed. by Robin Marris (London: Macmillan, 1974), pp. 178–213, p. 179.

35. Martin Benjamin and Daniel A. Bronstein, "Moral and Criminal Responsibility and Corporate Persons," in *Corporations and Society*, ed. by Warren J. Samuels and Arthur S. Miller (New York, N.Y.: Greenwood Press, 1987), p. 280. On the corporation's lack of "soul," see also Russell B. Stevenson, Jr., "Corporations and Social Responsibility: In Search of the Corporate Soul," *George Washington Law Review*, vol. 42, no. 4 (May 1974), pp. 709–736.

36. See, e.g., Charles Derber, *Corporation Nation: How Corporations Are Taking Over Our Lives and What We Can Do About It* (New York, N.Y.: St. Martin's Press, 1998), pp. 4–5. For an earlier look at the rise of the organization, see, e.g., Kenneth Boulding, *The Organizational Revolution: A Study in the Ethics of Economic Organization* (New York, N.Y.: Harper & Brothers, 1953).

37. U.S. Census Bureau, *Statistical Abstract of the United States, 2000* (Washington, D.C., 2000) p. 535.

38. For 1997, corporations accounted for 90 percent of sales in the retail sector. U.S. Census Bureau, *1997 Economic Census: Retail Trade*, "Establishment and Firm Size," Census Bureau Web page, 2000, p. 216 <http://www.census. gov/prod/ec97/97r44-5z.pdf> (March 13, 2002).

39. U.S. Census Bureau, "Statistics about Business Size, Employer and Nonemployer Firms by Legal Form of Organization," Census Bureau Web page, 1992, <http://www.census.gov/epcd/www/smallbus.html> (March 5, 2002). These data are based on the 1992 Characteristics of Business Owners Survey, a series that was discontinued.

40. Theodore Caplow, Louis Hicks, Ben J. Wattenberg, *The First Measured Century: An Illustrated Guide to Trends in America, 1900–2000* (Washington, D.C.: AEI Press, 2001), pp. 252–253.

41. Caplow, et al., pp. 246–247.

42. U.S. Census Bureau, *Statistical Abstract of the United States, 2000* (Washington, D.C., 2000), p. 552.

43. Data from National Science Foundation, "National Patterns of R&D Resources: 2000 Data Update," NSF Web page, March 2001, <www.nsf.gov/sbe/srs/ nsf01309/start.htm> (1 November 2001). Government spending includes both federal and nonfederal governments, with the exception of nonfederal spending on research and development performed by industry, which is

counted as industry spending. Industry consists of manufacturing and non-manufacturing companies.

44. Organisation for Economic Co-operation and Development, Directorate for Science, Technology and Industry, *University Research in Transition* (Paris: OECD, 1999), p. 95, Table 2.

45. Data from The Association of University Technology Managers, Inc., *AUTM Licensing Survey, FY 2000 Survey Summary* (Northbrook, Ill.: The Association of University Technology Managers, Inc., 2001), p. 9.

46. Relying on Federal Election Commission data, the Center for Responsive Politics estimates that for the 1998 election cycle, soft-money contributions totaled $186 million and PAC contributions totaled some $266 million for a combined total of $452 million. Of this amount, business accounted for $166 million of the PAC contributions and $167 million of the soft-money donations, for a total of $333 million. The Center for Responsive Politics, "Business, Labor, and Ideological Split in Donations from PACs," CRP Web page, <http://www.opensecrets.org/pubs/bigpicture2000/bli/bli_pacs.ihtml> (March 25, 2002); "Business, Labor, and Ideological Split in Soft Money Donations," <http://www.opensecrets.org/pubs/bigpicture2000/bli/bli_indiv.ihtml> (March 25, 2002). Note that this total overstates corporate contributions somewhat because it also includes contributions from trade and professional associations, although many of these associations are themselves supported by corporations. On soft-money contributions, see generally Joseph E. Cantor, "Soft and Hard Money in Contemporary Elections" (Washington, D.C.: Congressional Research Service, 1997).

47. U.S. Census Bureau, *Historical Statistics of the United States, Colonial Times to 1970*, Bicentennial Edition, Part 2 (Washington, D.C., 1975), p. 1105; U.S. Census Bureau, *Statistical Abstract of the United States, 2000* (Washington, D.C., 2000), p. 341. The combined total federal income tax paid by individuals and corporations was $50.6 billion in 1954 and $1.1 trillion in 1999. Of this total, corporations paid $21 billion in 1954 (42 percent) and $184.7 billion in 1999 (17 percent).

48. As cited in Stuart Kahan, "Played Out on the Ledger Sheets," *Practical Accountant*, vol. 32, no. 6 (June 1999), pp. 64–65. Kahan cites the Association of Certified Fraud Examiners "Report to the Nation on Occupational Fraud and Abuse" (1996) for white-collar crime data, and the FBI, "Crime in the United States, 1995—Crime Index Offenses Reported," pp. 27 and 39, for street-crime data. See <http://www.cfenet.com/media/reportnation.asp> (October 26, 2001) and <http://www.fbi.gov/ucr/95cius.htm> (October 5, 2001).

49. InterStudy Publications, *The Competitive Edge: 11.1 HMO Industry Report* (St. Paul, Minn: InterStudy Publications, 2000), p. 18.

50. Jon Gabel, "Ten Ways HMOs Have Changed During the 1990s," *Health Affairs*, vol. 16, no. 3 (1997), pp. 134–145. Gabel's figures are based on data from the American Association of Health Plans.

51. Florencio López-de-Silanes, Andrei Shleifer, and Robert W. Vishny, "Privatization in the United States," Working Paper No. 5113 (Cambridge, Mass.: National Bureau of Economic Research), pp. 9–10 and Table 1.

52. Nicholas V. Gianaris, *Modern Capitalism: Privatization, Employee Ownership, and Industrial Democracy* (Westport, Conn.: Praeger, 1996), p. 57.

53. Ladan Mahboobi, "Recent Privatisation Trends," *Financial Market Trends*, no. 79 (Paris: OECD Publications, 2001), pp. 43–65.

54. Maria K. Boutchkova and William L. Megginson, "Privatization and the Rise of Global Capital Markets," *Financial Management* (Tampa) 29 (Winter 2000), pp. 31–76, at 44–48.

55. Mahboobi, "Recent Privatisation Trends," pp. 48–49.

56. Information in this paragraph from William L. Megginson, "The Impact of Privatization on Capital Market Development and Individual Share Ownership," presentation at International Federation of Stock Exchanges (FIBV) Investor Education Workshop, Stockholm, November 20, 2000. See also Boutchkova and Megginson, "Privatization and the Rise of Global Capital Markets," at 35, 36, 44, 69. In addition, William L. Megginson provided a private communication on file with the author (July 5, 2001).

57. Boutchkova and Megginson, "Privatization and the Rise of Global Capital Markets," p. 37.

58. Neil Roger, "Recent Trends in Private Participation in Infrastructure," *Private-sector*, Note No. 196 (Washington, D.C.: The World Bank Group, Finance, Private Sector, and Infrastructure Network, September 1999).

59. Sarah Anderson and John Cavanagh, "Top 200: The Rise of Corporate Global Power" (Washington, D.C.: Institute for Policy Studies, 2000), pp. 3, 13, Institute for Policy Studies Web Page, <http://www.ips-dc.org/downloads/Top_200.pdf> (March 13, 2002). Although corporate sales do not measure a company's contribution to GDP, the comparison of sales to GDP provides some indication of the economic clout wielded by the world's largest firms.

60. OneSource Information Services, <http://globalbb.onesource.com> (August 15, 2001).

61. Anderson and Cavanagh, "Top 200," at p. 3.

62. Ibid., p. 10.

63. Organisation for Economic Co-operation and Development, *OECD Science, Technology and Industry Scoreboard: Towards a Knowledge-Based Economy* (Paris: OECD, 2001), p. 149.

64. For the difficulties faced by a private corporate manager of a formerly government-provided water service, see Lynn Sharp Paine, "Sideco Americana S.A. (A), (B), (C)," HBS Case Nos. 9-398-081, 9-398-082, 9-398-083 (Boston, Mass.: Harvard Business School Publishing, 1998).

65. Thomas Hobbes, *Leviathan*, ed. by Richard Tuck (Cambridge, U.K.: Cambridge University Press, 1991), Part I, Ch. 13, p. 89.

66. Ibid.

67. See, e.g., Francis Fukuyama, *Trust: The Social Virtues and the Creation of Prosperity* (New York, N.Y.: The Free Press, 1995); Robert D. Putnam, "The Prosperous Community: Social Capital and Public Life," *American Prospect*, no. 13 (Spring 1993), pp. 37–38.

68. For research on effects of corruption, see Paolo Mauro, "Corruption and Growth," *Quarterly Journal of Economics*, vol. 110, no. 3 (August 1995), pp. 681–712;

Shang-Jin Wei, "How Taxing Is Corruption on International Investors?" *The Review of Economics and Statistics*, vol. 82, no. 1 (2000), pp. 1–11.

69. Shang-Jin Wei, "How Taxing Is Corruption," p. 8.

70. Paolo Mauro, "Corruption and Growth," at p. 705.

71. For a similar view, see G. J. Warnock, *The Object of Morality* (London: Methuen & Co., 1971).

72. Maitland, "Moral Personality and Legal Personality," pp. 304–320, esp. pp. 314–315: "For the morality of common sense the group is [a] . . . right-and-duty bearing unit."

73. This example comes from Francis J. Aguilar, *Managing Corporate Ethics: Learning from America's Ethical Companies How to Supercharge Business Performance* (New York, N.Y.: Oxford University Press, 1994), p. 73.

74. Cited in James W. McKie, "Changing Views," in *Social Responsibility and the Business Predicament*, ed. by James W. McKie (Washington, D.C.: The Brookings Institution, 1974), pp. 22–23. For other examples, see Morrell Heald, *The Social Responsibilities of Business: Company and Community, 1900–1960* (New Brunswick, N.J.: Transaction Books, 1970), pp. 10–14.

75. Henry S. Dennison, *Ethics and Modern Business* (Boston, Mass.: Houghton Mifflin, 1932), p. 15.

76. Ibid, p. 9.

77. See codes collected in Edgar L. Heermance, *Codes of Ethics, A Handbook* (Burlington, Vt.: Free Press Printing Co., 1924); Everett W. Lord, *The Fundamentals of Business Ethics* (New York, N.Y.: Ronald Press Co., 1926), esp. pp. 141–173.

78. For analysis and review of these campaigns, see Roland Marchand, *Creating the Corporate Soul* (Berkeley, Ca.: University of California Press, 1998).

79. For the story of AT&T's campaign, see Marchand, "*AT&T*: The Vision of a Loved Monopoly," Chap. 2 in *Creating the Corporate Soul*, pp. 48–87.

80. Norton Long, quoted in Marchand, *Creating the Corporate Soul*, p. 87.

81. *A. P. Smith Manufacturing Company v. Barlow*, 13 N.J. 145 at 154 (Sup. Ct. of N.J. 1953).

82. See, e.g., Boulding, *Organizational Revolution*. Also John Kenneth Galbraith, *American Capitalism: The Concept of Countervailing Power*, rev. ed. (Boston, Mass.: Houghton Mifflin Company, 1956); Edward Sagendorph Mason, *The Corporation in Modern Society* (Cambridge, Mass.: Harvard University Press, 1959).

83. For a recent article tracing the literature on corporate social responsibility in the United States, see Archie B. Carroll, "Corporate Social Responsibility: Evolution of a Definitional Construct," *Business and Society*, vol. 38, no. 3 (September 1999), pp. 268–295.

84 A. A. Berle, "Economic Power and the Free Society," in *Corporation Takeover*, ed. Andrew Hacker (New York, N.Y.: Harper & Row, 1964), pp. 103–104.

85. A. A. Berle, Jr., "Corporate Powers as Powers in Trust," *Harvard Law Review*, vol. 44 (1931), pp. 1049–1074.

86. For an account of this era covering many of these corporate challenges, see Baldwin, *Conflicting Interests*.

87. See, e.g., Kenneth R. Andrews, "Can the Best Corporations Be Made Moral?" *Harvard Business Review* (May–June 1973), pp. 57–64; Thomas Donaldson,

Corporations and Morality (Englewood Cliffs, N.J.: Prentice-Hall, Inc., 1982), esp. pp. 18–35; Peter A. French, *Collective and Corporate Responsibility* (New York, N.Y.: Columbia University Press, 1984), esp. pp. 41–66; Kenneth E. Goodpaster and John B. Mathews, Jr., "Can a Corporation Have a Conscience?" *Harvard Business Review* (January-February 1982), Reprint No. 82104.

88. See generally Seymour Martin Lipset and William Schneider, *The Confidence Gap: Business, Labor, and Government in the Public Mind* (Baltimore, Md.: The Johns Hopkins University Press, 1983).

89. Fred D. Baldwin, *Conflicting Interests*, citing Seymour Martin Lipset and William Schneider, " 'How's Business?' What the Public Thinks," *Public Opinion* (July–August 1978), pp. 41–47.

90. Lipset and Schneider, " 'How's Business?' What the Public Thinks," p. 41. See also Baldwin, *Conflicting Interests*, pp. 75, 84.

91. In late 1977, Congress passed the Foreign Corrupt Practices Act which prohibited U.S. companies and all issuers of securities in the United States, including non-U.S. companies, from paying anything of value to foreign government officials for the purpose of obtaining or retaining business. The act, as amended in 1988 and 1998, is found at 15 U.S.C. §§ 78m, 78dd-1, 78dd-2, 78dd-3, 78ff. The heightened concern about corporate social responsibility was reflected, for example, in the stature of the executives actively involved in discussions and debates such as those found in *Social Responsibilities of Business Corporations: A Statement on National Policy by the Research and Policy Committee of the Committee for Economic Development* (New York, N.Y.: Committee for Economic Development, 1971).

92. See Francesco Cantarella, "The Growth of Corporate Responsibility Committees," *The Corporate Board*, vol. XVII, no. 101 (November–December 1996), pp. 16–20; J. Richard Harrison, "The Strategic Use of Corporate Board Committees," *California Management Review*, vol. 30 (1987), pp. 109–125, at pp. 109–110. For board-level ethics committees, see Ethics Resource Center and the Behavior Research Center, *Ethics Policies and Programs in American Business* (Washington, D.C.: Ethics Resource Center, 1990), p. 37.

93. See Lauren Talner, *The Origins of Shareholder Activism* (Washington, D.C.: Investor Responsibility Research Center, 1983), pp. 8–9, 22–23.

94. Philip Johansson, "Social Investing Turns 30," *Business Ethics* (January/February 2001), pp. 12–16.

95. For a study of the South African disinvestment issue, see Robert K. Massie, "Moral Deliberation and Policy Formation: A Study of Eight Institutional Investors' Approaches to South African Disinvestment," DBA thesis, Harvard University Graduate School of Business Administration, 1989.

96. Patrick E. Murphy, "Corporate Ethics Statements: Current Status and Future Prospects," *Journal of Business Ethics*, vol. 14 (1995), pp. 727–740.

97. Report by the President's Blue Ribbon Commission on Defense Management, *Control and Accountability*, June 1986.

98. The quotation is from Robert D. Kennedy, chairman and CEO of Union Carbide Corp. from 1986 to 1995, as found in George C. Lodge and Jeffrey F. Rayport, "Responsible Care," HBS Case No. 9-391-135 (Boston, Mass.: Harvard Business School Publishing, 1991), p.8.

99. John P. Kotter and James L. Heskett, *Corporate Culture and Performance* (New York, N.Y.: The Free Press, 1992), pp. 8–10, esp. footnote 9.

100. Christopher A. Bartlett and Sumantra Ghoshal, "Changing the Role of Top Management: Beyond Strategy to Purpose," *Harvard Business Review* (November–December 1994).

101. The rise of stakeholder theory in recent decades is often traced to the publication of R. Edward Freeman's *Strategic Planning: A Stakeholder Approach* (Boston, Mass.: Pitman Publishing, 1984). Freeman himself traces the use of the term "stakeholder" in the management literature to an internal memorandum of the Stanford Research Institute (now SRI International) in 1963 (Freeman, *Strategic Planning*, p. 32). Precursors of this idea date back to the 1920s and 1930s with, for example, the suggestion that managers might come to think of themselves as trustees for employees, consumers, and the public, as well as for investors. See E. Merrick Dodd, "For Whom Are Corporate Managers Trustees?" pp. 1145–1163 at 1160.

102. E.g., Tracy Kidder, *The Soul of a New Machine* (Boston, Mass.: Little, Brown & Co., 1981); Tom Chappell, *The Soul of a Business: Managing for Profit and the Common Good* (New York, N.Y.: Bantam Books, 1993); Robert W. Hall, *The Soul of the Enterprise: Creating a Dynamic Vision for American Manufacturing* (New York, N.Y.: Harper Business, 1993); C. William Pollard and Carlos H. Cantu, *Soul of the Firm* (New York, N.Y.: Harper Business, 1996); Thomas V. Morris, *If Aristotle Ran General Motors: The New Soul of Business* (New York, N.Y.: Henry Holt and Co., 1997); Alan Briskin, *The Stirring of Soul in the Workplace* (San Francisco, Ca.: Berrett-Koehler, 1998); Leonard L. Berry, *Discovering the Soul of Service: The Nine Drivers of Sustainable Business Success* (New York, N.Y.: Free Press, 1999).

103. For a recent article on trust, see Laurence Prusak and Don Cohen, "How to Invest in Social Capital," *Harvard Business Review* (June 2001) p. 86–93.

104. United States Sentencing Commission, *Guidelines Manual* (Washington, D.C.: USSC, 2001), Ch. 8C2.5(f)-(g), pp. 431–432.

105. American Law Institute, *Principles of Corporate Governance: Analysis and Recommendations*, vol. 1 (St. Paul, Minn.: American Law Institute Publishers, 1994), Section 2.01 (b) (2), (3), p. 55.

106. *Paramount Communications v. Time, Inc.*, 1989 Del. Ch. Lexis 77 (Delaware Chancery Court 1989). The decision was affirmed by the Supreme Court of Delaware. See *Paramount Communications v. Time, Inc.*, 571 A.2d 1140 (1990).

107. *Paramount Communications v. Time, Inc.*, 1989 Del. Ch. Lexis 77, 21.

108. For a listing of the states with "constituency statutes," see Guhan Subramanian, "The Influence of Antitakeover Statutes on Incorporation Choice: Evidence on the 'Race' Debate and Antitakeover Overreaching," Harvard NOM Research Paper No. 01-10, December 2001, Table 4, p. 30, Social Science Research Network Electronic Paper Collection, <http://papers.ssrn.com/abstract=292679> (February 26, 2002), forthcoming *U. Penn. L. Rev.*

109. These events were triggered by a "no-action" letter issued by the SEC to the management of the Cracker Barrel Old Country Store. Cracker Barrel's management sought the SEC's views on its intention to omit from its proxy mate-

rials a proposal submitted by one shareholder, the New York City Employees' Retirement System, calling on the company to prohibit employment discrimination on the basis of sexual orientation. The text of the SEC's letter can be found in *New York City Employees' Retirement System v. Securities and Exchange Commission*, 843 F. Supp. 858 (S.D.N.Y.1994), n. 3.

110. For commentary, see John C. Coffee, Jr., "Blocking Bias Via Proxy," *Wall Street Journal*, February 2, 1993, p. A14; Richard H. Koppes, "Corporate Governance," *National Law Journal*, December 29, 1997–January 5, 1998, p. B5.

111. Securities and Exchange Commission, Amendments to Rules on Shareholder Proposals, Exchange Act Release No. 34-4001817, 1998 SEC Lexis 1001 (May 21, 1998)(codified at 17 CFR 240.14a-8).

112. U.S. Labor Department, ERISA Opinion Letter 98-04 A (May 28, 1998). See Neal S. Schelberg and Craig A. Bitman, "Corporate Governance Under ERISA: The Power to Influence Corporations," *Employee Benefits Journal*, vol. 24, no. 2 (June 1999), pp. 21–28.

113. Environmental Protection Agency, "Incentives for Self-Policing: Discovery, Disclosure, Correction and Prevention of Violations," 65 Fed. Reg. 19618 (final version April 2000) as cited in Jeffrey M. Kaplan, "The Sentencing Guidelines: The First 10 Years," *ethikos*, vol. 15, no. 3 (November-December 2001), p. 3.

114. Exchange Act Release No. 44969 (October 23, 2001), as reported in Dana H. Freyer and Rebecca S. Walker, "How The SEC Will Credit Compliance Programs in Enforcement Decisions," *ethikos*, vol. 15, no. 4 (January–February 2002) p. 1.

115. Pensions Act, 1995, c. 26. See Occupational Pensions Regulatory Authority (OPRA), "Pension Scheme Trustees: A Guide to Help Occupational Pension Scheme Trustees Understand their Duties and Responsibilities," 2001, <http://www.opra.gov.uk/publications/guides/trusteeguide-49.shtml> (October 27, 2001).

116. Quoted in Melanie Wright, "Money-Go-Round: If you listen to your conscience will you feel it in your wallet?" *Daily Telegraph* (London), July 8, 2000, p. 3.

117. The new listing requirements incorporate the recommendations of the so-called Turnbull Report, prepared by the Institute of Chartered Accountants in England and Wales under the leadership of Nigel Turnbull, Finance Director of Rank Group. The report outlines what companies should do to comply with the internal control requirements contained in the corporate governance principles known as "The Combined Code of the Committee on Corporate Governance." See "Internal Control, Guidance for Directors on the Combined Code," Appendix (London: The Institute of Chartered Accountants in England & Wales, September 1999), p. 13.

118. Geoffrey Wheatcroft, "Gruesome Purposes and Counting Machines," *Wall Street Journal*, March 21, 2001, p. A20.

119. Quoted in Joseph B. White, "'Next Big Thing': Re-Engineering Gurus Take Steps to Remodel Their Stalling Vehicles," *Wall Street Journal*, November 26, 1996, p. A1.

Chapter 5   A Higher Standard

1. Robert Levering and Milton Moskowitz, "100 Best Companies to Work For, America's Top Employers," *Fortune*, January 8, 2001.
2. Walker Information Global Network and Hudson Institute, "Commitment in the Workplace: The 2000 Global Employee Relationship Report," Indianapolis, Indiana, October 18, 2000.
3. Daniel B. Turban and Daniel W. Greening, "Corporate Social Performance and Organizational Attractiveness to Prospective Employees," *Academy of Management Journal*, vol. 40, no. 3 (1996), pp. 658–672. Compare a 1999 Cone/Roper survey cited in Sue Adkins, *Cause Related Marketing: Who Cares Wins* (Oxford, U.K.: Butterworth-Heinemann, 1999), p. 97 (The most important factors in considering a future employer are ranked as: (1) career growth potential; (2) good corporate reputation; (3) starting salary; (4) fringe benefits; (5) record of high yield for shareholders; (6) good sports and social facilities).
4. A number of sources are gathered in John Weiser and Simon Zadek, *Conversations with Disbelievers: Persuading Companies to Address Social Challenges* (New York, N.Y.: The Ford Foundation, November 2000), pp. 64–68. See also Cone, Inc. and Roper Starch, *Cone/Roper Cause Related Trends Report: The Evolution of Cause Branding*SM (Boston, Mass.: Cone Inc., 1999), pp. 12–13 (Nine in 10 workers whose companies had a cause-related marketing program—a marketing effort linked to an important social concern—felt proud of their company's values, compared to 56 percent of those whose employers did not have such a program; 87 percent of employees whose companies had a cause-related marketing program felt a strong sense of loyalty to their company compared to 67 percent employed in companies without one); Council on Foundations, *Measuring the Value of Corporate Citizenship* (Washington, D.C.: Council on Foundations, 1996), p. vi (Employees involved in employer-sponsored community events were 30 percent more likely to want to continue working for the company and to help it become a success); Minette E. Drumwright, "Company Advertising with a Social Dimension: The Role of Noneconomic Criteria," *Journal of Marketing*, vol. 60, no. 4 (October 1996), pp. 71–87 (Cause-related marketing campaigns enhance employee morale).
5. Frederick F. Reichheld with Thomas Teal, *The Loyalty Effect: The Hidden Force Behind Growth, Profits, and Lasting Value* (Boston, Mass.: Harvard Business School Press, 1996).
6. These factors are used by the Reputation Institute, a New York-based research group whose executive director is Charles J. Fombrun, author of *Reputation: Realizing Value from the Corporate Image* (Boston, Mass.: Harvard Business School Press, 1996).
7. *Corporate Ethics in America*, A Research Study Commissioned by the Society of Consumer Affairs Professionals in Business Foundation and conducted by the Gallup Organization (Arlington, Va.: SOCAP Foundation, 1993), pp. 15–16. See also Ronald Alsop, "The Best Corporate Reputations in America," *Wall Street Journal*, September 23, 1999, pp. B1, B22; David J. Vidal, *Consumer Expectations on the Social Accountability of Business* (New York, N.Y.: The Conference Board Research Report 1255-99-RR, 1999).

8. Jennifer Reese, "America's Most Admired Corporations," *Fortune*, February 8, 1993, p. 44ff. See also Council on Foundations, *Measuring the Value of Corporate Citizenship*.

9. *1999 Cone/Roper Cause Related Trends Report*, p. 4 (83 percent of Americans have a more positive image of companies that support a cause they care about).

10. Isabelle Maignan, "Consumers' Perceptions of Corporate Social Responsibilities: A Cross-Cultural Comparison," *Journal of Business Ethics* (March 2001), pp. 57–72 (Consumers in France and Germany are significantly more likely than U.S. consumers to support responsible companies in their shopping activities, but consumers in all three countries were willing to make specific efforts to buy products from responsible organizations). See also *1999 Cone/Roper Cause Related Trends Report*, pp. 7–9 (Nearly two-thirds of American consumers say they would be likely to switch brands or retailers to one associated with a good cause if price and quality were equal. Among so-called "influential Americans," 68 percent said they would be likely to pay more for a product associated with a good cause). *Corporate Ethics in America*, p. V (Two-thirds of adult U.S. consumers surveyed said they gave consideration to a company's ethics when deciding to purchase its products or services). Council on Foundations and Walker Information study, *Corporate Character and Social Responsibility*, 1994, as cited in Walker Information, *Measurements*, vol. 7, no. 4 (Indianapolis, Ind.: Walker Information, Inc., 1998) (47 percent of U.S. consumers said they would be much more likely to buy from a company that was socially responsible). For a survey conducted in Hong Kong, see "Consumers Put a 'Surprisingly High' Priority on Clean Conduct: Public Demands Better Ethics, Says Survey," *South China Morning Post*, May 9, 1994 (In a 1994 survey, 81.3 percent of the Hong Kong public said that the ethical conduct of a company would affect their decision to buy goods and services from it; 95 percent said they'd be more likely to buy from a company with high ethical standards).

11. Sue Adkins, *Cause Related Marketing*, p. 74.

12. Maignan, "Consumers' Perceptions of Corporate Social Responsibilities." Also, compare Adkins, *Cause Related Marketing*, p. 84, with *1999 Cone/Roper Cause Related Trends Report*. Adkins cites survey data that showed the following percentages of consumers willing to switch brands or retailers to support a good cause: U.K. (86 percent); Italy (75 percent); Belgium (65 percent); United States (76 percent); Australia (73 percent). The Cone/Roper survey of U.S. consumers found about two-thirds of Americans said they were willing to do so. See also other sources cited supra n. 10.

13. Hill & Knowlton, *2001 Corporate Citizen Watch Survey* (New York, N.Y.: Hill & Knowlton, July 2001). See other surveys of U.S. consumers cited supra n. 10.

14. See, e.g., *Corporate Ethics in America*, p. 29.

15. Ibid., pp. 8–9.

16. Maignan, "Consumers' Perceptions of Corporate Social Responsibilities."

17. "Consumers Put a 'Surprisingly High' Priority on Clean Conduct."

18. Ronald Alsop, "The Best Corporate Reputations in America," *Wall Street Journal*, September 23, 1999, pp. B1, B22.

19. MORI survey cited in Adkins, *Cause Related Marketing*, p. 82.

20. "The Millennium Poll on Corporate Social Responsibility," Executive Briefing, conducted by Environics International, Ltd., in cooperation with The Prince of Wales Business Leaders Forum and The Conference Board, 1999, <http://www.environicsinternational.com/news_archives/MPExecBrief.pdf> (March 5, 2002).

21. For a look at business leaders' activities in this realm, see James E. Austin, *The Collaboration Challenge: How Nonprofits and Business Succeed through Strategic Alliances* (San Francisco, Ca.: Jossey-Bass, 2000). See also James E. Austin, "Business Leadership Coalitions," *Business and Society Review*, vol. 105, no. 3, pp. 305–322. Another study that calls for business involvement in solving societal problems is George E. Peterson and Dana R. Sundblad, *Corporations as Partners in Strengthening Urban Communities* (New York, N.Y.: The Conference Board Research Report 1079-94-RR, 1994).

22. See *1999 Cone/Roper Cause Related Trends Report*, p. 15 (U.S. societal problems business should work on: public education, crime, environment, poverty, medical research, hunger, child care, drug abuse, homelessness); Vidal, *Consumer Expectations on the Social Accountability of Business*; Council on Foundations, *Measuring the Value of Corporate Citizenship*.

23. Valerie P. Hans, *Business On Trial: The Civil Jury and Corporate Responsibility* (New Haven, Conn.: Yale University Press, 2000), esp. pp. 112–137.

24. Ibid., p. 121.

25. Ibid., p. 120.

26. V. Lee Hamilton and Joseph Sanders, "Corporate Crime through Citizens' Eyes: Stratification and Responsibility in the United States, Russia, and Japan," *Law & Society Review*, vol. 30 (1996), pp. 513–547, at p. 530.

27. See, e.g., W. Trexler Proffitt, Jr., *The Evolution of Institutional Investor Identity: Social Movement Mobilization in the Shareholder Activism Field*, Unpublished doctoral dissertation in organization behavior, Northwestern University Graduate School, Evanston, Illinois (submitted December 2001).

28. For a history of this development, see Lauren Talner, *The Origins of Shareholder Activism* (Washington, D.C.: The Investor Responsibility Research Center, 1983), pp. 8–9, 22–23.

29. Investor Responsibility Research Center (IRRC), "Summary of 2000 U.S. Shareholder Resolutions" (Washington, D.C.: Investor Responsibility Research Center, 2001). Compare IRRC, *Social Policy Shareholder Resolutions in 1999: Issues, Votes and Views of Institutional Investors* (Washington, D.C.: Investor Responsibility Research Center, 2000), pp. 3, 57–62 (230 proposals on social policy issues in more than 150 major U.S. corporations). Proffitt, *The Evolution of Institutional Investor Identity*, has compiled a database indicating a larger number of proposals than those tracked by IRRC. See also Interfaith Center on Corporate Responsibility, *The Corporate Examiner*, vol. 28, no. 3–4 (New York, N.Y.: ICCR, March 8, 1999).

30. IRRC, "SRI-Related Proposals, 2001" and "IRRC Proxy Voter Database" (Washington, D.C.: IRRC, 2001).

31. Survey conducted by the U.K. Social Investment Forum as reported by Ethical Investment Research Service (EIRIS), "Market Statistics—Cause-Based Investments," EIRIS Web page <http://www.eiris.org/pages/MediaInfo/Mar Sta.htm> (April 19, 2002).

32. Social Investment Forum, *1999 Report on Socially Responsible Investing Trends in the United States*, Section III, "Shareholder Advocacy Advances Issues of Social Concern," November 4, 1999, Available online at <http://www.social invest.org/areas/research/trends/1999-Trends.htm> (March 4, 2002).

33. The philosophy behind this approach was articulated in an influential book called *The Ethical Investor: Universities and Corporate Responsibility* by John G. Simon, Charles W. Powers, and Jon P. Gunnemann (New Haven, Conn.: Yale University Press, 1972).

34. Unless otherwise indicated, information in this paragraph comes from Social Investment Forum, *1999 Report on Socially Responsible Investing Trends in the United States.*

35. Asahi Life Socially Responsible Investment Fund, as reported in "Blow Whistles While You Work," *Economist*, April 28, 2001.

36. From a report prepared by Matteo Bartolomeo and Teodosio Daga for the Sustainable Investment Research Internationsl (SiRi) Group in cooperation with euronext and CSR Europe, "Green, Social and Ethical Funds in Europe, 2001," January 1, 2002 <http://www.sricompass.org/default.asp> (July 1, 2002). Ethical Investment Research Service (EIRIS) estimated the value of retail ethical investment funds in the U.K. at 4 billion pounds as of August 2001. See <http://www.eiris.org/pages/MediaInfo/FAQmn.htm> (September 25, 2001).

37. The growth rate for assets in socially screened portfolios is based on data reported in Social Investment Forum, *1999 Report on Socially Responsible Investing Trends in the United States.* According to this report, socially screened portfolios accounted for $162 billion in 1995, $529 billion in 1997, and $1,497 billion in 1999. For the $16.3 trillion in investment assets under management in 1999, the Social Investment Forum report cites *1999 Nelson's Directory of Investment Managers.* For growth in total mutual fund assets, see Investment Company Institute, *Mutual Fund Fact Book 2000* (Washington, D.C.: Investment Company Institute, 2000), p. 2. Total U.S. mutual fund assets grew from $2,811.5 billion in 1995 to $6,846.3 billion in 1999.

38. Dow Jones Sustainability Group Index Guide, Version 2.0, September 2000, p. 7. As of mid-2001, Dow Jones Sustainability Group Indexes Gmbh had 30 licensees in 12 countries who had created financial products based on the DJSGI Dow Jones Sustainability Group Index, June 2001 Quarterly Report <http://www.sustainability-indexes.com/pdf/DJSI_Newsletter_2000102.pdf> (October 18, 2001).

39. "FTSE Ethical Index Launches with Some Surprises," *Dow Jones International News*, July 10, 2001. Alex Skorecki and Simon Targett, "Big UK Names Fail the FTSE4Good Ethics Test," *Financial Times*, July 11, 2001.

40. These funds with their launch dates: Smith Barney Social Awareness Fund, 1997; Merrill Lynch Principled Values Portfolio, 1998; Credit Suisse Equity Fund (LUX) Global Sustainability, 2000 (previously set up in 1990 as Credit Suisse Equity Fund Eco-Efficiency); UBS (LUX) Equity Fund Eco Performance, 1997; Vanguard Calvert Social Index Fund, 2000. The data on European funds are from "The European Survey on Socially Responsible Investment and the Financial Community" conducted by Taylor Nelson Sofres in 2001 and available on the CSR Europe Web page <http://www.csreurope.org> (June 26, 2002).

41. Survey by SustainAbility, cited in Johansson, "Social Investing Turns 30," p. 16.

42. Aliya Inam, "In the Name of God," *Asian Business*, November 1, 1999, p. 43.

43. See, e.g., Jonathan M. Karpoff and John R. Lott, Jr., "The Reputational Penalty Firms Bear from Committing Criminal Fraud," *Journal of Law and Economics*, vol. XXXVI (October 1993), pp. 757–802. Researchers disagree about the magnitude of losses, and much depends on the type of misconduct as well as the time period within which the research was carried out. See, e.g., Melissa S. Baucus and David A. Baucus, "Paying the Piper: An Empirical Examination of Longer-Term Financial Consequences of Illegal Corporate Behavior," *Academy of Management Journal*, vol. 40, no. 1 (1997), pp. 129–151, at p. 131 (for short-term effects on stock price). See also, Jeff Frooman, "Socially Irresponsible and Illegal Behavior and Shareholder Wealth," *Business and Society*, vol. 36, no. 3 (September 1997), pp. 221–249.

44. Peter Wright, Stephen P. Ferris, Janine S. Hiller, and Mark Kroll, "Competitiveness through Management of Diversity: Effects on Stock Price Valuation," *Academy of Management Journal*, vol. 38, no. 1 (1995), pp. 272–287.

45. *Corporate Ethics in America*, p. 22.

46. Results of the survey conducted by the Council on Foundations and Walker Information in 1994 are noted in Walker Information, *Measurements*, vol. 7, no. 4 (Indianapolis, Ind.: Walker Information, 1998), p. 2.

47. Roger W. Robinson, Jr., "Are You Investing in Rogue States?" *Wall Street Journal*, July 6, 2001, p. A8.

48. Allan Kennedy, *The End of Shareholder Value: Corporations at the Crossroads* (Cambridge, Mass.: Perseus Publishing, 2000).

49. Perhaps the best known is Robert S. Kaplan and David P. Norton, *The Balanced Scorecard: Translating Strategy into Action* (Boston, Mass.: Harvard Business School Press, 1996).

50. The film referred to is "The Carpet" by Magnus Bergmar/Bergmar Produktion (Mariefred, Sweden, 1994), aired on Swedish television, March 1994. For news reports of the IKEA incident, see the following: Allen Glen, "Child Labor Used to Make IKEA Carpets," *South China Morning Post*, February 19, 1995, p. 1; Greg McIvor, "Child Labor: Pakistani Carpet Exports Under Swedish Scrutiny," *Inter Press Service*, March 16, 1994; John Tagliabue, "Europe Fights Child Labor in Rugmaking," *New York Times*, November 19, 1996, p. D9.

51. Between September 1, 1992, and September 1, 1993, the Nike brand grew in value by 18 percent. Paul LaMonica, "Brands," *Financial World*, September 1, 1993.

52. Nike's general manager in Jakarta, John Woodman, quoted in Adam Schwarz, "Running a Business," *Far Eastern Economic Review*, June 20, 1991, p. 16.

53. For a full account, see Lynn Sharp Paine, "Royal Dutch/Shell in Transition (A)," HBS Case No. 9-300-039 (Boston, Mass: Harvard Business School Publishing, 1999).

54. "Business Ethics Don't Travel Well," *The Times* (London), May 15, 1997.

55. "Nike Answers Critics on Sweatshop Issue," *Corporate Social Issues Reporter* (Washington, D.C.: Investor Responsibility Research Center, May 1998), pp. 1, 3–7.

56. For analysts' views, see the following: Josie Esquivel and Rob Milmore, "NIKE (NKE): Just a Head Fake—Still Too Early to Do It," Morgan Stanley Dean

Witter, U.S. Investment Research, February 24, 1998; Faye Landes, "Nike, Inc.: Upgrading to Buy—They're Just Doing It," Salomon Smith Barney Research, December 18, 1998; Michael J. Shea, "Nike, Inc (NKE/NYSE)," Sutro & Co., January 5, 1999.

57. Company press release, May 12, 1998.

58. Adam Smith, *An Inquiry into the Nature and Causes of the Wealth of Nations,* 5th ed. (London: 1789) as reprinted with an introduction by Max Lerner (New York, N.Y.: The Modern Library, Random House, Inc., 1937), pp. 700–713.

59. See Adam Smith, *The Theory of Moral Sentiments,* Ch. II, iii, 3.5 (Indianapolis, Ind.: The Liberty Classics, [1757, 1790] 1982), p. 107: ". . . the happiness of every innocent man is . . . not to be wantonly trod upon, not even to be . . . ignorantly and involuntarily violated, without requiring some expiation, some atonement in proportion to the greatness of such undesigned violation."

60. Susan Ariel Aaronson, "Oh, *Behave!* Voluntary Codes Can Make Corporations Model Citizens," *The International Economy,* March/April 2001. This article catalogues and describes 19 standard-setting initiatives. See also Business for Social Responsibility, *Comparison of Selected Corporate Social Responsibility Related Standards* (San Francisco, Ca.: Business for Social Responsibility, November 2000) (a summary and comparative guide to eight major initiatives); Oliver F. Williams, ed., *Global Codes of Conduct: An Idea Whose Time Has Come* (Notre Dame, Ind.: University of Notre Dame Press, 2000). As of early 2002, the committee on consumer policy of the International Organization for Standardization (ISO) was conducting a feasibility study on global standards for corporate social responsibility. See <http://www.iso.ch/iso/en/commcentre/pressreleases/2002/Ref816.html?printable=true> (March 29, 2002).

61. E.g., Organisation for Economic Co-operation and Development, Directorate for Financial, Fiscal and Enterprise Affairs, "OECD Principles of Corporate Governance," OECD Web page, 1999, <http://www1.oecd.org/daf/governance/principles.pdf> (March 4, 2002); *Corporate Governance, A Report to the OECD by the Business Sector Advisory Group on Corporate Governance* (Paris: OECD April 1998); The Business Roundtable, *Statement on Corporate Governance: A White Paper from the Business Roundtable* (Washington, D.C., September 1997).

62. E.g., International Labour Organization, "Tripartite Declaration of Principles Concerning Multinational Enterprises and Social Policy," ILO Web page, revised in 2000 (created 1977), <http://www.ilo.org/public/english/employment/multi/tridecl/> (December 7, 2001).

63. E.g., International Chamber of Commerce, *Fighting Bribery: A Corporate Practices Manual,* ed. by François Vincke, Fritz Heimann, Ron Katz (Paris: ICC Publishing, 1999).

64. E.g., International Chamber of Commerce, "The Business Charter for Sustainable Development—16 Principles," ICC Web page, 1991, <http://www.iccwbo.org/sdcharter/charter/principles/principles.asp> (March 4, 2002); Coalition for Environmentally Responsible Economies (CERES), "CERES Principles," CERES Web page, 1989, <http://www.ceres.org/about/principles.htm> (March 4, 2002); International Organization for Standardization, "ISO

14000—Meet the Whole Family," ISO Web page, 1998 (standards first published elsewhere in 1996), <http://www.iso.ch/iso/en/iso9000-14000/pdf/iso14000.pdf> (March 4, 2002).

65. United Nations Global Compact, "The Nine Principles," Global Compact Web page, 1999, <http://www.unglobalcompact.org/un/gc/unweb.nsf/content/thenine.htm> (March 4, 2002).

66. Caux Round Table, "Principles for Business," Caux Round Table Web page, 1994, <http://www.cauxroundtable.org> (March 4, 2002).

67. Organisation for Economic Co-operation and Development, "The OECD Guidelines for Multinational Enterprises," OECD online, revised in 2000 (created 1976), <http://www.oecd.org/daf/investment/guidelines/mnetext.htm> (March 4, 2002).

68. Global Reporting Initiative, "The GRI Guidelines," GRI Web page, 2000, <http://globalreporting.org/GRIGuidelines/index.htm> (March 4, 2002).

69. World Business Council for Sustainable Development, report by Richard Holme and Phil Watts, "Why Corporate Social Responsibility Makes Good Business Sense," January 2000, <http://www.wbcsd.org/newscenter/releases.htm> (March 4, 2002).

70. United Nations Development Programme, *Human Development Report 2000* (New York, N.Y.: Oxford University Press, 2000), p. iii.

71. Freedom House, "Democracy's Century: A Survey of Global Political Change in the 20th Century," Freedom House Web page, <http://www.freedomhouse.org/reports/century.pdf> (September 25, 2001).

72. Francis Fukuyama, *The End of History and the Last Man* (New York, N.Y.: The Free Press, 1992), p. 50.

73. Maria K. Boutchkova and William L. Megginson, "Privatization and the Rise of Global Capital Markets," *Financial Management* (Tampa) (Winter 2000), pp. 31–76 at p. 31. See also Nicholas V. Gianaris, *Modern Capitalism: Privatization, Employee Ownership, and Industrial Democracy* (Westport, Conn.: Praeger, 1996), p. 58.

74. Theodore Caplow, Louis Hicks, and Ben J. Wattenberg, *The First Measured Century: An Illustrated Guide to Trends in America, 1900–2000* (Washington, D.C.: AEI Press 2001), pp. 52–53.

75. Ibid., pp. 24–25.

76. Based on data from the U.S. Census Bureau, *Statistical Abstract of the United States, 2000* (Washington, D.C., 2000), pp. 771, 773; *Statistical Abstract, 1986*, p. 384. See also U.S. Census Bureau, *Census of Service Industries, 1982*, Geographic Area Series, SC 82-A-52.

77. Jon Gabel, "Ten Ways HMOs Have Changed During the 1990s," *Health Affairs*, vol. 16, no. 3 (1997), pp. 134–145. Gabel derived these figures using data from the American Association of Health Plans.

78. InterStudy Publications, *The Competitive Edge: 11.1 HMO Industry Report* (St. Paul, Minn.: InterStudy Publications, 2000), p. 18; Gabel, "Ten Ways HMOs have Changed."

79. Data from American Hospital Association, *Hospital Statistics* (Chicago, Ill.: Healthcare InfoSource, 2000), p. 3. See Gordon W. Josephson, "Private Hospital Care for Profit? A Reappraisal," *Health Care Management Review*, vol. 22,

no. 3 (1997), pp. 64–73. See also David M. Cutler and Jill R. Horwitz, "Converting Hospitals from Not-for-Profit to For-Profit Status: Why and What Effects?" in David M. Cutler, ed., *The Changing Hospital Industry* (Chicago, Ill.: The University of Chicago Press, 2000), pp. 45–79, 45 ("Between 1970 and 1995, 330 (about 7 percent) out of approximately 5000 not-for-profit hospitals have converted to for-profit corporate form, including a dramatic number in just the past few years.").

80. Caplow, Hicks, and Wattenberg, *The First Measured Century*, pp. 38–39.

81. Ellen Galinsky and James T. Bond, *The 1998 Business Work-Life Study: A Sourcebook* (New York, N.Y.: Families and Work Institute, 1998), pp. 34–35.

82. The rise in telecommuting is difficult to gauge, as is the precise number of telecommuters working from home. An October 2001 survey found 28 million teleworkers in the U.S., including those who "work at home, at a telework center, or on the road." See Donald D. Davis and Karen A. Polonko, "Telework in the United States: Telework America Survey 2001," Executive Summary, available at International Telework Association and Council Web page <http://www.telecommute.org/twa/index.htm> (June 18, 2002).

83. See Albert Z. Carr, "Is Business Bluffing Ethical?" *Harvard Business Review* (January–February 1968), Reprint No. 68102, pp. 5–7.

84. Mark L. Clifford, "Keep the Heat on Sweatshops," *Business Week*, December 23, 1996, p. 90.

Chapter 6   The New Value Proposition

1. This chapter draws on several of my previous publications, principally the following: Lynn Sharp Paine, "Does Ethics Pay?" *Business Ethics Quarterly*, vol. 10, no. 1 (January 2000), pp. 319–330; Lynn Sharp Paine, "Moral Thinking in Management: An Essential Capability," *Business Ethics Quarterly*, vol. 6, no. 4 (October 1996), pp. 477–492); Lynn Sharp Paine, *Cases in Leadership, Ethics, and Organizational Integrity: A Strategic Perspective* (Burr Ridge, Ill.: Richard D. Irwin, 1997).

2. This is not a new thought. In 1751 Scottish philosopher and historian David Hume wrote: "That *honesty is the best policy* may be a good general rule, but is liable to many exceptions. And he, it may perhaps be thought, conducts himself with most wisdom who observes the general rule and takes advantage of all the exceptions." David Hume, *An Inquiry Concerning the Principles of Morals*, ed. Charles W. Hendel (New York, N.Y.: Liberal Arts Press, 1957), p. 102.

3. This conception of the superior or exemplary person is found in Confucian thought. See *The Analects of Confucius*, Book 12.16.

4. Joshua Daniel Margolis and James Patrick Walsh, *People and Profits? The Search for a Link Between a Company's Social and Financial Performance* (Mahwah, N.J.: Lawrence Erlbaum Associates, Publishers, 2001), p. 8. The authors cite 49 accounting measures, 12 market measures, 5 measures mixing accounting and market indicators, and 4 additional outcome measures.

5. See Global Reporting Initiative Web site, <http://www.globalreporting.org> (February 19, 2002). For a different approach, see the self-assessment tool developed by the Caux Round Table based on the Caux Principles for Business, described in K.E. Goodpaster, T.D. Maines, and M.D. Rovang, "Stakeholder

Thinking: Beyond Paradox to Practicality," *Journal of Corporate Citizenship*, October 2000. For an overview of this topic, see Simon Zadek, Peter Pruzan, and Richard Evans, *Building Corporate Accountability* (London: Earthscan Publications, Ltd., 1997). See also Rob Gray, Dave Owen, and Carol Adams, *Accounting & Accountability* (New York, N.Y.: Prentice Hall, 1996).

6. Sandra Sugawara, "IBM Settles to End Bribery Case," *Washington Post*, December 22, 2000, p. E3.

7. Prohibitions on bribery are found, for example, in codes such as the Caux Round Table's "Principles for Business," section 2, principle 7, "Avoidance of Illicit Operations," Caux Round Table Web page, 1994, <http://www.cauxroundtable.org> (March 4, 2002) and "The OECD Guidelines for Multinational Enterprises," part 1, section 6, "Combating Bribery," p. 24, OECD online, revised in 2000 (created 1976), <http://www.oecd.org/daf/investment/guidelines/mnetext.htm> (March 4, 2002). For a history of the prohibition on bribery, see John T. Noonan, *Bribes* (New York, N.Y.: Macmillan, 1984).

8. Ethics, also called moral science, has been defined broadly as the "general enquiry into what is good" encompassing "all conduct which furthers or hinders ... the welfare of self or others." See, e.g., G.E. Moore, *Principia Ethica*, orig. 1903 (Cambridge, U.K.: Cambridge University Press, 1968), p. 2; Herbert Spencer, *The Principles of Ethics*, vol. 1, orig. 1892 (Indianapolis, Ind.: Liberty Classics, 1978), p. 309. For other definitions, see G. Wallace and A.D.M. Walker, eds., *The Definition of Morality* (London: Methuen and Co., 1970).

9. Scholars differ in dating the split between these disciplines. A recent account cites as pivotal an 1836 article by John Stuart Mill, the British philosopher and political economist. There Mill likened pure economics to geometry and offered a tidy categorization that set economics off from ethics as well as politics and other subjects having to do with values. Although Mill himself saw economic and ethical concerns as necessarily intertwined in practical affairs, his categorization enabled others to sharpen the boundaries between them. Adam Smith's *Wealth of Nations*, for example, came to be seen thereafter as a work of economics separate from his writings on moral philosophy and jurisprudence. See Alan Ryan's review of Emma Rothschild, *Economic Sentiments: Adam Smith, Condorcet, and the Enlightenment* (Cambridge, Mass.: Harvard University Press, 2001) in *The New York Review of Books*, July 5, 2001, pp. 42, 44.

10. For discussion of the long-standing debate about truth-telling in this situation, see Sissela Bok, *Lying: Moral Choice in Public and Private Life* (New York, N.Y.: Pantheon Books, 1978), pp. 39–42.

11. See <http://www.groucho-marx.com/> (February 19, 2002).

12. The headlines are from Richard S. Tedlow, "James Burke: A Career in American Business (B)," HBS Case No. 9-390-030 (Boston, Mass.: Harvard Business School Publishing, 1989), p. 11. The journalist quoted is Tom Blackburn, "A Capsule History of Corporate Morality," *Miami News*, February 21, 1986, as cited in Tedlow. Dr. Mark Novitch has spoken publicly about his experience as FDA Deputy Commissioner during the Tylenol crisis and also communicated privately with the author.

13. For recent research indicating that consumers find it acceptable for companies to benefit from civic contributions but are also leery of too much self-promotion, see Sue Adkins, *Cause Related Marketing: Who Cares Wins* (Oxford, U.K.: Butterworth Heinemann, 1999), p. 81; Ronald Alsop, "Perils of Corporate Philanthropy—Touting Good Works Offends the Public, but Reticence is Misperceived as Inaction," *Wall Street Journal*, January 16, 2002, p. B1.

14. "How come when I want a pair of hands I get a human being as well?" quoted in Stuart Crainer, *The Ultimate Book of Business Quotations* (New York, N.Y.: AMACOM, 1998), p. 234.

15. The estimate of college students taking economics courses comes from Eleena de Lisser, "Novel Economics: Putting Life and Love into the Dismal Science," *Wall Street Journal*, October 19, 2000, p. A1.

16. I borrow the characterization of this view as "sentimental" from Sharon Parks who reports the same objection from those who oppose the teaching of ethics in graduate schools of business. See Sharon Daloz Parks, "Is It Too Late? Young Adults and the Formation of Professional Ethics," in Thomas R. Piper, Mary C. Gentile, and Sharon Daloz Parks, *Can Ethics Be Taught? Perspectives, Challenges, and Approaches at Harvard Business School* (Boston, Mass.: Harvard Business School Press, 1993), pp. 13–72.

17. This paragraph is based on the following in order of reference: On "ego integrity," the state of psychological and moral wholeness attained in the eighth and final stage of life, see Erik H. Erikson, *Childhood and Society*, 2nd ed. (New York, N.Y.: W.W. Norton & Company, Inc., 1963), pp. 268–269. For stages of moral development, see Lawrence Kohlberg, *The Psychology of Moral Development: The Nature and Validity of Moral Stages*, vol. 2 of *Essays on Moral Development* (New York, N.Y.: Harper & Row, 1984), pp. 429, 431, 459–460. For other perspectives on moral development, see also Carol Gilligan, *In a Different Voice: Psychological Theory and Women's Development* (Cambridge, Mass.: Harvard University Press, 1982) (Gilligan challenges the Kohlberg theory as male-oriented); Parks, "Is It Too Late? Young Adults and the Formation of Professional Ethics," in Piper, Gentile, and Parks, *Can Ethics Be Taught?* For studies of the impact of moral education programs, see James R. Rest, *Moral Development: Advances in Research and Theory* (New York, N.Y.: Praeger Publishers, 1986), p. 177. On self-cultivation and moral maturity in Confucian thought, see, e.g., *The Analects of Confucius*, Bk. 2.4.

18. Survey data is from Ethics Resource Center, *Ethics in American Business: Policies, Programs and Perceptions* (Washington, D.C.: Ethics Resource Center, 1994), pp. 15, 31–32.

19. This account is taken from two sources: Bill Sells, "What Asbestos Taught Me About Managing Risk," *Harvard Business Review* (March-April 1994), pp. 76–84; and Lynn Sharp Paine, "Manville Corporation Fiber Glass Group (A)," HBS Case No. 9-394-117 (Boston, Mass.: Harvard Business School Publishing, 1993).

20. The lawyer's testimony is recounted in Saul W. Gellerman, "Why 'Good' Managers Make Bad Ethical Choices," *Harvard Business Review* (July–August 1986), p. 86.

21. The quote is from Sells, "What Asbestos Taught Me About Managing Risk," p. 7.

22. Ibid., p. 12.

23. Paine, "Manville Corporation Fiber Glass Group (A)," p. 12.

24. For a full account of the company's development and philosophy, see Lynn Sharp Paine, "Wetherill Associates, Inc.," HBS Case No. 9-394-113 (Boston, Mass.: Harvard Business School Publishing, 1993).

25. J. Scott Armstrong, "Social Irresponsibility in Management," *Journal of Business Research*, vol. 5 (September 1977), pp. 185–213. The study also included other groups that were given specific instructions as to their role. Some were designated as "stockholder boards" explicitly charged with maximizing returns to shareholders. Others were designated as "stakeholder boards" whose duty was to consider the interests of the company's various stakeholder groups. Altogether, the study, which was carried out over five years between 1972 and 1977, involved more than 300 groups in 10 countries.

26. The case is based on the situation described in Lynn Sharp Paine, "Sears Auto Centers (A)," Harvard Business School Case No. 9-394-009 (Boston, Mass.: Harvard Business School Publishing, 1993).

27. See, e.g., *The Analects of Confucius*, Book 2.12; Immanuel Kant, *The Moral Law, or Kant's Groundwork of the Metaphysic of Morals* (orig. 1797), trans. H.J. Paton (New York, N.Y.: Barnes and Noble, 1950), p. 95.

28. For legal scholarship on the power of social norms to shape behavior, see, e.g., Daryl K. Brown, "Street Crime, Corporate Crime, and the Contingency of Criminal Liability," *University of Pennsylvania Law Review*, vol. 149 (May 2001), p. 1295. See also Marshall B. Clinard and Peter C. Yeager, *Corporate Crime* (New York, N.Y.: The Free Press, 1980), pp. 58–60.

29. See Stanley Milgram, *Obedience to Authority* (New York, N.Y.: Harper & Row Publishers, Inc., 1974). The quoted comment comes from an account of the Milgram experiments found in Ruth R. Faden and Tom L. Beauchamp, *A History and Theory of Informed Consent* (New York, N.Y.: Oxford University Press, 1986), pp. 174–175.

30. This research was described by Professor Darley on Dateline (NBC), "Bystander Intervention," April 30, 1996. It is based on an earlier study reported in Bibb Latane and John M. Darley, *The Unresponsive Bystander: Why Doesn't He Help?* (New York, N.Y.: Appleton-Century Crofts, 1970).

31. For some examples of common ethical failings, see Solomon Schimmel, *The Seven Deadly Sins: Jewish, Christian, and Classical Reflections on Human Nature* (New York, N.Y.: The Free Press, 1992); Judith N. Shklar, *Ordinary Vices* (Cambridge, Mass.: Harvard University Press, 1984). On the "banality of evil," see Hannah Arendt, *Eichmann in Jerusalem: A Report on the Banality of Evil* (New York, N.Y.: Viking Press, 1963).

32. This talk was later published as Lynn Sharp Paine, "Regulating the International Trade in Hazardous Pesticides: Closing the Accountability Gap," in *Ethical Theory and Business*, 4th ed., Tom L. Beauchamp and Norman E. Bowie, eds. (Englewood Cliffs, N.J.: Prentice Hall, 1993), pp. 547–556.

33. On the necessity for a principle of noninjury, see, for instance, Sissela Bok, *Common Values* (Columbia, Mo.: University of Missouri Press, 1995), pp. 13–17, who cites many spiritual and ethical traditions for this principle: Christian, Buddhist, Jain, Confucian, Hindu. Legal scholar H.L.A. Hart points

out in *The Concept of Law* (Oxford, U.K.: Clarendon Press, 1961, pp. 187–191) that rules prohibiting the infliction of bodily harm on others are among the "rules of conduct which any social organization must contain if it is to be viable." He notes that these rules are found in all systems of law and conventional morality. See also the following, quoted in Bok: Charles Darwin, *The Descent of Man, and Selection in Relation to Sex, Part One* (orig. 1870), vol. 21, *The Works of Charles Darwin*, ed. by Paul H. Barrett and R.B. Freeman (New York, N.Y.: New York University Press, 1989), p. 121 ("No tribe could hold together if murders, robbery, treachery, etc., were common . . ."); Stuart Hampshire, *Innocence and Experience* (Cambridge, Mass.: Harvard University Press, 1989), pp. 32–33 (describing the classes of fundamental duties and obligations worked out in every society, including "restraints against harm and destruction of life"); and P. F. Strawson, "Social Morality and the Individual Ideal," in Wallace and Walker, eds., *The Definition of Morality*, pp. 101–103, 111 ("mutual abstention from injury" is among the rules of conduct needed for society's viability).

34. See, e.g., Caux Round Table, "Principles for Business," section 3, "Stakeholder Principles," Caux Round Table Web page, 1994, <http://www.cauxroundtable.org> (March 4, 2002). These principles call on business to protect the health and safety of its various constituencies and to "make every effort to insure that the health and safety of our customers, as well as the quality of their environment, will be sustained or enhanced by our products and services."

35. For the Brandeis reference, see *Guide to Microfilm Edition of the Public Papers of Justice Louis Dembitz Brandeis*, in the Jacob and Berthan Goldfarb Library of Brandeis University, Document 128. Testimony before the Senate Committee on Interstate Commerce, *Hearing on Persons and Firms Financed in Interstate Commerce* 1 (Pt. XVI), 62nd Congress, 2nd session, December 14–16, 1911, pp. 1146–91. As quoted in Robert A.G. Monks and Nell Minow, *Watching the Watchers: Corporate Governance for the 21st Century* (Cambridge, Mass.: Blackwell, 1996), pp. 102–104.

36. American Law Institute, *Principles of Corporate Governance: Analysis and Recommendations*, vol. 1, (St. Paul, Minn.: American Law Institute Publishers, 1994), section 2.01, p. 55. A legal source often referenced for the narrower interpretation of executive duty is the 1919 Michigan Supreme Court decision *Dodge v. Ford Motor Co.* (204 Mich. 459) which required Ford to pay out larger dividends, as demanded by the plaintiff minority shareholders, rather than reinvesting profits in the company, on the grounds that a corporation is to be run "primarily for the profit of the stockholders."

37. Quoted material is from the court's decision in *Paramount Communications, Inc. v. QVC Network, Inc.*, 637 A.2d 34, 44 (Del. 1994) (in change-of-control situations the directors are obligated "to secure the transaction offering the best value reasonably available for the stockholders"). See *Santa Fe Pacific Corp. Shareholder Litigation*, 669 A.2d 59, 71 (Del. 1995) for a statement of the situations that trigger the duty to maximize shareholder value. See also American Law Institute, *Principles of Corporate Governance*, vol. 1, section 6.02 (b), (c), p. 405. For general discussion and summary of the law in this area see Constance E. Bagley and Karen L. Page, "The Devil Made Me Do It: Replacing

Corporate Directors' Veil of Secrecy with the Mantle of Stewardship," *San Diego Law Review*, vol. 36 (Fall 1999), p. 897; R. Cammon Turner, "Shareholders vs. the World," *Business Law Today* (January–February 1999), pp. 32–35.

38. For a general statement of the "business judgment rule," see American Bar Association, Committee on Corporate Laws, *Corporate Director's Guidebook*, 3d ed. (Chicago, Ill.: American Bar Association, 2001), p. 13. A frequently cited judicial statement of this rule is in *Aronson v. Lewis*, 473 A.2d 805, 811–812 (Del. 1984). For full treatment of this topic, see Dennis J. Block, Nancy E. Barton and Stephen A. Radin, *The Business Judgment Rule: Fiduciary Duties of Corporate Directors*, 5th ed. (New York, N.Y.: Aspen Law & Business, 1998).

39. A contemporary version of this argument is found, e.g., in Martin Wolf, "Sleep-Walking With the Enemy: Corporate Social Responsibility Distorts the Market by Deflecting Business From Its Primary Role of Profit Generation," *Financial Times*, May 16, 2001. For an older version, see, e.g., Milton Friedman, "The Social Responsibility of Business Is to Increase Its Profits," *New York Times Magazine*, September 13, 1970, pp. 124, 126 (arguing that business support for social responsibility strengthens the "iron fist of Government bureaucrats").

40. See, e.g., Ethan B. Kapstein, "The Corporate Ethics Crusade," *Foreign Affairs* (September–October 2001), p. 105.

41. The Harkin Bill, sponsored for the first time by Iowa Democrat Thomas Harkin in 1992, was introduced in various sessions between 1989 and 1999. The Child Labor Deterrence Act of 1992, 102d Cong., 2d sess., S. 3133. At the time of this writing, it had not been enacted into law. See also Carol Bellamy, *The State of the World's Children 1997*, United Nations Children's Fund (UNICEF)(New York, N.Y.: Oxford University Press for UNICEF, 1997), pp. 23, 60.

42. Memorandum of Understanding (MOU) Between the Bangladesh Garment Manufacturers and Exporters Association (BGMEA), the ILO and UNICEF, (1995). For a critique of the program and suggested improvements, see Mohammad Mafizur Rahman, Rasheda Khanam, and Nur Uddin Absar, "Child Labor in Bangladesh: A Critical Appraisal of Harkin's Bill and the MOU-Type Schooling Program," *Journal of Economic Issues*, vol. XXXIII, no. 4 (December 1999), pp. 985–1003.

43. For a description of efforts underway, see International Labour Office, International Program on the Elimination of Child Labour (IPEC), *Action Against Child Labour 2000–2001: Progress and Future Priorities* (Geneva: International Labour Organization, 2001).

Chapter 7   Performing at a Higher Level

1. Stanley Ziemba, "Sears Slips to No. 3 in the Retail Kingdom," *Chicago Tribune*, February 21, 1991, Business Section, p. 1.

2. A full account can be found in Lynn Sharp Paine, "Sears Auto Centers (A), (B), (C)," Harvard Business School Case Nos. 9-394-009, 9-394-010, 9-394-011 (Boston, Mass.: Harvard Business School Publishing, 1993).

3. Quoted in Julia Flynn, Christina Del Valle, and Russell Mitchell, "Did Sears Take Other Customers for a Ride?" *Business Week*, August 3, 1992, p. 25.

4. Henry Gilgoff, "Sears Says Trust Us," *Newsday*, Nassau and Suffolk Edition, June 28, 1992, Business Section, p. 68.

5. Quoted in T. Christian Miller, "Sears Admits 'Mistakes' at Auto Service Centers," *San Francisco Chronicle*, June 23, 1992, p. A1.

6. Roger William Riis and John Patric, *Repairmen Will Get You If You Don't Watch Out* (Garden City, N.Y.: Doubleday, 1942), pp. 53–125.

7. Gregory A. Patterson, "Sears Is Dealt a Harsh Lesson by States—Mishandling of Auto-Repair Inquiries Proves Costly," *Wall Street Journal*, October 2, 1992, p. A9.

8. Lucette Lagnado, "Intensive Care: Ex-Manager Describes the Profit-Driven Life Inside Columbia/HCA," *Wall Street Journal*, May 30, 1997, p. A1.

9. Martin Gottlieb and Kurt Eichenwald, "Health Care's Giant," *New York Times*, May 1997, sec. 3, p. 1.

10. Columbia/HCA Healthcare, December 31, 1996 10-K (Nashville, Tenn.: Columbia/HCA Healthcare), filed with the SEC. The account presented here is based on previously cited sources as well as Susan Headden, Stephen J. Hedges, and Gary Cohen, "Code Blue at Columbia/HCA," *U.S. News & World Report*, August 11, 1997, p. 20; Lucette Lagnado, Anita Sharpe and Greg Jaffe, "Doctors' Orders: How Columbia/HCA Changed Health Care, For Better or Worse—It Rapidly Bought Hospitals, Cut Costs; Then Came Profits—and Subpoenas—Diseases as 'Product Lines,'" *Wall Street Journal*, August 1, 1997, p. A1; Lucette Lagnado, Eva M. Rodriguez, and Greg Jaffe, "What He Knew: How 'Out of the Loop' was Dr. Frist During Columbia's Expansion?— Hospital Giant's New CEO Had a Top Title But Says He Deferred to Mr. Scott—Making the 7 A.M. Meetings," *Wall Street Journal*, September 4, 1997, p. A1.

11. Lucette Lagnado, "Columbia Taps Lawyer for Ethics Post; Yuspeh Led Defense Initiative of 1980s," *Wall Street Journal*, October 14, 1997, p. B6. For a description of the company's ethics program, see Alan Yuspeh, et al., "Above Reproach: Developing a Comprehensive Ethics and Compliance Program," *Frontiers of Health Services Management*, vol. 16, no. 2 (Winter 1999), pp. 3–38.

12. Albert J. Dunlap, *Mean Business: How I Save Bad Companies and Make Good Companies Great* (New York, N.Y.: Random House, 1996), p. 197.

13. All the information in this paragraph is from John A. Byrne, "Chainsaw," *Business Week*, October 18, 1999, p. 128. The article was adapted from Byrne's then-forthcoming *Chainsaw: The Notorious Career of Al Dunlap in the Era of Profit-at-Any-Price* (New York, N.Y.: HarperBusiness, 1999).

14. Jonathan Weil, "Five Sunbeam Ex-Executives Sued by SEC," *Wall Street Journal*, May 16, 2001, p. A3; "'Chain Saw Al' Schemed to Inflate Sunbeam Earnings, SEC Alleges," *Boston Globe*, May 16, 2001, p. D2.

15. For a full account of the recall, see Lynn Sharp Paine and Michael Watkins, "Recall 2000: Bridgestone Corp. (A)," HBS Case No. 9-302-013 (Boston, Mass.: Harvard Business School Publishing, 2001). Note that this case is based entirely on public sources.

16. Calvin Sims, "A Takeover with Problems for Japanese Tire Maker," *New York Times*, August 10, 2000, p. C4.

17. Robert L. Simison, Norihiko Shirouzu, Timothy Aeppel, and Todd Zaun, "Pressure Points: Tension Between Ford and Firestone Mounts Amid Recall Efforts," *Wall Street Journal*, August 28, 2000, p. A1.

18. Estimated costs to Bridgestone as reported in Todd Zaun, "A Blowout Blindsides Bridgestone," *Wall Street Journal*, August 7, 2000, p. A8; Todd Zaun, "Japan's Bridgestone to Inject $1.3 Billion into Firestone," *Wall Street Journal*, December 5, 2001, p. A12. Estimated costs to Ford as reported in Norihiko Shirouzu, "Ford Earnings Decline on Firestone-Tire Recall," *Wall Street Journal*, October 19, 2000, p. A3; Norihiko Shirouzu, "Ford Motor May Trim Dividend to Help Conserve Funds," *Wall Street Journal*, October 8, 2001, p. A20.

19. Keith Bradsher, "Documents Portray Tire Debacle as a Story of Lost Opportunities," *New York Times*, September 11, 2000, p. 1.

20. Edmund Sanders, Judy Pasternak, John O'Dell, "State Farm Says It Alerted Firestone to Problem in '97," *Los Angeles Times*, August 16, 2000, p. C1.

21. "Ford vs. Firestone: Firestone Was Aware of Tire Flaws Back in 1998," *Newsweek*, September 18, 2000, p. 26.

22. The report, prepared by Safetyforum.com, was released on September 10, 2000. Bradsher, "Documents Portray Tire Debacle as a Story of Lost Opportunities."

23. Ibid.

24. Statement by Bridgestone/Firestone executive vice president Gary Crigger, Bridgestone/Firestone Web page, August 9, 2000, <http://www.bridgestone-firestone.com/news/corporate/news/00809c.htm> (February 8, 2001).

25. Quoted in James R. Healey, "Documents Imply Firestone Knew of Tire Trouble in '94," *USA Today*, October 4, 2000, p. B1.

26. Yoichiro Kaizaki, Press Conference, September 11, 2000.

27. "Firestone's Thorny Way; Global Strategy, Weak Situational Judgment Impact Stock Value from the Start," *Nikkei Sangyō Shimbun*, October 25, 2000; "Risk Minimization Management, Company Breakage," *Nikkei Bijinesu*, October 2, 2000.

28. All information in this paragraph is from Bradsher, "Documents Portray Tire Debacle as a Story of Lost Opportunities."

29. Simison, et al., "Pressure Points."

30. David Welch and John Protos, "John Lampe: A Mr. Fixit for Firestone?" *Business Week*, October 23, 2000, p. 56.

31. See "Firestone's Thorny Way; Starts Again with American CEO, Deep Wounds from Lack of Sense of Crisis Management," *Nikkei Sangyō Shimbun*, October 24, 2000; Sara Nathan, "Firestone Reassurances Fall on Skeptical Ears," *USA Today*, December 20, 2000, p. B3.

32. For a description of other corrective actions taken, see Lynn Sharp Paine and Michael Watkins, "Recall 2000: Bridgestone Corp. (B)," HBS Case No. 9-302-014 (Boston, Mass.: Harvard Business School Publishing, 2001). Note that this case is based entirely on public sources.

33. Unless otherwise noted, the material in this section is based on the following case studies: Lynn Sharp Paine and Ann K. Leamon, "AES: Hungarian Project

(A), (B)," HBS Case Nos. 9-300-045, 9-300-089 (Boston, Mass.: Harvard Business School Publishing, 2000); Lynn Sharp Paine, "AES Global Values," HBS Case No. 9-399-136 (Boston, Mass.: Harvard Business School Publishing, 1999); Lynn Sharp Paine, "AES Honeycomb (A), (B)," HBS Case Nos. 9-395-132, 9-395-122 (Boston, Mass.: Harvard Business School Publishing, 1994).

34. The quoted phrase comes from Suzy Wetlaufer, "Organizing for Empowerment: An Interview with AES's Roger Sant and Dennis Bakke," *Harvard Business Review* (January–February 1999), p. 121.

35. Described, for example, in Oliver E. Williamson, *The Economic Institutions of Capitalism: Firms, Markets, Relational Contracting* (New York, N.Y.: The Free Press, 1985), pp. 43–52.

36. AES, Summary Fact Sheet, December 2001, as updated to February 2002 by company officials.

37. See, e.g., AES Corporation Annual Report, 2000, pp. 7, 14.

38. AES Corporation Proxy Statement, "Compensation Committee Report on Executive Compensation," SEC Filing, March 23, 2000.

39. Wetlaufer, "Organizing for Empowerment," p. 116.

40. This issue is posed in Paine, "AES Global Values," HBS Case No. 9-399-136.

41. For details, see Paine and Leamon, "AES: Hungarian Project (A)," HBS Case No. 9-300-045.

42. This term covers conceptual errors such as mistaking a general category for a subtopic within it, such as when a child asks whether "math" is part of "algebra," or locating a species within the wrong general category. The term was used most famously by Oxford philosopher Gilbert Ryle who argued in *The Concept of Mind* (London: Hutchinson, 1949) that our common ways of thinking about the relation between mind and body rest on a category mistake.

43. This incident is detailed in Paine, "AES Honeycomb (A), (B)," HBS Case Nos. 9-395-132, 9-395-122.

44. See, e.g., Kathryn Kranhold, "Balancing Act: 'Surf City' Power Plant Brings Hope for Crisis, Fear for Environment," *Wall Street Journal*, April 18, 2001, p. A1; Nancy Vogel, Dan Morain, "The Energy Crisis: State Renews Demand for Power Price Relief Energy," *Los Angeles Times*, May 26, 2001, p. A1. See also Deepak Gopinath, "The Divine Power of Profit (Dennis Bakke of AES Corp.)," *Institutional Investor*, March 1, 2001, p. 39.

45. Chris R. Ellinghaus and Raymond C. Niles, Salomon Smith Barney, Equity Research: United States Power & Natural Gas, "The AES Corporation," September 20, 2000.

46. Quoted in Michael M. Phillips, "AES's Nile Dam Project in Uganda Hits Snag with Bribery Concerns," *Wall Street Journal*, July 3, 2002, p. A4.

47. The quoted material is from the video accompanying Richard S. Tedlow, "James Burke: A Career in American Business," HBS Case No. 9-389-177 (Boston, Mass.: Harvard Business School Publishing, 1989). For a discussion of the Johnson & Johnson Credo, see Laura L. Nash, "Johnson & Johnson's Credo," in *Corporate Ethics: A Prime Business Asset* (New York, N.Y.: The Business Roundtable, 1988).

Chapter 8   A Compass for Decision Making

1. Questioning of Gary Crigger, BFS executive, by Representative Heather A. Wilson (Republican, New Mexico), House Committee on Commerce, *The Recent Firestone Tire Recall Action, Focusing on the Action As It Pertains to Relevant Ford Vehicles: Hearings Before the Subcommittee on Telecommunications, Trade, and Consumer Protection and the Subcommittee on Oversight and Investigations*, 106th Cong., 2d sess., September 6 and 21, 2000, p. 130.

2. Quotes as reported in Jeanne Cummings, Tom Hamburger, and Kathryn Kranhold, "Law Firm Reassured Enron on Accounting," *Wall Street Journal*, January 16, 2002, p. A18.

3. This chapter draws on two of my previous publications. See Lynn Sharp Paine, "Moral Thinking in Management: An Essential Capability," *Business Ethics Quarterly*, vol. 6, no. 4 (October 1996), pp. 477–482; Lynn Sharp Paine, *Cases in Leadership, Ethics, and Organizational Integrity: A Strategic Perspective*, Part III (Burr Ridge, Ill.: Richard D. Irwin, 1997), pp. 223–235.

4. "After all, our discussion is not about something incidental, but about how we ought to live our lives." Plato, *The Republic*, ed. by G.R.F. Ferrari, trans. by Tom Griffith, Book 1:352d (Cambridge, U.K.: Cambridge University Press, 2000), p. 34.

5. This usage follows the American philosopher William James, who described the pragmatic mentality as one oriented to "last things, fruits, consequences," as opposed to "first things, principles, 'categories.'" See William James, "What Pragmatism Means," *Essays in Pragmatism* (New York, N.Y.: Hafner Publishing Company, 1948), p. 146.

6. Contemporary approaches to stakeholder analysis vary widely. For a recent roundup, see Thomas Donaldson and Lee E. Preston, "The Stakeholder Theory of the Corporation: Concepts, Evidence, and Implications," *Academy of Management Review*, vol. 20, no. 1 (1995), pp. 65–91. For stakeholder analysis as it was envisioned by an early proponent, see R. Edward Freeman, *Strategic Planning: A Stakeholder Approach* (Boston, Mass.: Pitman Publishing, 1984). Although some have criticized stakeholder theory, the typical criticisms do not apply to the type of stakeholder analysis recommended here. See, e.g., Elaine Sternberg, "Stakeholder Theory Exposed," *Corporate Governance Quarterly*, vol. 2, no. 1 (March 1996), p. 4.

7. Frederick B. Bird and James A. Waters, "The Moral Muteness of Managers," *California Management Review*, vol. 32, no. 1 (Fall 1989), p. 16. See also Robert Jackall, *Moral Mazes: The World of Corporate Managers* (New York, N.Y.: Oxford University Press, 1988).

8. Unless otherwise indicated, the material in this section is based on Lynn Sharp Paine, "Lotus Marketplace: Households," Harvard Business School Case Nos. 2-396-162, 2-396-163 (Boston, Mass.: Harvard Business School Publishing, 1995).

9. The quoted E-mail message is reported in Michael W. Miller, "Computers: Lotus Is Likely to Abandon Consumer-Data Project," *Wall Street Journal*, January 23, 1991, p. B1.

10 *Trans Union Corp. v. FTC*, 345 U.S. App. D.C. 301 (2001), available at <http://www.ftc.gov/opa/2001/04/tuappeal.htm> (February 15, 2002).

11. Excerpts from the Fair Credit Reporting Act reflect the language in effect at the time of the events described in the text. See Fair Credit Reporting Act, 15 U.S.C.S. sec. 1681b.(3)(E), as in effect in 1990. As amended in 1996 by the Consumer Credit Reporting Reform Act, the FCRA narrowed the permissible distribution of credit reports without the consumer's authorization to situations that involve a "legitimate business need . . . in connection with a business transaction that is *initiated* by the consumer [my emphasis]." As reported in Fred H. Cate, "The Changing Face of Privacy Protection in the European Union and the United States," *Indiana Law Review*, vol. 33 (1999), p. 174, at 211. The discussions in Europe would eventually result in the 1995 European Union Data Privacy Directive, which took effect in 1998. See Gregory Shaffer, "Globalization and Social Protection: The Impact of the EU and International Rules in the Ratcheting Up of U.S. Privacy Standards," *Yale Journal of International Law*, vol. 25, no. 1 (Winter 2000).

12. The examples of marketing to dieters and selling a confidential list of Jewish singles are reported in John Ward Anderson, "Va. Bill Would Curb Abuse of Computerized Mail Lists; Users Lobby Against Privacy Measure," *Washington Post*, February 5, 1992, p. C1. On direct marketing and predatory lending, see Andy Jacob, "Arrows from Ivory Towers: Subprime Lending vs. Predatory Lending," *Bank News*, October 1, 2000, pp. 14–16. See also Henry J. Sommer, "Causes of the Consumer Bankruptcy Explosion: Debtor Abuse or Easy Credit?" *Hofstra Law Review*, vol. 27 (Fall 1998), pp. 33, esp. 37–40.

13. Gordon Fairclough, "Philip Morris Says It's Sorry for Death Report," *Wall Street Journal*, July 26, 2001, p. B1.

14. The CEO is quoted in Fairclough, "Philip Morris Says It's Sorry for Death Report."

15. Oliver Wendell Holmes, Jr., *The Common Law* (Boston, Mass.: Little, Brown and Company, 1881), p. 3.

16. On rights and interests, see Ronald Dworkin, *Taking Rights Seriously* (Cambridge, Mass.: Harvard University Press, 1978).

17. This discussion is based on the facts as recounted in Kenneth E. Goodpaster, "Managing Product Safety: The Ford Pinto," HBS Case No. 9-383-129 (Boston, Mass.: Harvard Business School Publishing, 1984).

18. Milo Geyelin, "Lasting Impact: How an Internal Memo Written 26 Years Ago Is Costing GM Dearly," *Wall Street Journal*, September 29, 1999, p. A1.

19. The amount was reduced from the jury's original award of $4.9 billion. Ibid.

20. J. Scott Armstrong, "Social Irresponsibility in Management," *Journal of Business Research*, vol. 5 (September 1977), pp. 185–213 at 202–205.

21. The quote from the CEO is taken from the video accompanying Richard S. Tedlow, "James Burke: A Career in American Business," HBS Case No. 9-389-177 (Boston, Mass.: Harvard Business School Publishing, 1989). Information about the debate teams is from John Deighton, "McNeil Consumer Products Company: Tylenol" (Hanover, N.H.: Amos Tuck School, Dartmouth College, 1983).

22. The quote from marketing consultant Jerry Della Femina is found in Deighton, "McNeil Consumer Products Company," p. 10.

Chapter 9   The Center-Driven Company

1. Information about Shell is taken from Lynn Sharp Paine and Mihnea Moldoveanu, "Royal Dutch/Shell in Transition (A), (B)," HBS Case Nos. 9-300-039, 9-300-040 (Boston, Mass.: Harvard Business School Publishing, 1999).

2. The amounts in the text are rounded to the nearest $5 million and were calculated from the original estimates in Swedish kroners using exchange rates as of January 1, 1999. For the financial analysis of Telia's redeployment plan, see Roland Hansson, *Personalförsörjningsmodellen—Ett Projekt i Tiden: Övertalighetshantering i Telia (The Redeployment Model—A Project of Today)* (Stockholm: Svenska Strukturforskningsinstitutet, 1999).

3. For a full account, see Lynn Sharp Paine, "Manville Corporation Fiber Glass Group (A), (B)," HBS Case Nos. 9-394-117, 9-394-118 (Boston, Mass.: Harvard Business School Publishing, 1993).

4. For a full account, see Lynn Sharp Paine, "Charles Veillon, S.A. (A), (B)," HBS Case Nos. 9-398-011, 9-398-010 (Boston, Mass.: Harvard Business School Publishing, 1997).

5. Jacques Zwahlen, "Policy Followed by a Mail Order Company to Prevent Forced Child Labor," presented at the Institut Universitaire d'Etudes du Développement, Geneva, September 1995, p. 1.

6. Unless otherwise stated, this account is based on Louis B. Barnes and Lynn Sharp Paine, "Guaranty Trust Bank PLC Nigeria (A), (B), (C), (D)," HBS Case Nos. 9-399-110, 9-399-111, 9-399-112, 9-399-116 (Boston, Mass.: Harvard Business School Publishing, 1999).

7. GTB is cited as a "reference point" in Ayodele Aminu, "Nigerian Business; Money Transfer: GTB Set to Add Value to Customers," *Africa News*, May 10, 2000. See also "Nigeria; The Age Barrier," *Africa News*, February 5, 2001 (GTB and Zenith credited with having "changed the face of banking . . . to provide what is today regarded as qualitative banking service").

8. Barnes and Paine, "Guaranty Trust Bank PLC Nigeria (A)," p. 7.

Index

Note: Boldface numbers indicate illustrations.